COMRADE CORBYN

PRAISE FOR *COMRADE CORBYN*

"Fascinating and forensic – a real insight into the making of Labour's
accidental leader. Meticulously researched and always even-handed,
this is a very human portrait of a figure who has become a byword for
controversy. Essential reading for anyone who follows politics."

• Mary Riddell, *Daily Telegraph*

"*Comrade Corbyn* is a real political thriller with a revolutionary ending.
This is British politics' most incredible political journey."

• Kevin Maguire, *Daily Mirror*

"Engaging and accomplished analysis."

• Jason Cowley, *Sunday Times*

"Prince has produced a well-researched and balanced account of
the rise of this most unlikely politician."

• *The Spectator*

"An accomplished study and the most lucid explanation yet of
the Labour Party's present state."

• *New Statesman*

"Rosa Prince's explosive new biography reveals why the Labour leader
has not changed with the times."

• *Daily Telegraph*

"A clear, well-researched and
fair-minded account."

• *Daily Mail*

"[Rosa Prince] has described in extraordinarily close detail exactly how,
methodologically, it happened that Corbyn became leader."

• David Sexton, *Evening Standard*

"Comprehensive and forensic."

• *Progress*

COMRADE CORBYN

A VERY UNLIKELY COUP: HOW JEREMY CORBYN STORMED TO THE LABOUR LEADERSHIP

ROSA PRINCE

Biteback Publishing

This new edition published in Great Britain in 2016 by
Biteback Publishing Ltd
Westminster Tower
3 Albert Embankment
London SE1 7SP
Copyright © Rosa Prince 2016

ISBN 978-1-78590-118-8

10 9 8 7 6 5 4 3 2 1

A CIP catalogue record for this book is available from the British Library.

Set in Minion Pro and DIN by Adrian McLaughlin

Printed and bound in Great Britain by
CPI Group (UK) Ltd, Croydon CR0 4YY

CONTENTS

For my grandparents, Comrades Harold and
Bea Freeman, who would have found
Jeremy Corbyn far too right-wing

PREFACE

I HAD ORIGINALLY PLANNED to call this book *Comrade Jeremy*. The two words seem to me to capture the perfect paradox of Jeremy Corbyn's life: his first name suggests the epitome of the middle-class, middle-aged, former grammar school boy who grew up in ease and privilege amid the pastoral delights of the English Shires. And yet from his early teens, the man who is now Labour leader has devoted himself to the international socialist class struggle, the causes and values of the left. As time went on, however, and Corbyn's ascent to the leadership became first a possibility then a probability and finally a reality, events overtook me. It was 'Comrade Corbyn', rather than 'Comrade Jeremy', that seemed to have gained traction on Twitter and elsewhere. The people had spoken. The title was changed. As this book recounts, it is by no means the first time during the story of Jeremy Corbyn's rise to power that best-laid plans have been overthrown by the whirlwind of social media surrounding him.

The book's subtitle (a reference to Chris Mullin's 1982 novel *A Very British Coup*) highlights the most unexpected nature of Corbyn's victory. When he entered the Labour leadership race in the spring of 2015, it seemed doubtful he would receive enough nominations from his fellow MPs to make it on to the ballot, let alone emerge triumphant from the contest three months later. The story of how Corbyn stormed the barricades of New Labour to capture his party while inspiring a new mass movement of energised and excited left-wing 'Corbynistas' is as unlikely – and as gripping – as any plot a novelist could have dreamed up.

Corbyn is uneasy about any examination of his past, and uncomfortable with what he views as intrusive interest in his personal life. He did not cooperate with this book, and initially discouraged his friends and family from speaking to me. Like his mentor Tony Benn, Corbyn believes that the personal is irrelevant; the political is everything. But as one of my interviewees said to me, Benn espoused this view 'while establishing one of the greatest personality cults of the last century'. Corbyn too now finds himself a leader (unlike Benn, an elected one), and it is little surprise that his many followers – as well as those who have their doubts – want to find out more. This book attempts to answer some of their questions, and seeks to explain the extraordinary events of the summer of 2015, when a rank outsider from the far Labour left swept to the leadership of one of Britain's great parties. The personal *is* political.

In writing this account, I have not sought to create a hagiography, but nor is it a hatchet job; it is a first attempt to understand and define the phenomenon that is Labour leader Jeremy Corbyn. In the course of my research, I have come to see him as a complex figure, with a clear thread running through his life. From the young activist who had to be persuaded to stand as an MP, to the dedicated campaigner who only gradually assumed the role of left-wing figurehead, to the political veteran who took weeks to agree to enter the 2015 leadership contest, Corbyn likes to be seen as a reluctant, almost unambitious figure who has had greatness thrust upon him. The man who emerges from these pages is, however, far more than an accidental hero. Once Corbyn accepts a challenge, he seizes it and fights to the very last: a formidable, uncompromising operator lurks beneath his gentle demeanour. This, then, is Comrade Corbyn.

If Corbyn himself was unwilling to be interviewed, I have been extremely fortunate in the large numbers of people from all stages of his life, from family and schoolfriends to fellow MPs and political activists, foes as well as fellow travellers, who have agreed to participate in this book, with interviews given both on and off the record. For ease of reference, it should be assumed that unless otherwise attributed all quotes are taken from interviews conducted during the course of the summer and autumn of 2015, or from further interviews conducted over the spring and summer of 2016. This applies equally to quotes which appear anonymously. To help the flow of the narrative, when referring to members of the House of Lords I have tended to use first names rather than titles for politicians who are rather better known by the former. I hope their Lordships will forgive me.

I am grateful to all the many people who generously gave up their time and memories. I would also like to thank the team at Biteback Publishing, particularly Iain Dale, James Stephens and Olivia Beattie for taking on this project and turning it around with the (crazy) speed we felt necessary to meet the thirst to know more about Corbyn. Thanks too to my agent, Victoria Hobbs from AM Heath; everyone at the *Telegraph*, especially Chris Evans, Robert Winnett, Robert Mendick and Kate Mayer; Bobbie Gillespie, for his kindness in sharing his research; Matthew Bell and Matthew Tempest.

My warmest thanks and love too to my family, Beth, Nick, Linda, Clara, Anya, Stephen and Laurie, for their patience and many kindnesses, with special thanks to my husband, Conor, and father, Peter, early and sage readers..

Rosa Prince,
December 2015

PROLOGUE

12 SEPTEMBER 2015

THE LAST TIME I had stepped inside the concrete and glass of Westminster's Queen Elizabeth II Conference Centre it had been as a reporter to hear Tony Blair defend himself at the Iraq Inquiry, the seemingly interminable public investigation into the 2003 toppling of Saddam Hussein and invasion of Iraq. Now, five and a half years later, I was back, this time to watch Blair's nemesis Jeremy Corbyn, the man who helped found the Stop the War Coalition and called for the former Prime Minister to be impeached, crowned his successor as Leader of the Labour Party.

The contrast between the two occasions should have been stark. While 20 January 2011 had been bitterly cold, the sun was shining for Corbyn's big day. Many of those who had waited outside to jeer Blair five years ago had also returned, their rage turned to jubilation at Corbyn's victory. And yet for all the differences, the atmosphere was no less tense. It didn't feel like a happy occasion. Around me people stood in small groups whispering; many were angry and bitter at the way the contest had played out.

Even Corbyn's supporters seemed somehow joyless, the hostility of those around them taking away something of the pleasure of victory. Their cries of 'Jez We Can, Jez We Did' felt defiant.

Inside the large but somehow claustrophobic hall where the result of the contest was to be announced, rows of seated Labour activists eyed each other warily. It was stiflingly hot, and the mood was fractious. On stage, in front of an electric red backdrop lit up with platitudinous slogans, the speakers – all men – called for unity and comradeship, but the audience didn't feel very friendly. Sitting directly in front of the stage, the candidates smiled and chatted quietly to one another; their supporters could not hide their emotions. 'I want to kill half the people in this room,' one texted me.

When Corbyn spoke, he too seemed less gladdened by his victory than vindicated. He accused the media of 'abuse' and vowed to take on the Conservative government over its welfare cuts and attacks on trade union power, concluding: 'Poverty isn't inevitable. Things can, and they will, change.' A man behind me complained when I failed to join the standing ovation. Under New Labour, my chair would have been kicked for not rising for the leader, he muttered.

I left the cavernous red room as quickly as possible and emerged into the by now brilliant sunshine. Outside, more ecstatic Corbyn supporters waited to welcome their new leader, while camera crews and journalists pounced on emerging politicians, offering outlets for their bile. There was no shortage of takers. Corbyn headed to the pub, where he sang 'The Red Flag', before attending his first event as leader: a protest in Parliament Square in support of refugees. Comrade Corbyn was making clear at the outset where his priorities lay: with the people and causes he had fought on behalf of for more than forty years.

I left him to it, got in my car and set off out of London along the M40, M42, M6 and finally the M54, into the heart of middle England. It took three hours, and while I drove I listened to the radio as MPs past and present expressed amazement at what had transpired, along with fears about the future of the party in Corbyn's hands. Just across the Shropshire border, I left the motorway and, after driving for ten minutes along an A-road, took a left turn at a sign for the Lilleshall national sports centre, where many of Britain's Olympians train, and found myself on the country lane where Corbyn grew up.

It took quite a while to find his actual house, the former Corbyn family home being so posh that it doesn't have a number, just a name. Lost, I drove a mile or so down the length of the lane and found myself in Newport, his nearest town when he was a boy, today home to about 15,000 people. There were parades of pretty Victorian shops and a fine church, St Nicholas, now Anglican but dating back in parts to the thirteenth century, 300 years before the Church of England came into being. Wikipedia told me that Newport was a Britain in Bloom finalist. It seemed an incongruous place for a people's revolutionary to have spent his formative years.

Back on the lane, beside a row of tall leafy trees blocking the house beyond, I finally spied an entrance gate with a plaque: Yew Tree Manor. This was it, the place Jeremy Corbyn had lived from the age of seven until he left home, where he first learned what it meant to be a socialist, discussed politics with his three lively brothers and was taught by his improbably left-wing parents to empathise with those less fortunate than himself. I was reminded of a story I had been told by his brother, that on purchasing the property in the 1950s, their mother Naomi had renamed it Yew Tree House, believing it sounded more modest. The current owners had changed it back again.

As I drove through the gates and crunched down the gravel drive, the word 'manor' certainly seemed to fit. I had seen photographs of the house beforehand, but they didn't do justice to the size and splendour of what I beheld. The handsome red-brick, seventeenth-century manor house was made up of three distinct sections, with a lovely old outbuilding attached. There were climbing vines around the windows and pink flowers blooming beside the front door. A shiny black Jag was parked out front, and flanking the house were trim green lawns and beautifully maintained gardens. The day was still warm and beautiful; somewhere nearby a horse whinnied.

David Askin, Yew Tree Manor's current owner, who bought it from the Corbyns for £40,000 in 1979, met me at the front door, gave me a cup of tea and kindly agreed to show me around. The house was all low ceilings and wooden beams, generously sized rooms extending off into yet more rooms; a large, open kitchen with a utility area and sculleries; living rooms, reception rooms, dens. It was a wonderful place to bring up a family up, we agreed.

Mr Askin took me outside and showed me the paddocks where his daughter-in-law now kept her horses: two ponies and two impressive bay thoroughbreds. As the horses cropped the grass, he pointed out in the middle of the field a strange brick tower, about four feet high, which, Mr Askin said, Corbyn's closest brother Piers, now a somewhat controversial long-range forecaster, had used as a weather station.

We leaned on the gate to the paddock and surveyed the scene in the last of the afternoon sun. So this was where Comrade Corbyn had come from, this tranquil, prosperous bubble of ease and order. It seemed a world away from the heat and recrimination of Westminster. What an extraordinary journey Labour's new leader has gone on, I thought to myself.

Now let me take you on it.

CHAPTER ONE

UNLIKELY SOCIALISTS

THE YOUNG MAN listened rapt as the trade union official regaled his audience of electrical engineers with stories of meeting his Communist hero, Leon Trotsky. It was 1936 and David Corbyn was twenty-one years old and newly apprenticed to learn the trade. Discussion among the men moved on to the horrors unfolding a thousand miles away in Spain, where a brave coalition of anarchists, Communists and peasants was fighting and dying in olive groves and medieval towns, in ultimately futile resistance to the brutality of General Francisco Franco's fascist Republican Army. 'Look, look, comrades,' the speaker cried. 'We've got to go and support the Spanish Relief Committee here.' Casting his eye around the room, his gaze alighted on David. 'Corbyn, you go!' he ordered.[1]

David was not an obvious radical, having been brought up in middle-class comfort as the son of a suburban solicitor, but on taking up his engineering apprenticeship he had joined the trade union along with the other young workers. He found their discussions inspiring. Ultimately, his membership of the union would change the course of British politics, thanks to the huge influence his politics, and those of his soon-to-be wife, would have in forming those of their youngest son, Jeremy.

While David was politically aware, he was still a very young man, living at home with his parents in Ealing, west London. When, as instructed, he went to the meeting of the Spanish Civil War Redress Committee, it is perhaps no surprise that his thoughts began to wander from the plight of his Nacionales comrades on the Spanish front to the alluring figure of a young woman seated close by. Naomi Josling was also twenty-one, born a month after David, in June 1915. Years later David would tell his third-oldest son Piers the story of how he came to be at the committee meeting, concluding: 'And that's where I met your mother.' 'How did you know it was my mother?' the child Piers asked, making his father laugh.[2] When Piers pushed David to say what had attracted him to his wife-to-be, he replied, 'I remember her hips and she wore a hat.'[3]

Jeremy Corbyn viewed his parents' first meeting somewhat differently, once telling an event in his constituency that the 'committed socialists' had met 'in solidarity' at Conway Hall, Holborn.[4] On another occasion he said: 'Mum and Dad met campaigning on the Spanish Civil War. Both were active peace campaigners.'[5] There was no mention of hats or hips. It was a characteristically impersonal account. The new Labour leader does not like to talk about his early life; he prefers to give the impression that he arrived in north London from nowhere, his beliefs amorphously arrived at, his background a blur, the first decades a mystery. In fact, Corbyn is very much the product of his upbringing; a middle-class boy born to highly unlikely socialists.

For all Corbyn's decades of devotion to the causes of struggling peoples in far-flung places, from Latin America to Palestine, the Chagos Islands to Russia, his own roots are decidedly European. His family tree, which can be traced back centuries, is littered with Williams and Johns, Emilys and

Charlottes, Jameses and Edwards. And, while strikingly similar to each other, there is little in either David or Naomi's backgrounds to suggest they would be drawn to fight for social justice for the working classes. Indeed, in some branches of Corbyn's ancestral line the reverse is true. Soon after his election, the *Sunday Express* claimed to have found a rather sinister figure in Corbyn's lineage, a James Sargent, born to a family of clothworkers in Gloucestershire in 1822, who went on to run a workhouse in Farnham in Surrey, described at the time as 'a scandal and a curse to a country which calls itself civilised and Christian'.[6] At his first conference address, the new leader joked: 'I want to apologise for not doing the decent thing and going back in time to have a word with him.'

According to family legend, the original Corbyns were French Huguenots, Protestants who fled persecution by the Catholic authorities, arriving in England in the early eighteenth century. He has also suggested there is a 'Jewish element in the family, probably from Germany'.[7] Corbyn's paternal grandfather Benjamin was also the child of a garment worker, one of seven children born to William and Louisa Corbyn, from Lowestoft in Suffolk. William was a prosperous tailor with more than one shop in the town, which brought in enough money to enable him to pay for his son to train as a solicitor. Benjamin married Dorothy Bush in 1914, the year before David was born, when he was twenty-nine and she twenty-seven. It was the eve of the First World War. Dorothy had been born in New Southgate, north London, close to the area Jeremy Corbyn would later represent. The daughter of a chemist from Hethersett in Norfolk, it was perhaps her father's connection to the east of England that led Dorothy to take a job in Lowestoft working as a primary school teacher.

After training as an articled clerk in Lowestoft and qualifying as a solicitor, Benjamin moved with his wife and young son to Ealing, west London. Their home was a comfortable Edwardian terraced house. He became active in a local discussion group devoted to the work of the League of Nations, the body set up following the First World War that became a precursor to the United Nations. League of Nationers tended to be those who saw internationalism as a solution to the horrors of war, a view Benjamin's grandson Jeremy would go on to share.

When Dorothy died in 1945 she left £214, 6s., 3d. to her husband. Benjamin lived for another twenty-three years until the age of eighty-three, leaving £22,460, a not inconsiderable amount for the time. His own son David's estate would be valued at just £20,000 more when he died nearly two decades later, worth rather less than Benjamin's in real terms. Jeremy's oldest brother, who is also called David, says of his father's family:

> They were good honest workers. It was not significantly inherited wealth. It had come from a tailor's business in Lowestoft. They had plenty of struggling, you could tell that. I don't think my father's side were particularly well off, to be honest. I wouldn't say they were wealthy. Although he was a solicitor, which is a fairly good job, it wasn't up in the top lot [conducting] high-level cases; he was dealing with the hardworking lot. He was partner in a business in Ealing for a long time.

After school, David Senior attended Acton Technical College, receiving a diploma in electrical engineering. Despite the flair he showed for his subject, and the good job he landed with Westinghouse Brake and Signal Company, his father Benjamin is said to have been disappointed that he had gone into a trade rather than a profession. Naomi's father Ernest Josling was also unimpressed by his daughter's beau. According to Piers Corbyn, Ernest was a 'terrible snob' who believed David was beneath Naomi socially.[8]

The accusation of snootiness is slightly surprising, given that, while Ernest was born in prosperous West Dulwich, south London, his wife, Caroline

Stott, was from the Isle of Dogs, in the East End, which at the time of her birth in 1879, four years after her husband, was primarily home to workers on the local docks. Following their marriage in Plymouth in 1903, Corbyn's maternal grandparents, the Joslings, moved around the country several times before settling back in London. By the time of the 1911 census they were living in North Finchley, just to the west of Jeremy Corbyn's future constituency of Islington North, and were well enough off that Caroline Josling was not working and had the help of a live-in domestic servant, seventeen-year-old Margaret Shilling. Ernest entered his occupation on the census as a 'surveyor and valuer'. His projects as a quantity surveyor included Chatham Docks in Kent, and the harbour at either Malta or Gibraltar (his grandsons cannot now recall which). Naomi is said by her oldest son David to have spent her childhood in a village in Berkshire, before the family returned to London once again.

One of Naomi's brothers, Kenneth, who would become a Church of England vicar, went to Oxford University (where he was a rowing blue) and it was perhaps this that inspired Naomi to seek a higher education for herself. She attended London University, graduating, like her husband, in a ceremony held at the Albert Hall. Her son David says women were 'discouraged' from going to college at the time: 'My mother Naomi went to university, which was very unusual in those days and I think [her] parents didn't entirely approve. Chemistry and Psychology were her degrees. She did a lot of teaching over the years using her university education.'

By coincidence, when David and Naomi met, the Joslings were living a few minutes' walk from the Corbyns, in Ealing, west London, in a house that – despite Ernest's snobbishness – was similar in size and scale to that of her soon-to-be in-laws. The times were heady ones politically for the couple, and indeed the wider world; within a few years there would be few people anywhere on the globe whose lives would be untouched by the horrors of war. Already, Spain was falling to Franco's fascists and Germany was in the full grip of Hitler's Nazi Party. Corbyn would later say that his father had hoped to serve with the International Brigade in Spain, but 'his health wouldn't allow it'.[9] He did not specify the nature of his father's complaint. Across Britain, Sir Oswald Mosley held rallies where he mesmerised crowds with stirring rhetoric against Communists and Jews. He marched his thuggish band of paramilitary followers, known as the British Union of Fascists (BUF), through city streets, intimidating the UK's small Jewish communities. With Hitler, Franco and Mussolini all in ascendence, Mosley's progress seemed equally inexorable until one day in October 1936, around the time that David and Naomi met, when a rag-tag army of anti-fascists and Jews fought a pitched battle against the BUF Blackshirts through the streets of the East End of London. Naomi Josling was among them; her presence a future badge of honour for her son Jeremy.

On the outbreak of war with Germany in 1939, David and Naomi decided to marry. Ernest was not happy about the betrothal. The couple's third son, Piers, has suggested that his parents felt unable to wed until after Ernest's death, adding that it was something Naomi always felt guilty about. 'My mother believed in justice,' Piers has said. 'She had big disagreements with her father and her father didn't want her to marry my father. He thought she was marrying down.' In fact, death records show it was Caroline Josling who passed away shortly before the couple, by now both aged twenty-five, wed in Brentford in 1940. Caroline's will bequeathed £446, 2s., 11d. in effects to her daughter, 'Naomi Loveday Josling (spinster)'. Ernest did not die for another three years, his substantial fortune of £9,525, 18s., 1d. going to Naomi's brother Harold, suggesting she had remained estranged from her father.

Having wed during the war, Naomi must have been concerned that David would be drafted to fight. To her relief, at the outbreak of hostilities, Westinghouse was awarded a contract with the Ministry of Defence, and David was soon employed in top-secret work for the war effort. His job was officially listed as a 'reserved occupation', a post considered too important to the course of the conflict for him to be enlisted for active service. Instead, as the Battle of Britain raged around them, both Naomi and David worked as air raid wardens in London. Days after his election as leader, after being criticised for remaining silent during the singing of the national anthem at a memorial service at St Paul's Cathedral to commemorate the Blitz, Corbyn explained that his thoughts had been with his parents: 'I was thinking about my family, my mum and dad, who were there at that time in London.'[10]

And what of David and Naomi's politics? How did two children of the Edwardian middle classes come to hold such idealistic views? In an interview given to the academic and social researcher John Davis in 2010, Piers Corbyn suggested that his parents' beliefs had at root a pragmatic, scientific aspect, the Corbyns viewing socialism as the most logical method of running the planet. 'The[y] were sort of radical ... well, they were socialist sorts,' he said. 'They probably believed in ... science and socialism being the salvation of mankind.' But while both David and Naomi considered themselves left-wing, their politics went no further than that. Their hero was Clement Attlee, the post-war Labour Prime Minister whose administration saw the creation of the National Health Service and the welfare state, rather than Joseph Stalin. Although Piers claims David was at one point approached and invited to join the Communist Party (presumably his war work made him an attractive proposition to the Russians), he preferred to stay within the environs of mainstream politics.

'They weren't into that sort of covert operations,' Piers said. 'They were straightforward political activists of a sort in the Labour Party.'[11]

When Westinghouse moved their war operations to their plant in Chippenham in Wiltshire, located near the railway station, the Corbyns went with the firm. David's speciality before and after the war was rectifiers – electrical devices that convert alternative currents (AC) into direct currents (DC) – but the precise nature of his war work is shrouded in mystery. His oldest son David says: 'It was mostly railway stuff they were making, but they almost certainly did other, possibly secret, things.'

The couple made their home at 57 Greenway Gardens, a three-bedroomed semi with a pleasant garden in the back. Their first child was born in 1942, at the height of the war, when the future of humanity itself seemed in peril. They named him after his father, and began the custom, broken only with the birth of Jeremy, of referring to their children by their middle names. David Junior was known as Edward to his family. A second son, John Andrew, followed two years later, and a third, Piers Richard, in 1947. While David and Piers later reverted to their first names except with very close family, Andrew would be known by his middle name until his death in 2001.

After the war, David would regale his sons with tales of serving with the Home Guard: 'Real *Dad's Army* stuff', the younger David Corbyn says, including a story of the platoon receiving a consignment of boots, only to realise they were all for left feet. 'Sharper than the average lot', David Senior's crew tracked the right boots down to the Home Guard HQ in the nearby town of Malmesbury, and, after scrounging some petrol, at the time subject to rationing, and despite the absence of sign posts, removed to confound a possible invasion by the Germans, made their way there to retrieve them.

Despite the fun stories, the younger David now realises that the war must have placed an enormous strain on both his parents, as it did on everyone of their generation – made a little easier perhaps by their relief that, unlike most men his age, his father's life was not directly at risk. 'I probably didn't appreciate it at the time, but you began to as you grew up because there were other people at school who had obviously lost parents. I remember that in the village as well,' David says.

The village was Kington St Michael, about three miles outside Chippenham, where the Corbyns moved in 1948. And it was here, having come into the world in Chippenham Cottage Hospital on 26 May 1949, as the Attlee government was in the process of nationalising the gas industry, six weeks after the North Atlantic Treaty Organization (NATO) was signed into being, and a fortnight before George Orwell published *Nineteen Eighty-Four*, that their youngest child, Jeremy Bernard Corbyn, was taken home.

CHAPTER TWO

AN IDYLLIC CHILDHOOD

BY ANY RECKONING, Jeremy Corbyn enjoyed an idyllic childhood, with loving parents who took care over his education, paid close attention to his boyish interests and hobbies and had the funds to make his life one of ease and comfort. His three siblings were so close in age as to be proper friends, and there were enough of them that there was always someone to play with. He was educated – at times, expensively – at exclusive, selective schools considered among the best in the area. The two homes he grew up in were spacious, beautiful and historic; despite the size of the family, he always had his own bedroom. Outside, there were gardens, lawns and paddocks; workshops and outbuildings, where he could mess about with engines with his father and brothers. If he tired of all that, he could wander off and explore some of the most beautiful countryside in England, fish in the local river, take a look around nearby stately homes or simply soak up the atmosphere of the ancient villages and towns where his parents made their home.

For two Londoners, David and Naomi Corbyn clearly had a love of the outdoors and enjoyed the pastoral life. They chose to live in quaint hamlets and remote villages, in sprawling, beautiful old buildings that dated back two, three or even four hundred years. One was a manor house so large it had once been a hotel. Their final decade was spent in a thatched cottage in a picture postcard village in Wiltshire, in the shadow of one of that county's famous chalk horses.

The couple began their country life in Hillside House, a large stone property close to the picturesque village of Kington St Michael. Dating back to before the Domesday Book of 1086 and with a plethora of stunning listed buildings and attractive holiday cottages, Kington St Michael is today home to around 700 inhabitants, and has become something of a tourist destination for those exploring England's idyllic West Country. Among its many attractions is Priory Manor, which dates back to the twelfth century, when it served as a nunnery and a home for paupers. Even in the Corbyns' day, the village was an extremely pleasant place to live: comfortable, affluent and largely untouched by post-war austerity. David Corbyn, Jeremy's father, continued to work in Chippenham, and acquired a car to drive the three miles into town and back every day. The purchase of a car set the Corbyns apart from most people in post-war England. As late as 1960, only one in forty of the population owned a motor vehicle. Work was going well for David, and with the war out of the way, his firm, Westinghouse, could afford to give him a decent pay rise. Around the time of Jeremy's birth, he had applied for a patent for an 'electrically operated vibrator apparatus',[12] and perhaps this too was bringing in money.

The Corbyn's third son Piers has insisted that his parents bought the large homes the boys grew up in at 'giveaway prices'.[13] Today the detached, five-bedroom, seventeenth-century Hillside House is valued at £610,000. Although the Corbyns' new home was large, Jeremy's oldest brother David Edward, who was six at the time of the move, remembers it as rather bleak. 'That was quite an unusual house, quite individual,' he says.

It was called Hillside and it was built into a hill. To me, it faced the wrong way. It faced north, so it was always cold. Initially there were no windows on the west side, so they put windows in and it was much better then. I don't know why it was built like that.

Along with the house, the Corbyns bought half an acre of land, and with plenty of open fields beyond the garden, the boys were encouraged to run around outside as much as possible. David Senior built himself a garage, in which he installed a workshop for his mechanical projects, and his sons enjoyed helping him out. It was finished around the time of the 1951 Festival of Britain. His son David Edward says: 'He put a stone Festival of Britain symbol high up on the front of the garage we helped him build.' Piers also remembered the garage:

> I think an important thing about me and my brothers and our upbring-
> ing was space … My father was always keen on us having lots of space
> and being able to do things and try things out. So we had this big gar-
> den … and there was a map of the world on the wall in the hallway,
> and we had a car. There was a little workshop attached to the garage.
> He was always making things; he was into science, telling us how things
> worked. So I was brought up thinking, 'Well, every child has to have
> a map of the world and garage and a workshop, and that's how things
> ought to be, and you could do things in gardens, and make things.'
> So it was a very creative environment in the true sense.[14]

Jeremy too must have gazed at the map of the world and begun to wonder about the lives of those living far away; he would develop an interest in international issues at a remarkably young age.

David says that with plenty of space to play, the four children enjoyed the outdoor life, getting into lots of 'active scrapes'. The boys gave each other silly nicknames: Jeremy's was 'Jelly' while Andrew was 'Dumbo'. 'We were known as the Corbyn boys,' Piers has said. 'We would all dress the same but in colour-coordinated knitted jumpers. [David] Edward's was green, Andrew's was red, I was blue and Jeremy wore yellow. They couldn't be passed down because they were the wrong colour.' Perhaps Naomi's somewhat utilitarian approach to dressing her children resulted in her youngest son's now famous lack of care over his clothes. David Edward claims that Piers and Andrew were even scruffier dressers than Jeremy, and confesses he himself is not overly concerned with fashion.

Despite the ease of their lifestyle, the boys were raised to believe that they were not especially well off. In his interview with John Davis, Piers rejected the suggestion that the Corbyns were 'comfortable', insisting that David and Naomi 'didn't get paid much'.[15] Still active socialists, it is perhaps not a surprise that the Corbyns were keen to ensure their boys did not grow up with a sense of entitlement or privilege. The Corbyns joined and became active members of the local Labour Party, where David in particular was busy with committees, occasionally getting into quite heated arguments with other members about tactics and strategy. 'My father was a very organised sort of man,' Piers has said. 'They were always political.'[16] Politics was discussed at home too, even when the boys were very small. The Corbyns watched with approval as the new Labour government set up the National Health Service and welfare state, and were disappointed when the party lost to the Conservatives at the 1951 general election. 'I remember round the dinner table, they were always talking politics,' Piers has said. 'They were big supporters of Attlee.' With three politically engaged, left-leaning older brothers, and parents devoted to the Labour Party, Corbyn effectively grew up within his own debating chamber; a private salon for discussion and argument.

A glimpse into the Corbyns' world view can be seen in a history Naomi wrote later of Stanton St Bernard, the Wiltshire village they moved to in 1979. Although the handsome, prosperous hamlet was owned for centuries by the Earls of Pembroke, Naomi's introduction sternly makes clear: 'This is a history of ordinary people.' She goes on: 'How they survived the disasters of famine, flood, the destruction in war by ravaging bands, the recurring epidemics and maiming by accident, the changing economic and political systems.'[17] It is immediately noticeable that Naomi's account makes no mention whatsoever of any of the many aristocrats who lived in Stanton over the years. For her, they simply didn't exist: she airbrushed them from her history as effectively as the Kremlin removed purged Communists from photographs. Her work, which she sold to fellow villagers for a small price, makes clear her close connection to the countryside, as well as her empathy for those who worked it. 'Through all the years, the endless search for food and fuel, the unremitting toil in fields and farm, there has been the gladness of hills,' her history concluded. 'In summer the sky and larks and beauty of the tiny downland flowers too rejoiced those who once walked our ways. The scudding clouds and dark hills of winter were seen as well by other eyes. We remember those who went before.'[18] A love of the land and the people who worked it; her son Jeremy would have approved.

When it came to educating their children, however, the Corbyns took a less egalitarian approach. Their boys would not mix with the sons and daughters of the working classes whom Naomi so admired, but would go to the best schools in the area, even if that meant paying. When the family was still living in Kington St Michael, they sent their children not to the primary school situated conveniently in the village church, where, according to one contemporary, 'everybody went', but to a convent school called St Margaret's. There the boys were known as 'Nons' because they were Protestant and therefore non-Catholic. Corbyn himself has said of his religious instruction:

My mum was a Bible-reading atheist – no, agnostic, probably. She had
been brought up in a religious environment, and her brother was a
vicar, and there was quite a lot of clergy in her family ... My father
was a Christian, and attended church, and the school that I went to
was religious – we had hymns and prayers every morning.[19]

A belief in education clearly trumped Naomi and David's faith in the Church
of England, however. Piers has said of his parents:

They sent us off to schools where we would learn something. We
were all sent to St Margaret's Convent School, although we're not
Catholics. My father was some sort of believer, I would say. But
my mother was a militant non-believer. I suppose it sort of taught
you a few things there. They were good at doing reading, writing
and arithmetic.[20]

Presumably the establishment Piers was referring to was St Margaret's
School, on the other side of Chippenham from Kington St Michael, in the
village of Calne. It is a prep school, with fees of £3,500 to £4,200 a term,
depending on the age of the child. The Corbyns saw no contradiction
between their socialism and their sons' attendance at private and selective schools. They would send the boys to a private preparatory school in
Shropshire a few years later too, and Naomi would become a teacher at a
grammar school. Despite their offspring's later insistence that they were
not wealthy, school fees for four children would have been a substantial
financial drain. The decision to enrol the boys at fee-paying and selective
establishments rather than the local schools their village friends went to
was perhaps viewed by Corbyn as hypocritical, even at the time. He would
take starkly different choices when it came to his own sons' education,

not yielding from his belief in sending children to local state schools even when it cost him his second marriage.

In 1953, the Corbyns' oldest son David Edward passed the feared eleven-plus exam, which enabled him to attend Chippenham Grammar School. The system at the time required children to sit a test that to a large extent determined their future: those passing were entitled to go to grammar schools, where they received a fine education; failures went to the secondary modern, where they were put on a track designed to lead to a job in a manual, non-professional trade. All four of the Corbyn boys would go on to pass the eleven-plus, which, given their strong interest in their children's education, must have been a relief to their parents. It also saved on school fees; the Corbyns clearly believed that the quality of the education on offer at grammar schools was good enough that they need not opt out of the state system altogether.

Soon after his oldest son began attending Chippenham Grammar, David Corbyn was headhunted by English Electric, a larger firm than Westinghouse, based in Stafford, which would later become part of the global conglomerate General Electric Company (GEC). By now he was gaining a name for himself in the industry as a brilliant electrical engineer, working long hours on projects around the country, which took him away from home and cut into the amount of time he had to spend on the Labour Party. He often discussed his work with his boys. David Edward, who followed his father into engineering, first with cars and later aeroplanes, becoming a test pilot for Concorde, was gripped by his talk.

> He'd been doing work at Westinghouse on germanium semi-conductor rectifiers. It was a very new technology, and they were pioneering the use of it. He later specialised in high-power electrical engineering, big currents, big problems. I don't know how he got to English

Electric in Stafford, but they were investigating the use of semi-conductor rectifiers and succeeding in so doing. He'd do things like [work on] big changes to the salt industry in Cheshire, where electrolysis was used to turn it into sodium and chlorine. So he'd be toddling off to salt processing mines in Cheshire, trying to make all this stuff work.

With his new job several hours' drive from their Wiltshire village, David Senior was forced to stay away from home during the week. He filled his lonely hours by exploring the local countryside, and began to spend his nights at a small country hotel called Yew Tree Manor, about half an hour's drive from Stafford, across the county border in Shropshire. In the nearby market town of Newport was the highly regarded Adams' Grammar School, a state establishment but with the unusual option of offering boarding. With Andrew approaching secondary school age, the decision was taken to send him to board at the Adams' School. Piers has suggested his parents' motivation may have been that Andrew had failed the eleven-plus in Wiltshire but, because there were not standardised tests, was able to re-sit in Shropshire.[21] There was the added bonus that Andrew could keep David company on the long drives home to Wiltshire at the weekend.

Piers has said that Andrew did not enjoy boarding,[22] and after a year the family made plans to join him in Shropshire, moving in 1956, when Jeremy was seven. David did not look far when deciding where the family should live. Having fallen in love with the country hotel he had been staying in, Yew Tree Manor, he made the owners an offer and it was accepted. When the Corbyns sold the property more than twenty years later, the purchasers were amused to see that there were still numbers over the bedroom doors, testimony to the property's past.

The Corbyns' new home was even more splendid than the last one had been. The seventeenth-century property had originally been part of the estate of the Duke of Sutherland, whose peerage was created by William IV in 1833 and whose country seat was the nearby Lilleshall Hall, now run by Sport England as a national sports centre. It had five bedrooms upstairs and another two downstairs, which were converted into living rooms by the Corbyns. Outside there were gardens, lawns and a paddock. As she did in all her homes, Naomi planted a vegetable patch, where she grew food for the family to eat. The house was set back from what was then a busy main road but has since become a sleepy country lane thanks to the construction of a relief road. The Corbyns' closest town was Newport, where the boys would all go to school. Although small, with just 4,000 inhabitants, it was prosperous. One of Corbyn's contemporaries at the Adams' School later described Newport as: 'A market town with a proper cattle market, and it was not a natural Labour Party constituency.'

All the Corbyns sought to play down the magnificence of the home the family would live in for more than two decades. Piers has claimed that their father renamed it Yew Tree House to make it sound more modest,[23] while David remembers it being his mother's decision, saying she found the term 'manor' inappropriate, although that was the name on the deeds. 'We weren't to have delusions of grandeur,' David says. 'It was just a home. It was quite a big house [but] it wasn't that unusual in those days. It's not in London. There were farm houses around us that were much better.' Jeremy Corbyn also attempted to downplay the magnificence of the home he spent his formative years in, describing it as an 'old farm'.[24] 'It was far too big but we had a whale of a time,' Piers added.[25]

Friends would later describe the Corbyns' as a 'chaotic, bohemian household',[26] with little parental interference. As well as the vast playing space outside his front door, Corbyn was free to roam the local laneways. He enjoyed fishing in a nearby river and visiting local farms, sometimes helping out in the fields. Of the four boys, the others brothers say,

Corbyn was the least interested in his parents' passions of science and engineering, although he did enjoy helping his father out with his car. While Piers in particular pestered their father with constant questions about the way things worked, Jeremy was content to curl up with a book.

A favourite game of both Piers and Jeremy was bicycle polo, which they would play on their lawn with other children from the village, chasing after a ball with hockey sticks while the Davids, father and son, tinkered away on the car in the outbuilding they had converted into a workshop. They even had a forge, which they used to make all manner of contraptions. Occasionally, Naomi, who had got a job as a maths teacher at Stafford Grammar School, would come out to complain about the noise, before disappearing again. It is said that the only time the house would be locked was when the family went on their annual holiday – when invariably they could not find the key. Often, David Senior took the boys potholing and caving, inspiring Andrew's interest in geology – he would later becoming an expert mining engineer – and the Corbyns' second son assembled an impressive rock collection. His brother David says: 'Many family outings he would overload the car with his rock and fossil samples. We would say, "You have to work out, Andrew, that your small samples all add up to a lot of weight!"' Piers, already interested in weather, built his own observation station, complete with 'thermometers, a homemade rain gauge and, to measure wind speed, an anemometer cobbled together from pieces of copper sheet, some curtain rod and part of a bicycle wheel'.[27] It was a comfortable existence, where the intellectual curiosities of each of the boys were encouraged.

One of the local children who came to Yew Tree Manor to play, David Mann, has fond memories of the Corbyns. He confirms that, however ordinary the boys believed their home to be, to other people it was an impressive sight. 'It seemed huge ... with big reception rooms and a large fireplace.' Mann, who grew up in a bungalow half a mile from the Corbyns' home, has said: 'Jeremy's mum was the first woman our family knew who had been to university. The house was a bit chaotic and very bohemian. There were books everywhere. Jeremy was very mechanical. We built wooden go-karts, which we pushed from behind, and set up a race track in the garden.'[28] Another local boy says his main memory of Yew Tree Manor was of 'delivering the milk to them', adding that locally the Corbyns were thought of as some of the 'affluent ones'. However, yet another schoolfriend, Phil Williamson, describes the Corbyns' as an 'ordinary middle-class household'. 'They weren't impoverished. He wasn't brought up by coal miners, but this idea that he was brought up in the lap of luxury isn't quite right,' Williamson says.

Although they had become instant friends as seven-year-olds when the Corbyns moved to the village, Jeremy and David Mann did not attend the same primary school. While Mann was sent with most of the rest of the village children to the local state school, St Nicholas's in Newport, Jeremy and Piers were dispatched to the fee-paying Castle House Prep School, located in a Grade II-listed building a few minutes' walk further up the high street. It was known at the time as 'Miss Pitchford's School' after Zellah Pitchford, the long-serving headmistress, who was something of a character. Fees at Castle House currently stand at £2,275 for younger children, £2,425 for older, and for the Corbyns the main advantage of the school, then as now, would have been the far smaller class sizes than at Mann's primary school. It was also a 'feeder' for the Adams' School. If Jeremy was cognisant of the privileged education he was receiving, Mann was under no illusions. 'Castle House pupils wore smart blue uniforms. We were too young to be aware of a class thing, but everyone knew Castle House was a cut above the rest.'[29]

Despite attending different schools, the two boys remained close, with Mann spending every Saturday at Yew Tree Manor. His friend Jeremy was quiet by nature, and very serious for his years. 'I can't remember having a laugh with Jeremy,' Mann has said. 'He was always very focused. He did strike me, even at that young age, as an individualist who knew his own mind. If you want to be along with me, fine. If you don't, well, you go and do something else.'[30] And then, in 1960, the friends were brought together during the week as well as at weekends. Despite the differences in their early education, both passed their eleven-plus and, in September, David Mann and Jeremy Corbyn joined David Edward, Andrew and Piers Corbyn at the Adams' Grammar School, Newport.

CHAPTER THREE

BOY TO MAN

THE ADAMS' SCHOOL in Newport was founded in 1656, during the brief period of English history known as the Interregnum, when Parliament, and not a monarch, ruled the country. It seems a wonderfully apt place for Jeremy Corbyn, who as an MP would call for the royal family to be moved to a more 'modest' abode, to have studied. Sadly for the young Jeremy, however, the Adams' School never really embraced its radical roots. On the restoration of the monarchy four years later, the school applied to have its articles of foundation confirmed by the new regime. A copy of the 1660 Act of Parliament that did so can be seen in the school's archives to this day. For the remainder of its existence, the Adams' School has been a pillar of the establishment, described by one former pupil as a 'grammar school with public school pretensions'. The school hymn is 'Jerusalem'; its sport rugby; and its motto 'serve and obey'. Corbyn absolutely hated it.

During his first year at Adams' in 1960, all four of the Corbyn boys were enrolled, and none of them seems to have been particularly keen on the place. Eighteen-year-old David sat his A-levels that academic year and did poorly; all his life he would blame an inadequate maths teacher for his failure to master the subject. Andrew must have been a little happier than previously, now that he was living at home with the rest of the family rather than boarding. He was in his final year of O-levels when Jeremy started at the school. Piers has said of Andrew: 'I don't think him being a boarder did him any good at all. It was a seriously screwed-up place.'[31] Both Piers and Andrew did well academically, getting good A-levels and winning places at Imperial College, London, Andrew to study mining engineering and Piers, physics.

In his interview with John Davis, Piers expanded on life at the Adams' Grammar School. Although the teaching was 'quite good,' he said that, like many schools in both the state and private sector at the time, it was a place of casual violence, with parents thinking little of teachers and older pupils physically chastising their children, and fights common between boys of all ages. Piers had an interesting theory of why violence which would today seem utterly out of place in an educational establishment was then generally accepted: the ordeal of the Second World War had perhaps inured an entire generation to physical brutality. '[In] the environment of those schools, beatings were normal,' Piers said.

> You'd be thrashed by somebody for doing something wrong. It was the standard six whacks … The prefects could do it with a plimsoll. The teachers could cane you. But you see, all schools in those days were like this. If it were beatings going on in any schools now it would be riots … But it was normal … after the war.[32]

A former pupil who attended Adams' at the same time as the Corbyns adds: 'It was a fairly brutal place. Prefects were entitled to flog children and I remember they would make you bend your head down under a table, so that when they hit you, you would hurt yourself by involuntarily banging your head on the underside of the table.' Another former pupil says boys were flogged for 'having your cap at a rakish angle', after which they would 'have to shake the fucker's hand'.

With three older brothers already at the school, Adams' was familiar to Corbyn even before he walked into the seventeenth-century building for his first day as a grammar school boy. On arrival, he was put into one of the two houses for non-boarders, Clive House, named for Lord Clive, 'Clive of India', the eighteenth-century coloniser whose actions Corbyn would come to abhor. Day boys were segregated according to geography, with those from the town of Newport in one house and 'country bumpkins', as Piers once described his brother,[33] in another. As a fellow country boy, Corbyn's village friend David Mann was also in Clive, and the pair became even closer. Mann remembers smoking a first cigarette together,[34] although Corbyn never picked up the habit. Despite the presence of a pub, The Fox, directly opposite Yew Tree House, there are no stories either of the young Corbyn sneaking in for an underage pint. The future Labour leader never developed a taste for alcohol and is today virtually teetotal. Most of Corbyn's contemporaries remember him as serious and studious but Mann claims he had to work hard to keep up in class. 'Jeremy never struck me as the brain of Britain, but he was doggedly determined,' he said.[35] Corbyn himself has said he just wasn't interested enough in what he was being taught to be a high achiever, preferring to educate himself by reading books of his own choosing, picked up at home. 'I wasn't a very good student. I liked reading about things, doing my own course of study.'[36] It was an early sign of his confidence in setting his own direction in life.

As he entered his teens, Corbyn began to get a name for himself as something of a rebel. He was thirteen during the 1962 Cuban Missile Crisis and while the world teetered on the brink of nuclear Armageddon for two nail-biting weeks, he, along with many teenagers of his generation, was both swept up in the drama and appalled by the prospect of the possible annihilation of the planet. Two years later, he joined the Campaign for Nuclear Disarmament (CND), and remains a member to this day. Corbyn also signed up to the League Against Cruel Sports, a move that was to prove problematic in a provincial school where some teachers were enthusiastic riders to hounds and many of his classmates earned pocket money as beaters on local shoots. 'It's a hunting county,' he once told an interviewer,

> so I was in a minority in my school in being totally opposed to blood sports and shooting for that matter. I remember on Monday mornings at school, one of the teachers would start on about who had been shooting at the weekend. I said, 'That's stupid, it's cruel, it's not sport,' and the same with hunting and all that. I was kind of in a minority of one; there were lots of arguments at school.[37]

Arguments were not entirely frowned on, however. Philip Davies, who was in the year above Corbyn at the Adams' School and is now a professor of American Studies, says: 'While it was a boys' school of a particular time and type, it was a school that encouraged plenty of political debate.' Corbyn joined the debating society and began to read as much as he could about politics. Somewhat unusually, the school library subscribed to the far-left *Morning Star* newspaper, which Corbyn devoured. His sense of right and wrong was acute. One former schoolmate, a prefect, remembers besting Corbyn in a debate by threatening fellow pupils with detention if they didn't vote for his side. Corbyn was outraged by the injustice and never spoke to him again.

Those who discussed politics with Corbyn remember him as calm and considered. Philip Davies, who was friendly with Piers and also knew Corbyn, says: 'He was very serious about his politics, but in a sincere rather than overbearing way. He really wanted you to understand, but he was also funny with a tremendous humour.' Another boy, Peter Pasquill, says Corbyn was 'self-effacing, modest, and a very genuine person'. He adds: 'He was always totally himself, maybe at times some teachers found it a little difficult to get through to him, but he always stuck to his guns and was prepared to argue his corner in a gentle but firm way. I have fond memories of him.' Pasquill says that Corbyn was 'a bit of an eccentric' but 'popular in his own way and enjoyed stirring up debate'.

Indeed, the attitude of many of Corbyn's classmates to this left-wing cuckoo seems remarkably similar to that his fellow MPs would later have of him: although they shared few interests, they respected his commitment to his various causes and found him always to be calm, polite, kind and serious. 'I take my bloody hat off to him, because he was swimming against the tide,' says one contemporary of Corbyn's commitment to left-wing causes. Another fellow pupil remembers him as something of a 'dilettante, into all sorts of things, and quite studious'. And another contemporary says: 'I wasn't in his circle, in fact I wasn't sure he had a circle. I had the impression that he was a bit insular and not a great mixer.' Corbyn was described by one schoolfriend as 'off in his own little world'. His friends also report that Corbyn did not bother overly about his appearance, often finding himself hauled off to the prefects' study for minor breaches of the rules, such as wearing odd socks, another form of mild dissent that he would carry with him into the House of Commons.

When Corbyn reached his fifteenth birthday, his rebellion escalated, as he refused to fall into line with the Adams' School custom of enrolling in the Combined Cadet Force (CCF), the Ministry of Defence-sponsored scheme that gives teenagers a flavour of the military and, then as now, was largely the preserve of private schools. National Service had come to an end only four years earlier, in 1960, the year Corbyn started at Adams', and the cadet force played a large role in the school's life, with many pupils going on to Sandhurst, the Royal Air Force College and the Royal Naval College. Cadets took part in the annual Remembrance Day commemorations in Newport and underwent overnight exercises at the nearby Ministry of Defence training camp at Swynnerton. Corbyn wasn't having any of it. 'We were all supposed to join a cadet force at the age of fifteen and prance around in uniform every Wednesday,' he said. 'The big thing was to visit an army camp at some point. I was again in a minority of one and refused to join this thing, so I was put on gardening duties.'[38]

Corbyn's boast that he was in a minority of one may have been accurate if he was referring to his year, but both Piers and the brothers' friend Philip Davies, who also came from a left-wing family, had already refused to serve. Davies says those who chose not to take part in the cadet force were known as 'conscientious objectors'. 'I have a vague memory that the school made it more difficult to opt out after this, but that they had always accepted that the Corbyn family were intellectually committed objectors,' he says. 'Mr Knott, the school caretaker, had our services on CCF afternoon – he taught a group including me the proper way to use a scythe, and we successfully scythed and cleared a complete field.' Another boy, who despite being a fellow 'conchie' was not of Corbyn's political persuasion, says: 'I remember we were banished to the confines of the library on Wednesday afternoons. We discussed things fairly vigorously, and how we never came to blows, I'll never know.'

Soon after Corbyn declined to join the CCF, in October 1964, a mock election was held to coincide with the general election called by the Conservative Prime Minister, Alec Douglas Home. With David and Andrew having departed Adams', and the always more politically adventurous Piers standing as a Communist, Jeremy was one of just two Labour supporters in the entire school, and was roundly mocked by his Tory peers for his political beliefs. It was the first election he would take part in, and his worst ever result. His friend Bob Mallett later said: 'Jeremy was the Labour candidate and I his campaign manager. At a middle-class boarding grammar school in leafy Shropshire, there weren't many socialists. We were trounced.'[39] One classmate who did not vote for Corbyn says he was able to 'handle a lot of the barracking. He stood his ground.'

Labour may have lost the election to the Conservatives at the Adams' School, and indeed in the Corbyns' constituency of The Wrekin, named for the prominent hill that overlooked much of Shropshire, but nationally the party proved rather more successful, with Harold Wilson becoming Prime Minister on a wave of optimism and excitement. His promise that the 'white heat of technology' would deliver the country into a new era seemed to herald a break from the grim years of post-war austerity and the stifling conformity of the 1950s. The Beatles were at No. 1, hemlines were rising and war was once again on the horizon, this time thousands of miles away in Vietnam. In Shropshire, the teenage Corbyn must have been aware that it was he, rather than his Conservative schoolmates, who was in tune with the times. The following year, Corbyn joined his parents and Piers as a member of the Wrekin Labour Party, enrolling in the Young Socialists, the party's newly constituted youth wing. He later said: 'I joined as a sixteen-year-old wanting to see a more peaceful and just world. I still believe the Labour Party is the vehicle through which that change can be achieved.'[40]

After seventeen months in office, in October 1966, Wilson decided to call a second election in an attempt to shore up his slim majority of just four. This time around, Corbyn set his aspirations somewhat higher than the Adams' School. The Wrekin was a swing seat, and the incumbent Tory MP, a colourful character called William Yates, who once took a party of 500 constituents on a trip to the French town of Le Touquet to celebrate his birthday, had a majority of just 2,000. Corbyn and his new friends from the Young Socialists were confident they could beat him. Along with Piers, Corbyn went out canvassing on behalf of the Labour candidate, Gerald Fowler. They handed out posters and wore bright yellow badges with the somewhat uninspiring slogans 'Follow Fowler' and 'Fowler is our Fancy'.

In this, his first proper campaign, Corbyn would display the organisational skills he would later become famous for as a parliamentary agent in north London. To raise money for Fowler's election war chest, Corbyn volunteered to sell tickets for a dance, to be held at the Royal Victoria Hotel in Newport. The event proved a sell-out, but when the night arrived, hardly anyone showed up. Corbyn had been far more successful at selling tickets than he had been in persuading reluctant dancers they might actually want to attend. Philip Davies, who was there with Piers, was horrified, not least because he had brought along a Conservative friend who was thrilled when he saw the low turn-out, which compared unfavourably to that at the Tory garden party he had taken Davies to. 'Attendance was crap,' Davies says. 'I remember feeling slightly mortified about this.' Davies was soothed by someone – he cannot now remember whether it was Jeremy, Piers or even Gerald Fowler – pointing out that the most important thing was that the dance had raised a good deal of money.

On election night, 31 March 1966, Jeremy, Piers and their friends from the Young Socialists stayed up late to listen to the results. Fowler had snuck in by just 846 votes, while nationally Wilson's majority increased to ninety-six, a great victory. A few weeks later, on the international workers' holiday of May Day, Piers came up with a fun escapade to celebrate Wilson's triumph and Fowler's success. As dawn broke on 1 May, the Young Socialists cycled the ten miles to The Wrekin. On mounting the 400-metre summit, and surveying the breathtaking views of Wales and the Midlands stretched out before them, one of the party, Phil Williamson, recalls that they stuck a red flag in the ground and sang the Labour anthem, 'The Red Flag', which begins: 'The people's flag is deepest red, it shrouded oft our martyred dead,' ending with the words Corbyn seems to have taken as a personal motto: 'Though cowards flinch and traitors sneer, We'll keep the red flag flying here.'

Both Jeremy and Piers Corbyn now began to take an interest in the unfolding drama of the Vietnam War. Just as it was around the country, the conflict became a big topic of conversation at the Adams' School. Piers later remembered that Vietnam led to his interest in far-left politics: 'We used to debate, argue, endlessly in the sixth form common room about the Vietnam War, and that was my moment of motion, I suppose.'[41] Asked what his interests were as a teenager, Corbyn once said: 'Peace issues. Vietnam. Environmental issues.'[42] When Piers began to develop more left-wing views, Corbyn held back. Piers has said: 'My younger brother, Jeremy, was very interested in the Labour Party Young Socialists and I was involved in them a bit, but not as much as he was. I always thought of myself more of a Communist.'[43] Jeremy's friends got the impression that he was more orthodox than his brother. Philip Davies says:

> Piers was always slightly more radical in his perspective, but Jeremy was always rather more a straightforward Labour Party supporter, believing in sorting out a proper working-class organisation. It was a slightly old-fashioned perspective. He and Piers both were lovely, thoughtful and committed. My dad [who was also left-wing] enjoyed talking with them on the few occasions they came around.

At the sporty Adams' Grammar, Corbyn took no interest in rugby and he seems to have paid little attention to the national game of football, which was not played at the school. Although he would later become an Arsenal season ticket holder and one of his sons is a Premier League coach, Corbyn also apparently took little notice when, in June 1966, a month after his seventeenth birthday, the England football team gathered at Lilleshall Hall, just a few hundred yards down the lane from Yew Tree House, to train for what would eventually become their victorious World Cup campaign. If Corbyn attempted to take a peek at the squad, he appears never to have mentioned it.

At home, Corbyn's parents continued to encourage their children's interests, political and otherwise. Yew Tree House became a regular meeting place for the Wrekin Young Socialists, the big old manor a somewhat unlikely setting for a gathering of would-be radicals. One member, Phil Williamson, says: 'His parents were very welcoming. We'd go to their house and plan the next event, and were served tea and soft drinks.' Given his upbringing, Corbyn's interest in politics was less an expression of rebellion than one of conformity with his parents. For his sixteenth birthday, Naomi, who had always encouraged his interest in modern fiction and history, gave him a collection of George Orwell essays, telling him he should decide his own beliefs and be prepared to stand up for them. He once said: 'My mum gave me a lot of books – indeed, I've got all her Left Book Club books at home.'[44] Naomi's influence on her son's politics manifested itself in ways both large and small; he told a local history project that his mother had taught him to pay attention to manhole covers. They liked to see if they dated from before or after the nationalisation of the water industry. 'My mother always said there's history in drain covers,' Corbyn said. 'I take pictures of them. People think it's a little odd but there we are.'[45]

David and Naomi were by now less active in the Labour Party themselves, partly because David had become more successful and busy at work, often travelling internationally. His son, David Junior, says that, highly unusually for the time, his father's electrical engineering work took him to Russia, where he worked with the railways. Perhaps as a result, David Senior built up a large collection of books about the Soviet Union and Communism.

At one stage, he even tried his hand at learning Russian, but gave up, finding it too challenging. It was an unlikely interest, given that this was the height of the Cold War, and with Stalin's purges now beginning to come to light. David does not seem to have been a Communist, however. Piers, enthused by the space race and the Soviet Union's achievement in launching *Sputnik*, the first man-made satellite, in 1957, had been interested in the Soviet Union for some time. Now he began getting a copy of the freesheet *Soviet Weekly* delivered to the house. He said: 'My father, I remember, looking through it said, "It's propaganda. But it's harmless." He'd seen all [the] propaganda and understood the nature of Stalinism more than I did, probably.'[46]

After leaving the Adams' School, Corbyn's oldest brother, David Junior, had moved to Luton to take on an engineering pupillage at a car company, while Andrew had gone first to Imperial College, where Piers joined him in 1965, and later to the Royal Mining College. As he drove Piers to Stafford Station to catch the train to London at the start of his first term at university, David Senior gave his third son a rare piece of parental advice: 'Work hard and don't be distracted by girls and politics.'[47] They were words of wisdom that would have been only partly relevant for Jeremy. His friend David Mann says that at this stage the future Labour leader was relatively uninterested in girls, preferring to spend his weekends with the Young Socialists or tinkering with the family car.[48] Although his passion for politics would abide, Corbyn would soon reverse the order of his other interests, spurning cars in favour of his bicycle and public transport, and going on to marry three times.

With his two middle brothers away at university in London, Jeremy began to go on trips to the capital, joining Piers on anti-Vietnam demos. Not long after his eighteenth birthday, he took part in a 24-hour fast for Oxfam at Piccadilly Circus. Phil Williamson confirms that, even at this stage, Corbyn saw himself as a backroom figure: 'He certainly didn't walk around saying I want to be Prime Minister, however, his strong political interest for justice was always there.' Philip Davies remembers Corbyn as 'sincere' and driven by 'a very moral sense of what was right for society and good for people, and a genuine wish to improve things for the population as a whole. It was a naive but a deeply moral route.'

In 1967, Corbyn sat his A-levels, emerging with two E grades, a disappointing result that would be insufficient to get him into university. On his last day at the Adams' School, he claims, the headmaster, John Roberts, told him: 'You'll never make anything of your life.' Corbyn, whose aversion to confrontation and argument would become well known, simply replied: 'Thank you.'[49] These days he shrugs off his poor educational attainment. Comparing himself to Sir John Major, the former Conservative Prime Minister who left school at sixteen, he once said: 'John Major said I was better qualified than him. He [only] got O-levels.'[50]

Despite his failure to get into university, Corbyn had no intention of remaining in Shropshire any longer than he had to. By now fascinated by international affairs, and, as one of his friends suggests, perhaps inspired by US President John Kennedy's recently formed Peace Corps, Corbyn applied to the Voluntary Service Overseas (VSO) project and was accepted and sent to Jamaica, then just emerging from colonial rule. His brother David believes he arranged the placement for himself, and it does seem to make sense that a boy who, like his parents, was a joiner, having been a member of various local political and campaigning groups since his early teenage years, would turn to a philanthropic organisation to provide a path for his future when all educational routes seemed blocked. At this stage, the VSO was male-only. Volunteers were largely unskilled, as Corbyn was, and newly graduated from either school or university. In return for two years' labour, they received basic accommodation, pocket money and the adventure of a lifetime. With few prospects back home in Shropshire, the VSO must have seemed like a lifeline to Corbyn. 'He was up the creek without a paddle after school,' his brother David says. 'He'd got not very good results. He'd got the usual handful of O-levels but he'd not excelled at A-level. So he went on the Voluntary Service Overseas scheme to Jamaica. It was something he wanted to find out more about; he could go as a volunteer, to do good. He obviously learned a lot and probably did do good.'

One friend who knows Corbyn well believes that by going on VSO rather than to university at the age of eighteen, his political views were arrested, to the extent that he has failed to move on intellectually since his teenage years. 'I personally have always seen Jeremy as a Peter Pan figure, just not a grown-up,' the friend says.

> I don't mean that in a mean way, I see that in quite a sweet way, someone who basically grew up pretty middle class in the Shires, went to prep school, went to grammar school, bright, definitely bright … latched onto politics in a kind of geeky way, and rather than going off to university and really getting stuck in, that period ends up [in] going to do VSO, which is a bit like the Peace Corps in a way.

At a time when few Britons travelled abroad, let alone to such an exotic destination as the West Indies, Corbyn's Jamaican odyssey must have been quite an experience. The first VSO volunteers had gone overseas only in 1958, while Jamaica had gained its independence in 1962, just five years before Corbyn arrived, making him something of a pioneer. In his letters home, he told stories about the strangeness of his new home, although his brother David, who would later become a Concorde test pilot, was just as interested in hearing about the journey by air. 'We used to quiz him and he'd tell us stories: how different life was there, and the difficulties of getting to or from there,' David says.

Once in Jamaica, Corbyn was sent to work as a teacher in a school in a deprived part of the capital, Kingston. It was a world away from the north coast of the island, where rich Americans and Europeans played in the sun. David believes the Foreign Office kept an eye on the VSO recruits, with volunteers summoned to the High Commission for pep talks. Peter Croft, who was in Jamaica for VSO at the same time as Corbyn, has said:

> They [the Jamaicans] had gained their independence but there were vestiges of the colonial times. I remember that we had a talk from one of the embassy staff on the etiquette of responding to cocktail parties at the embassy. And I think even for us coming from England it was really a rather dramatic illustration of the contrast in terms of privilege and relative deprivation. Going out to Jamaica at that time changed the way that we looked at the world and changed how we were when we came back to Britain.[51]

At the Adams' School, Corbyn had been painfully aware of the disconnect between the world as experienced by most people and the lives of the establishment. In Jamaica, that contrast was even starker. It was an era when the playwright Noël Coward hosted royalty and prime ministers at his hillside home Firefly, while Bob Marley and his fellow reggae musicians inspired the nation's black youth to embrace their African roots and rise up against the poverty they had been condemned to since their forebears were brought to the island as slaves to pick sugar cane. Corbyn himself has said of his VSO adventure:

> The most interesting experience in my life was being sent to Jamaica at the age of eighteen and being told to work with young people. I was only about two years older than most of the kids I was working with.

> It was pretty hard going actually, but it was wonderful. I didn't go to
> university, I did that instead.[52]

The new job was a challenge. Describing his teaching experience to regional
reporters in Westminster, he later said:

> It was a really defining moment of my life because I was thrown in at the
> deep end as an eighteen-year-old who arrived in Jamaica and somebody
> said: 'Would you teach geography?' But it was not just general geography,
> it was Caribbean geography.
>
> I was then confronted with a class of seventy kids to teach geogra-
> phy to, something I was barely aware of. I worked out what all teachers
> do. If you are a chapter ahead of the class, you are OK until you have a
> really bright kid, and then you have got a problem. You say: 'Don't be
> so pushy, give a chance to the others.'
>
> So I learnt tactics of crowd control during that process and also a
> great deal about people and how you deal with a crisis, because you have
> to deal with it because you have got no choice.

There was also plenty of time for reflection and contemplation. He has said
that while in Jamaica he took to poetry; so pleased was he with one verse
that he submitted it to the *New Statesman* for publication.[53] Sadly, he heard
nothing back. A few months into his Jamaican odyssey, Corbyn first grew
the beard that has since become iconic, earning himself the nickname with
the locals of 'Beardman'.[54]

Although marijuana was relatively common in Jamaica with the rise
of the Rastafari religion, which encourages the smoking of cannabis
for spiritual purposes, Corbyn claims not to have used pot as a young
man. When, during a hustings organised by LBC for the 2015 leadership

contest, the four candidates were asked if they had ever smoked cannabis, Corbyn was the only one to reply in the negative: 'Really boring, no never,' he said.[55]

With its romantic sights and smells, Jamaica must have been a thrilling place to visit for a boy whose experiences to date had been confined to rural Wiltshire and Shropshire. David Lammy, the MP for Tottenham, who has known him for twenty-five years and whose own background is black Guyanese, believes the time Corbyn spent in Jamaica was life-changing, leading him, on his return to England, to seek out a life among neighbours of more varied backgrounds than those his parents chose to make their home among. 'In Jamaica he kind of falls in love,' Lammy says.

> Jamaica in those days would have been emerging [into] independence, lots of heated politics … Bob Marley, an Afro-centric perspective, but also tensions with the colonial empire. Basically, psychologically, what he does is he comes back to England, but he comes back to the bit of England that is the closest he can get to Jamaica. He comes to [north London], the heart of multicultural Britain.

Once his time with the VSO had come to an end, Corbyn set off on his own around Latin America, including long stays in Bolivia and Peru, and arriving in Chile in 1970, just in time for the election of Salvador Allende. In an era before the internet, communication from home was patchy. As he told the Huffington Post in December 2015:

> I was away from home for a long time. I made one phone call the whole time I was away. And when I phoned my home, they were out. We communicated by letter. They had no idea where I was going, I didn't have much idea where I was going. I thought it was all perfectly OK.

What Corbyn saw of the inequality in Jamaica and Latin America seems to have left an indelible impression. His family confirms that he was struck by the inequality he encountered. He returned radicalised, and for the rest of his life would be on the far left of British politics. His experiences also fostered a sense of independence and self-sufficiency unusual in a grammar school boy from a close-knit, loving family.

It must have chaffed to have to return to England after three years away. He resumed living with his parents at Yew Tree House and took a job on a local farm. He developed a rapport with the animals and became a vegetarian, a relatively unusual choice for the time, and one he has stuck to for more than forty-five years. He has said of his decision: 'I got attached to the pigs and I couldn't stand the thought that they would have to go off to be slaughtered.'[56] So enthusiastic is Corbyn about vegetarianism that he once put down a humorous Early Day Motion (a type of parliamentary petition) congratulating the House of Commons' canteen on an 'excellent bean casserole'. Corbyn also worked in the fields and, like his mother, developed a lifelong interest in growing his own fruit and vegetables, later spending many happy hours on his allotment in Islington.

But life back in Shropshire wasn't exactly inspiring. In an attempt to shake things up, he next decided on a career in journalism, getting a job on the local paper, the *Newport Market Drayton Advertiser*. 'Oh dear, a hick newspaper if ever there was one,' his brother David says. 'I don't think he was a good newspaper reporter.' Although most of his time was spent covering weddings and funerals, Corbyn seemed to enjoy himself at the paper, rushing around on his bicycle and getting into scrapes with 'Scoop Norton,' the *Advertiser*'s 'ace reporter' who wrote most of the major news stories, such as they were.

On returning from his travels, Corbyn also renewed his association with the Wrekin Labour Party and in May 1972 he travelled to the Lincolnshire seaside town of Skegness to attend the Young Socialists' Annual Congress. There, in what would later become a habit for Corbyn, he played down his rural background, telling fellow delegates he was from Telford, the new town ten miles and a world away from Newport and Yew Tree House. Among the people he met during the congress were a young politically active married couple, Valerie and Keith Veness, who would go on to be lifelong friends and colleagues in the Labour Party, Keith acting as his agent for some years. Keith Veness remembers Corbyn as 'the bright young bloke who was the delegate from Telford New Town in Shropshire, where he lived'. For what must have been the first and only time, Corbyn and his new friends found themselves on the right of the gathering, which, Veness says, was 'full of left groups'. 'By that time the Militant Tendency had taken it over so we on the hard left, [Labour] party members, were hence on the right of the conference.'

Despite the fraternal battles, Corbyn enjoyed himself with the Young Socialists. It was a relief to spend time with like-minded spirits such as the Venesses after long years feeling like an outsider in Shropshire. Compared to their lives as political activists in London, the daily beat as a rural local newspaper reporter seemed pretty unexciting. Corbyn's mother, Naomi, also felt that a career in journalism was not for him, and began pestering him to resume his studies. Soon after the congress, he handed in his notice at the *Advertiser* and made his way to the capital. He was twenty-two years old and he would never live anywhere but north London again.

CHAPTER FOUR

JANE — AND DIANE

WHEN JEREMY CORBYN arrived in north London in 1973, he felt himself immediately among friends, in a world instantly more of a fit than that of his upbringing. Here were fellow thinkers who shared his vision of a more equal society, and a place where people of all colours and creeds mingled, and no one judged what you wore or how you spent your time. Politics was in the air in the way that it hadn't been in the countryside; people were engaged, interested in their fellow men and women, and prepared to become involved, to fight for what they believed in. For David and Naomi Corbyn, politics had reached its logical conclusion in a total war, their flight from a London under bombardment by the Nazis leading them to find a sanctuary in the pastoral life. To their youngest son, however, politics was liberating, not threatening. The countryside in contrast was stifling, parochial. In an interview with the *New Statesman* many years later, Corbyn named as his favourite novel Gustave Flaubert's *Madame Bovary*,[57] the story of a bored French housewife who seeks escape from the banalities of her provincial life in adulterous adventures. For Corbyn, London and the activism he undertook there became a means of escape from the cloying confinement of his rural upbringing. Moving to north London, for the first time, in a way that Wiltshire, Shropshire, Jamaica, and certainly not his grammar school had not been, he was at home.

That he ended up in north London was a happy accident. Worried by his lack of prospects and sensing his restlessness in Shropshire, Naomi persuaded Corbyn to apply for one of the few courses that would have him: Trade Union Studies at the Polytechnic of North London, now part of London Metropolitan University. Based on the Holloway Road, a busy thoroughfare cutting through the area of Islington he currently represents, North London Poly, as it was known, had recently been formed from the merging of two other polytechnics, the Northern and the Western, and had a respectable reputation, with the great historian A. J. P. Taylor on the lecturing staff.

Corbyn moved to London with a friend from the Wrekin Young Socialists, Jim Brown, and the pair found themselves temporary accommodation near the polytechnic in Islington while they looked for permanent digs. Fired up by his new surroundings, Corbyn set about seeking out likeminded souls. Bored of his studies one day, he wandered into the offices of *Tribune*, the fortnightly socialist newspaper, in the hope of striking up a conversation. By coincidence, working there was Valerie Veness, whom he had first met the year before at the Young Socialists' Camp in Skegness. Her husband Keith Veness says: 'Valerie rang me and said: "Do you remember that Jeremy Corbyn bloke? He's just walked into the office." He'd obviously just moved to London.'

Keith and Valerie Veness were thrilled to learn that Corbyn was in Islington, and not just because they enjoyed his company. Their local branch of the Labour Party, Islington North, had become split, with the Member of Parliament, Michael O'Halloran, unpopular with members on the left of the party. As an energetic young man who seemed to share their political outlook, the Venesses hoped that the new arrival Corbyn would become an ally in the constituency party. Ultimately, the couple would win their war against O'Halloran – but not for more than a decade. To the couple's disappointment, Corbyn's stay in Islington lasted only a few months before he found cheaper accommodation three miles away in Hornsey, moving into a studio flat on Etherley Road. He joined the Hornsey Constituency Labour Party (CLP) and the local branch of the Young Socialists, quickly becoming one of the leading lights of both organisations. Islington North would have to wait.

Toby Harris – now Lord Harris of Haringey, a former leader of Haringey Council – first got to know Corbyn at this time. He says:

> I was a very sad young teenager and joined the Labour Party at the age of sixteen. I had been an active branch secretary when I was still at school, went to Cambridge and came back during the holidays, and somehow while I was in my first year at Cambridge he appeared on the scene. He was at that time what would have been known as a 'bedsit infiltrator'. He lived in a bedsit, he just turned up, was very left-wing and gradually took over the local party. Each time I came back and re-engaged I discovered that Jeremy was a more significant figure.

Around the time that he moved to Hornsey, Corbyn quit his studies at North London Poly. Still smarting from his experiences at the Adams' School, Corbyn found it no easier to deal with authority when he resumed his education. His brother Piers told *The Sun*: 'Jeremy had his studies terminated because he had big arguments with the people in charge. He probably knew more than them.' During his brief period in higher education, Corbyn enjoyed student politics, going on rallies and taking part in debates. The writer and commentator Leo McKinstry, who knew him a little later, claims Corbyn never moved on intellectually from his time at the poly. '[H]e is an unreconstructed Trotskyite whose views have remain frozen ever since he attended his first demonstration in the late 1960s. Corbyn is the permanent rebellious adolescent,' McKinstry has said.[58]

After quitting college, in need of work and still interested in trade union-ism, Corbyn heard of an opening at the National Union of Tailor and Garment Workers (NUTGW). Based in Hoxton Square in Shoreditch, the union's membership was largely made up of Jewish tailors from the East End of London, who had a long tradition of involvement with the Labour Party. Even by the early 1970s, their trade was dying, with skilled tailors pushed out as department stores and cheap, mass-produced clothes, often made overseas, became the norm. Although it had been the tenth largest union in the country after the war, with nearly 130,000 members, by the time Corbyn began working there, the NUTGW was somewhat moribund; fellow trade union-ists jokingly referred to it as the 'National Union of Jewish Stalinists'. Keith Veness says: 'Jeremy was basically office boy at their place in Hoxton Square. That was his first job. He just applied for it – in those days there wasn't huge numbers of people wanting to be a filing clerk for a trade union.' Corbyn himself referred to his new employer as 'the other T&G',[59] the 'real' T&G being the Transport and General Workers' Union, the country's biggest. His work included challenging employers who claimed to have gone bankrupt just before the Christmas (and Hanukkah) holidays, owing their staff pay.

Corbyn worked hard at the NUTGW but his primary interest was the Labour Party. He became chairman of the Hornsey Young Socialists and put all his free time into the cause, increasing his influence over the local party as much by the hours he put in as the strength of his personality. Lord Harris says that without being a particularly forceful character, Corbyn's relentless activism meant that, within a couple of years, he came to exert almost total control. Those who knew him at this time describe him as a classic backroom boy, pulling levers behind the scenes on behalf of more appealing but less driven personalities. Harris goes on:

He was always there as the organiser. He persuaded people to do things. He certainly over a period of five, ten years, really energised the local Constituency Labour Party so that it became very active, one of the largest in the country. He was a very hard worker. There was a pejorative phrase, a 24-hour-a-day politician, but he really was. He lived and breathed it.

Keith Veness, who remained close to Corbyn and worked with him on campaigns straddling their neighbouring constituencies, agrees that he put in the hours: 'He was very keen, very active. I suppose we all were but he was particularly so. He seemed to operate without much sleep. He didn't let anything like that get in the way.' Corbyn's new friends did not detect any personal ambition in his makeup, and, given that, it remains a mystery to many of them why he was so consumed by politics. Lord Harris says:

You were never quite clear what the personal motivation was, it was never explicit. It was all about 'We've got to win these council seats, we've got to win.' He wanted Labour to do well [and] he did create a good local election machine. He was quite charismatic in that way.

Although he raised a few hackles among the 'old guard' of the Hornsey party, many of whom were to his right politically, no one could doubt Corbyn's dedication. And soon his work paid off. The local council, Haringey, had become Labour-controlled only in 1971, and Corbyn put in long hours building membership and support in the borough. He also began to rise through the ranks of CND, having joined as a boy, eventually becoming a national vice-chair. Corbyn was by now a popular, if slightly aloof, figure. 'A lot of people liked him and nobody doubted his commitment to making things happen and delivering Labour votes, which obviously is critical, it's what the Labour Party is all about,' Harris says. 'When he first arrived he was a very energetic organiser, [and] slightly pushed aside some of the older people in the party who had always done it their way. [He was] much more active, energetic, and adopted a left-wing posture.'

Within a few years, the Hornsey CLP had grown to become the largest in the country, with around 4,000 members, including a strong youth contingent. Keith Veness says: 'He had a group of quite a few younger people who worked with him. They wanted to build a very active and strong campaigning party.' The young new members were also no doubt attracted by the active social scene that began to spring up, centred around a few Irish pubs close to the party's headquarters. Lord Harris says Corbyn was less interested in this aspect of party life.

> He was social and friendly but that wasn't the purpose. Yes, he would go to the pub, but that was so people knew they were supposed to be canvassing the following morning. He would turn up with several bags of leaflets for people to take home. I don't remember him drinking much. If there was a social event he would always look in but he wouldn't necessarily stay for very long.

Tariq Ali, the left-wing commentator and writer who socialised with Hornsey party activists at the time, agrees:

> He was never a social butterfly, far from it, but he wasn't anti-social, and he was always a very caring guy. Like Jeremy, I'm not a great pub-goer at the best of times, and wasn't then, but occasionally I would join them for a jar. We were all very political. Our generation was a political generation. We lived for politics and it was the most important thing in our lives, and still is for Jeremy.

Others remember Corbyn as more convivial company. The documentary-maker Nick Rosen has written:

> [H]e was chairman of Hornsey Labour Party Young Socialists. I was a much younger YS member and he was my mentor in all things political. After meetings, a group of us would go to the Irish pub around the corner … and then back to one of our flats … We would talk all night about the coming collapse of capitalism. And we would sing songs. Protest songs, folk songs – all kinds of songs. Whatever else we sang around the kitchen tables of north London, Irish protest songs were the backbone of the evenings. I still remember all the words to songs like 'Off to Dublin in the Green' and 'The Wearing of the Green'. Once these sessions started Jeremy would also usually insist on at least one round of that rather repetitive ditty 'One Man Went to Mow', about farming a meadow. He would really get into it – racing down the numbers from ten men, nine men, eight … to one man and his dog.[60]

While the nursery rhyme 'One Man Went to Mow' may be uncontroversial, the other songs Rosen remembers bellowing out with Corbyn are associated with the Irish Republican Army; indeed, the first contains a reference to a ploughboy saying: 'I'm off to join the IRA and I'm off tomorrow morn.' Corbyn would later come under fire for his championing of Irish Republicanism. At a time when the murders of fourteen civil rights protesters by paratroopers in Derry on Bloody Sunday 1972 had turned Northern Ireland from a trouble spot to a war zone, and with the IRA bringing the conflict to the British mainland with the 1974 Guildford and Birmingham pub bombings, in the cosy world of north London's Irish bars, Corbyn's sympathies were clear.

Hornsey Labour Party had attractions for Corbyn other than nights out in the pub. During the course of 1973, he began chatting to fellow member

Jane Chapman, at the time a postgraduate student, at party meetings. While campaigning together for Harold Wilson during the February 1974 general election, they fell in love, enjoying what she has described as a 'whirlwind romance'. 'He was friendly and lively and seemed bright and committed,' Chapman later said. 'And he wasn't bad looking in those days. He was quite charming.'[61] Three months later they were married; like Corbyn, Chapman was twenty-five years old. 'We were political soulmates,' she says. 'The relationship was very much based on shared political ideas and involvement.' Corbyn proposed with an antique emerald engagement ring, and the wedding, a civil ceremony at Haringey Town Hall, was followed a few days later by a reception for friends and family at her father's bowling club in the Somerset seaside resort of Weston-super-Mare. Chapman's parents were lifelong Tories and while they did not speak out against the marriage, she said her mother 'would have probably hoped for something different' from this fervently left-wing young man.[62]

Two days before the wedding in May 1974, both Corbyn and Chapman had been elected to Haringey Council, where they were soon nicknamed 'Haringey's Nye Bevan and Jennie Lee' after the left-wing husband-and-wife MPs who were prominent in the 1950s and '60s. Colleagues who did not share their left-wing beliefs referred to them instead as 'The Dreadful Duo'.[63] Chapman later told the *Daily Mail*: 'Politics became our life. He was out most evenings, because when we weren't at meetings he would go to the Labour headquarters and do photocopying.'

With the election of a minority Labour government in February 1974, it became clear that another general election would soon take place, and it was duly called by Harold Wilson for October. Chapman was selected to fight the safe Conservative parliamentary seat of Dorking for Labour, while Corbyn took on the role of election agent in Hornsey. Neither was successful, but both performed respectably, Chapman increasing the Labour vote, and the candidate in Hornsey, Irving Kuczynski, coming within 800 votes of snatching the seat from the Tories. Lord Harris says of Chapman: 'She was much more overtly the ambitious one. She did want to be an MP.' Chapman agrees that she was 'more senior than Jeremy' politically, adding that she never detected any personal ambition in her husband: 'He never expressed an interest in the past in that kind of leadership; it was more about raising the discussion and representing ordinary people.'

The following year, during the referendum on the European Economic Community (EEC) that confirmed Britain's membership of what would later become the European Union, Corbyn voted against the mainstream. 'I did vote and I voted "No",' he later said.[64] He maintains a suspicion of Europe to this day, a traditional stance of the left viewed by today's Labour mainstream as impossibly old-fashioned.

Not long after the referendum, Corbyn and Chapman moved a few minutes' walk away to a one-bedroom, ground-floor flat on Lausanne Road, one of a series of streets running in straight lines between two major thoroughfares, the A105 and the B138, giving them the nickname 'The Ladder'. Many of their neighbours were Greek Cypriot, to be succeeded as the years passed by members of the Kurdish community. They had chickens in the back garden and acquired a black mongrel dog called Mango and a tabby cat, which they named Harold Wilson, after the Prime Minister on whose campaign they had fallen in love. It was yet another illustration of the centrality of politics to the couple's lives. They now were part of the zeitgeist, participating in meetings on matters national and international, organising demonstrations, campaigning, debating. The couple became friendly with people from exotic backgrounds, including the Pakistan-born Tariq Ali and the late Bernie Grant, the Guyanese black rights campaigner who would go on to become the MP for Tottenham. Shropshire and Somerset must have seemed a long way away.

The Corbyn family remained close, however. The middle two Corbyn brothers, Andrew and Piers, were sharing a flat in west London and, after getting into a dispute with their landlord, took over a large house in Elgin Avenue, Notting Hill, as squatters. As first friends and then other members of the radical, left-wing circles they moved in learned of what they had done and decided to join them, numbers swelled, and they went on to found what became known as the Squatters' Movement. Within a few years, Piers was heading a community that included hundreds of squatters in homes across the capital, including a number of families, becoming caught up in frequent brushes with the police and local authorities.[65] Corbyn did not join the squat, preferring to concentrate on electoral politics, but he saw his brothers often. Piers in particular would frequently drop over to Hornsey, joining in with the activities of the CLP.

The Corbyn brothers tended to keep quiet about their middle-class background. 'I think his parents [were] radical, in a very decent way,' Tariq Ali says. Leo McKinstry, who knew him a little later, says it was only Corbyn's 'slightly refined' tones that made him stand out from the Irish and cockney voices of north London. 'Other people on the left tried to put on a proletarian accent,' McKinstry says. 'To his credit, Jeremy never did.'

Corbyn did adopt the universal look of the revolutionary socialist, a peaked cap and grubby green jacket covered in grease from his motorbike, which he got from an army surplus store close to one of his brothers' squats near Euston Station.[66] When a member of his trade union, a Savile Row tailor, offered to make Corbyn a bespoke suit, he gracefully declined, saying: 'I'm not a great one for expensive clothes.'[67] Speaking to a local historian years later, he added: 'I said that would be corrupt, and bribing a trade union official.' As the anecdote suggests, Corbyn's was an austere existence; he did not drink, smoke, take drugs, crave material possessions or have cultural interests; to him, politics was so all-consuming it left little room for other interests, hobbies, or even vices. When Veness lent him books, he returned them unread. Chapman says he lacked intellectual curiosity. 'We were both very poor,' she has said.

> He was a union organiser and I was a postgraduate student on a schol-
> arship grant so we didn't have much money. It wasn't exactly lunch at
> the Ritz. It was mainly meetings and then seeing me afterwards. But
> he's never drunk or smoked so we didn't get drunk together. There
> was a slightly puritanical ethic, which I wasn't used to.[68]

Politics, the nuts-and-bolts version that involved helping people and promoting the causes you believed in, was everything.

Corbyn's hard work began to be noticed outside of his fiefdom of Hornsey. In 1975, he was recruited to join the National Union of Public Employees (NUPE) as an organiser by its charismatic general secretary, Alan Fisher. Keith Veness already worked for NUPE, as did Bernie Grant, whom Corbyn now got to know. Veness says:

> NUPE had had this huge growth in membership very suddenly. They
> had a very good bloke called Alan Fisher who was general secretary.
> He went out and deliberately recruited some very good young, radi-
> cal, left-wing sort of people to be full-time officers in the union. That
> included Bernie Grant, and Jeremy was one of those. What made
> them different was they weren't the older, clapped-out people a lot of
> the older officials were. He recruited this team of young, keen radical
> people and they did transform NUPE, they recruited loads of members.

Corbyn's work involved representing cleaners and dinner ladies employed by the now-defunct Inner London Education Authority. It left him plenty of freedom to continue his political work in Hornsey.

What there was little time for, however, was fun, and his wife Jane began to feel restless. Lord Harris says that while she might have been keen to invite people over for dinner and conversation, Corbyn would not have seen the point. Conversation unrelated to politics was meaningless and as for the food, well, as Chapman has said, he could always eat cold baked beans out of a tin when he was hungry.[69] Tariq Ali cannot remember attending many social events with Corbyn either. Jane and Jeremy did manage a few camping holidays, touring Europe on Corbyn's 250 CC Czech CZ motorbike, but on their return it was back to politics. Although she was ambitious, keen to become an MP, having been selected to fight the parliamentary seat of Deal in Kent at the next election, Chapman felt she was too young to forgo all other interests. 'He's a genuinely nice guy,' she has said. 'The problem is, his politics are to the exclusion of other kinds of human activities, like spending longer going out for a meal, or going out to the cinema, buying clothes, watching *EastEnders*. It's the work–life balance.'[70]

Although she herself was not yet ready for children, Chapman knew she wanted them one day, and became increasingly concerned that Corbyn might never agree to it. 'Jeremy was 100 per cent dedicated to his work,' she says. 'Of course, we both were very active together [but] I ... wanted more from life, some time for personal things. We were still very young and he didn't want children then.'

'I got burnt out by politics, I was exhausted by it all and he wasn't,' Chapman went on. 'I wanted to do other things – go to the cinema, go clubbing. He has remained very focused politically but, although I was committed, I just didn't have it to the same extent.'[71]

Friends of the couple remember Chapman's complaints about Corbyn's failure to do any housework. 'She probably wanted more of a social life but he genuinely was 24-hours-a-day driven,' Lord Harris says. 'He's totally committed to politics, so your emotional life as part of a relationship takes a back seat,' Chapman herself added. 'He just didn't attach much importance to the domestic side or to anything other than [his] interest in politics.'[72] There were no rows but the couple drifted apart, and by 1979 the relationship was over. 'In all honesty, they didn't split up, it just unravelled,' Keith Veness says. 'He never came home very much and Jane gave up on him in the end.' Corbyn bought out Chapman's share of the flat, and by the end of the year they were divorced.

Corbyn was not single for long. Chapman has since said that she still half held out the hope that they might reconcile, but within a few months of the separation, her husband had met the woman with whom he would have one of the most long-standing relationships of his life: Diane Abbott. While his love affair with Abbott would barely last the year, from the embers of their romance they would go on to form a deep friendship and alliance that sustains both and continues to this day. Abbott, who was then twenty-six, was working as a race relations officer for the National Council of Civil Liberties (NCCL) when they met. The child of Jamaican immigrants – Corbyn would have enjoyed discussing his adventures on the island a decade earlier with her – Diane's mother was a nurse and her father a welder, and she grew up in north London. Like Corbyn, Abbott was the product of a grammar school education; unlike him, she took full advantage of the opportunities it provided, going on to Cambridge University, where contemporaries remember her as cutting quite a dash. 'She was one of the few black students at university, so one very much noticed her,' one recalls. 'Even then she moved in left-wing circles. She was a glamorous figure, good-looking, and seemed an interesting person.'

Abbott has said that having initially found the experience of going to university daunting, it became the making of her, giving her a confidence she would require in her later careers. 'In every profession I've worked in, from TV journalist to MP, I've never been afraid to be the only woman or ethnic minority,' she has said. 'I've always worked in male-dominated careers and politics is no different.'[73] After university, Abbott entered the civil service, where she worked at the Home Office, going on to join the NCCL shortly before meeting Corbyn. There, she got to know future Labour luminaries including Patricia Hewitt, the then general secretary; its legal officer Harriet Harman; and Harman's husband Jack Dromey.

Some of Corbyn's friends in the local Hornsey party received a somewhat rude introduction to his new lover. In September 1979, undeterred by Labour's defeat nationally a few months earlier, Corbyn summoned a small group of activists together early one morning to hit the campaign trail. A party member who was present that day says:

> One Sunday autumn morning, he had broken up with Jane, and we were out leafleting. And for some reason he called four or five of us and said: 'Oh, we've got to go back to my flat and pick up some leaflets.' It seemed a bit odd – 'Why the hell didn't you bring them with you, Jeremy?' So we all bowl along to his bedsit, follow Jeremy into the room; there on the mattress on the floor in the one room is Diane with the duvet up to her neck, saying: 'What the fuck's going on?' We were quite shaken. You know what it's like when people you know both sides of break up – you have no inkling they're going to break up, then suddenly they break up. So there was a bit of people's surprise at that. It was [the] late '70s, it was still a point of interest, a white man with a black woman, so he was slightly showing off: 'I've got a new girlfriend, and she's black.'

Another member of the north London left-wing scene heard a similar anecdote from an acquaintance living in Hornsey at the time, which may in fact relate to the same incident. The source says they were told: 'I remember once knocking on Jeremy's door ... and who came down to the front door wearing his nightshirt but Diane Abbott?' Corbyn and Abbott's was a meeting of minds, and they have remained close for thirty-five years. Unusually for the man who likes to play down his privileged roots, he regaled her with stories of his childhood in Shropshire, once telling his local paper: 'Diane Abbott always says to me, "You learned everything you know in Shropshire, and unfortunately you have forgotten none of it."'[74]

Abbott too was treated to a motorcycle holiday, with the couple embarking on a trip around France. When Corbyn first entered the 2015 leadership election, a diary story emerged suggesting that the amorous adventure had involved a tour of Communist East Germany, then in the iron grip of Comrade Erich Honecker, general secretary of the Central Committee of the Socialist Unity Party of Germany since 1971. The story became common currency in the weeks following Corbyn's election, leading Westminster gossips to wonder how the pair had fared in a country closely monitored by the Stasi, the East German secret police, and where visits by Westerners, even two young revolutionaries, were not common events. Two writers even began work on a play about the unlikely romantic getaway, until Abbott herself burst the bubble by telling the *Sunday Times* in November 2015: 'I have never been to East Germany with Jeremy. Jeremy did have a motorbike and we went to France.'

Abbott's words may have ruined the joke for Westminster wits, but they marked the first public confirmation from one of the protagonists themselves that the affair had taken place. Until then, Corbyn had maintained a strict silence about their relationship, while Abbott had given only the smallest of hints. In a 1985 interview with *She* magazine, she had said her 'finest half-hour' had been romping with a naked man in a field in the Cotswolds, which is en route to the Wiltshire village Corbyn's parents moved to in 1979. When gossip columns suggested she was referring to Corbyn, the pair did not deny it. So smitten was Abbott with Corbyn that, according to an item that ran in the satirical magazine *Private Eye* soon after her election to Parliament eight years after the relationship ended, she wrote down a series of sexual fantasies about him in a diary which was discovered by her colleagues at the NCCL. The magazine claimed they expressed 'her desire to be manhandled by her then lover Jeremy Corbyn – a bearded Fenian and NUPE national organiser'.

While fun, the relationship was not without its problems, however. Although Corbyn and Chapman were in the process of divorcing, it irritated Abbott that they continued to see each other at Haringey Council meetings. Chapman has claimed that a 'nervous, tense and slightly hostile' Abbott turned up on her doorstep one evening and demanded that she 'get out of town'.[75] Chapman later told the *Daily Mail*: 'She wanted a clear run. I was in the media a lot then because of my political work and she wished I wasn't.'[76] Insecure about the relationship, Abbott too began to tire of the amount of time Corbyn devoted to politics. But again, with Corbyn the master of avoiding confrontation, there were no rows. Keith Veness says:

> I had Bernie Grant ring up one day and say: 'Diane's had enough of Jeremy, she's moving, come and give us a hand', so two or three of us had to go round, put all the furniture on the van. It was nothing spectacular, it just died a death. He was hugely committed to the cause, every campaign going. It was more a shrug of the shoulders [from Abbott], saying: 'It's hard to have a relationship with someone who doesn't come home for two weeks.' [But] him and Diane have always stayed friends, and him and Jane were always friends.

Single again, Corbyn was free to devote himself to his first and lasting passion: politics.

CHAPTER FIVE

ON THE LEFT

TONY BENN, THE former Cabinet minister and unofficial leader of the left, sat behind the podium at the 1981 Labour conference in Brighton, anxiously waiting to learn if his bid to become deputy leader of the party had succeeded. With him were the hopes and aspirations of hundreds of thousands of left-wingers. Benn's followers were convinced that victory in the contest would help them reclaim their party after what they saw as the betrayals of the Wilson and Callaghan years and compromises of the then leader, Michael Foot. Benn's decision to challenge the incumbent Denis Healey, a respected figure who until recently had been Chancellor of the Exchequer, was controversial, and he had been bitterly denounced for it. The debate within the party that summer had grown ugly. Disgusted by what they saw as a power grab by the left and by Foot's failure to control the Bennites, some on the Labour right decamped and formed a new party, the Social Democratic Party (SDP). The denouement of Labour's civil war came at the party's annual conference, at 5 p.m. on Sunday 27 September.

Benn was not confident of victory. That morning he had been disappointed to learn that despite the efforts of his acolyte Jeremy Corbyn, who worked as one its senior organisers, NUPE, one of the largest unions in the country, would be voting for Healey. It was a heavy blow. Benn had been counting on NUPE's support and did not now think he had enough backing among the trade union bloc of Labour's electoral college to win. When the result came through, his fears were realised – although only just. Benn had 49.547 per cent of the vote compared to 50.426 for Healey. He would later complain that a number of MPs had stayed in the Labour Party only long enough to vote against him before defecting to the SDP. Labour's left was shattered by the defeat; the wounds of many who hurt with Benn that afternoon would not heal until Corbyn's own election as leader thirty-four years later.

Corbyn was at conference for Benn's loss and was among a small group of friends who comforted the left's defeated king at Brighton's Queens Hotel that night. Watching Corbyn take to the conference stage thirty-four years later to accept the Labour crown, many older figures in the party felt as if history was being re-run – with a strikingly different outcome. Roy Hattersley, who succeeded Healey as deputy leader in 1983, wrote: 'Listening to Jeremy Corbyn's leadership election speech was like travelling forty years back in time. It was as if Tony Benn had been reincarnated.'[77] Within two years of the bruising 1981 deputy leadership contest, it would be Corbyn, not Benn, who would be the de facto leader of the left in Parliament. So how did the young trade unionist go from being a local party activist, albeit an energetic and relentlessly effective one, to a figure of national prominence?

Corbyn had come to Benn's attention in the early 1970s. Moving in the same left-wing circles, it was inevitable that their paths would cross. Born Anthony Wedgwood Benn, the son of a hereditary peer who campaigned to change the law in order to renounce his title and stand as an MP, he served in the Wilson and Callaghan Cabinets but by the start of the '80s had moved firmly to the left, becoming, as Jane Chapman puts it, a kind of 'father figure to the left'. Bennites believed in nuclear disarmament, redistributive taxation and withdrawal from NATO and the EEC, all stances Corbyn shared. He soon had an open invitation to visit his mentor's house on Sunday evenings. By the middle of the decade, Corbyn was acting as an 'unofficial adviser' to Benn at the Department of Industry, where the latter was serving as Secretary of State under Harold Wilson. Another friend of the left, Tony Banks, joined the team, and he and Corbyn did their best to provide Benn with assistance against what he complained was obstruction from the civil service as he sought to pass labour-friendly legislation and create a National Enterprise Board. It was to be Corbyn's first – and only – taste of life at the centre of government.

After Benn's death, Corbyn said of him: 'He was an original thinker. And yeah, he got the most amazing attacks and was ridiculed throughout his life but ended up a much-loved, old-school institution. Tony was a legend in many, many ways.'[78] It was a lesson Corbyn seems to have taken on board: stick to your guns and eventually you become a national treasure.

At the general election of May 1979, Corbyn had no thought of following his hero Benn into Parliament, and no ambitions beyond keeping Margaret Thatcher out of power and seeing his local parliamentary constituency of Hornsey, which had been Tory since the war, fall to Labour. While he would ultimately fail at both, he threw himself into campaigning for the party locally. So determined was he that he arranged for groups of Labour supporters from elsewhere in London to help out in the constituency, and even roped his mother into campaigning on behalf of his candidate, 'Red Ted' Knight, who would go on to head Lambeth Council at the time of its bitter war with the Thatcher government over rate capping. During one of her visits to London, Naomi was tasked with folding leaflets alongside young activists in Corbyn's 'dingy' flat on Lausanne Road. James Le Fanu, a Stoke Newington Labour member who would later become a doctor and writer, was one of those sent to Hornsey to help out. 'My recollection is of sitting in the room across the table from Mrs Corbyn, Jeremy's mother, and stuffing envelopes,' he says. 'I remember her as being very sparky. There was something rather touching about it. She must've come up to stay with Jeremy, and part of the deal was she took part. It's the sign of a true Labourista.' Le Fanu remembers Corbyn's flat as 'dismal'. 'It was an absolute tip,' he says. 'Not stylish. There was quite a lot of coming and going.'

Two days before polling day, Margaret Thatcher herself paid a visit to Hornsey, and on election night the long-time Conservative MP Hugh Rossi was returned with his highest ever majority. Later that year both Corbyn and Ted Knight were called in for questioning by the police after accidentally failing to declare £30 in election expenses, which would have tipped them over the legal spending limit. As agent, the chronically disorganised Corbyn was legally responsible for the error, but the police accepted that the mistake was an oversight rather than anything more sinister.[79]

With the electoral defeats of 1979 and the upheavals in his personal life, which had seen him split from both his wife Jane Chapman and his girlfriend Diane Abbott, Corbyn entered the 1980s a somewhat lonely figure. That Christmas he did not join his parents in their thatched cottage in Wiltshire, where they had moved after selling Yew Tree Manor in 1979. Lord Harris, who had grown closer to Corbyn after the latter acted as his agent in the 1978 council elections, believes he saw the holiday period as little more than a distracting break from the important business of politics.

> I remember after he had broken up with Jane seeing him at Christmas time, saying, 'What are you going to do for Christmas?' He'd got custody of the dog, Mango, and [he said,] 'Oh, I'm going to take Mango to the Suffolk seaside, she can run along the beach.' It wasn't cadging for an invitation; actually, given that no one else would be interested

in political activity [because it was Christmas] there was no point [being in London].

The ructions in the Labour Party continued as the Bennites began the decade by pushing for greater power for the grassroots. At a local level too, parts of the country began to drift towards the left, and north London in particular became a microcosm of the drama playing out on the national stage, as the two sides of the party battled for control. Haringey Town Hall may not have had an actual bust of Lenin in its entrance hall, as neighbouring Islington proudly boasted, but with Corbyn playing a leading role, it now moved sharply to the left. While Corbyn himself was never confrontational, those around him were in no doubt that he was involved in what some saw as a drive to edge out the moderates in the local CLP. Lord Harris says:

> This is where the nice guy bit slightly frays at the edges. Although he wouldn't be personally nasty to people, he would be part of whipping up an atmosphere of hostility. The old guard in the [constituency] party, who were characterised as being traditional right-wingers – although anywhere else might have been regarded as quite left-wing – were sidelined, became less prominent, less able to hold senior positions in the party. The [Hornsey] party itself had always been fairly left-wing in traditional terms … but it became more that way inclined. As things moved on into the early '80s it became really very intolerant of people who ultimately left for the SDP. Jeremy was never quite at the forefront of that but he often helped stir up an atmosphere.

Although Corbyn had seemed to have few personal friends in the '70s, he now began to draw close to a group (virtually all men) who would become his closest allies in the more than three decades of struggle before his own election as leader. In 1981, he became involved with *London Labour Briefing*, a newspaper set up by one charismatic new friend, Ken Livingstone, the future MP and Mayor of London, who would soon become leader of the Greater London Council (GLC) in a dramatic putsch. In his autobiography, Livingstone credits Corbyn as being one of his most effective allies in his battle to win the capital for the left in May 1981 by unexpectedly seizing the leadership of the GLC.[80] The tactics and planning for the coup were game-played in the pages of the *Briefing*. Livingstone described the paper as being for 'active militants within the Labour Party and the unions in London',[81] but his biographer, Andrew Hoskins, suggests it was more than that. 'People described it as an organisation, almost a force within the Labour movement: for some, necessary; for others, malignant and divisive.'[82]

Le Fanu, who encountered Livingstone at around the same time that he met Corbyn, describes them as very different characters:

> That persona [Corbyn] has now is actually how I remember him; slightly self-effacing, softly spoken, certainly he wasn't a loud-mouth, demagogic character. By contrast we had that young Ken Livingstone come to address the [Stoke Newington Labour] party in 1979. He must have been at that time in his early thirties, and he made an incredibly powerful impression. He was incredibly fluent and persuasive and witty. The contrast was really quite striking. With Jeremy you would never have thought [that he would become leader]. Were Ken in Jeremy's position, you could sort of understand it. He was a real politician, in the sense of being a wheeler and a dealer. The point about Jeremy is precisely that he isn't.

Another friend of Benn's, Chris Mullin, the future MP for Sunderland South, also met Corbyn at this time. Mullin says:

He was active in the deputy leadership election, he was active in all the arguments going on in the late 1970s, he was particularly active in the Winter of Discontent, in his capacity as an [NUPE] employee. I just remember him being around, really, not that he was necessarily a very significant player.

Along with Tony Benn and Ken Livingstone, Corbyn became involved in the Campaign for Labour Party Democracy (CLPD), which then as now pushed for more participation for grassroots members. In June 1980, under pressure from the CLPD, the incumbent leader James Callaghan agreed to hold a Committee of Inquiry in Bishop's Stortford, Hertfordshire, where a number of Bennites' demands were met. Among them was a proposal for the mandatory re-selection of MPs, a procedure that would give activists at constituency level enormous power over their elected representatives. One of the most forceful advocates of re-selection was Jon Lansman, a left-wing activist who would go on to work on Corbyn's 2015 campaign, as he did Benn's in 1981. Re-selection struck terror into the hearts of MPs on the right and centre of the party, and was abolished by Neil Kinnock four years later amid complaints that it put them at the mercy of unrepresentative but active left-wingers in local constituency parties. When, during Corbyn's 2015 election campaign, Lansman raised the spectre of mandatory re-selection again, it sent a chill down the spine of many MPs.[83] Their worst fears appeared to be confirmed less than three months after Corbyn's election, in the wake of the internal row within Labour over airstrikes against Syria. Days after being appointed by Corbyn as Labour's defence adviser, Ken Livingstone used his LBC radio show to declare that those who had defied the new leader on Syria should be challenged, adding: 'This is politics. Democracy can't just be for the MPs, it has to be for the rank and file as well.'

Buoyed by their success at Bishop's Stortford, the Bennites used the 1980 annual party conference to push for more reforms, including ending the power of MPs to elect the leader. The move was agreed in principle, and conference voted to establish another special meeting, this time at Wembley, north-west London, where details of the new scheme would be agreed. In a desperate bid to thwart Tony Benn and stop him being elected leader under a new system which, it was envisaged, would give the trade unions and ordinary members a say for the first time, Callaghan now resigned as leader. He had stayed on despite the loss of the 1979 election in the hope that the rise of the left would prove a passing phase and that he would be able to hand the baton over to his favoured successor, Denis Healey. Although that would prove impossible, his move to stand down in November 1980, before the Wembley conference could agree the new voting system, meant the competition to replace him was run under the old rules: election by the Parliamentary Labour Party (PLP). Furious, Tony Benn refused to take part, describing the contest as illegitimate. It was little consolation when the new leader was announced as not Healey but Michael Foot.

In January 1981, the Wembley conference duly voted to approve the new electoral college system, giving trade union leaders the whip hand. Trade unions enjoyed 40 per cent of the vote, with the PLP having 30 per cent and members represented via CLPs the remaining 30 per cent. Furious that, as they saw it, Foot had allowed the transfer of power to left-wing local parties and trade unionists, some on the Labour right, led by the Gang of Four – Shirley Williams, Bill Rodgers, David Owen and Roy Jenkins – announced the formation of their new SDP the day after Wembley. Having missed out on the leadership, Benn now began to mull using the new electoral college to challenge Healey for the deputy leadership, which the latter had won as a consolation prize, having stood for both posts in the November contest.

By the summer of 1981, the mood was tempestuous; Labour came to resemble a grumbling volcano, occasionally flaring into fiery eruptions. One of the most serious flashpoints broke out in Corbyn's back yard, when Tariq Ali, a friend of his brother Piers, tried to join the Hornsey CLP. While Hornsey welcomed Ali with open arms, Labour's ruling National Executive Committee (NEC) ordered his application be rejected on the grounds that he had been a long-standing member of a rival hard-left socialist party, the International Marxist Group (where he had met Piers Corbyn). A battle royale ensued. Ali says now: 'Jeremy, he was very supportive and said, "We accept Tariq Ali as a member and he should be given a card regardless of the NEC decision."'

The row dragged on for years, becoming known as the 'Battle of Hornsey'. Corbyn was one of Ali's staunchest allies, even ordering the Hornsey membership secretary to issue him a membership card in contravention of explicit instructions from the NEC. Such was the sense of anger in the air that Hornsey Labour HQ came under attack: one window was broken and another had a pitchfork thrown through it. A small bomb was set off in the street outside, at a time when CLP members had been due to meet to discuss Ali's case (although the gathering had been called off at the last minute). An unruffled Corbyn, as the branch secretary, told the local press the violence was the work of 'fascists and racists'.[84]

Disgusted at the defiance of Corbyn and others, some on the right of the Hornsey CLP, including Lord Harris, resigned, joining many nationally who found the bitter, unhappy atmosphere within Labour too much to bear. Harris says:

> That, of course, was a quite intolerant time in the party, with a lot of hostility to those who were not convinced by Bennite rhetoric. I suppose I went along with some of it but became increasingly worried

about the direction of travel ... and I was one of those saying things have gone too far. [Corbyn] was part of that Bennite view. He wouldn't be the one to respond, it would be the other people around [him]. There were others who would do his bidding, people he'd encouraged to flourish in the party.

Ultimately, despite all Corbyn's efforts, the ructions were for nothing: he could not deliver for Ali any more than he could for Benn. In 1983, Ali gave up the fight. He says now: 'I finally thought it wasn't worth the whole row and I said bye bye. But Jeremy's been a friend ever since.'

The first mention of Corbyn in Tony Benn's extensive diaries comes in September 1981, when, in his capacity as a NUPE official, he drove the MP to the Trades Union Congress (TUC) annual conference. On the way, he is recorded as having told Benn that '70 per cent of the London NUPE branches were backing his deputy leadership bid.[85] Either Corbyn miscalculated or London's backing was offset by a lack of support in the union elsewhere in the country. The last-minute move by right-wing trade union leaders to save Labour from a Bennite takeover has gone down in party folklore. Despite the narrowness of the defeat, the loss was a bitter disappointment for the left. It must have been acutely painful for Corbyn, who by now revered Benn, and is described by Ali as 'one of the leading campaigners to make Benn [deputy] leader of the Labour Party', particularly given that it was the actions of his own union, headed by Alan Fisher, that had delivered the decisive blow.

Following his defeat, Benn's friends, including Tariq Ali and Ralph Miliband, the Marxist writer and father of Ed and David, grew worried about him. Ali says: 'When Tony Benn lost the deputy leadership of the party he was quite depressed. Ralph Miliband and I felt that we should see him regularly, just to keep his morale up. So we set up this little group, the "Corresponding Society". It took place at Benn's house at Holland Park.' But the 'Independent Left Corresponding Society', as it was formally constituted, was more than a means of lifting Benn's spirits. It became an important intellectual forum, a place where like-minded, left-wing individuals could share their ideas. One of those usually present, Robin Blackburn, then editor of the *New Left Review*, says: 'It was … a rolling seminar or discussion group that included prominent people from political life, people who were … working on policy and foreign policy and issues to do [with that], theoretical discussions of one sort of another, or cultural discussion.'

As well as Benn, Miliband, Ali and Blackburn, regular attendees were the historian Perry Anderson, the economist Andrew Glynn, Labour's general secretary Jim Mortimer, and Hilary Wainwright of the Socialist Society. Ken Livingstone, busy with the GLC, turned up occasionally, as did John McDonnell, then a local government worker, who would later become Corbyn's closest friend in politics. Corbyn was also particularly struck by the views of another attendee, the late Mike Marqusee, an American activist and writer who would go on to be a founding member of the Stop the War Coalition. For the 33-year-old Corbyn, the society's discussions proved to be the university education he never had.

The Corresponding Society provided an environment devoted to ideas rather than action, a novelty for Corbyn, who until now had seen politics in terms of campaigns and strategy, and was at this stage viewed by his friends as a classic apparatchik rather than a deep thinker. Tariq Ali says:

> Jeremy didn't speak much but he certainly came to those meetings and I think they had an impact on him, because it was politics discussed on a very serious level, and not just as immediate tactics, what should we do about A or B, but politics in the broader sense of the word; what is the future of the Labour Party?

The atmosphere was serious rather than convivial. Blackburn says:

> There wasn't a great deal of alcohol. I'm sure Tony would be very punctilious and polite and would occasionally offer such a thing, but it wouldn't get very far. There would certainly be tea and coffee. On the whole, we didn't discuss narrowly organisational issues; that was what was nice about the meetings. Very often something had happened or there was some political issue of the moment, and that would spark off a discussion. So it wasn't too formalised, though there would be a certain agenda. We did organise ourselves to publish the very occasional pamphlet.

Of Corbyn's role in the group, Robin Blackburn says:

> I don't think he was leading the discussion very much. He would report on things that were happening, because he was very much a grassroots activist. These were actually quite dark years, where the left wasn't making lots of headway. Tony always had an incredible series of meetings that he was doing and it was always quite nice to get his reflections [because] they were always quite optimistic. Jeremy would be a little bit more cautious and down to earth.

John McDonnell has said: 'They would discuss everything under the sun. Jeremy was very close to Tony right up until the end.'[86] Corbyn himself has recollected how Benn had a chair in the room the group met in, which had once belonged to Keir Hardie and which was so uncomfortable that no one wanted to sit in it. Invariably rushing in late from a meeting or demo, Corbyn would usually be the last to arrive and would be forced to take Hardie's chair.

There was a lot to discuss. Determined to cure the country of the 'British disease' of low productivity, industrial strife and below-par economic performance, the Conservatives began a brutal programme of cuts. London's local government, including the GLC and councils such as Haringey, saw it as their role to take a stance against Thatcherism. The tone of the debate was strident. It was an era of marches and demos, of spiralling unemployment, sky-high interest rates and riots in Brixton, south London. Pit closures brought the country close to another miners' strike; it was clear that industrial action was on the horizon and trade unions prepared for a standoff with the government. In May 1982, a group of women peace campaigners began a protest outside the Greenham Common airbase in Berkshire, over the siting of US nuclear weapons there. Naomi Corbyn, by now living in rural Wiltshire, stunned her new neighbours in the staunchly Tory hunting-and-shooting community by setting out on fifty-mile round trips on her tiny scooter to bring food parcels to the peace women.

After the relative calm of the post-war consensus, politics had shifted into an era of stark discord. Corbyn was in his element. In the summer of 1982, when a Conservative councillor on the Haringey authority proposed a motion offering 'loyal support' for British troops sent to resist the Argentine invasion of the Falkland Islands, Corbyn resisted, declaring the war a 'Tory plot'.[87] Offering 'sympathy' for British servicemen – twenty-two of whom had lost their lives a few days earlier in the sinking of HMS *Ardent* – he tabled an alternative motion to the council, reading:

> We resent this waste of unemployed men who are being sent to the Falklands to die for Thatcher and [Argentine dictator General Leopoldo] Galtieri. A tide of jingoism is sweeping the country. Already £1.5 billion has been spent on this invasion. It is a nauseating waste of money and lives. We are spending all this at a time when we can't find money for houses, hospitals or wages, not for world hunger, not for

aid to north-east Africa. Yet they can commandeer ships like there's no tomorrow, and send people to die in the south Atlantic.

Lord Harris says of Corbyn's politics at this time:

> He had a line: he pushed left-wing policies on the council. He wanted an interventionist local authority trying to deliver more to the local area. He believed in community development. He was against cuts. His views have not changed, essentially. Very interested in foreign affairs, a legacy of the Vietnam era, very anti-American, pro-Palestinian, Republican causes, all of that.

David Lammy adds:

> In the '80s, Haringey, Islington and Hackney were at the forefront of what was dubbed the 'loony left'. The thing about Jeremy is that a lot of people have changed their views over the years, Jeremy's literally one of the only people [not to]. Jeremy, he absolutely is not acting, and has stayed in exactly the same place.

Corbyn's political work continued through the early 1980s, driven by a determination to oppose the Thatcher government. His campaigns were various, but, ironically, like that of Margaret Thatcher herself, his philosophy had an underlying intellectual coherence: help for the underprivileged and marginalised, a belief in the universal welfare state, and the promotion of peace and human rights on a global level. In his capacity as chair of the Haringey Council Planning Committee, he introduced a scheme to build council housing in private residential areas, criticising 'the arrogance of all those doctors and lawyers, talking about the environment when what they're scared of is black kids'.[88] With NUPE and Tony Benn, he launched a successful campaign to save St Mary's Hospital in Paddington from closure.[89] Nick Rosen remembers being alarmed when Corbyn came up with a scheme to turn some school playing fields behind his parents' house into a campsite for travellers.[90]

Nineteen eighty-two saw the publication of *A Very British Coup*, a novel by Chris Mullin loosely based on Benn, which imagines a left-wing politician unexpectedly becoming Prime Minister. Set seven years in the future in 1989, its opening sentence reads: 'The news that Harry Perkins was to become Prime Minister went down very badly in the Athenaeum.'[91] Members of the venerable club today would almost certainly be equally alarmed were Corbyn to make it to No. 10. Mullin still finds it hard to believe that it is Corbyn, of all his friends on the left at the time, who has come closest to bringing his fiction to life. 'If you'd said to me a couple of months ago he was going to become leader, I'd have laughed out loud,' Mullin says today.

> I think most people, including him, would have laughed. He's not charismatic, he's very low key. He's not a great orator. I remember him as being mild-mannered. Over the years I've come to regard him as essentially a rather otherworldly figure. He's always stuck absolutely to what he's believed in and never really changed appreciably. He's always lived according to his principles, he's always led a modest lifestyle.

But if he didn't quite have the same reputation as a firebrand as Ken Livingstone, or display the authority and leadership of Tony Benn, by the end of Thatcher's first term in government, Corbyn had quietly built a name for himself as a substantial figure on the left. And now, almost by accident, he would take the next step in his journey to the Labour leadership: he would be elected as a Member of Parliament.

CHAPTER SIX

ISLINGTON NORTH

THE OLD PRIEST was found slumped over the wheel of his car. Father McNamara had long been a heavy drinker, even an alcoholic, and now it had brought about his death. While his flock in the north London borough of Islington mourned, many of their non-Catholic neighbours saw McNamara's passage into the next world as something less than a tragedy. Under his watch, the Catholic Church had become inextricably entwined with the local Labour Party, exerting, some members felt, a pernicious influence over the way it was run. Their MP, Michael O'Halloran, a member of the tight-knit north London Irish community, had been a drinking buddy of the priest. He was unpopular, particularly among newer members of the local Labour Party, and widely seen by his colleagues in the House of Commons as ineffective. Despite this, with its tight grip on the local party, he seemed to enjoy the holy protection of the Church. With McNamara's death, it was as if a cloud had lifted. Within a few years, O'Halloran would be out of a job, and Jeremy Corbyn would be the new Member of Parliament for Islington North.

The story that ends with Corbyn becoming an MP begins with another sudden death: that of O'Halloran's predecessor, Gerry Reynolds, in June 1969, while Corbyn was still in Jamaica. Islington North seems to have been something of a cursed constituency. Reynolds, just thirty when he entered Parliament, was himself elected in a by-election caused by yet another untimely death, that of the sitting MP Wilfred Fienburgh in a car crash in 1958. Reynolds was seen as a rising star in the Wilson governments of the 1960s, serving as a defence minister, and had already been spoken of as a future Labour leader. When he collapsed from a heart attack and died at the age of only forty-one, his loss was felt deeply across the party and the country at large.

The contrast between Reynolds's dynamism and the mediocrity of his successor was stark. Encountering O'Halloran on the campaign trail ahead of his by-election, Auberon Waugh wrote in *The Spectator*:

> Mr Michael O'Halloran cannot think of a single issue on which he would ever differ from the leadership, whoever it was. He seems to have a certain amount of difficulty in thinking at all, and must be almost unique among his race in appearing tongue-tied … It is sad that the constituency which produced Gerry Reynolds should settle for anyone quite so speechless.

Corbyn's friend Keith Veness says of the MP: 'O'Halloran was probably the most useless person elected to the House of Commons, and that's saying something.' In his obituary of O'Halloran, which ran in *The Independent* in 1999, Tam Dalyell, the West Lothian Labour MP who later became Father of the House, wrote: 'Michael O'Halloran was, in my experience, the least coherent man ever to come to the House of Commons.'

O'Halloran himself once told Dalyell he had not sought to be an MP, and initially felt uncomfortable in the role, although it was one he came to love.[92] The former railwayman was born in County Clare in the Irish Republic and 'drifted', as he put it, to London and Islington to find work. When Reynolds died, O'Halloran was as surprised as anyone to find himself anointed by the dominant Irish faction in the Islington North Labour Party, led by Father McNamara. Dalyell wrote:

> He himself was disarmingly open about the fact that he had never ever intended to be a Member of Parliament, was astonished that he had been selected, openly admitted it was the work of 'the Irish mafia' and said that he would do his best, but that he was a fish out of water.[93]

The *Sunday Times* would later run an exposé on O'Halloran's selection, alleging that the process had been rigged. Keith Veness says:

> North Islington was part of the Irish diaspora which ran from Hammersmith into Camden and Islington. The Catholic Church had a hugely disproportionate influence. A lot of people moved into North Islington but they refused to let anyone in who hadn't come through the Church. Someone would go round the Labour Party headquarters and ask to join and be told, 'Sorry, it's full up, but we'll put your name on the list.' You could have run a whole comedy series about what North Islington was like. They packed the Labour Party with very right-wing Catholics, mainly Irish. We used to call them 'the Murphia'.

O'Halloran won the by-election with a 10 per cent fall in Labour's share of the vote and, amid continuing disquiet over his selection, Labour's ruling NEC launched an inquiry. The allegations were serious: Father McNamara's cabal was accused of drafting in new, mainly Irish, members following

Reynolds's death in order to secure O'Halloran as his replacement. The row has striking parallels with another selection scandal nearly half a century later, in the Scottish town of Falkirk, which would lead to the inquiry that eventually brought about a change in the rules governing Labour leadership elections – resulting, in turn, in victory for the current MP for Islington North, Jeremy Corbyn. Back in 1970, the NEC concluded that O'Halloran's selection had been above board. Some local members, including the Venesses, believed that the controversy had been 'hushed up' to allow the national party to focus on the general election that had been called for later that year.

The bad taste lingered on through the following decade, as increasing numbers of younger people, often university-educated, left-wing and middle class, moved into the borough. Tam Dalyell wrote:

> Islington, which when [O'Halloran] inherited it from Gerry Reynolds had been what Labour was pleased to call a solid working-class constituency, had undergone gentrification. Some very articulate people came in to the constituency and O'Halloran, by no stretch of the imagination, was their cup of tea. They were determined to winkle him out of his seat.[94]

As the complaints against O'Halloran and Father McNamara escalated, Labour's NEC held a series of inquiries into Islington North, without ever being able to uncover a decisive piece of evidence that would justify deselection. Following his death in 1999, *The Times* wrote: 'There were charges of personation, vote rigging, packing of key meetings and victimisation. It is true that O'Halloran was not involved in many of these events … but it is also fair to say that he would not have been out of place in South Boston's [notoriously corrupt] Democratic Party.' At one point, as his grip on the local party began to slip, O'Halloran was forced to appeal to Michael Foot, the then leader, after he was barred from attending the constituency's general management committee.

Corbyn was one of those who complained to the NEC on behalf of his old friends the Venesses. 'We fought this huge battle, and every neighbouring constituency, Islington South and Islington Central and Hornsey, they all wrote into the NEC demanding an inquiry,' Keith Veness says. 'It was a huge set-to. Jeremy was one of the people, because he was the agent for Hornsey, who managed to mobilise a bit of support for us.'

Despite the best efforts of the Venesses and others, the '80s began with O'Halloran firmly in place in Islington North, having been re-elected with a majority of more than 4,000 at the 1979 general election. Things were about to change, however, and, appropriately, Corbyn's friend Tony Benn was to prove the catalyst. The agony of the split that now took place, as Corbyn's mentor fought to seize control of the Labour Party for the left, is indelibly impressed on every MP who was in the Commons at the time. Jack Straw, the former Foreign Secretary who was an MP from 1979 until 2015, has described this period as his worst in Parliament.[95] The direction Benn was pushing Foot caused as much disquiet in the Islington North CLP as it had in Hornsey and elsewhere, leading a group of members to drift off to the SDP. In Islington as in the rest of the country, those who departed were naturally on the right of the party, and so tended to be O'Halloran supporters, making his position less stable. At around the same time, Father McNamara, as Keith Veness puts it, 'drank himself to death'. His replacement, a Father Clancy, attended an Islington North CLP meeting where he told members that the Catholic Church would in future keep out of Labour Party business. 'Once that happened, O'Halloran's support started giving up,' Veness says. 'We [on the left] captured all the key positions in the party.'

O'Halloran too had had enough. In September 1981, three weeks before Benn's defeat, he followed his supporters to the SDP, the sixteenth Labour MP to do so. He blamed his departure on both Tony Benn and Ken Livingstone, labelling them 'bigoted and unrepresentative of millions of Labor supporters'.[96] But who would the party choose to replace him? Lord Harris, Corbyn's long-time colleague in the Hornsey CLP and on Haringey Council, says: 'There were big ructions in the Islington party [when] O'Halloran [left]. It was quite difficult circumstances. He had been around a long time. There was turmoil locally. At what point [Corbyn] emerged, I don't know.'

He may never have given any indication to his friends in Hornsey that he was ambitious, but, unbeknownst to Harris, the Venesses, who remained highly influential in the local Islington North party, were clear from the start that Corbyn should be their new MP. Margaret Hodge, now the MP for Barking, was leader of Islington Council at the time, and met Corbyn when he emerged in the running to become the candidate. She says:

> He was chosen to replace Michael O'Halloran when he went to the SDP in late 1981. The Venesses were his mates because [he and Keith Veness] were in the union together, they were both in NUPE. The Venesses were instrumental in securing the seat for him, and then Valerie [Veness] went to work for him.

Following the bitter infighting of the previous decade or more, and conscious that they wanted a fresh start following the bad feeling and taint of corruption that had clung to the O'Halloran era, many on the left in the Islington North party were wary of selecting one of their own to replace him. Keith Veness says:

> We had it for years: 'You only oppose O'Halloran because you want

the seat for yourself.' So all of us who had been involved in the battle against him, we took a self-denying ordinance to say none of the people in North Islington would go for his seat. So we had to look around for a good candidate who knew the constituency. That's how we came up with Jeremy, who lived about a hundred yards outside the constituency in Hornsey. Jeremy was just someone you saw everywhere. London was a whole series of small villages; when you had a London-wide campaign it was always the same people turning up to things. Everyone thought that Jeremy was a good bloke, very active, we thought he would make a good MP. When the selection came up, Jeremy was a good person to have because he supported us in the battle against O'Halloran. He wasn't a North Islington person, so you couldn't say he was only doing that because he wanted the seat. He lived a hundred yards outside North Islington so there was no question he'd been involved in things.

When Keith Veness approached Corbyn to suggest he stand for selection to replace O'Halloran, his response was underwhelming, however. 'Jeremy's never up for anything,' Veness says. 'You usually have to talk him through it.' Not for the last time, Corbyn would have to be persuaded to take on a leadership role; and not for the last time, once he had displayed due reluctance and then agreed to run, he threw himself into the battle with everything he had.

The initial selection process went smoothly enough. Corbyn stood as a candidate of the left, according to one long-standing local activist, and with most right-wing members having departed the CLP, at the end of 1982, he was chosen as the Labour candidate for Islington North. Lord Harris for one was initially shocked, never having seen Corbyn as someone who wanted to be a 'star'. 'It was almost a surprise when he emerged as the candidate in Islington North,' Harris says. 'Six months before, you wouldn't have said, "Jeremy's after the Islington seat." Maybe others were aware but I certainly wasn't. I hadn't realised that was what motivated him. I wasn't clear what motivated him.' Corbyn's ambition must have been apparent to others, however. At around the time that he was seeking selection, Ken Livingstone asked him to consider running for the GLC rather than Parliament, but he declined, leaving the future Mayor of London mildly 'pissed off', according to Veness. 'Jeremy was one of the very few who resisted Ken's blandishments, otherwise history would have taken a very different course,' he says.

As the 1983 general election approached, matters became more complicated. With just three months to go until polling day, the selection had to be run again when boundary changes resulted in the three Islington constituencies being merged into two, with parts of Islington Central moving into Islington North and Islington South. In any other era, that would have meant that, as the newly arrived candidate, out of courtesy Corbyn would have been obliged to stand aside for the sitting MP to run in his seat. But, in one of the strokes of good fortune that have characterised Corbyn's journey to prominence, the two other Islington MPs, John Grant in Islington Central and George Cunningham in Islington South, now joined O'Halloran in defecting to the SDP.

Things then became even more confused, as O'Halloran began to regret his decision and sought to re-join Labour, to no avail. The re-run selection in Islington North confirmed Corbyn's candidacy. But when John Grant was selected by the SDP to fight Islington North, O'Halloran decided to run as an independent. Keith Veness says:

> We never did things by half in Islington – we had three MPs who
> defected to the SDP. The first time Jeremy stood, O'Halloran tried to
> join the SDP but they didn't want him, so he just stood as 'O'Halloran

Labour'. You can't legally use the words 'Labour Party' [as a non-Labour candidate] but there's no patent to just calling yourself 'Labour'. So Jeremy's first election, he had to defeat two sitting MPs, which is Guinness Book of Records stuff.

To counter the confusion of having the long-time sitting MP, who would have carried significant name recognition for constituents, standing against him under a 'Labour' banner, Corbyn's campaign team deployed volunteers to parade up and down outside polling stations with sandwich boards declaring that he was the true Labour Party candidate. Among them was Naomi Corbyn, who was again drafted in to help, and must have enjoyed campaigning for her son far more than she had for Hornsey's 'Red Ted' Knight in 1979. Keith Veness says: 'We had to get people with poster boards walking outside the polling station saying: "Corbyn is the real Labour candidate." It was one of the short straws in the Labour Party, you'd got to walk around with a sandwich board.'

The 1983 general election was a difficult one for Labour: the SDP was at its zenith, Margaret Thatcher riding a patriotic wave of triumphalism following the successful recapture of the Falkland Islands the previous year, and Michael Foot, with his donkey jacket and wild white hair, close to being regarded as a national joke. The party's manifesto, famously described as 'the longest suicide note in history' by Sir Gerald Kaufman, Labour MP for Manchester Gorton, included unilateral nuclear disarmament, the abolition of the House of Lords, the renationalisation of British Telecom and British Aerospace and withdrawal from the EEC, policies foisted on Foot after, under pressure from Benn and the Campaign for Labour Party Democracy, he agreed to allow party conference to decide his offering to voters. Corbyn believed in them all at the time and in the main continues to do so to this day. His campaign literature declared: 'Under the Tories, Britain has become an even more divided and unequal society.' He condemned the 'cuts, closures and poverty' of the Conservative government, issued a clarion call for the end of nuclear weapons, and demanded an extensive programme of home building.

Many traditional Labour voters around the country found the manifesto too left-wing to stomach and were attracted to the exciting new SDP. Among them were Eileen and Roy Burnham, parents of Andy, who, perhaps unwisely, encouraged them during the 2015 leadership contest to speak out about their defection. Their words provide an insight into the views of many former Labour voters at the time. Eileen Burnham said: 'Tony Benn was driving me mad. Michael Foot was leader but every time we thought Labour was making real progress, Benn came out with his extreme statements and I'd think, "You are just going to bugger this up." And he did.'[97] The SDP went on to poll 25 per cent of the vote at the 1983 election, just 3 per cent less than Labour. Margaret Thatcher scored her most decisive result, winning a Commons majority of 144.

Despite the tough conditions for Labour, Corbyn was duly elected a Member of Parliament on the night of 9 June 1983. Thanks to the SDP splitting the vote, Labour's share was down by 12 per cent but he retained a respectable 5,607 majority over the Conservative David Coleman, 1,000 more than O'Halloran had enjoyed. John Grant for the SDP was third and, despite the confusion over his use of the name 'Labour', O'Halloran himself came fourth. And so it was that, in a roundabout way, Tony Benn's actions in splitting the party led to Jeremy Corbyn's election to Parliament, with a little heavenly help in the form of the death of a hard-drinking priest.

Despite his initial reluctance to stand as the Labour candidate, Corbyn soon found he had a natural aptitude for life as a hard-working MP. By the time of his election as Labour leader in September 2015, Corbyn had been the MP for Islington North for more than thirty-two years. He is undoubtedly hugely popular in the area. At an event held in 2013 to celebrate his three decades in Parliament, he said that representing the people of Islington had been an 'amazing experience'.[98] Corbyn is known as a 'good constituency MP', meaning he takes great pains over helping those who need him, and he is universally considered to do an exemplary job. His brother David says: 'If you've been to Islington, as we have many times, you would see he's viewed by the residents as "one of us". You can't move in that place without someone coming up to you and wishing him well.' Emily Thornberry, who has represented the neighbouring constituency of Islington South since 2005, adds: 'He's a fantastic constituency MP, there's no doubt he is. He's incredibly active and goes to everything and does all the casework. Nobody has complaints about him in that way, at all. It's difficult to fault what he does as a constituency [MP].' Another neighbour, David Lammy, who represents Tottenham, agrees: 'Personally, my experience of him, he's always been super-polite, very dedicated, very kind and incredibly committed to his constituents.' Neil Kinnock, the former Labour leader who himself lives in the area, says: 'Since 2007 he's been my MP and, clearly, he is a very diligent constituency representative who is liked and respected by constituents. He's also, of course, a pleasant man with no affectations. I've seen those natural qualities confirmed at local CLP social functions.'

As he had in Hornsey, Corbyn built up the Islington North CLP. Below his offices at 129 Seven Sisters Road, the party owned a bar, the Red Rose Centre, which became a hang-out for enthusiastic young activists. There was a lively social scene and the centre proved a draw, attracting such leading lights from the Labour movement as Corbyn's old friend Tony Benn, and Barbara Castle, one of the first female Cabinet ministers, to give lectures. Comedians from the left-wing, alternative comedy scene, including the poet John Hegley, would perform. Leo McKinstry was branch secretary of Islington North until the mid-1990s. He says of the Red Rose Centre:

It was a great place if you were deeply into politics; our whole lives revolved around it. The bar was very well run. Friday and Saturday nights were regular cabarets, often raising funds. It was part of that whole north London comic scene, all jeering at Thatcher, quite a lively scene. It was always cavernous, there didn't seem to be any natural daylight, it always had a nocturnal air about it.

Corbyn was a regular at the bar, if an abstemious one. 'I don't think he drank, Jeremy, maybe occasionally half a glass of beer or wine,' McKinstry says.

Islington North is not an easy place to represent. At just 1,820 acres it is the smallest constituency in the country and perhaps its most unequal, home to some of the richest people in London as well as many of its poorest. It includes Arsenal Football Club, which Corbyn immediately became a passionate supporter of, in sport as in life choosing the glamorous metropolis over his roots in the provinces, snubbing the West Midlands teams that as a Shropshire lad would have been more natural choices. He names England's Ian Wright as his favourite player, followed by the Dutchman Dennis Bergkamp.

The northern part of Islington is exciting, troubled and energising. As fellow resident Damian McBride, a former special adviser to Gordon Brown, put it in an article for the *Mail on Sunday* days before Corbyn's election as leader:

Forget the name of his constituency – Islington North – and forget every stereotype about poetry recitals and posh restaurants that you associate with that London borough … This is not the gentrified Islington made famous by Tony and Cherie Blair … More than 100,000 people live in an area the size of 1,000 football pitches … Despite their similar populations, you could fit Corbyn's Islington North inside

David Cameron's rural Witney seat one hundred times over. In Witney, 93 per cent of the population define themselves as white British. In Islington North, fewer than half do. Just one in 250 of David Cameron's constituents is black; for Corbyn, it is one in seven ... [F]or thirty-two years, Corbyn has seen the changing face of Britain on his streets, as large groups of Irish, Caribbean and Asian immigrants in the community were joined by Turks, Somalis and Poles. He has also wrestled with the impact on his constituency of gangs, drugs and violent crime, and he represents hundreds of residents at risk of becoming homeless because of cuts in housing benefit.

A number of people who know Corbyn as a constituency MP suggest that his political philosophy has been moulded by what he has encountered in Islington. Gary Heather, who is Corbyn's local councillor, says the MP is 'totally and utterly dedicated to the people of Islington. His world view is informed by meeting people here in Islington. That fact that there is lasting inequality in Islington has shaped him. People who are not politically active would miss it, but Islington is an area of high deprivation.' Emily Thornberry adds:

Essentially, Jeremy's idea of being an MP is working really hard as an MP and learning from his constituents. You have to remember that an awful lot of people in Islington weren't born in this country. So Jeremy's concern for human rights and what's going on in the world is something that resonates with people whose families are still living in those countries.

In return for his dedication to them, the voters of Islington North have proven staunchly loyal to an MP whose outlook has often placed him considerably at odds both with the country at large and, particularly during the New Labour era, with his own party. In all but two of the seven general elections he has fought since his first, Corbyn has increased his majority. At more than 21,000, it is today higher than ever before. Emily Thornberry says:

> There are a lot of people who vote for Jeremy who don't agree with his politics, who don't agree with the stance he takes on things, but see him as the genuine article, like the fact that he's in Parliament, like the fact that they have an MP they don't necessarily agree with but they will vote for. And Jeremy accepts that.

Corbyn made his first address to the House of Commons on 1 July 1983. If he had initially been reluctant to run for Parliament, there was no sign of any reticence now. Those listening to him in the Chamber must have been taken aback both by his confidence and by the fire he exuded. As is customary for a maiden speech, he dedicated it to his new constituency; less traditionally, he broke with the convention that opening remarks be uncontroversial. 'This is the first time that I have spoken to the House,' he began.

> It seems a million miles away from the constituency that I represent and the problems that the people there face. Islington North is only a few miles from the House by Tube or bus. We are suffering massive unemployment and massive cuts imposed by the government on the local authorities. That is a measure of the contempt with which the government have treated Islington North. Within a few minutes of the House are areas in Finsbury Park where there are black people of twenty and older, both women and men, who have never worked since leaving school at the age of sixteen. They have little but a great

deal of contempt for the government ... They have little regard for a system that seems destined to force them to stay permanently on the dole. I shall convey that spirit to the House as often as I can. The people in my constituency are bitter and angry.

He concluded:

I represent an area of London that has suffered as much as any other from the policies of this government, and I shall be telling the House repeatedly that we do not intend to take these issues lying down. We shall not allow unemployment to go through the roof. We shall not allow our youth to have no chance and no hope for the future. We shall return to these issues because justice has to be done for those who are worst off and unemployed in areas such as the constituency that I represent.

So began the parliamentary career of Comrade Corbyn.

CHAPTER SEVEN

OPPOSITION MP, 1983–1997

THE SIXTH VOLUME of Tony Benn's diaries, *End of an Era*, includes a black-and-white photograph of Jeremy Corbyn taken three days after the 1983 general election. He is sitting in the garden of Chris Mullin's Brixton flat, where a group of left-wingers had gathered to pick over the entrails of Labour's defeat, and looks somewhat dejected, despite having been elected MP for Islington North at the age of just thirty-four. Although there were congratulations at the meeting for Corbyn, the mood among the assembled party was downbeat. Of all the blows on what had been a truly terrible election night, the hardest to bear was the loss of Benn's own seat of Bristol East. With their leader out of Parliament, and Ken Livingstone not entering for another four years, it would now fall to Corbyn to take up cudgels in the Commons on behalf of the left. He was ready for the fight. Benn's diary reports Corbyn as being in an unusually combative mood that Sunday in June. 'Jeremy Corbyn (who is now MP for Islington North) didn't want a binge of recrimination,' wrote Benn, who then records Corbyn as doing just that. 'The campaign had started well and then everything had been fudged,' Benn writes of Corbyn's view of the campaign, before quoting him directly: '"There was great incompetence in the party machine; the leaflets put out were absolutely bland crap."'

When Corbyn arrived in Parliament, he immediately joined the Socialist Campaign Group of MPs. Set up the previous December by the Bennites as an alternative to the left-wing Tribune Group, which had split over Benn's decision to challenge Denis Healey for the deputy leadership, the Campaign Group, as it is now generally known, was unapologetically on the hard left. When it was formed it had twenty-one members, but the loss of the 1983 general election and particularly Benn's ejection from the Commons (although he would return in a by-election within a year) meant it would never again be the force it was at its inception. Corbyn has remained a member throughout his time in Parliament and served as its secretary in the late 1980s.

At the group's first meeting following the 1983 election, with around twenty attendees including Benn (who, as a former MP, retained access to the Palace of Westminster), the discussion centred on who they should back in the contest to replace Michael Foot. The candidates were Neil Kinnock, the ambitious shadow Education Secretary who already had the support of the trade unions; Roy Hattersley, a former Cabinet minister under Callaghan who served Foot as shadow Home Secretary; Peter Shore, who had been in both Wilson and Callaghan's Cabinets and was now shadow Chancellor; and Eric Heffer, a former member of the Communist Party who had backed Benn's deputy leadership bid in 1981. Corbyn was clear that the Campaign Group should endorse Heffer, and he railed against Kinnock for having led a group of soft-left MPs to abstain in the second round of the 1981 deputy leadership contest, arguing it had swung the result for Denis Healey. Benn's diary quotes Corbyn as saying: 'Kinnock lost the deputy leadership for Tony in 1981, deliberately and specifically, and he was busy preparing himself for the leadership campaign during the general election. There must be a left candidate.'

In the event, when the result was announced in October 1983, Kinnock won comfortably, with more than 70 per cent of the vote. Hattersley, who was also running for the deputy leadership, came second, but won the latter post over the Campaign Group's Michael Meacher. Kinnock and Hattersley were described as a 'dream team' in the press, combining old and young (although there is just nine years' difference in their ages), left and right. (Perhaps not surprisingly for the times, there was no widespread call for a woman to be on the leadership ticket as there would be by the time of the 2010 and 2015 elections.) Corbyn was not impressed by either the Dream Team or most of his new colleagues in Parliament, telling the Campaign Group: 'People are saying that the job of the PLP is to go for the middle suburban vote, but the Campaign Group must be there on the picket lines, and at the workplace level.'

As Labour settled into long years of opposition, Corbyn set off on a campaign of his own, one that saw him become a mini-opposition within his own party. It was a battle he would wage until his own election three decades later. The whips, whose job it is to ensure party discipline, soon learned they could not rely on Corbyn. Professor Philip Cowley, the University of Nottingham academic who has made a specialism of parliamentary rebellions, has said of Corbyn:

> He's always been rebellious. In the first parliament that he entered, in 1983, he was the sixth most rebellious Labour MP. From then on, he was always in the top ten, and between 1997 and 2010 he was the most rebellious. Over those thirteen years in government, he defied the whip 428 times. In the last five years, he dropped into second place but only just, one vote behind [his close friend and ally] John McDonnell.[99]

Kinnock, who served as Labour leader for nine years, says that he does not believe he ever held a meeting with Corbyn, an extraordinary statement and one that underlines the new MP's alienation from the leadership from the start. Kinnock says today:

> I've known Jeremy since he was elected in 1983, of course, but I've never had any real acquaintance with him. In the '80s and early '90s he was – as everyone knows – a member of the Campaign Group awkward squad so we had virtually no contact because they had little effect in the Commons and, as changes in policy and organisation were achieved, declined as a presence in the party. I don't recall either of us seeking a meeting with each other, and we had no social political common ground or interests.

Charles Clarke, a former Labour Home Secretary who worked as Kinnock's chief of staff between 1981 and 1992, has said of Corbyn:

> Jeremy would always be seen at the core of every element of rebellion of the party on any issue you were talking about: economics, liberty, international. His politics were the politics of opposition. If he had his way, we would never have reformed the party in the 1980s, we would never have had a Labour government in 1997.[100]

When Corbyn moved into the offices of the Leader of the Opposition in Parliament's Norman Shaw building in September 2015, he admitted it was the first time he had ever stepped foot inside.

Corbyn never developed a love of Parliament in the way MPs often do. He wasn't seduced by its traditions and conventions, or awed by its history and majesty. Nor was he clubbable, choosing to isolate himself with his friends from the Campaign Group, including Dennis Skinner, Stuart Holland, Tony Benn, later his ex-girlfriend Diane Abbott and former NUPE colleague Bernie Grant, who both entered Parliament in 1987, and John McDonnell, elected in 1997. His reticence around those who do not share the purity of his beliefs means he has acquired few close friends in the Commons. David Winnick, who is himself broadly on the left but is not a member of the Campaign Group, says: 'When Jeremy came into Parliament he was always on the hard left ... I think it would be fair to say he was a very detached member of the PLP. I never saw him at the Monday 5 p.m. meetings. I can't recall Corbyn ever being present.' Even Chris Mullin does not consider Corbyn a friend despite their long years of campaigning together. 'I've known him for more than forty years [but] I can't claim to have known him very well,' he says. For Corbyn, personal friendships were always less important than politics.

David Lammy says of Corbyn:

> He's a campaigner who is more at home outside Westminster than doing the rounds in the House of Commons bars. As such I don't associate him with having lots of friends in Westminster. There are a few: his old allies like Diane Abbott and before that Bernie Grant, close neighbours including Frank Dobson, Emily Thornberry and myself, and the Campaign Group of MPs. He's also got links with former Islington Council leaders like Mary Creagh and Catherine West, but beyond that I can't think of many people who know him.

Largely teetotal, Corbyn avoided the House of Commons' many bars. Unlike his colleagues with homes in far-flung constituencies, he could return to Islington at night, and was not forced to while away the hours between votes by socialising. In the Commons' Tea Room, before his election as leader, he chose not to mingle with his fellow Labour MPs but perched at a small table close to where the Conservatives and Liberal Democrats sat. There he would usually be joined by Abbott, and, after 2010, sometimes the Green Party MP, Caroline Lucas. Andrew Mitchell, the former Conservative Chief Whip, is another rare friend from outside his party, sharing an interest with Corbyn in foreign affairs. Emily Thornberry is one of the few Labour MPs from outside the Campaign Group to have a relationship with Corbyn, and has found him extremely supportive. She says:

> It was really interesting talking to other women who had been elected [along with Thornberry in 2005]. They found the neighbouring MPs were not helpful, they would put them down, and Jeremy was absolutely never like that at all. He was incredibly helpful and tolerant of the fact that I was different to him and I did have a different approach. And fact that we did have differences was not a big deal, and he would never put me down and I would never put him down.

Lammy agrees that Corbyn is not a parliamentary man: 'You don't get the sense that Jeremy has liked this place [the Commons]. But having said that, he is someone who knows how to work this place. Jeremy understands the rules, he's visible in debates.' In the Chamber, Corbyn always sat at the very back of the Commons' green benches. While his friend Dennis Skinner, another long-standing left-winger, jealously guarded his space on the front row, which by convention long-serving MPs are entitled to, Corbyn was content to take a more modest, less prominent position. Considering the length of his service in the Commons, Corbyn's name features remarkably infrequently in the national press prior to the 2015 leadership contest. Part of the reason for this was his refusal to court the lobby, the group of political reporters accredited to cover Parliament. When Corbyn entered the leadership race, lobby correspondents who were on familiar terms with his three rivals complained that he and his team were virtual strangers.

Corbyn also rarely appeared on television, unlike Tony Benn and most MPs preferring not to pop in and out of Millbank, the office building close to Parliament where the BBC and other broadcasters have their studios. Old footage of Corbyn during his early years in Parliament is difficult to come by. The televising of the House of Commons did not begin until May 1989, during Corbyn's second term in office, and no tape of him speaking in the Chamber has emerged prior to 1990, by which time he had been an MP for seven years. In the first available clip, he is seen at Prime Minister's Questions (PMQs) on 8 May 1990, one of Margaret Thatcher's last, angrily demanding to know what she intends to do about the plight of the homeless. He is a confident speaker, his language plain and clear, allowing the facts rather than rhetoric to make his point. Why, he asks, are there more than 27,000 homeless people in the capital, when there were no more than 2,750 when Thatcher came to power in 1979? Her retort about the failure of councils such as Islington to make use of empty homes is accompanied by jeers from the Labour benches.

At this first televised PMQs, Corbyn was dressed in cream slacks, an open-necked shirt and a beige jacket; he wore no tie. It was a look he had adopted early on. Six months after his election, the Conservative Terry Dicks called for scruffily dressed Labour MPs to be barred from the Chamber; Corbyn was one of those he had in his sights, leading to a rare and memorable appearance on *Newsnight*. Wearing the rattiest of blue corduroy trousers, a shabby beige jacket and, the *pièce de résistance*, a jumper hand-knitted by his mother Naomi in a sickly shade of mustard, the new MP for Islington North insisted he was appropriately attired for Parliament. 'It's not a fashion parade, it's not a gentlemen's club, it's not a bankers' institute. It's a place where the people are represented,' he protested. 'Furthermore,' Corbyn went on, turning the tables on the Tories, late at night here it's quite disgusting. After the debates are over and the division bell rings for ten o'clock, there's a fleet of limousines drawn up and out get large Tory MPs with even larger stomachs, wearing dinner jackets and they stride in to vote … I don't think that's the job of an MP. The job of an MP is to represent their people.

Over the course of his first parliament, Corbyn and the Campaign Group became increasingly sidelined. The wind had turned. Following the Thatcher government's crushing defeat of the miners at the 1984–85 strike (described by the BBC and others as the most bitter industrial dispute in British history) Neil Kinnock took advantage of the left's weakness to launch an attack on Militant, the Trotskyist, entryist organisation that had taken over the party in Liverpool and parts of London. Kinnock's purge meant the left would be marginalised within Labour for the next thirty years. Although not a member himself, Corbyn came to the defence of Militant, taking on the chairmanship of a body called 'Labour Against the Witch Hunt', which opposed the group's expulsion. Some of Corbyn's colleagues found his support for the Militant Tendency tantamount to disloyalty. Robert Kilroy-Silk, the flamboyant Labour MP turned chat show host who was targeted for deselection by Militant and later defected to the UK Independence Party, claims to have taken a swing at Corbyn, only for the latter to run away. Corbyn remembered the fracas differently:

I had been on a programme on television the day before talking about why Militants shouldn't be expelled from the Labour Party. He thought they should, and he was extremely abusive, threw me against a wall in the voting lobby. His quote was: 'I'm an amateur boxer, I can sort anybody out.' I said: 'I'm an amateur runner.' I walked off. He thought it was a great triumph for his macho prowess.[101]

Corbyn's long hours in Parliament and commitment to a variety of left-wing causes left him little time for a social life – or family. He began to see less of his brothers and parents, although they remained on loving terms. In February 1986, Corbyn's father David died of cancer of the intestines. He was seventy and still working as an engineering consultant. Corbyn has said that his father's refusal to retire inspired his own decision to stay on in Parliament past his sixty-fifth birthday. 'I've never gone through life with the intention of retiring. My dad didn't retire. He died working. Not because he was forced to but because he wanted to. It's a family thing.'[102] His mother, Naomi, died eighteen months after her husband. She was seventy-two and left an estate worth £236,333. News of their mother's death reached Corbyn and his brother Piers while they were in the East Midlands, attending a political meeting. Piers has told how the pair decided not to leave the event, remaining where they were overnight: 'We said, "Well, Mum would have said just get on with it," so that's what he did.'[103] The anecdote was later written up as a sign of Corbyn's heartlessness, but in fact he was deeply affected by the loss of both his parents. On the anniversaries of what would have been their 100th birthdays, in the spring of 2015, he held two quiet dinners with Piers and his third wife, Laura Alvarez, to remember his parents. It is Corbyn rather than his two surviving brothers who is the keeper of the family's photographs and other mementoes.

By the time of Naomi's death in 1987, Labour's journey towards the centre was well under way, its new director of communications Peter Mandelson at the forefront of moves to ditch policies of the Foot era seen as having made Labour unelectable. Reforms brought in under pressure from the Campaign for Labour Democracy, such as the increased role for conference in policy-making, and mandatory re-selection for MPs, were pushed back. Corbyn, however, remained true to his cause. Leo McKinstry, who was an Islington Labour councillor at the time, says: 'He was extremely left-wing, even then. I remember being amazed at one meeting when he said:

"Our job is not to reform capitalism, it's to overthrow it." This was just before the Berlin Wall came down, and he was still talking in that 1920s language.'

In 1987, the Independent Corresponding Society and the Campaign Group, both of which Corbyn was a member of, decided to make their discussions public. They convened an event known as the Chesterfield Socialist Conference, after the constituency Benn now represented, and where they gathered. The conference's aim was to 'reaffirm and redefine the socialist project in Britain for the 1990s', in the words of one left-wing publication, *Radical Philosophy*. In his address, Corbyn attacked what was described as the 'yuppification' of Labour under Kinnock.[104] But despite his increasing discomfort with the direction of travel under first Kinnock, then John Smith and, in particular, Tony Blair from 1994, Corbyn was never tempted to leave the Labour Party. What kept him going? Tariq Ali says:

> It's always a question for people on the left, socialists, how do you live with times of defeat? And the defeat came with Thatcher's victory. And then Blair and [then shadow Chancellor Gordon] Brown were basically Thatcherites and saw themselves as such. The only option is to carry on. What else to do? Either you sell out, which quite a few people on the left did, you become Blairites, [or you carry on]. Why [did Corbyn] not sell out? It would never have crossed his mind. He was rock solid.

And so Corbyn just kept going. His causes and campaigns read like a history of left-wing protest of the '80s and '90s. He defended a miner accused of breaking a policeman's jaw in a fracas outside a pit at the peak of the miners' strike, and he was arrested outside the Old Bailey during a protest over the strip-searching of female defendants. He manned the picket at Wapping, scene of the second major industrial dispute of the 1980s, when the media mogul Rupert Murdoch moved News International, publisher of *The Sun*, *The Times*, the *News of the World* and the *Sunday Times*, out of Fleet Street, in a move designed to break the hold of the print unions. The all-night protests often turned ugly, as the police clashed with picketers, and there were thousands of arrests before the year-long protest came to an end in 1987. 'The News International dispute was an example of an oppressive government which paid thousands of police officers to keep 5,000 people out of work,' Corbyn told the House.[105]

He called on the government to use the money it was spending on the 1986 wedding of Prince Andrew to Sarah Ferguson to improve Department of Social Security advice services, called for hereditary peers to be ejected from the House of Lords, and spoke out against Britain's independent nuclear deterrent. An early campaigner for gay rights, he voted against Section 28, the much-hated clause of the 1988 Local Government Act that banned the 'promotion of homosexuality' by councils or in schools, and he introduced, unsuccessfully, a Bill to ban deer hunting. In 1990, he helped Tony Benn secretly install a plaque in the crypt of the House of Commons to mark the spot where the suffragette Emily Wilding Davison (who later died by throwing herself in the path of the king's racehorse) hid on the night of the 1911 census in order to record her residence as Parliament. The plaque remains there to this day.[106]

Corbyn was at the rally in Trafalgar Square in March 1990 that turned into a riot against the government's loathed Community Charge, known as the poll tax (which would ultimately lead to Thatcher's ousting later that year). One of thirty Labour MPs who refused to pay the charge, in 1991 he appeared at Highbury Magistrates Court, telling *The Times*: 'I am here today because thousands of people who elected me just cannot afford to pay.' Three years later he took up the cause of a headmistress from Hackney who was suspended for refusing a charity offer of subsidised tickets for her pupils to a Royal Ballet production of *Romeo and Juliet* because it was a 'blatantly heterosexual love story'.[107] He voted against Britain's signing of the Maastricht Treaty creating the European Union in 1993, and chaired a rally in Hyde Park over the extension of police powers of stop and search in the 1994 Criminal Justice Act. He served on the Commons' Social Security Committee, and spoke out against the contentious Child Support Agency, which chased errant fathers for maintenance payments. In the Commons, he was on parliamentary groups representing the National Union of Rail, Maritime and Transport Workers and the Public and Commercial Services Union.

Corbyn was at every demonstration and every meeting. And if he never quite captured the public's imagination, his rhetoric failing to reach the heights of the miners' leader Arthur Scargill, his character less appealing than that of Ken Livingstone or Tony Benn, he laid down a steady track record of campaign work and showed true dedication to the causes he espoused. Margaret Hodge says: 'He doesn't walk into a room and command presence like some people do. It's rather odd, if you talk to me about other people I spent a lot of time with … in those days, Jeremy was never a strong presence for me. He feels slightly in his own world.' Ronnie Campbell, a fellow member of the Campaign Group, says: 'He's always at the back. It was always Tony Benn or Dennis Skinner or the rest of them, but not Jeremy. Jeremy's always the quiet one. Jeremy's not a noisy sort of fellow, he's very unassuming. You wouldn't think he was leadership material.' Leo McKinstry adds:

> Jeremy hates confrontation. You could say it's an honourable thing and he dislikes the personal kind of politics, but you could also say it's a bit weak. It's the very opposite of, say, George Galloway or Tony Benn or Ken Livingstone, who would love to take people on. Jeremy wouldn't like to take people on at all. If you had said to me in 1985, 1986

that in twenty years' time Jeremy Corbyn would have been Leader of the Labour Party, I would have just burst out laughing. He wasn't the great, impressive, charismatic figure. He certainly wasn't like Benn or Galloway, or even McDonnell. One activist once described him to me as a 'souped-up councillor'.

Tariq Ali, however, believes the modesty and record of activism that define Corbyn are precisely the gifts that the Labour selectorate in the 2015 contest responded to. He says: 'My abiding memory of him: not a trace of arrogance like some have, willing to talk to anyone, to convince anyone, going to meetings even though he knew there would be ten people and a dog at the meeting. He just turned up.' David Lammy agrees:

> [What] a lot of people don't realise is every march, every campaign, every intersection between the Labour Party and the SWP [Socialist Workers' Party], Respect, the anti-war coalition, Jeremy is there. He never turns down an invitation. He is at everything. Jeremy's there. When people talk about a movement, Jeremy's always been the head of that movement outside [Parliament].

From the very outset, Corbyn saw it as his duty to represent not just his constituents in Islington North, nor even the working people of the United Kingdom, but also the underprivileged and persecuted in every corner of the globe. Many of the causes he took up were at the time unfashionable but have since become universally recognised as righteous ones. Margaret Hodge recalls that one issue that occupied much of Corbyn's attention during the 1980s was Nicaragua, where the Sandinista government was under attack from the US-backed Contra rebels. She says: 'He was most concerned about Nicaragua. He spent his time on foreign policy issues.

He would do the very local, the constituency stuff, and then he was more interested in Nicaragua than Westminster.' Corbyn's focus was not just local or national; it was global.

Corbyn was an early supporter of the African National Congress (ANC) in its struggle against apartheid in South Africa. While Thatcher declared Nelson Mandela a terrorist and opposed sanctions, Corbyn joined the executive of the Anti-Apartheid Movement and protested outside the South African embassy in Trafalgar Square. On 22 July 1984, he and fellow MPs Stuart Holland and Tony Banks were among 100 demonstrators who were arrested. Corbyn was photographed holding a banner reading: 'Defend the right to demonstrate against apartheid – join this picket'. During the tributes to Mandela following the death of the freedom fighter turned President in 2013, Corbyn regaled the House with an account of his arrest, which led to him being awarded £250 in compensation:

> It was one of those strange moments when you are arrested by the police and you say, 'On what charge am I being arrested?', assuming one is going to be told 'obstruction'. They said no. It was under the Diplomatic Immunities Act. It was behaviour that was offensive to a foreign diplomatic mission. And the policeman said to me: 'What do you plead and why have you come here?' I said: 'I have come to be as offensive as possible to the South African apartheid regime, but I enter no plea so you will have to offer a plea on my part of Not Guilty.' The cases all went to court and we were all exonerated on the grounds of our moral outrage at apartheid, all given compensation and all that compensation was given to the ANC and the Anti-Apartheid Movement.

Corbyn was a patron of the Palestinian Solidarity Group; he travelled to Grenada soon after the American overthrow of the democratically elected left-wing government there; he opposed the sale of weapons to Iraq; and he was among the first to highlight Saddam Hussein's mistreatment of the Kurds, also taking part in protests and demonstrations outside Downing Street and Parliament against the bombing of Iraq in the late 1980s and early 1990s. According to his official parliamentary biography,[108] he was chairman of the All-Party Parliamentary Group on Angola, vice-chairman of the Human Rights Group, vice-chairman of the Latin America Group, treasurer of the Mexico Group, chairman of the Parliamentary CND Group, a member of the Dalit Solidarity Campaign and, just for some local light relief, patron of the Mitford Under-Fives Centre in Islington.

Corbyn is known as an indefatigable campaigner on behalf of the causes he believes in. Just once has he faced serious accusations of failing to do enough for those who needed his help. In 1992, he was approached at his constituency office by five social workers who raised serious allegations of sexual abuse in children's homes in the borough. It was one of the first indications of what would later become a huge scandal involving child abuse and Islington Council. Dozens of victims are now known to have been sexually assaulted by paedophiles who may have included the late Jimmy Savile, the notoriously prolific abuser. Although there is no suggestion that Corbyn was aware of these crimes at the time they took place, campaigners on behalf of victims do accuse him of failing to act once they told him of their concerns. One of those who attended the 1992 meeting, Liz Davies, has claimed that although Corbyn listened politely, he appeared to do nothing.[109] Campaigners are also critical of what they see as a failure by Corbyn to come to the defence of whistleblowers who lost their jobs in Islington after trying to raise the alarm, and of victims, who were often dismissed as fantasists.[110]

During the 2015 leadership campaign, the claims of Davies and others that Corbyn had failed to act were raised by John Mann, the Labour MP for Bassetlaw and a backer of Yvette Cooper, who suggested they showed he was unsuitable to become leader.[111] Mann also referred to a 1986 incident when Corbyn had criticised a Conservative MP, the late Geoffrey Dickens, who was seeking to uncover a suspected paedophile ring operating in Islington, accusing Dickens of 'getting cheap publicity at the expense of innocent children'. Corbyn had made a formal complaint to the Commons Speaker when Dickens visited Islington without abiding by the convention of first informing him, as the local MP. Corbyn's campaign dismissed Mann's remarks, saying: 'Jeremy Corbyn has a long record of standing up for his constituents. He called for an independent inquiry into child abuse in Islington at the time, and has taken this strong line ever since.' The team produced an article that had appeared in the *Islington Gazette* not long after his 1992 meeting with the social workers, in which he called on the council to hold an inquiry, and asked Virginia Bottomley, the then Health Secretary, to investigate. Margaret Hodge, who as leader of Islington Council at the time has also been criticised for failing to do more to tackle the crisis, says that as elected officials rather than front-line council workers, both she and Corbyn could not have known about the scandal, and did all they could once they learned of it.

The departure of Neil Kinnock following the shock loss of the 1992 general election and the coming to power of the popular John Smith did little to improve Corbyn's relationship with the leadership of his party. By 1993, and despite Labour's healthy twenty-point opinion poll lead, he was accusing Smith of 'failing to articulate the views of the mass of the people'. When Tony Blair came to power following Smith's sudden death the following year, Corbyn was emphatically out of the loop. He had voted not for Blair but for Margaret Beckett, who had been Smith's deputy. In fact, as an MP Corbyn never backed the winning candidate in a Labour leadership election until his own, opting for Eric Heffer in 1983, Tony Benn in 1988, Bryan Gould in 1992, Beckett in 1994, John McDonnell in 2007 and Diane Abbott in 2010. None polled higher than Beckett now did, and she received only 18.9 per cent of the electoral college. Ken Livingstone had initially hoped to stand for the leadership against Blair in 1994, even announcing that he would run on a ticket with Corbyn as his deputy (forgetting to tell Corbyn himself, who was horrified at the suggestion) but gave up the plan when it swiftly became apparent that he could not secure enough support in the parliamentary party.[112]

With the ascendence of New Labour, Corbyn was utterly out in the cold. Tony and Cherie Blair may have lived in Corbyn's borough of Islington, but their lifestyle and outlook were vastly different. Where he had once campaigned against the excesses of Thatcher's Conservative government, as the general election approached and it became clear that Labour would be returning to office after eighteen long years in opposition, he and his friends on the left increasingly found themselves protesting over the policies of their own party. Ronnie Campbell says: 'We had our times with the Blairites. We had to keep our mouths shut because the left was just about knackered. All through the Blair years we had to be subdued, we couldn't open our mouths too much.' Tony Benn's diary for July 1996 records the extent of New Labour's antipathy towards Corbyn:

> I had tea with Jeremy Corbyn, who said that he had been asked to appear on *The Midnight Hour* [a political discussion television show]. Labour Party Headquarters evidently rang up and said, 'If you use Jeremy Corbyn you will never get another shadow Cabinet minister to appear.' So the TV producers pulled out.

Corbyn bitterly opposed Blair's move to scrap Clause IV of Labour's constitution, which committed the party 'to secure for the workers by hand or by brain the full fruits of their industry and the most equitable distribution thereof that may be possible upon the basis of the common ownership of the means of production, distribution and exchange...' Clause IV had become emblematic of Labour's self-identification as a socialist party. Under Blair, it was seen as outdated and undesirable, and getting shot of it became a totemic moment for New Labour. In May 1995, Corbyn put his name to a letter to *The Independent* that read: 'The destruction of Clause IV is an attempt to change the fundamental character of the British Labour Party and accept the situation in which ownership of private capital confers over-whelming economic, social and therefore political power.'

In the run-up to the 1997 general election, Corbyn accused Blair of aping Tory policies on schools and the criminal justice system, and was among a large group of Labour MPs who objected vociferously when shadow Chancel-lor Gordon Brown raised the possibility of cutting child benefit. He remained a vocal critic too of Rupert Murdoch, then being wooed by Blair, who was keen to harness the might of the press baron's stable of newspapers, par-ticularly the tabloid *Sun*. Corbyn didn't trust the hype around New Labour, then as now rejecting the suggestion that it was necessary to compromise in order to gain power. 'There is a real danger of us upsetting our core sup-port, which could lose the election,' he said.[113] Labour at this stage was at 60 per cent in the polls. On the eve of New Labour's first election victory in May 1997, as Brown, desperate to shed the identification in voters' minds between Labour and high taxes, promised not to put up taxation, Corbyn declared: 'Most people are not opposed to raising the top level of tax. And those who made lots of money under Thatcher should pay more.'[114]

In 1996, Corbyn stood for the shadow Cabinet, which at the time was chosen by election by the PLP, coming last with thirty-six votes. He would not run for another office in the Labour Party for nearly twenty years. Blair for one saw him as no threat. Attending a smart dinner party in Islington around this time, the Labour leader struck up a conversation with another guest, who mentioned that she was a constituent of Corbyn's. 'Ah, Jeremy,' Blair said complacently. 'Jeremy hasn't made the journey.'[115]

CHAPTER EIGHT

IRELAND

'**T**HIS IS THE six o'clock news,' the BBC newsreader announced on Thursday 26 September 1996. The Liberal Democrat annual conference in Brighton was drawing to a close and the Conservative Cabinet was going through yet more paroxysms over Europe. As for Labour, the party's usual façade of steely discipline under Tony Blair had been challenged by the unorthodox actions of a trouble-making backbench MP, Jeremy Corbyn. With less than a year to go before a general election, the leadership could not be seen to tolerate such indiscipline.[116] 'Two Labour MPs, Tony Benn and Jeremy Corbyn, are facing expulsion from the Parliamentary Labour Party tonight…' the newsreader went on. Labour's Chief Whip Donald Dewar was preparing to throw the recalcitrant MP for Islington North and his friend and mentor Tony Benn out of the parliamentary party. Had he done so, Corbyn would have been ineligible to stand as a Labour candidate at the 1997 general election and the 2015 leadership election would have looked very different.

The issue that brought the wrath of the whips down on Corbyn was one both close to his heart and over which, for more than a decade, he had found himself at odds with most of his fellow MPs and the overwhelming majority of British voters: Northern Ireland. A few weeks earlier, Corbyn had invited Gerry Adams, the president of Sinn Féin, the political wing of the Irish Republican Army, to the House of Commons to launch his autobiography, *Before the Dawn*. (Adams had originally planned to call the book *Tiocfaidh Ar Lá*, which translates from the Irish as 'our day will come' and has been an IRA slogan since being adopted by the dying hunger striker Bobby Sands in 1981.) Adams was himself a former Member of Parliament, having represented Belfast West between 1983 and 1992, although, in line with Sinn Féin's policy of not recognising the Westminster Parliament's legitimacy in Northern Ireland, he had not taken up his seat. As a former MP, he had the right to launch his book at the Palace of Westminster, and the Speaker, Betty Boothroyd, had initially allowed Corbyn to reserve the Jubilee Room for the event. However, the Serjeant at Arms, responsible for the safety of the Commons, then withdrew permission on the grounds that the Sinn Féin man posed a security threat.

In the mid-1990s, Sinn Féin still was seen as a pariah organisation by most British people, as the Troubles continued to exact a terrible toll. The broadcast speaking ban on Adams and other Republican leaders had been lifted only in 1994, with the first IRA ceasefire; until then, television viewers had been treated to the bizarre spectacle of their words being voiced by actors. A bar on certain figures, including Gerry Adams, travelling to the British mainland was lifted at the same time. Frustrated by what it saw as a lack of progress in the peace talks, however, the IRA brought the ceasefire to a bloody end with a 'spectacular' seventeen months later, driving a truck bomb into the new London financial centre of Canary Wharf, killing two men in a newsagent's shop. Seven months on, and just three days before Adams's proposed book launch in September 1996, Diarmuid O'Neill, an English IRA volunteer of Irish parentage, was shot dead by police who opened fire on a hostel in Hammersmith, west London, where he had allegedly been plotting to build another lorry bomb.

Adams had been barred by Boothroyd from launching a previous book, *Free Ireland*, the year before at a function organised by Corbyn. Now, in defiance of the Serjeant's ban, Corbyn issued a press release announcing that the second event would go ahead. With timing that must have made Tony Blair and his communications supremos Peter Mandelson and Alastair Campbell groan, it was scheduled to take place four days ahead of the last Labour conference before the general election. A public meeting between a Labour MP and the leader of the Irish Republican movement was not the ideal prelude for what Mandelson hoped would be a shop window for New Labour to show off to voters how fundamentally the party had changed since the dark days of Michael Foot and the 1983 manifesto. Corbyn was unmoved. 'Gerry Adams is entitled to speak in this House. Dialogue with all parties remains essential if the peace process is to continue,' he said.[117] It would be a line he would repeat often over the years when being condemned for meeting controversial groups and figures. His critics complain that, as with Sinn Féin, Corbyn only seems to take part in one side of the dialogues he calls for.

And there was widespread criticism now for his insistence on pressing ahead with the Adams event. Andrew Hunter, chairman of the Conservatives' Parliamentary Northern Ireland Committee and a member of the Orange Order, said: 'It is entirely inappropriate that a man whose party is not unequivocally committed to the democratic process should be given a platform in the mother of parliaments.'[118] Blair quickly distanced himself from Corbyn, saying: 'I condemn this event without reservation and totally dissociate the Labour Party from it.'[119] Mo Mowlam, the shadow Northern Ireland Secretary, and Clive Solely, chairman of the Commons' Northern Ireland Committee, both also condemned Corbyn. The shadow

Cabinet voted unanimously to deplore his invitation to Gerry Adams and even the usually sympathetic *Guardian* questioned in an editorial why a 'serious' person such as Adams would bother with a 'clown' like Corbyn, dismissing him as a 'fool, and a fool whom the Labour Party would probably be better off without'.

The day before it was due to take place, Corbyn moved the event to the London Irish Centre, in his Islington constituency, and instead invited Adams to the Commons for a private meeting, which, unlike a book launch or press conference, the House authorities were powerless to prevent. He telephoned Tony Benn to discuss the matter, and his mentor agreed to take part in the discussion with Adams too. When the leadership learned of the meeting, Donald Dewar issued a statement saying that Corbyn would face disciplinary action, and that night's six o'clock news announced that both Corbyn and Benn would have the Labour whip withdrawn.[120] But the involvement of Benn had changed things. As *The Times* reported at the time: 'While Mr Corbyn would have been a relatively easy target, Mr Benn was not and the leadership would have been loath to become embroiled in a battle with such a senior figure, still popular on the left of the party.' Benn's diary records his fears for Corbyn:

> I have taken a considerable risk, and Jeremy has too, but he's much
> weaker because to kick him out would be easier. I wish I hadn't got
> into this, because I don't want a confrontation with anybody. It did
> frighten me in a deep way, and Jeremy said that [the broadcaster] ITN
> were camping outside his house.

In the event, it was Adams who decided that discretion was the better part of valour; saying the row over his presence at the Commons had become a 'distraction', he met Corbyn elsewhere. Benn saw Mandelson's work in subsequent briefings to newspapers that described 'Blair's fury' with the pair, and included the suggestion that Dewar had been instructed to table a motion at the next meeting of the PLP withdrawing the whip from Corbyn.[121] The man himself was unrepentant. 'If there's to be a peace process, clearly it's got to involve Sinn Féin and Gerry Adams,' he said.[122] It seems certain now that it was only the shield provided by Benn that saved Corbyn from deselection, allowing him to remain in the parliamentary party.

In an article in *New Left Review* soon after the row, Ronan Bennett, the novelist and screenwriter who would be employed by Corbyn in controversial circumstances, criticised New Labour's attitude towards Corbyn and Adams. He suggested it compared unfavourably to what he saw as an inappropriate warmth for the Ulster Unionists at a time of riots over the authorities' refusal to allow the Orange Order to parade through a Catholic neighbourhood in Drumcree, Co Armagh. 'It seems an obvious and unedifying case of double standards that Blair and Mowlam should have threatened Jeremy Corbyn for inviting Gerry Adams to the House of Commons while they invited David Trimble [the Ulster Unionist leader] to [Labour conference at] Blackpool,' Bennett wrote. 'Barely twelve weeks elapsed between Blackpool and the appalling events sparked after Trimble played general at of the "second siege of Drumcree".'

In the event, the row over the Adams invitation fizzled out, and Corbyn was returned to Parliament for his fourth term in Blair's landslide of 1 May 1997.

That it should be Northern Ireland that would bring Corbyn closest to being ejected from the Labour Party came as no surprise to those who had followed his parliamentary career from the start. Leo McKinstry, who is himself from Northern Ireland, believes that Corbyn's experiences in Islington, with its strong Irish community clustered around the constituency's two main thoroughfares of the Seven Sisters Road and the Holloway

Road, helped shape his views in the early 1980s. 'The Irish influence was really strong,' McKinstry says.

> Islington North and that belt of strongly Labour London constituencies were the absolute epicentre of the pro-Irish, Labour, Troops Out movement. They were all part of this hard-left movement, very involved with Ken Livingstone. That did inform Jeremy Corbyn, that north London mix of Republicanism and the hard left. There were a number of Irish clubs, Irish bars, Irish nightclubs, it was the absolute heart of the whole Irish community. I had absolutely no time for the violent, blood-soaked side of Irish Republicanism. I really found some of his [Corbyn's] stuff pretty contemptible.

In October 1984, eighteen months after becoming an MP, Corbyn played host at the Commons to two members of the IRA: Gerard MacLochlainn, who had served several years in jail for bomb-making, and Linda Quigley, who was convicted of terrorism offences after being arrested at the funeral of one of the hunger strikers in 1981. Extending an invitation to two convicted terrorists, albeit to a private meeting to discuss prison conditions in Northern Ireland, would have been controversial at any time. With what would be seen as inflammatory timing, Corbyn's meeting took place just two weeks after the IRA's attack on the Grand Hotel, Brighton, during Conservative Party conference, which had come close to assassinating Prime Minister Margaret Thatcher, and left five dead. Dozens more were severely injured, including Margaret Tebbit, wife of the Tory chairman Norman Tebbit, who was paralysed.

The Brighton bomb was the closest the IRA came to striking at the heart of the British establishment. It was also a human tragedy, the dead including Lady Jeanne Shattock, the wife of a provincial veterinarian;

the Conservative MP Sir Anthony Berry; and Eric Taylor, chair of the party's North West Area Association. Corbyn's meeting, which took place before one of the fatally injured succumbed to her wounds and prior to the funerals of other victims, was seen as both insensitive and reckless, given the security risk involved in allowing known terrorists inside the nation's legislature. When news of the meeting emerged, a few weeks after it had taken place, the party's then leader Neil Kinnock was furious; Corbyn was hauled to a meeting with the Chief Whip, Michael Cocks, and given a severe ticking-off. Cocks told reporters: 'I was very shocked. In fact, I was appalled ... In the present climate for someone to ask people like this is highly irresponsible and not understood either by fellow Members of Parliament or the general public.'[123] Corbyn was unmoved: 'Mr Cocks and I don't agree,' he said. 'He thinks it was unwise to have such a meeting in the House of Commons, I think otherwise. I made it very clear that I felt it important that any individual MP who wishes to meet anyone from anywhere should have the right to do so.'[124]

He used the same argument on other occasions when he irritated the leadership by extending invitations to Gerry Adams and other Republicans. As well as hosting the Sinn Féin leader at the Commons several times, in 1989 Corbyn asked Adams to address a fringe meeting at Labour conference in Brighton, scene of the IRA's attack on the Conservatives five years earlier, to the fury of Kevin McNamara, the shadow Northern Ireland Secretary and a Nationalist sympathiser, who said of Adams: 'As far as I am concerned, there is no place for people who defend murderers at the Labour Party conference.'[125]

In 1994, Corbyn took himself off on a motorcycle tour of Ireland, speaking at rallies in Dublin, Galway and Cork on behalf of the Troops Out Movement.[126] Two years later, Corbyn and Ken Livingstone invited a Sinn Féin delegation led by Mitchel McLaughlin, the party's chairman, to Parliament, where they had tea in a Commons' cafeteria known as 'Plods' because of its popularity with Palace of Westminster police. MPs on both Corbyn's side and the government's were aghast when it emerged that, during their tour of Westminster, one member of the Sinn Féin delegation had disappeared off on their own seeking a lavatory. Donald Dewar again read Corbyn the riot act. One Labour source was quoted as saying of Dewar's dressing-down: 'He said this House had been the target in the past and could well be in the present and the future.'[127]

A senior officer in the Northern Ireland security apparatus at the time, who is now retired, says Corbyn's invitations to Gerry Adams and other Sinn Féin politicians, as well as to members of the IRA, caused great alarm among the security services. The source says:

> You're talking about … bringing into Parliament … very senior members of the Provisional movement, whether they were Sinn Féin or whether they were the Army [IRA], they were all seen as very big players in the Republican movement and the Provisional Republican movement. They were … major players … prominent in what they would class as their war against the British. There would have been concerns that they would have been able, once they had gone over, to go back and talk about the layout of the place. And to find out details of when conventions were happening, and when fringe meetings were happening, and where people lived. Certainly there would have been a number of people uneasy at his invites at that time, in the '80s and early '90s when the [IRA] campaign still continued. It was hard for MPs or his colleagues who would have been maybe going into government to accept that he was bringing them there. There were dangers, definitely, particularly for those people like your Secretary of State [for Northern Ireland], Home Secretaries, who were seen as most at risk.

Another former senior Royal Ulster Constabulary (RUC) officer quotes Lenin to describe Corbyn as a 'useful idiot' for the Republican movement – the approval of a British Member of Parliament conveying some form of legitimacy on their cause. This source says:

> I used to look at him when he would visit Belfast in the 1980s, when he was running around with guys who had done some pretty horrible things, and think: 'Who is this guy? What is he thinking coming here?' I think our colleagues in England would have been more concerned with some of his antics. They would have panicked at some of what he got up to.

Corbyn's willingness to truck with the Republicans before the ceasefires of the 1990s remains controversial. When he first came to Parliament in the 1980s, most Labour MPs broadly supported the non-violent Nationalist cause in Northern Ireland, expressed through Labour's sister party, the Social Democratic and Labour Party (SDLP), with an ultimate belief in a United Ireland. Labour backed the Anglo-Irish Agreement, which Margaret Thatcher and the Irish Taoiseach Garret FitzGerald signed into being in November 1985, and which gave the Republic of Ireland an advisory role in Northern Ireland while confirming there would be no change in the latter's constitutional position without the consent of its people. Corbyn was among a minority of a dozen Labour MPs, including Tony Benn, Dennis Skinner and Tam Dalyell, to vote against the agreement in the Commons, telling the House: 'We believe that the agreement strengthens rather than weakens the border between the six and the twenty-six counties [of Northern Ireland and the Republic], and those of us who wish to see a United Ireland oppose the agreement for that reason.' Despite a small Tory rebellion and the dissent of the Unionist parties, Thatcher received her largest ever Commons majority that night.

David Winnick says that Corbyn's close association with the Republican cause set him apart from most of his Labour colleagues.

> Where he differed was Ireland. I strongly disagreed with the line that he took ... I constantly argued that there was no justification for the IRA. I thought he was wrong. It's totally false to say those talks with Adams led to peace negotiations. What led to peace negotiations was the decision of the Provisional IRA to enter into peace negotiations.

Lord Bew, Professor of Irish Politics at Queen's University, Belfast, who is an expert on Northern Ireland, agrees with Winnick: 'Corbyn was always out on a limb with the Provos [the Provisional IRA]. He was to a large degree irrelevant. He was so far out there. Everyone knew to keep a distance from Corbyn.'

The senior security source maintains that Corbyn's contacts with Sinn Féin were in fact counter-productive, because he allowed its leaders space to put pressure on the London government:

> It was a very unusual thing to do, when you're in the middle of the [IRA] campaign. Quite clearly at that stage the Republican movement had an agenda and a strategy to continue with the campaign. They made that very clear. [He was] someone who was bringing these people [Sinn Féin] over there just to put pressure on the government, as opposed to ... saying: 'You need to get these people [the IRA] to stop [the violence] and then we can do business. That was the big thing all along, that these people [the Republicans] need to stop it [the violence], need to make a declaration of intent to say we are going to stop, and that wasn't coming from Jeremy Corbyn.

Lord Bew suggests that to claim Corbyn played a role in the peace process by entering into a dialogue with Adams and Sinn Féin, at a time when no one else would, fundamentally misrepresents the eventual Northern Ireland settlement. While the British government insisted Republicans accept the principle of self-determination by peaceful means, as a supporter of the Troops Out movement, Corbyn shared Sinn Féin's view that Irish unity need not be predicated on either consent or a ceasefire. 'The terms on which Corbyn was in dialogue with Adams was on the basis of Adams wins', Bew says.

> The way that Blair did this peace process was by ... moving Labour away from [Irish] unity, it's got to be a principle of consent if they're going to get the union. There was never any ambiguity among [John] Major or Blair about what the settlement was: it was unity by consent.

Corbyn himself credits not the British and Irish governments but the leaderships of the Northern Ireland political parties, particularly Sinn Féin and the SDLP, for the peace, and argues that the presence of the British Army exacerbated the conflict, as the Nationalist community was subjected to repeated human rights abuses. 'The violence was wrong on all sides and I have said so all along', Corbyn has said.

> My whole point was, if you are to bring about a peace process, you weren't going to achieve it by military means. Talk to anyone who was in the army in Northern Ireland at that time. Did kicking in the doors on streets, on terraces, all through Derry bring about the peace process, or did ultimately the political dialogue that [SDLP leader] John Hume had, Gerry Adams had, that all of the Ulster Unionists ultimately came to? Surely that was an incredible achievement.[128]

Lord Bew dismisses Corbyn's view as overly romantic, and argues that he has never moved on from his days singing Irish protest songs in the pubs of north London. The academic believes that given the practicalities involved – particularly the financial drain of maintaining peace in the face of the ongoing threat from loyalist paramilitaries and the further expense of being forced to pick up a large tab in the form of benefits for hundreds of thousands of Northern Irelanders – the modern Irish state does not want to take on the North in the short term. 'You cannot simply withdraw from Northern Ireland. The Irish state wants stability, not unity,' he says.

> Irish troops would need 60,000 [soldiers to keep peace] – they have
> 11,000. The British can't afford the welfare bill [in Northern Ireland],
> let alone the Irish. I'm not sure that Corbyn ever understood that.
> I suspect that common sense about Ireland isn't there. The Irish state
> is much more prosaic than left-wing people singing Irish songs in
> London realised.

The security services in Northern Ireland also considered Corbyn to have no real sense of the nature of the conflict there, and felt that he, unlike his friends Tony Benn and Ken Livingstone, lacked the high profile that would have given his attempts to involve himself in the peace process some legitimacy. The senior security officer source says: 'I think he was very naive, Jeremy Corbyn. It's easy to look across [from England] and not have any depth of knowledge about it all. Yes, an independent view is good and it can help, but it still needs some kind of context and I don't think Jeremy had that.'

It is characteristic of Corbyn that, through all of his campaigning on behalf of the Republicans, he managed to remain on friendly terms in the Commons with Sinn Féin's greatest opponents. Eileen Paisley, widow of the firebrand preacher and Democratic Unionist Party leader Ian Paisley, has recently said her late husband 'liked' Corbyn, adding: 'He didn't share his politics and he didn't approve of Jeremy Corbyn meeting Gerry Adams and Sinn Féin people when the IRA campaign was still going on. But he always found him very courteous and polite. He said Jeremy was a gentleman.'[129] Some of Corbyn's Labour colleagues remain exasperated, however, by what they see as his insensitivity over the Irish issue, then and now. One senior MP was astounded when, following his election as leader, Corbyn used his speech to the 2015 Labour women's conference (part of Labour conference in Brighton) to call for a memorial to Countess Constance Markievicz, the first woman elected to Westminster, who was a member of Sinn Féin and second-in-command at Dublin's St Stephen's Green during the 1916 Easter Rising. The MP says:

> Fancy going to conference and talking about Constance Markowitz. He references her as this historical figure, she's had a portrait hanging up in the House of Commons as part of the women MPs [official tribute], so [he could have] done that properly [by speaking in Westminster] instead of being totally insensitive and doing it next to the bloody Grand Hotel in Brighton [scene of the 1985 IRA attack]. Jesus Christ.

New Labour certainly wanted no formal role for Corbyn in the peace process. In his autobiography, Ken Livingstone suggests that the November 1996 meeting he and Corbyn had set up with Mitchel McLaughlin, provoking Donald Dewar's fury, had been convened in order to pass secret messages from Mo Mowlam, who would shortly become Northern Ireland Secretary, to the leaders of Sinn Féin and the IRA, adding that he had not been able to appraise Donald Dewar of the real motive for their meeting at the time.[130] But when, in 1997, David Winnick became the British co-chair of the British–Irish Inter-Parliamentary Body, one of the cross-border agencies created out of the Anglo-Irish Agreement, he suggested appointing Corbyn to the organisation, only to have the Whips' Office cross his name off the list. 'One of the whips came up to me and said we didn't include Corbyn because he wouldn't accept any form of discipline,' Winnick says. During his thirty years in Parliament, first Labour's leadership, then (after elections for Commons' select committees were introduced in 2010) his MP colleagues kept Corbyn off the Northern Ireland Committee, which holds investigations into major issues relating to the Province.

Corbyn continues to meet Sinn Féin politicians to this day, even posing for a photograph as he shared a cup of tea with Gerry Adams and Martin McGuinness, Sinn Féin's chief negotiator and self-confessed former IRA leader, in the canteen at Westminster's Portcullis House during the 2015 Labour leadership race. The Catholic Northern Irish writer Eilis O'Hanlon, who is often highly critical of Republicans, has written of left-wing English politicians who associated with Sinn Féin in the 1980s and 1990s:

> From Corbyn to [John] McDonnell to Ken Livingstone, they all justify it these days by saying it was OK because it led eventually to the peace process. But that's disingenuous in the extreme. When they were out defending the IRA, its fellow travellers also didn't know when, or if, that campaign would end. They still happily supported, or had an ambivalent attitude towards, Republican violence. They knew exactly what they were doing, and how their solidarity was used by the Republican movement to paint its murder campaign as part of some wider struggle for social justice.[131]

Thirty years later, Corbyn remains unrepentant about his meetings with Irish Republicans, including at periods of great tension in the peace process.

Asked following his election as leader in 2015 about his conversations with Gerry Adams and others at the 'worst of times' in the Troubles, he said: 'Isn't that the time to speak to people?'[132] Of the 1984 meeting shortly after the Brighton bomb, he went on:

> I invited people who were former prisoners, who had served their sentences, into the House of Commons … for a discussion about the prison situation and conditions in Northern Ireland, for a discussion about the possibility of a political development and a political solution. All through the 1980s, yes, I did make myself very unpopular with some people with a preparedness to reach out into the Republican tradition in Ireland … At the same time, secretly the British government was also engaged in that … I wanted the fighting to stop and I said that to many, many people on many, many occasions,. I don't want violence, I don't want killing, I don't want all the horrors that go with it.[133]

Corbyn's friend Tariq Ali says that his public dialogue with Sinn Féin through the 1980s, when the Troubles were going through a spike in violence, should be viewed through the prism of the peace process that followed. Indeed, one of those who met Corbyn at Westminster that October in 1984, Gerard MacLochlainn, would go on to play a role in the negotiations that led to peace, being part of the Sinn Féin delegation that met Labour's front-bench team after the first IRA ceasefire in 1994. Ali says:

> The British ended up having to talk to the IRA. When the left talked to the IRA, Ken Livingstone, Jeremy, myself, others, totally we were denounced. But then finally they had to do the deal, and they did it. And it was John Major, a Tory Prime Minister, who started it off,

and then Blair completed it. So I don't take too seriously, 'You shouldn't talk to some people' or share a platform. Obviously it's been used against him, but I don't think it's affected him.

Chris Mullin concurs, saying:

A succession of ministers of all main parties have had dealings with Adams and McGuinness. I suppose [Corbyn] was slightly ahead of his time, that's all. I wasn't particularly concerned about it. I took the view, which others did, that it would be necessary to talk to Sinn Féin and even the IRA to get over the war. Even the Conservative government took that view in the end.

The Campaign Group MP Ronnie Campbell adds: 'As for talking to the IRA, the Blair government, the Major government, was talking to the IRA, in secret, that is. At least Jeremy did it openly.'

If the verdict on Corbyn's relationship with the Republicans is equivocal, he appears fully vindicated in his work highlighting abuses of the justice system in both England and Northern Ireland, and championing the victims of miscarriages of justice arising from the Troubles. In 1985, he and Tony Benn flew to Belfast to observe one of the 'Supergrass' trials, hearings in which accused paramilitaries were tried on the basis of testimony from former associates given in return for inducements such as non-prosecution, lighter sentences or even cash. The trials were held in 'Diplock courts', presided over by a judge with no jury, to avoid the intimidation of jurors by paramilitaries. Benn's diary tells the story of their trip to Belfast. When they arrived at court, they found the screens and speakers in the public gallery broken, so officials, recognising the two MPs, suggested they take seats in the empty jury box. On seeing them there, the defence barrister turned to the judge and said: 'I'm surprised at how small the new jury is but I'm happy to accept their verdict instead of yours.'[134]

Corbyn's most significant contribution to the cause of justice in Ireland and the UK was his work on behalf of the Guildford Four, Maguire Seven and Birmingham Six, groups of wrongly accused men, women and even children – the youngest was just fourteen – convicted on spurious evidence with the use of forced confessions of responsibility for a series of IRA bomb attacks in 1974 on pubs in English towns, in which twenty-three people died. They were not all finally freed until 1991, by which time some had spent as many as sixteen years in prison. All would eventually receive formal apologies from the British government. When Corbyn first began campaigning on their behalf, however, with feelings among the public still running high over the loss of civilian lives on the British mainland, he was one of the few prepared to take a stance on what was a highly unpopular cause. Even Lord Bew concedes: 'I think you've got to give the devil his due. He's got to claim it as a win and that's it.'

One member of the Guildford Four, Paul Hill, had been living in Islington at the time of his arrest, and after Corbyn's election he began to visit him in prison, even attending his 1988 wedding to Marion Serravalli in HMP Long Lartin and tabling an Early Day Motion to congratulate the couple. 'I'm convinced he's innocent,' he said of Hill.[135] The following year, when Hill was released on bail pending an appeal, it was Corbyn who put up his £2,000 surety.[136]

Corbyn was also staunch in the defence of Ronan Bennett when the House authorities tried to block his employment. As an eighteen-year-old in Belfast in 1974, Bennett was convicted on what was later found to be cooked-up evidence of the murder of an RUC police inspector during a bank robbery. He was sentenced to life imprisonment, but freed on appeal after thirteen months. On moving to London a few years later, he was arrested again and accused of conspiracy to cause explosions, before being acquitted at a high-profile trial at the Old Bailey. When Commons Speaker Bernard Weatherill learned that Corbyn had taken him on as a research assistant, he stripped Bennett of his Commons pass. Corbyn condemned the 'disgraceful attack and character assassination of an innocent man', who was by now a respected academic, arguing that Bennett's help was invaluable in his work on behalf of victims of miscarriages of justice.[137] The Speaker did not change his mind and Bennett remained barred from the Commons.

And what of Corbyn's views on Ireland today? During the 2015 leadership contest he was criticised for refusing five times during an interview with BBC Radio Ulster to condemn IRA atrocities.[138] Asked in another interview if he still believes in a United Ireland, he said:

> It's for the Irish people to decide. My own view is, historically: yes. I am very much on the record as that. But quite honestly, the peace process has brought about a huge step forward ... You go to Belfast, you go to Dublin, people travel back and forth all the time ... There is that sense that there is an island of Ireland ... That's a good step forward.[139]

CHAPTER NINE

CLAUDIA — AND A FAMILY

TONY BLAIR WAS having a difficult Christmas. Just five months earlier, in July 1994, the young, energetic Leader of the Labour Party had been swept to office by an overwhelming majority, and, with the Tories under John Major increasingly moribund, he was already confident he was on his way to Downing Street. The 'New' Labour Party he was building seemed, like him, fresh, exciting and terribly modern compared to the ageing Conservatives with their whiff of scandal and corruption. But all was not well within the Labour family. Blair's oldest child, Euan, was approaching secondary school age, and he and his wife Cherie were facing a dilemma common to many left-leaning, middle-class parents in London at the time. The state schools in their borough of Islington were officially classified as the third worst in the country, yet Blair led a party that proudly viewed comprehensive education as one of the great cornerstones of the welfare state.

The first comprehensives were created just after the war, mainly in Labour education authorities, and they became standard for most schoolchildren under Harold Wilson's first government of 1964–66. They were non-elitist, catering to pupils of all aptitudes and social backgrounds. By the 1990s, however, comprehensives had become something a political football. Between 1988 and 1998 the Conservatives, long perceived as somewhat hostile towards the comprehensive model, created a new category of grant-maintained schools, 'opted out' of local authority control, and therefore free from the influence of often left-wing councils. The Blairs felt that the grant-maintained Catholic London Oratory School in Fulham, west London, eight miles from their home in Islington, was right for Euan. There were fifty comprehensives closer to their house. When the news of their decision to send the boy to a grant-maintained school broke in December 1994, the sense of disappointment and betrayal among many in the party Blair led was acute.

The diaries of Tony Benn and Chris Mullin make clear how furious large parts of the Parliamentary Labour Party were at Blair's decision. Harriet Harman, a member of the shadow Cabinet, had made the same choice for her son the year before, leading to an outcry in the national party. Harman had only just kept her job, staying in office largely due to the unwavering support of Blair himself. Now the leader was adding to the insult by following Harman's lead. In ignoring those who had raised their discomfort and despair at her decision, Blair seemed to confirm to many in the party – even those on the 'soft' rather than the 'hard' left – not only that he did not care about their concerns but, crucially, that the new leadership did not share their traditional Labour values. Mullin's CLP was so disgusted at Blair's move that they sent him a formal letter of objection.[140] A series of delegations from the PLP, as well as individual MPs, remonstrated with Blair to no avail. The row was personal and unpleasant. It seemed to confirm to many that New Labour was a different creature from the Labour Party its followers understood and believed in.

The views of one left-wing Member of Parliament, Jeremy Corbyn, on Blair's decision to snub his local comprehensive schools in Islington go unrecorded in the diaries and press of the time. Always loath to discuss family matters, his own and others, and understanding better than most the complexities involved, Corbyn deliberately chose to keep his counsel. It was an issue that would have a far greater bearing on his life than on those more vocal than he. Corbyn was now a father himself, with three boys, the oldest, Benjamin, just three years younger than Euan. As the MP for Islington North, Corbyn's family, like the Blairs', fell within the Islington Education Authority catchment area. And like Cherie Blair, Corbyn's wife Claudia Bracchitta was unimpressed with the local schools. Their nearest comprehensive, Holloway Boys, had extremely poor exam results, even by the low standards of Islington. Fewer than one in five pupils gained five or more GCSEs at grade C or above, compared to the national average of 46 per cent. Yet Corbyn was committed to comprehensive education, and had already borne criticism from his constituents when Bracchitta had insisted on enrolling Ben in a private Montessori nursery as an infant. Their disagreements over their sons' education pushed a wedge between the couple they would never recover from. By 1998, Corbyn's marriage was over. Bracchitta could not, as she saw it, jeopardise her son's life chances by sending him to Holloway Boys; like his father before him, Ben would have a grammar school education. With Corbyn unable to accept her decision, the couple reluctantly separated.

When they met and married twelve years earlier, Corbyn's and Bracchitta's politics had been very much in line. Bracchitta's background was as exotic as Corbyn the romantic could have hoped for. Her family was originally from Spain, and if the Civil War there had played a role in bringing Corbyn's parents together, it would also prove, in a roundabout way, instrumental in leading him to the woman who would become his second wife. Bracchitta's grandfather Ricardo had been the Spanish consul in Chile at the outbreak of the Spanish Civil War in 1936. He returned to Spain to fight on the side of the Republic but fled back to Chile via Mexico when Franco's fascists prevailed. A generation later, the family was again forced into exile when the military dictator General Augusto Pinochet seized power in a coup d'état in 1973, deposing the democratically elected Marxist President Salvador Allende. Bracchitta's uncle, Oscar Soto, was Allende's personal doctor, and was with him when the presidential palace was surrounded by Pinochet's troops, only narrowly escaping with his life. More than 40,000 people are now known to have been persecuted by the Pinochet regime, of whom 3,000 were murdered. Among those forced to flee were Claudia Bracchitta and her mother, who was also a doctor. They arrived in London on her eleventh birthday.

Chile was a popular cause among left-wing intellectuals in Britain, and the Bracchittas soon found themselves drawn into the left-wing circles of 1980s north London. There, they settled in Corbyn's former council area of Haringey. Bracchitta's mother became friendly with Tamara Deutscher, wife of Isaac Deutscher, the great Polish historian and biographer of Leon Trotsky and Joseph Stalin, and an intimate of both Tony Benn and Ralph Miliband. Tariq Ali says: 'Claudia's mother I used to meet quite often because she was a very close friend of Tamara Deutscher. And I think that's where I first met Claudia, before she married Jeremy, at Tamara's house.' As she grew up, Claudia Bracchitta too became politically aware and active in the Chilean exile community, gaining a reputation as 'very left-wing'.

Following his experiences in Latin America as a young man and as a member of Amnesty International, Corbyn had taken an interest in Chile and Pinochet for a number of years. Moving in the same social and political milieu, it was inevitable that he would come across Bracchitta. The pair began their relationship after they got chatting while both in the audience of a speech given by Ken Livingstone at the GLC in 1986. Bracchitta, a painter and decorator, had recently married a man called Edmund Benge, but would soon be divorced. Corbyn had been single since his divorce from Jane Chapman and split from Diane Abbott in 1979. They immediately struck up a rapport and formed a relationship. Tariq Ali says that given Bracchitta's background and Corbyn's interest in Latin American politics, they made a good couple. 'It was totally natural,' he says. 'Jeremy ... he's not one of these Labour Party MPs, many of whom, including on the left, are quite provincial-minded. He's always been an internationalist.' Bracchitta became pregnant with their first child a few months later, and the couple wed at Camden registry office in May 1987. Benjamin Amaru Corbyn, named for his paternal great-grandfather, was born that July.

If Ali was not surprised by Corbyn's marriage to Bracchitta, others were – when they finally found out about it. Wanting to spare his new bride the attention that comes from being the wife of an MP, and allergic to any discussion of his family, Corbyn did his best to keep her out of the spotlight. For years, Corbyn's was the only entry in the parliamentary companion *Roth's*, a textbook compiled by Andrew Roth comprising short biographies of MPs, to contain a question mark next to the space devoted to spouses. 'Roth asked me and I refused to tell him,' Corbyn once said. 'He said that everybody else answered the question, and I said I thought it was nobody else's business. I wish we had the French system, where public figures have genuinely private lives and there is no *Daily Mail*.'[141] One of Tony Benn's friends who met Corbyn at a tea party at the Commons hosted by Benn's mother, Lady Stansgate, remembers being astonished when he introduced her to the stunning woman beside him – Bracchitta – as his wife.

In 1994, Bracchitta made a rare foray to Westminster, joining a group of wives of Labour politicians led by Keith Vaz's wife Maria, to campaign for shorter hours. Using the name 'Claudia Corbyn', she told the BBC that her husband came home at night 'green with exhaustion'. 'In the end I had to insist on taking him to hospital,' she added. Until their separation in 1998, the only other appearance in the media by Bracchitta came in 1992, when she informed an *Evening Standard* diarist that the family's pet terrapins had died.

Despite her low public profile, Bracchitta remained a member of the left-wing circles that had first brought her into contact with Corbyn. Tony Benn's diary recalls a pleasant day spent with the couple and their youngest sons at Stansgate, his Essex family seat. Robin Blackburn, Corbyn's friend from the Corresponding Society, believes Bracchitta played an important role in shaping his politics. He became increasingly interested in the democratically elected socialist leaders of South and Central America, including Allende and, later, Hugo Chávez of Venezuela. It was a starkly different approach to that of the New Labour political class, including his future leadership rivals Andy Burnham, Yvette Cooper and Liz Kendall, who had as their lodestar the United States' Democratic Party. Blackburn says of Corbyn:

> I think the Latin American left did have some impact on him. Jeremy must have been to the United States but I don't think it's been a special destiny for him, and he must have been to Latin America much more often. Venezuela became very important, especially because Hugo Chávez [came] to power in a democratic way and actually retained large, popular support, despite chaos in the country and problems of all sorts. He still commanded a lot of genuine support up until his death.

Four years after Ben's arrival, Bracchitta gave birth to a second son, Sebastian Jeremy; known as Seb, he would go on to work as a parliamentary researcher for Corbyn's great friend John McDonnell. A third boy, Thomas, was born two years later. Corbyn was an attentive father, despite the long hours he devoted to politics. His constituents grew used to seeing him cycling to school with one or other of the boys on the back of his bike. When Ben was three, Corbyn and Bracchitta received their first intimation of the trouble that would lie ahead over their sons' education. With Bracchitta keen to return to work, the couple began looking around for a nursery for Ben. In the days before political parties vied with each other to capture the middle-class family vote with the promise of free pre-school places, there were few publicly funded nursery slots in the country, and none in Islington for those not on low wages. Corbyn reluctantly agreed that Ben could go, at a cost of £600 a term, to a nearby Montessori nursery, an international system of education that emphasises non-structured learning through play and the natural development of the child. He was not comfortable with the decision, however, particularly when a local paper, the *Islington Chronicle*, got wind of it. Defending himself, Corbyn said his salary as an MP was too high to qualify for the council pre-school, adding: 'I believe every child should have the opportunity to go to a state nursery. That's not possible under this [Conservative] government.'

Although he did his best to spend time with the boys, Corbyn's long hours spent at the Commons and on his various campaigns meant Bracchitta had always borne the bulk of the responsibility for caring for the boys and overseeing their education. She was keen to make the right decisions for them. Bracchitta later said:

> Jeremy is very involved with the children. He adores them. He is constantly shuttling between here and Westminster, he tries to pick up the children from school, but invariably he is back at the Commons or at meetings in the evening. The hours the House of Commons keeps make it impossible to have a normal family life. It is difficult to find the time to give the children the extra help other parents might be able to, so the schooling had to be right.[142]

When he reached the age of four, Ben was sent to the local state primary school, but never settled. After the school lost a succession of headteachers, Bracchitta began looking around for an alternative. 'From the start he was unhappy,' she later said. 'He began to deteriorate to the point where I felt I had to do something.'[143] For some time, Bracchitta dithered, believing it would be 'incorrect' politically to give up on the local school.[144] It was an agonising decision. 'But some time later I went to a parents' evening and saw Ben's books and thought, "That's it." I felt he had to leave,' she said. 'I was lucky enough to get a place at a lovely little school that works well. Ben changed overnight. When I saw how happy he was and how well he was doing, I felt guilty for not doing something sooner. I vowed I would not make the wrong decision again.'[145]

When the time came to apply to secondary school for Ben in 1997, and determined not to compromise on his education again, Bracchitta put down as her first choice Acland Burghley, a local comprehensive with a good repu-tation. Unfortunately, as a result, it was heavily oversubscribed. When the family heard back from Islington Education Authority, they learned that Ben was eighty-seventh on the waiting list for Acland Burghley, and had been given a spot at Holloway Boys, a school officially listed as failing. Bracchitta was in despair. 'I would have liked to have sent Ben to a good local school that I felt comfortable with and where he would have thrived and fulfilled his potential. But there wasn't one,' she later said.[146] Bracchitta was well aware of Corbyn's views on comprehensive education, and became frustrated as he refused to discuss the problem further. The tensions between them grew. Almost as an afterthought, Bracchitta had also submitted an application for the Queen Elizabeth's School for Boys, a grammar school in Barnet, ten miles from their house in Islington, running to the school to deliver it by hand after missing the last post. Ben was invited to sit the entrance exam and, to Bracchitta's surprise given that he had received no coaching or preparation, he passed.

Founded in 1573, even before Corbyn's alma mater, Adams' School, Queen Elizabeth's has striking similarities to the institution he loathed. Following the trends in education, it became a comprehensive in 1974 but reverted back to its grammar school status twenty years later. With a reputation for academic excellence, it also enjoys enviable facilities, including an Olympic-sized swimming pool and state-of-the-art music rooms. It has the best record of any state school in the country for sending pupils to top-thirty universities and to Oxbridge. In 2007, when Corbyn's middle son Sebastian was still there, it was named *Sunday Times* state school of the year. Corbyn detested everything it stood for. It was not just his own experiences thirty-five years earlier at a grammar that prized obedience, conformity and academic achievement over individual flair and free thinking. He also felt deeply for the children left behind in schools such as Holloway Boys when middle-class families went elsewhere. And as the area's local MP, he could not abide the hypocrisy of seeking to represent voters whose children were forced to attend schools deemed not good enough for his own sons. How could he look those parents in the eye?

Corbyn and Bracchitta went round and round in circles for months. She would not send Ben to Holloway Boys and Corbyn could not bear for him to go to Queen Elizabeth's. The option of moving house, which many middle-class Londoners did to get into the catchment area of a better school, was not open to them; even if Corbyn didn't have to live in Islington as the local MP, he would have seen it as cheating. 'I feel very strongly about comprehensive education, yes,' he once said simply.[147] Ultimately, as the parent who had always taken charge of the boys' education, it was Bracchitta's decision to send Ben to Queen Elizabeth's. 'I didn't have a premeditated idea that I had chosen this school years ago,' she said later. 'I didn't know until after Ben got in that it was one of the top five in Britain. I only wanted a school that was near here and would be really good for Ben.'[148]

In choosing Queen Elizabeth's, Bracchitta was aware that she was ending her marriage. The couple's differences over their son's education was not their only problem, but it was significant enough to be one of the major causes of their separation. At its heart, the argument captured the essence of Corbyn's character: it was not that he would not compromise on his beliefs; it was that he could not. Once again, Corbyn had put politics above his relationship. Margaret Hodge says:

> The fact he leaves his wife because she sends his children to grammar school is sort of crazy, but it's Jeremy. When he told me, I remember thinking, 'This is completely mad.' You have fall-outs with your partner but you don't leave your family on the basis of that sort of an issue.

Chris Mullin adds: 'As far as one can see ... his marriages failed because he was so absorbed with politics to the exclusion of everything else.' Corbyn moved out of the family home and into a temporary flat. But the couple remained close. When Pinochet was arrested in London in October 1998, they campaigned together for his extradition, Corbyn describing it as an issue 'on which the entire, extended Bracchitta–Corbyn clan are totally united'.[149]

Alone in his flat after twelve years of marriage, Corbyn missed the boys, and two years after separating, the couple decided to buy a new house together, which they set about converting into two flats. Not long afterwards, while the work to divide the new property was still going on, word got out about their split, the reasons for it, and their new living arrangements. After the scandals involving Harriet Harman and the Blairs' choice of school for their children, Corbyn's unconventional decision to lay down his marriage for his beliefs made him, briefly, a celebrity.

Fittingly, Corbyn was away from home at a political gathering when he learned the story was about to break. Describing the moment he found out, he said later:

> I was in The Hague for a peace conference and I had a tip-off that the *Daily Mail* were phoning around trying to find things out about me. Then they phoned my Commons office and said they had got this information, and that I had two hours to respond ... I had to spend most of my time in The Hague in phone boxes.[150]

The attention engulfed the couple like a wave. They gave interviews, separately and together, and for a few days found themselves public property. Camera crews and reporters camped outside the door; columnists debated the merits of the difficult choices each had made. They were, by turn, praised and pilloried. Lifestyle features were written about the benefits and downsides of sharing a house with an ex. Corbyn absolutely hated the fuss. He had never enjoyed attention being paid to his family, and now he came to loathe it. Later, during the 2015 leadership election, he would have his most difficult moments when he felt the intrusive gaze of the media swinging onto his family. His friend Tariq Ali says: 'Jeremy is quite ... withdrawn is the wrong word ... but he values his privacy.' After 1998, Corbyn would never again discuss his personal life in any depth.

In his first interview about his family, he said of the divorce:

> We agreed amicably to separate on the grounds that we were incompatible. There were other problems. In lots of cases where people separate, it's not for one reason alone. But the only one of legitimate public interest is our disagreement over the choice of school for Ben. We both remain devoted to our children and love them very much. We both give them love and support, and that will continue.[151]

In a later interview, given just after he entered the Labour leadership race, he refused to discuss the episode any further, but explained how the unwanted attention had scarred him.

> I hated that period. I hated the publicity for it. I hated the pressure put on my kids as a result of it, and it was … very unpleasant and very intrusive. We divorced. We have three kids; we get on very well; we talk to each other; and I don't like dragging personal things into my political life. And I think it's very sad when that happens. I don't criticise anybody else for what happens with their children, and I don't expect people to interfere with my children's lives. It's gone, it's past and people should leave personal stuff out of it if they can.[152]

Bracchitta, too, found the experience of trial by media bruising. 'I knew that at some point it would become public in some way. I didn't expect it to come out in quite the way it did, in a very sensationalised and polarised manner. I thought it might be a small thing in the local paper.'[153] On the other hand, she seemed to find the experience of being interviewed by sympathetic journalists somewhat therapeutic: perhaps it was a relief to share her thoughts after worrying over them for so long. 'There is no one correct answer,' she mused in the *Sunday Times*.

> Every child is different, every family has different circumstances. What may on paper be the best school in the land is not the right one if your child is not happy. Our family is in the public eye and that made it hard. Anything we did would be a public statement. But in the end, you can only do what's right for your child.

Explaining the background to the split, she went on:

A break-up is never for one specific reason, but this did not help. I took the decision about Ben's schooling alone. I knew Jeremy was against it and that it was causing him great difficulties. I felt very isolated. When you are unable to make decisions about the most important thing in the marriage – the children – then the tensions are very great. I didn't willingly do it, but I was in an impossible situation. In his own way, it must have been very difficult for Jeremy, too. But he's always been very clear on what he believes. For Jeremy the education issue was clear-cut, but for me it was not so.

In a separate interview, Bracchitta said:

I am concerned Jeremy has been portrayed as a hard-left MP who couldn't care about his children, which is absolutely not the truth. I was put across as the pushy parent who wanted a grammar school place for her son and nothing else. It isn't a story about making a choice but about having no choice. I couldn't send Ben to a school where I knew he wouldn't be happy. Whereas Jeremy was able to make one sort of decision, I wasn't. It's a position you are pushed into rather than one you choose.[154]

The break-up was classic Corbyn: no confrontation, no bitterness, just a gradual realisation that the relationship was coming to an end. In failing to accept Bracchitta's decision, and therefore allowing the marriage to slide into divorce, Corbyn was able to maintain the purity of his belief system. Throughout it all, and to this day, the couple respected each other's points of view and continued to be fond of each other. 'It's not that he doesn't care, or that he's happy with any old thing for his children, or that his stance is somehow selfish,' Bracchitta said. 'He is simply a person of true conviction. It is not a pose, but a genuine commitment to something he's campaigned for all his life.'[155]

CHAPTER TEN

OPPOSITION MP, 1997–2010

WITH THE ELECTION of a Labour government on 1 May 1997, Jeremy Corbyn found himself in a peculiar position. He was a member of the governing party but often at odds with it, sometimes seeming like a one-man opposition to New Labour and everything it stood for. Already a paid-up 'member of the awkward squad', as he described himself, he now became a fully-fledged serial rebel. 'I'm one of the usual suspects,' he once said cheerfully to a broadcaster, before launching into yet another attack on a piece of legislation promoted by the Blair government. By 1997, Corbyn was reconciled to a life on the back benches; in the golden sunshine that bathed the country the morning after the election, he was not waiting by the phone for an invitation to join the new government. David Winnick says: 'Jeremy Corbyn came into Parliament in 1983; by 1997 he knew he wasn't about to be made Minister for Paperclips. I don't think it was any great surprise that he didn't get a post till now. For him it was either the top job or nothing.' Tariq Ali agrees: 'Ambition never entered into his political makeup. For one thing, he and everyone else on the left knew, especially after Blair took the party, that their days were numbered.'

When Labour's 418 MPs returned to the Commons after the general election, it was the first time most of them, Corbyn included, had ever sat on the government benches. Most found it a thrilling experience. But for the MP for Islington North, little changed. He continued with his campaigns and he continued – often – to vote against the government, never mind that the government was now headed by a Labour Prime Minister. That Corbyn was out of step with the new regime was obvious to all. Following this, his fourth election, and having increased his majority by 11 per cent, Polly Toynbee asked in *The Independent*: 'What's Jeremy Corbyn doing in the same party as Tony Blair?' Matthew Parris in *The Times* added that Corbyn was 'loathed by the leadership of his party'. Almost relishing his role as the enemy within, Corbyn enjoyed telling the story of how, when a new Labour MP joined him for a cup of tea in the Commons Tea Room soon after election day, she was immediately approached by a whip, who told her: 'If you're seen talking to him again, you're finished.'[156]

One new MP who chose to ignore warnings from the whips about Corbyn (although knowing his history it is unlikely they would have bothered) was his old comrade John McDonnell. He entered the Commons as the representative for Hayes and Harlington in 1997, and would rapidly become Corbyn's closest friend in politics, even eclipsing Tony Benn as a brother in arms. McDonnell was a former trade unionist who had been a close ally of Ken Livingstone on the GLC, serving as his deputy before the pair had a spectacular fallout over rate capping. McDonnell wanted the GLC to follow Liverpool in refusing to publish a budget, as a means of challenging the Thatcher government's policy of capping the rates that could be set by some – in practice, always left-wing – councils. Even for Livingstone this was too much.

Despite being the senior parliamentarian, David Winnick noted how, from the start of their time together as backbench MPs, Corbyn appeared to defer to McDonnell, particularly on economic policy. Over time, Corbyn would focus increasingly on foreign affairs, leaving domestic matters to McDonnell – a dynamic, although they would not relish the comparison, not dissimilar to that of Blair and Brown. Winnick says: 'The relationship between them was clear right from the beginning. From time to time in the Chamber, Corbyn would go over and sit with McDonnell in his place and whisper in his ear about something; never the other way around.' Winnick is not the only Labour MP to describe Corbyn as the junior partner in the relationship.

Eighteen years after McDonnell's election to Parliament, and following his own anointment as leader, Corbyn sat alongside his ex-girlfriend Diane Abbott and watched with pride as his friend and newly appointed shadow Chancellor addressed Labour conference. Taking out his phone, he sent her a text message: 'Can you believe me, you and John are here?'

Philip Cowley's 2005 book *The Rebels: How Blair Mislaid His Majority*[157] contains a telling passage about Corbyn's voting record during Labour's first two terms in office.

> The most rebellious MP between 2001 and 2005 was Jeremy Corbyn, the Labour MP for Islington North, who voted against the party whip on 148 occasions. This will be of little surprise to Westminster-watchers – he was also the most rebellious Labour MP between 1997 and 2001 … He once claimed that he did not vote against the party willy-nilly, only being willing to defy the whip over three types of issues: war and peace, issues of liberty, and socio-economic policy. Point out to him that this covers almost everything that the government could possibly do, and he laughs. 'I suppose it does.'

Corbyn rebelled when the government tried to restrict debate over the nomination of select committees; he rebelled over the Anti-Terrorism, Crime and Security Bill; over the Education Bill, over the Nationality, Immigration and Asylum Bill and over the NHS Reform and Health Care Professions Bill; he rebelled over Iraq, over the fire-fighters and over the railways; he rebelled over the Criminal Justice Bill, the Social Care (Community Health and Standards) Bill, over the Asylum and Immigration (Treatment of Claimants) Bill and over the Higher Education Bill; he rebelled over the Gambling Bill, the Children Bill, the Housing Bill and the Serious and Organised Crime Bill; he rebelled over the Identity Cards Bill; and last, but certainly not least, he rebelled over the Prevention of Terrorism Bill. In short, Corbyn took part in almost all of the rebellions involving Labour.

With their large majorities, the Blair governments of 1997 to 2007 could afford to overlook the waywardness of one recalcitrant, left-wing MP, the whips becoming accustomed to leaving Corbyn out of their equations. When he was absent from the Commons, as he often was to attend meetings around the country or on overseas trips, he generally did not bother to 'pair', the system by which the whips of the two major parties agree to excuse an MP from voting by standing down an opponent. A diary item from 2002 recorded that when a mischievous backbencher took a peek into a notebook belonging to one of the Labour whips, it contained a somewhat heavy-handed joke at Corbyn's expense: '"Jeremy Cor-Bin Laden" it read. The ribcage repair kit, Matron, if you please.'[158]

When Blair was succeeded by Gordon Brown in 2007, and despite the latter being considered more sympathetic to the left, Corbyn found it no easier to toe the line. In Brown's first year in office he rebelled more than fifty times, including over the new Prime Minister's ill-starred attempt to introduce a measure making it possible to detain terrorist suspects without trial for forty-two days. Emma Crewe's book *The House of Commons: An Anthropology of MPs at Work* contains an anecdote about Corbyn's relationship with the Whips' Office at the start of the Brown regime, when Sadiq Khan, the MP for Tooting, was assigned as his whip.

> A phone call between then whip Sadiq Khan and Jeremy Corbyn tended to go something like this: Whip: 'Hello there Jeremy, just wanted to check how you are planning to vote on Tuesday.' Jeremy: 'I'm going to vote against.' Whip: 'OK.' Jeremy: 'I mean against the government.' Whip: 'Yes, I know.' Jeremy: 'Sadiq, at this point you are supposed to persuade me to support the party.' Whip: 'I can't be bothered. Would you consider abstaining?' Jeremy: 'No, sorry, I can't do that.' Whip: 'OK.'[159]

Some are highly critical of Corbyn's long record of rebellion. Alan Johnson, the former Home Secretary, has said: 'He's been cheerfully disloyal to every Labour leader he's ever served under.'[160] Tom Baldwin, who ran Ed Miliband's media operation, added: 'He's spent thirty-two years on the margins of Labour and the margins of British politics.'[161] Others see his behaviour differently. Catherine West, the new MP for Corbyn's old stomping ground of Hornsey and Wood Green, and an early supporter, has said: 'He's a purist. He's always been the same and that's what people like about him.'[162]

Although he may have come close a few times, Corbyn always just about stayed the right side of the line, and never had the whip withdrawn. At times it was a tightrope, but Corbyn managed to stay true to his principles while remaining within the Labour fold. 'I suppose it's to his credit that he's remained faithful to his views,' says David Winnick. 'Why should he change if he has strong convictions? He's never begged for anything.

He's always been a fairly detached member of the PLP. He's got a safe seat, he's getting on in years, why should he change?'

During the 2015 leadership contest, Corbyn faced questions over whether his serial failure to toe his party's line would come back to haunt him. How could he justify rebelling so often, and how did he expect to command loyalty when he had failed so abjectly to give it to his predecessors? The questions were to prove prescient. Soon after his election, having initially declared that he would impose the party whip on Labour MPs ahead of a Commons vote to approve airstrikes against ISIS in Syria, Corbyn found himself forced to grant the PLP a free vote; given his history, he nakedly lacked the authority to demand obedience.

Asked by the BBC's *Panorama* programme shortly before his election about his years of disloyalty, Corbyn himself said: 'I am somebody that believes in what they do and stands up when they do it.' And, anyway, it wasn't all opposition. Soon after becoming leader, Corbyn named as his proudest moment in politics cycling home from the House of Commons at 5 a.m. one Tuesday morning in March 1998 after voting in favour of the minimum wage.

Despite his voting record, it could be argued that Corbyn has in fact remained remarkably loyal to Labour. During these long years in opposition to his own government, a different character might have gone off in another direction, as indeed his friends George Galloway and Ken Livingstone did, standing for office, respectively, for a new party and as an independent. While Corbyn may have cheered both on, incurring the wrath of many for tweeting congratulations to Galloway for beating the Labour candidate in the 2012 Bradford West by-election, there was no question of him leaving the party he had joined as a sixteen-year-old grammar school boy. Tariq Ali says:

> I really wanted Jeremy and John McDonnell and the handful of lefties
> to break from New Labour and set up a little group in Parliament

outside New Labour as a basis for building a new party. And of course that was not their view. I felt, 'What's the point of staying with this bunch of thieving rogues?' But they were very committed to Labour, unlike me. There was a handful of people who just wouldn't capitulate. It was as simple as that. We never thought, and he never thought, and John McDonnell never thought, that he could win the party.

Corbyn himself was recently asked why those on the left such as John McDonnell, Tony Benn and him had stuck with Labour. He responded:

> I've often been extremely frustrated with the Labour Party, particularly over Iraq and, earlier on, Vietnam. Then you think of what the Labour Party has achieved and that it is the electoral home to millions of people, so I'm still in it. Always have been. I remember discussing this with Tony Benn many times, and he said: 'You know what, comrade, we're just in it, aren't we?'[163]

And so, through the New Labour years, Corbyn, McDonnell and Benn continued as they always had, with meetings and demonstrations, speeches and rallies. Gradually, those around him grew to realise, Corbyn was taking over Benn's role as the leader of the left, albeit in his own understated way. Benn himself had always assumed it would be the more charismatic Ken Livingstone or the left-wing MP Alan Simpson who would succeed him, but was happy to see Corbyn, his close friend and ally, grow into the role. His diary through the early years of the Blair government paints a picture of the transition as – concerned for the health of his wife, Caroline, who would die from cancer shortly before Benn stood down from Parliament in 2001 – he allowed the next generation of left-wingers to shoulder some of his responsibilities.

Benn describes his proudest moment in Parliament after his own victory in the peerage battle as watching his son Hilary be sworn in as MP
for Leeds Central having won a by-election in 1999. Many of those who
knew all three men, however, say that given Hilary's rather more moderate views, by the start of the new century Corbyn had become more of a
political son to Benn than his own offspring. David Lammy saw the pair
together at a demonstration shortly before Benn's death in 2014. He says:

> Tony was weak and could hardly stand up. As Tony sat down, and
> Jeremy was helping him with water and making sure he was OK, that's
> when I realised ... that Jeremy was almost the anointed individual to
> continue that struggle. Of course there are pre-eminent left-wingers in
> Parliament, people like Dennis [Skinner] [but] in terms of the circuit,
> the intellectual hard-left circuit that emanates from ... north London,
> west London, Tony represented that and Jeremy was anointed. Jeremy
> has a huge respect in that world.

Corbyn also kept up his friendships on the far left. One former senior
Labour Party aide says of Corbyn:

> Of all of those on the left, including Diane Abbott and Ken Living-
> stone, Corbyn is the only one who keeps in with the left-wing splinter
> groups, all those hardcore, seriously quite dangerous Trot groups.
> Everyone else finds them unacceptable, as does anyone who entered
> the Labour movement after 1994. But Corbyn keeps in with them.

Again, Corbyn's campaigns through the later years of the 1990s and into
the 2000s read like a roll-call of left-wing protest, his interests often eclectic in character but always ideologically coherent, and all catalogued and

neatly filed in his tidy Commons office. In 1998 he nominated the jailed whistleblower Mordechai Vanunu, an Israeli nuclear scientist, for the Nobel Peace Prize, lectured Labour conference on the ills of the arms trade and, always suspicious of NATO, condemned the bombing of Serbia, which Blair supported. A year later, when the Kosovan Liberation Army was given air support from NATO in its battle against the Serbs, he was among a tiny minority opposed to the campaign, leading Clare Short, the International Development Secretary, to call Corbyn and his fellow rebels a 'disgrace to the Labour Party'.[164] Corbyn protested at Labour's acceptance of a donation from Bernie Ecclestone, the owner of Formula One, which coincided with the government's decision to exempt the sport of motor racing from a ban on tobacco advertising (the money was eventually returned), and (along with many) described the Millennium Dome as a waste of money. Arguing that pacifists should pay lower taxes, he told the House of Commons: 'British taxpayers have a right of conscience not to be in the armed forces in time of war. Why shouldn't they have the same right in time of peace?'[165]

Corbyn drew up Early Day Motions criticising the fast-food giant McDonald's for suing two environmental activists in what became known as the 'McLibel' case, and opposed the government's cuts to single-parent benefits. He organised a rally in Hyde Park over the introduction of university tuition fees and cuts to student grants. (*The Times* reported him as addressing the crowd with the words 'Fuck the rich'. A few days later they issued a correction amending the quote to 'Tax the rich'; Corbyn rarely swears and never in public.)[166]

He was vice-chair of the All-Party Parliamentary Human Rights Group and raised the plight of the Chagos Islanders over their expulsion from their homeland. And there was rare praise from Corbyn for a New Labour Cabinet minister when, after years of campaigning alongside his by now ex-wife Claudia Bracchitta, he saw Home Secretary Jack Straw approve the extradition of the former Chilean dictator General Augusto Pinochet in 1999. 'Jack Straw has made a correct, brilliant and courageous decision that coincides with the fiftieth anniversary of the Universal Declaration of Human Rights,' he said.[167] In response to his campaigning over Pinochet, Corbyn received death threats, with posters pasted to his constituency office in Islington reading: '3,000 dead, Jeremy Corbyn you're next.' (Straw reversed his decision the following year.)

At the start of the new century, and having turned fifty, Corbyn's public hard-line image showed signs of beginning to mellow. In 2001 he won the 'Beard of the Year' competition, his facial hair described as a form of rebellion against New Labour. He would go on to win the associated Parliamentary Beard of the Year prize five times. Corbyn, however, was not for going quietly into the night. Just to underline his status on the left, and having never enjoyed any relationship to speak of with the journalists who make up the Parliamentary Lobby, in 2004 Corbyn took over Benn's column in the *Morning Star* newspaper. David Winnick describes his choice of outlet as illuminating. 'Those who take a very hard line in the Communist struggle control the *Morning Star*,' he says. Corbyn did not generally read mainstream national newspapers, referring to them as the 'right-wing press'. Instead, he preferred to get his news from the *Morning Star* and two Irish papers: the *Irish Post* and the *Leinster Leader*.

A long-standing republican, in 2000 Corbyn called for the 'relocation of the royal family to some smaller and more modest accommodation' than Buckingham Palace.[168] When the Queen Mother died two years later, he scandalised the Commons by wearing his trademark red blazer to the sombre eulogies. A newspaper diary item claimed that when Corbyn's house in Islington was burgled a few years later, so disgusted were the thieves at the meagre offerings that they threw the offending jacket out of the window of their getaway car.[169] What didn't make it into the piece was a postscript:

seeing Corbyn's famous red blazer lying in the street, some of his constituents assumed that their MP had been hit by a car and run over, leading a reporter from the BBC to call his office to check he was alright.

Corbyn travelled widely during the Blair years, taking part in delegations to Palestine, the World Social Forum in Mumbai, and to Moscow on behalf of the people of Chechnya. He continued his work with CND and signed an EDM calling for action on climate change (an issue on which he found himself at odds with his brother Piers, who is a climate change sceptic). In 2005, Corbyn helped organise and spoke at a conference called Hands Off Venezuela. 'He is such a brilliant man,' Benn wrote admiringly in his diary. 'He's known Latin America for thirty years.' The pair later met Venezuelan President Hugo Chávez in London, where the socialist leader had been invited to address City Hall by Livingstone, before attending a reception at the Commons.

Through it all, Corbyn remained committed to Islington North, dedicated to his constituents and an assiduous local campaigner. Gary Heather, his local councillor in Islington, says: 'When he goes out campaigning, he knocks on doors and more often than not ends up inside speaking to people about their problems for an hour and a half. We call it "doing a Jeremy".' When it came to raising local issues with ministers, Corbyn had a useful ally in his neighbour in Islington South, Emily Thornberry. 'The way it worked was, if we had an issue locally which needed to be discussed with a government minister, frankly if Jeremy approached the minister they might think twice, whereas I would apply and then we would both go.'

Corbyn may have been well known in his constituency, in left-wing circles and among the growing protest movement that emerged during the latter part of the Blair years as people, particularly the young, found an outlet for their concerns about New Labour away from party politics, but he remained relatively friendless in Parliament. He continued to stay away from the bars and other MP hang-outs and avoided the weekly meeting of the PLP. When it was said in 2015 that one of Corbyn's first responsibilities on becoming leader would be to address the PLP, one senior MP was heard muttering, 'He'll have to find it first.'[170] After the chaotic appointment of his first shadow Cabinet, Lucy Powell, who had been close to Ed Miliband as his election coordinator, was forced to admit that when Corbyn invited her to serve as his shadow Education Secretary it was the first time they had ever spoken.[171] Jon Trickett, the MP for Hemsworth and another Miliband ally who would go on to help organise Corbyn's leadership campaign, also barely knew Corbyn before the summer of 2015. 'The Commons is a very odd place,' Trickett says.

> You can spend half your life here, be in the same ideological space as somebody else, but you're not necessarily a bosom buddy. Obviously we know each other, we talk to each other. He's a very pleasant guy, warm and friendly, not dogmatic but highly principled. I don't go in the bars, he doesn't. I don't drink, I don't think he drinks. If you're a London MP it's a quite different rhythm. You don't need to spend as much time here if your constituency is on the doorstep.

As Blair's time in office drew to a close (chivvied along by Gordon Brown), those on the left considered their options. John McDonnell decided to run against Brown to prevent a coronation, but was frustrated when fellow left-winger Michael Meacher also entered the fray. By the time of Blair's resignation in 2007, Meacher had agreed to stand aside for McDonnell, but not all his backers followed suit. With candidates needing the support of 12.5 per cent of the PLP, equating to forty-five nominations, McDonnell fell sixteen votes short of the target. Brown stood unopposed. Corbyn himself briefly considered a try for the deputy leadership, telling *The Guardian*: 'Nothing's decided ... but there needs to be an anti-[Iraq] war candidate.

None of the existing ones are.'[172] The plan came to nothing, and Harriet Harman narrowly beat Alan Johnson for the post. But both men had learned valuable lessons, McDonnell in particular taking great satisfaction at getting Corbyn onto the ballot eight years later.

Brown's premiership was dominated by two events: the 2008 financial crash and the expenses scandal of 2009. Both would play an important role in Corbyn's passage to power in 2015. Corbyn was described by the *Daily Telegraph*, which broke the expenses story, as an 'angel', and he is officially listed as one of the lowest parliamentary claimants. However, while Corbyn boasted that his house off the Holloway Road was 'my first home, my second home, my third home, my fourth home',[173] as a London MP he was never entitled to a taxpayer-funded second property and therefore could not have been tempted into the abuses of public money that his colleagues representing areas away from the capital were caught out in: the moats and duck houses of the Conservatives, the sparkly lavatory seats and LCD televisions of his Labour peers. The much-reported story[174] that Corbyn made the lowest claim of any MP – for a £8.95 printer cartridge – is essentially apocryphal; the receipt had been left out of the relevant quarter's expenses and so was filed separately.[175]

But Corbyn is rightly praised for his attitude towards parliamentary expenses at a time when most MPs saw them as a clandestine extension of the salaries they were too afraid to increase for fear of voter opprobrium. 'I am a parsimonious MP,' Corbyn once said. 'I think we should claim what we need to run our offices and pay our staff but be careful because it's obviously public money.'[176] The rent on Corbyn's constituency office in Finsbury Park is between £12,000 and £14,000 a year. His landlord is the Ethical Property Company, which describes itself as 'a unique social business, managing commercial property that supports the work of some of the UK's most dynamic and influential charities and not-for-profit organisations'.

Just as anger over the austerity measures introduced in the wake of the banking crisis helped drive the desire for a left-wing candidate during the 2015 leadership election, so the expenses scandal would help to shape the conditions for Corbyn's victory by creating a widely felt dissatisfaction with mainstream politicians and politics. Although his rival Andy Burnham correctly identified a public desire to burst the pomposity of what he described as the 'Westminster bubble', he failed to recognise that his own New Labour background as a former special adviser and Cabinet minister disqualified him from benefiting from it. Instead, it would be Corbyn who would capture the hearts of the disaffected and capitalise on the mood for change. One former member of Ed Miliband's team says wryly: 'I blame the *Telegraph* for doing the expenses thing.' He adds: 'Large parts of the anti-politics mood was caused by the expenses scandal. It probably would have happened anyway but would it have happened to the same extent without expenses? I don't think so.'

Another overlooked factor in Corbyn's capture of the Labour leadership also has its basis in these years of opposition, which often saw him at odds with his own party. Both his Islington friend Keith Veness and David Lammy believe that Corbyn's dedication to so many causes over forty years of campaigning gave him a valuable head start when it came to the leadership election. 'The one thing about Jeremy is that hundreds of thousands of people know him,' Veness says.

> They've been on the picket line with him, or he spoke at their meeting, or he did this, that or the other. You go to any Labour Party meeting you get all these people coming up and say[ing] 'I remember when I met Jeremy.' He has supported every cause. That's his main thing. He's like that in Islington North: everyone knows him.

Lammy adds:

> The Labour Party wanted a movement; Jeremy has been leading a movement for years; hard left, on the fringes, but many, many, many, many campaigns, and many noble campaigns, honourable campaigns, fighting; deeply anti-racist, deeply anti-fascist. That's Jeremy. Jeremy is not a shirker, he puts the hours in. He enjoys it, he thrives on a crowd. At the moment it becomes fringe, Jeremy's still there. The Lawrences [parents of the murdered black teenager Stephen Lawrence] are in the news, deaths in police custody is in the news, Mark Duggan [whose death at the hands of a police firearms officer triggered the 2011 riots] is in the news, then it fades, Jeremy's still there. Nuclear disarmament's in the news, Trident's in the news, it fades, Jeremy's still there. That's the point. Time and time and time again he's done that work. These movements know him. What's hard I think at the moment for [people in the mainstream of the] party to understand is that these movements have been going on and they haven't been inside the party.

The foundations of Corbyn's people power movement had been laid.

CHAPTER ELEVEN

IRAQ

JEREMY CORBYN TOOK to the platform and began to address the crowd gathered before him. 'Everybody in the world has a chance to say no, absolutely no, to war in Iraq,' he cried. 'Thousands more deaths in Iraq will set off a spiral of conflict, of hate, of misery, of desperation that will fuel the wars, the conflict, the terrorism, the depression and the misery of future generations.' Watching him on the stage that day, 15 February 2003, were his mentor Tony Benn, his ex-wife Claudia Bracchitta and their three sons. In front of the platform in London's Hyde Park, wrapped up against the freezing winds, a million people listened to Corbyn's warning, while behind them, hundreds of thousands more snaked in a continuous line for miles through the streets of the capital. On that February weekend, millions marched on every continent of the globe, in 789 towns and cities in seventy-two countries, from Cairo to Hobart, Tasmania; Reykjavik to New York; Rome to Buenos Aires; Damascus to Madrid; Tokyo to Johannesburg; Manchester to Tel Aviv. A group of scientists working at the McMurdo research base in Antarctica joined in with a half-hour rally, making a peace symbol by lying down in the snow. In Baghdad, protesters walked through streets which would soon be bombarded from the air. In all, as many as 30 million people are estimated to have taken part in the Stop the War marches of 15 and 16 February 2003.

The plea for peace was ignored. Just over a month later, on 20 March, Operation Iraqi Freedom began. The United States and the United Kingdom-led invasion of Iraq resulted in the capture of Baghdad and toppling of the dictator Saddam Hussein, who would be executed by hanging in December 2006. Corbyn's words proved prophetic. The war in Iraq would last nearly nine years, result in the loss of perhaps as many as a million lives (the total figure remains in dispute), including 179 British service personnel, and lead to a bloody sectarian civil war which continues to this day. In October 2015, Tony Blair would admit that the war helped contribute to the rise of the hard-line, bloodthirsty terrorist group ISIS.

As one of the leaders of the Stop the War Coalition, which organised the march, Corbyn can claim his share of credit for what the veteran American activist Jesse Jackson has described as 'the biggest demonstration in the history of the entire earth'.[177] And, although he could not have foreseen it, the ensuing disenfranchisement felt by those million-plus Britons who heard him that day would later play a direct role in his capture of the leadership, to the outrage of the man who now turned a deaf ear to those Corbyn led in march to Hyde Park: Tony Blair. The friends and contacts Corbyn made during those tension-filled months leading up to the Iraq invasion would also form the basis of the tight-knit and highly effective team he would gather around him in the summer of 2015, while his opposition to the war gave him a moral authority his New Labour rivals lacked.

The Stop the War Coalition was founded in anticipation of an impending war not in Iraq, but Afghanistan, in 2001. Corbyn and his friends on the left had been as horrified as anyone by the events of 11 September, the attacks which became known as 9/11 leaving an indelible mark on all who witnessed them on their television screens. Tony Benn wondered initially if the atrocities in New York and Washington DC could be the work of far-right terrorists, such as Timothy McVeigh, who murdered 168 people by bombing a federal office building in Oklahoma City in 1995.[178] When, within a few days, it became apparent that Islamist jihadists were responsible, in the form of a shadowy group called al-Qaeda led by the sinister figure of Osama bin Laden, it was immediately clear that the United States would respond with force. The left, already largely alienated from the Labour leadership under Blair's premiership, feared Britain would follow suit. As the drums of war began to beat in Washington, it became glaringly obvious that an attack on Afghanistan, where the fundamentalist Taliban regime was accused of sheltering bin Laden, was imminent. On 20 September, US President George Bush declared that America was now engaged in a 'War on Terror', which would begin with al-Qaeda.

Even at this early stage, the left feared the conflict could spread more widely through the Middle East. Peter Kilfoyle, a prominent backbencher who had served as a Labour defence minister, mentioned Iraq as a potential US target less than two weeks after 9/11. In words which would prove remarkably prescient, he said: 'Hawks in the American administration, I fear, are trying to shape an agenda which settles old scores rather than meet the needs of a campaign against terrorism. The last thing we need to do is encourage a whole new generation of potential suicide bombers.'[179] In an article in the *Morning Star* written in 2003, Corbyn himself said: 'Historians will study with interest the news manipulation of the past eighteen months. After 11 September, the claims that bin Laden and al-Qaeda had committed the atrocity were quickly and loudly made. This was turned into an attack on the Taliban and then, subtly, into regime change in Afghanistan.'

As their alarm grew, Corbyn and his friends from the peace movement hit the phones, and began working on a plan to stop the drift to war. On 25 September, a fortnight after 9/11, a group of around 2,000 left-leaning politicians, activists and peace campaigners gathered at the Friends House in Euston, central London. They called themselves the Stop the War Coalition after a protest group formed a few days earlier at the University of California, Berkeley, and which had already spread to campuses across the United States. Lindsey German, a leading member of the Socialist Workers' Party and then editor of *Socialist Review*, took the chair. She has described the run-up to the formation of the coalition and the scene at the Friends House that day:

> The day after 9/11 they immediately started talking of the war [in Afghanistan] and linking al-Qaeda with the Taliban. The second day after the attack, they started talking about Iraq ... We all thought: 'This is going to be something *big*, we've got to do something' ... We decided ... we'd go for a really big meeting ... When we got there, we'd not only filled the big hall – about thirteen or fourteen hundred people – but also filled the small hall, and then we had 500 people outside that couldn't get into either hall. So we had an outdoor meeting too. It was absolutely *incredible*.[180]

The audience, made up of members of CND, the Communist Party of Britain, Labour Left Briefing, and the Alliance for Workers' Liberty, as well as a number of figures on the left such as Tony Benn, Tariq Ali and Mike Marqusee, listened as German warned that Afghanistan faced 'destruction', with the conflict leading to 'possibly a wider conflagration in the Indian subcontinent, Iran and the Middle East'.[181] Other speakers included Bruce Kent, the former chairman of CND, and Corbyn himself. The broad aims of the coalition were agreed: to prevent and end wars everywhere, with a particular focus on the coming conflict in Afghanistan. Corbyn has since said that his hope for the coalition was that it would represent 'peace, hope and justice' in a world lurching towards war. German was appointed convenor, while Corbyn became a member of the steering committee. Benn was made president.

In the weeks following 9/11, President Bush issued a series of demands of Afghanistan's ruling Taliban government to hand Osama bin Laden over. When the regime wouldn't or couldn't comply, on 7 October 2001, the US and UK launched Operation Enduring Freedom, a war against the Taliban that would drag on for the next thirteen years. The attack began with the bombing of Taliban military bases in Kabul, Kandahar and Herat. But while the joint force, supported by the Afghanistan opposition Northern Alliance, initially found it relatively straightforward to reoccupy the country, they failed to capture or kill the majority of the Taliban's fighting force, which melted away into neighbouring Pakistan and the formidably remote hill and desert regions of Afghanistan. A protracted guerrilla war now took hold.

As soon as the conflict was under way, Stop the War began a programme of protests, beginning with a rally in Trafalgar Square and followed, a month later, by a march through central London. Numbers grew quickly, with 25,000 people taking part in the November 2001 march. A pattern began to emerge of large rallies and protests, addressed by leading members of the British Muslim community as well as figures from politics, the Church and the arts: Corbyn, Benn, Ali, playwright Harold Pinter, the writer and broadcaster John Pilger, the political activist Bianca Jagger, George Galloway, Ken Livingstone. 'In whose interests is this madness? How many more people must die?' Corbyn asked in one impassioned speech to an anti-war rally towards the end of 2001. 'What kind of civilisation is it where the richest nation on earth finds its answers in bombs?'[182] 'We have a passive parliament and a cringing Cabinet that does not even demand the right to discuss Britain's involvement in the war,' Benn added.[183]

In January 2002, the left's fears that the War on Terror would spread appeared to be confirmed when President Bush used his annual State of the Union address to declare the existence of an 'axis of evil' formed of three rogue states which were aiding and abetting terrorists and therefore posed a threat to the US. They were named as Iran, North Korea and Iraq, Bush reserving his strongest rhetoric for Iraq under the dictatorship of Saddam Hussein, whom his father, President George H.W. Bush, had come close to toppling in the First Gulf War eleven years earlier. Even at the time of the first conflict, Corbyn and others had voiced suspicion about America's designs on Iraq and the Middle East. In an article for the Campaign Group newsletter in 1991, he wrote: 'The aim of the war machine of the United States is to maintain a world order dominated by the banks and multinational companies of Europe and North America.'[184]

Tony Benn's diary through 2002 and into 2003 highlights the trepidation felt by many on the left – and not just on the left – as it gradually dawned on the world that Bush was indeed turning his gimlet eye to Iraq. So began the sorry story of the road to war: the dodgy dossier, the 45-minute claim, the weapons inspectors, the failed diplomatic attempts to secure a United Nations resolution, the rebellion in the House of Commons, which could not prevent the war. In September 2002, a Stop the War march billed as 'the biggest yet' was held in London, attracting around 400,000 people. Ahead of the march, Corbyn said the protest would show the world that Blair 'does not speak for ordinary people in Britain. He speaks for the relationship with George Bush.'[185] 'Opposition to this war in this country is the most incredible coalition I have ever seen,' he added. 'You will see Christians, you will see Muslims, you will see the young and the old, trade unionists and peace campaigners ... We speak for the peace-loving people of this country.'[186] Having spent so many years among a tiny minority of left-wing activists committed to turning out in demonstrations and protests year in, year out, Corbyn admits he was surprised and energised by the strong public response to the Stop the War campaign. At one point, as the numbers taking part grew to the tens and later the hundreds of thousands, he said he realised 'we were the mainstream'.[187] It was a novel experience.

Corbyn was at the forefront of the campaign in the Commons, too. Just before the September 2002 march, he was among a group of fifty-six Labour MPs who staged a rebellion on a technical motion to register their opposition to the march to war. Corbyn has described his astonishment as he read the now infamous 'September dossier', produced by the government that day as justification for going to war, citing apparent proof that Iraq held weapons of mass destruction (WMD), based on evidence which would later largely be discredited. 'I remember arriving at Parliament at eight o'clock in the morning to read this historic document,' he said. 'I was the first there at the Table Office [where government papers are published], at one minute to eight, [and] at the moment they opened up I put my hand in and grabbed two copies.'[188] Corbyn gave one copy to an academic friend, and after the two men went off to read them separately, they phoned each other, saying: 'This thing is nonsense, this thing is utter nonsense, who could possibly believe this stuff?'[189] Five months later, when US Secretary of State Colin Powell attempted to win over the United Nations General Assembly with diagrams of Saddam's supposed WMD, the absurdity of the claim struck Corbyn immediately. The diagrams resembled ice cream vans, he remarked. 'In fact, they may well have been ice cream vans.'[190]

Corbyn had by now grown close to his fellow members of Stop the War, many of whom would go on to provide invaluable support during his leadership campaign. By pooling the personnel of a disparate group of far-left and pro-peace groups, Stop the War could draw on the talents of a far larger group than would be available to a normal single-issue campaign; naturally, the cream rose to the top, creating a coterie of people as professional as they were motivated. Those who cut their teeth at Stop the War would later prove their organisational superiority when they outflanked their theoretically more experienced rivals during the summer of 2015; veterans of a movement that had brought more than one in sixty of the population on to the streets of London in 2003 felt no compunction in putting together what would become a triumphant tour of the country by their unexpected favourite twelve years later. Among those Corbyn met at this time was Carmel Nolan, who would become his press officer during the leadership race.

Through the autumn and winter of 2002 and into 2003, more marches and protests were staged, culminating in the giant Stop the War protest of 15 February 2003. The scale of it took everyone by surprise; those who marched as much as those gung ho for war. The sheer numbers involved briefly gave hope that, surely, the government could not ignore the demand for peace. Speaking of his experiences that day, Corbyn told the House of Commons in January 2015:

> I was there with many others in this House on that huge platform we had looking out on Hyde Park, with a million people there and hundreds of thousands more who could not even get into Hyde Park. I saw people there who politically profoundly disagree with me. I saw people who had never been at a public demonstration or meeting in their lives, who were so moved by the obvious lies that they had been told that there were weapons of mass destruction in Iraq, and that is why we had to go to war, and they opposed it. Everyone there learned a lesson that day. And the cynicism we meet on the doorstep ... is in part because of the contempt Parliament showed on that particular day.

Tariq Ali too believes that the Blair government's failure to heed the over-whelming call for peace left those who took part in the march with a sense of grievance against Labour which would not fully die away until Corbyn's election. Indeed, he feels that Corbyn's passage to the leadership can in no small part be attributed to Iraq, not just because of the disastrous conse-quences that would flow from the invasion but also because of the feeling of alienation imprinted on those who marched that day. He says: 'There were a million people out against the Iraq War. The huge turn-out on Iraq was the beginning of the end of New Labour.'

Even as late as 18 March 2003, when the House of Commons gathered to formally vote on whether to send British troops to Iraq, many hoped war could yet be averted. The Labour whips launched a heavy-handed operation to keep rebellious MPs in line, and a number of Cabinet ministers threat-ened to resign. In the event, only Robin Cook, the Leader of the House, would do so, along with two more junior ministers. On the television foot-age of Cook's dramatic resignation speech in the Commons, Corbyn can be seen sitting directly behind him. He leads the applause (highly unusual in the Commons, where MPs rarely clap) and later described the speech as 'astounding'.[191] Of the 139 Labour MPs who rebelled against the war, none would regret it; of the 244 who did not, only a handful would not come to rue their decision.[192]

Shortly before the vote, Blair somewhat optimistically gathered a group of anti-war MPs, including Corbyn, to a meeting in his little office behind the Commons Chamber. After half an hour or so, and with the conversation going in circles, Blair began glancing at his watch. Corbyn later described the exchange that followed: 'I said: "Tony, just one question: Why are we doing it?" He slapped his hand on the table and said: "Because it's the right thing to do." I said: "That's not an answer." He said: "It's the only one you're going to get."'[193]

When the bombing of Baghdad began, with a 'shock and awe' bombardment in the middle of the night, the mood in Britain swung around to support the troops. But as the months passed and the public grew sickened by the death and destruction taking place, particularly as the promised WMD never materialised, public opinion began to turn back again. Through it all, Corbyn and Stop the War maintained their opposition to the conflicts in both Afghanistan and Iraq. Following the coalition's annual general meeting in February 2004, nearly a year after the invasion of Iraq, Tony Benn recorded in his diary: 'Jeremy Corbyn made a brilliant speech. I must say, Jeremy is so thoughtful and experienced and clear.'

Then, as now, Corbyn considered his Labour Party colleague Tony Blair a war criminal. In March 2006, on the third anniversary of the war, he attended a protest in Trafalgar Square where twenty-eight war crimes charges against the governments of Blair and Bush were read out, including 'crimes against peace' and 'planning and conducting an aggressive war using deceit'. That year, he rebelled in order to vote in favour of the establishment of what would become the Chilcot Inquiry into the war, resisting what he described as the 'extraordinary pressure' of the whips.[194] Like many, he is intolerant of the delays that have dogged the Chilcot Inquiry. And he continues to believe that Blair should be put on trial, telling the BBC's *Newsnight* during the 2015 leadership contest: 'If he has committed a war crime, yes. Everybody who has committed a war crime should be. It was an illegal war. I am confident about that.'

The Middle East had always been a source of fascination for Corbyn. Now, in the wake of the conflicts in Afghanistan and Iraq, he began increasingly to explore political avenues and connections to groups in the region which have since left him open to widespread opprobrium. Perhaps as a result of his experiences with Iraq and other causes he has championed, particularly in the international arena, of receiving retrospective vindication for campaigns which at the time were dismissed as at best wrong-headed and at worst dangerous, it is criticism he chooses not to accept. A long-standing champion of internationalism and human rights, Corbyn is clear in his mind about his views on the Palestinian conflict and other trouble spots. On occasion, however, he has been accused of stubbornness, in failing to understand how some of his associations appear to others. Like the man he has spent so long opposing, Tony Blair, Corbyn has come to believe in his own personal sense of right and wrong, and will not be deflected by the disapproval of others.

One of the most serious charges against Corbyn, an issue which arose several times during the 2015 leadership campaign, is that he has entertained and shared platforms with Islamist leaders whose public statements include anti-Semitism, homophobia, misogyny and the defence of terrorism and jihad. As with Northern Ireland, Corbyn insists that he is willing to speak to all sides of the Middle East debate; as with Northern Ireland, he is accused of holding that debate with only one side of the conflict. When some of the worst utterances of those he has associated with are pointed out to him, Corbyn often protests that he was unaware of them at the time, a defence which suggests either carelessness or, his critics say, disingenuousness.

When Corbyn first entered the leadership race and then unexpectedly emerged as the favourite, journalists on newspapers he dismisses as 'the right-wing press' found easy fodder in his long history of association with Islamist groups. There are numerous references in the cuttings files to meetings with representatives from organisations including Hamas, the Palestinian group responsible for terrorist attacks in Israel, and Hezbollah, the political movement founded in the wake of the 1982 Israeli invasion of Lebanon, which has a violent military wing. Corbyn is both sensitive yet strangely deaf to criticism of his stance on the Middle East, becoming touchy when challenged. Near the beginning of the 2015 contest, he was caught up in a memorably irritable exchange with the *Channel 4 News* journalist Krishnan Guru-Murthy, who pushed him on his use of the word 'friends' to describe representatives from Hamas and Hezbollah. Accusing Guru-Murthy of 'trivialising' the debate and of 'tabloid journalism', he testily explained his language thus:

> I use it in a collective way, saying these are our friends. Does it mean I agree with Hamas? No. Does it mean I agree with Hezbollah and what they do? No. What it means is, I think, to bring about a peace process you have to talk to people with whom you may fundamentally disagree.

Peter Tatchell, the gay rights campaigner and long-time ally of Corbyn, believes the term 'friend' is, however, highly inappropriate in this context: 'I don't buy the excuse that Jeremy's use of the term "friends" was diplomatic language to win over extremists and encourage dialogue,' he has written.

> He would rightly not accept a similar explanation by an MP who used those words about, and shared a platform with, the BNP [British National Party], EDL [English Defence League, both far-right groups] or European fascist parties. Islamists are a religious version of the far right. They want a clerical dictatorship without democracy and human rights. They do not merit friendship, praise or uncritical association of any kind.[195]

With his stated aim of conducting a dialogue over the Middle East, Corbyn has entered into a series of 'friendships' with a 'remarkable number of unsavoury types', in the words of *The Spectator*, and has taken a series of trips to the region, sometimes accompanied by his third wife, Laura Alvarez, funded by pro-Palestinian groups. These include Interpal, a British charity banned in the US, where it was described as 'part of the funding network of Hamas'[196] (a claim the charity strongly denies), and the Palestinian Return Centre, which has links to Hamas.

Corbyn's Middle East associates include Ibrahim Hewitt, a radical preacher who has said that homosexuality damages the fabric of society,[197] whom he entertained at the Commons, saying: 'I consider him to be a very good friend and I think he's done a fantastic job.'[198] Corbyn also attended events organised by Deir Yassin Remembered, an organisation named after a Palestinian village, the site of a massacre by Zionist paramilitaries, and run by the self-proclaimed Holocaust denier Paul Eisen. 'Fifteen years ago [Eisen] was not a Holocaust denier,' Corbyn said when challenged about the meetings. 'Had he been a Holocaust denier, I would have had absolutely nothing to do with him. I was moved by the plight of people who had lost their village in Deir Yassin.'[199]

In 2009, Corbyn invited to the Commons Dyab Abou Jahjah,[200] a Lebanese political activist who has referred to homosexuals as 'AIDS-spreading fagots' [sic][201] and who described British soldiers as legitimate targets,[202] writing personally to Jacqui Smith, the then Home Secretary, to urge her to grant his 'friend' a visa. When their meeting was raised by *The Sun* during the leadership campaign, Corbyn first denied it, then, when a photograph of the event emerged, said he had forgotten about it. 'The idea that I'm some kind of racist or anti-Semitic person is beyond appalling, disgusting and deeply offensive,' he insisted when asked about Jahjah. 'I have spent my life opposing racism.'[203] In a blog post, in which he denied being an anti-Semite and insisted his words about British soldiers had been misinterpreted, Jahjah wrote of his links to Corbyn:

> Yes, I do support Jeremy Corbyn, and I am hopeful he will win the
> leadership of Labour and help build a better future for the British

> people. I am like Mr Corbyn a socialist, and we do share similar
> values. This does not mean that I agree with him on everything and
> I am sure that he also disagrees with me on some things. He was not
> my cheerleader then and I am not his cheerleader now, serious peo-
> ple do not reason in these terms.

Corbyn also intervened with the Home Office on behalf of Sheikh Raed
Salah, who has claimed that 'a suitable way was found to warn the 4,000
Jews who work[ed] every day at the Twin Towers to be absent from their
work on 11 September 2001',[204] and describes homosexuality as a 'great
crime',[205] inviting him to tea on the Commons Terrace in 2012. Corbyn
defended their meeting, saying: 'We had quite a long conversation and I
made my views very clear. He did not at any stage utter any anti-Semitic
remarks to me.'[206] In another episode which would later prove controversial, in 2012 Corbyn wrote a letter in defence of Stephen Sizer, an Anglican
vicar barred from social media by the Church of England for posting an
article on Facebook which linked wealthy Jews to 9/11.[207]

A month before the 2015 Labour leadership result, and with Corbyn the
overwhelming favourite to win, the *Jewish Chronicle*, the UK's oldest Jewish
newspaper, challenged him to explain some of his associations. To the private concern of some in his team, he initially failed to respond, leading the
Chronicle to run a front-page editorial saying:

> We are certain that we speak for the vast majority of British Jews in
> expressing deep foreboding at the prospect of Mr Corbyn's election
> as Labour leader. Because, although there is no direct evidence that
> he has an issue himself with Jews, there is overwhelming evidence of
> his association with, support for … Holocaust deniers, terrorists and
> some outright anti-Semites.

When Corbyn did finally respond to the *Chronicle*, he described his portrayal as a friend of anti-Semites as 'ludicrous and wrong'.[208]

The *Times of Israel* also expressed concern about the prospect of a Corbyn victory, describing his election as 'the Rosh Hashanah present unwanted by the majority of British Jews', a reference to the Jewish holiday which in 2015 took place the day after his coronation. It included a statement from Jonathan Arkush, president of the Board of Deputies of British Jews, referring to 'very deep concerns' in the Jewish community about 'Corbyn's reported links to a Holocaust denier and other individuals with anti-Semitic track records and about his hostile views on Israel'. Joan Ryan, chair of Labour Friends of Israel, urged voters in the leadership contest not to back Corbyn, saying: 'We recognise the deep concerns which exist about positions taken, and statements made, by Jeremy Corbyn in the past and recognise the serious questions which arise from these.'[209]

Corbyn's team took a robust response to allegations of anti-Semitism, at one point issuing a statement saying:

> Jeremy has involved himself in Middle East issues for many years, meeting many people and groups with whom he has huge differences of opinion – but he believes that only dialogue can bring about peace. The Holocaust was the most vile period in human history and the Jewish people were scapegoated by the Nazis. Some people in Britain, including Jeremy's own parents, stood in Cable Street in 1936 to halt the rise of Nazism in our country.[210]

Some members of Corbyn's team fear privately, however, that he has become so accustomed to hostile press that he can no longer identify when potentially legitimate concerns are being expressed. One prominent Corbyn supporter says privately that, even if he disagrees with the criticism by the

Jewish community, it behoves the Leader of the Labour Party to try to ease fears, rather than simply rejecting them. 'It is clear that some members of the Jewish community regard him as anti-Semitic,' the source says. 'He is not, but he has been so clearly associated with Hamas and Hezbollah that that is what they think. He has to be aware of that. He has got to tackle it, he can't let it simmer.'

Tariq Ali, however, believes Corbyn's record on the Middle East is clear, and charges of anti-Semitism, or, more accurately, of tolerance of anti-Semitism, unjustified: 'It's nonsense. I don't think that has had a big effect on him, the criticism from the Jewish Board of Deputies or the *Jewish Chronicle*. His commitment to Palestine has been exemplary, and that will never change.' Chris Mullin adds: 'He's being done over for saying we should talk to Hamas; when I was in government that was always the advice coming from MI6.' Ronnie Campbell says: 'He was great with the Palestinians, he wanted peace there. This idea that he's against the Jews is a load of shite. He would love the conflict to end, some sort of settlement.'

Other old friends are more critical. In his long article on Corbyn's foreign policy, Peter Tatchell wrote:

> He has been careless in not checking out who he shares platforms with and been too willing to associate uncritically with the Islamist far right. While I'm certain that Jeremy doesn't share their extremist views, he does need to explain in more detail why he has attended and spoken at meetings alongside some pretty unsavoury bigots who advocate human rights abuses – and especially why he did so without publicly criticising their totalitarian politics.[211]

In another scathing assessment of Corbyn's foreign policy positions, the journalist Taylor Parkes wrote in the online magazine The Quietus:

Whatever Corbynites claim, this is not international diplomacy. These were not summit meetings, nor were they peace talks; more like publicity stunts. Publicity stunts for peace, perhaps, or something similarly asinine and Lennonish, but still, the fact remains: there's no conceivable way that anything constructive – not one thing – could ever have come from any of them.[212]

Some of Corbyn's more controversial remarks on the Middle East have been made on Press TV, the official television channel of Iran's Republican government, which human rights campaigners say has been used to broadcast the forced confessions of those opposed to the regime. He has consistently called for an end to sanctions against Iran, even before Tehran's promises to restrict its nuclear programme, and laments the 'demonisation' of Iran by the West.[213] Days before the conclusion of the leadership race, a clip emerged of him on Press TV describing the execution of Osama bin Laden at the hands of US Navy Seals who stormed his compound in Abbottabad, Pakistan, in 2011 as a 'tragedy'. 'This was an assassination attempt, and is yet another tragedy, upon a tragedy, upon a tragedy,' he said. 'The World Trade Center was a tragedy, the attack on Afghanistan was a tragedy, the war in Iraq was a tragedy. Tens of thousands of people have died.'[214] More footage, this time of an interview with Russia Today, emerged during the contest in which he appeared to equate the barbarous ISIS terrorist group with American forces in Iraq. Asked what would shift the balance of the conflict in Iraq, he responded:

An acceptance and understanding of why so many people in some of the cities in the north have apparently been prepared to accept the ISIS forces. Yes, they are brutal, yes some of what they have done is quite appalling. Likewise, what the Americans did in Fallujah and other places is appalling.[215]

A Corbyn campaign spokesman responded to criticism of his words by saying: 'Jeremy Corbyn believes the violent ideology of ISIS is a vicious, repugnant force that has to be stopped.'[216]

It is customary for politicians, particularly those at senior levels, to steer clear of commenting on the leadership elections of rival parties. However, such was the indignation with which Corbyn's ISIS remarks were greeted, that David Cameron was moved to enter the fray. 'I think this is absolutely the wrong approach and will make Britain less secure,' he said.[217] In his speech to the 2015 Conservative Party conference following Corbyn's election, the Prime Minister went further, condemning his description of bin Laden's death by saying:

> A tragedy is nearly 3,000 people murdered one morning in New York. A tragedy is the mums and dads who never came home from work that day. A tragedy is people jumping from the towers after the planes hit. We cannot let that man inflict his security-threatening, terrorist-sympathising, Britain-hating ideology on the country we love.

Cameron has also refused to apologise for referring to Corbyn as a 'terrorist sympathiser' on the eve of the December 2015 Commons' vote that approved the use of airstrikes against ISIS in Syria.

Corbyn remains a member of Stop the War and continues to argue against military intervention in the Middle East. Both positions have led to criticism. His opposition to airstrikes in Syria, and in particular a somewhat clumsy and ultimately unsuccessful attempt to force his new shadow Cabinet to follow his lead and vote against the government in the Commons, led to the greatest crisis of his early leadership. Having been proved right on Iraq, he could not bear to see Labour MPs commit the folly, as he saw it, of embroiling the country in another open-ended, American-led mission in the region. But his stance brought him close to losing half his shadow

Cabinet, including Hilary Benn. When he finally gave way and allowed a free vote, the Commons witnessed the bizarre spectacle of Benn closing the debate with a powerful and much acclaimed speech in support of airstrikes hours after his leader had set out the opposite position.

Soon after the vote, John Rees, a national officer for Stop the War, launched an online petition calling for Benn's deselection. An article attacking the shadow Foreign Secretary appeared on the group's website, apparently blaming the Paris terrorist attacks of 13 November 2015 on the West, and comparing ISIS to the International Brigades of the Spanish Civil War. 'The jihadist movement that ultimately spawned Daesh [ISIS] is far closer to the spirit of internationalism and solidarity that drove the International Brigades than Cameron's bombing campaign – except that the international jihad takes the form of solidarity with oppressed Muslims, rather than the working class or the socialist revolution,' it read. Corbyn was urged to distance himself from Stop the War – but declined to do so. While his friend Caroline Lucas resigned from her role as vice-chairman, the Labour leader attended the group's Christmas party ten days after the Syrian airstrikes vote.

As with many of the causes Corbyn has espoused, the new Labour leader's foreign policy, particularly as it relates to the Middle East, is polarising. Ultimately, those who voted for Corbyn accept that, despite his somewhat questionable associations of the past, he is a man of peace. His clear-sightedness in opposing an unpopular war his New Labour rivals supported (both Andy Burnham and Yvette Cooper voted in favour of the Iraq invasion) lend him an authority they could never aspire to. His long years of campaigning have imbued in Corbyn a legitimacy and an authority which gave those who turned away from politics in disgust after March 2003 a reason to return to the Labour Party. As Corbyn told the House of Commons in January 2015: 'I don't want to go to war memorials, I don't want to go to memorial services, I want us to be a real influence for peace, for justice, in the world.'[218]

CHAPTER TWELVE

A CONTENTED MAN

JEREMY CORBYN SPENT polling day, 7 May 2015, knocking on doors in Islington North, asking his constituents to once again trust him with their votes. He was three weeks shy of his sixty-sixth birthday. At an age when most people are contemplating retirement, if they haven't already taken it, there was never any doubt that he would stand for election for an eighth time. Politics had been his life for more than fifty years, it had contributed to the break-up of two marriages and it dominated his thoughts, friendships and time. He could not imagine a life away from Parliament and, more importantly, he did not want to. However, anyone encountering Corbyn now would have described him as a settled, contented man. Gone was the restlessness and anger of his youth, to be replaced, if not by a more mellow outlook on life, then certainly one which had perhaps grown somewhat philosophical. He was comfortable in his own skin; happy with the way his life had turned out.

In Islington North, Corbyn continued to be admired and respected by his constituents, putting in long hours on their behalf, and they would go on to reward him by increasing his majority to more than 21,000, making his the thirtieth safest Labour seat in the country. Margaret Hodge recalls attending an event in Islington North at the start of 2015, at the request of the local party. 'I hadn't been there for thirty years, and Jeremy was there and he made a speech and what really absolutely hit me was that this was the same speech he'd made thirty years earlier,' she says.

At work in the House of Commons, Corbyn had spent the past five years in very much the same vein as he had the previous twenty-seven: opposing the government, regardless of its persuasion. The fall of Labour under Gordon Brown and the coming to power of the Conservative and Liberal Democrat coalition headed by David Cameron in May 2010 had very little impact on his political activity. While he continued to be a serial rebel, Corbyn felt rather more comfortable in Ed Miliband's Labour Party than he had for some time. Jon Trickett, one of Miliband's closest advisers, says that during the 2010 to 2015 parliament, Corbyn ceased to be viewed as a thorn in the side by the leadership. He was clear about what he would and would not support, and was not obviously fomenting insurrection on the left. 'I think he would have thought that Ed was in a better place than some of his predecessors,' Trickett says.

> Jeremy doesn't have a personality which goes out of his way to upset other people or cause them difficulties. My feeling would be at that time that you could predict that Jeremy would find some things that Ed was doing unprincipled and wouldn't vote for them. It wasn't a surprise. He never really in recent years attempted to organise. I saw him as a man of principle who spoke his mind on what he thought was right. I wouldn't describe him as a loner but I wouldn't describe him as an organising tendency trying to overthrow the system. He was more like: this is who I am, this is what I stand for.

On becoming leader, Corbyn would seek Miliband's counsel on several occasions, finding his advice helpful.

While he may have felt a little more at home in the Labour Party during the 2010 to 2015 parliament, Corbyn had not, however, compromised on his beliefs. Asked later about the perception that the party's offering under Miliband had been too left-wing to win a general election, he said:

> It certainly wasn't an ultra-left manifesto. What was it proposing? A limited amount of public ownership of the national railways, which is actually very popular, quite good stuff on the minimum wage and so on, but on the economy, it wasn't fundamentally redistributive, which is what we need to be putting forward. We live in a very unequal society.[219]

As it had been throughout his time in Parliament, Corbyn's main political concern was international affairs. One senior Labour adviser who worked first for Brown and later for Miliband said that in his ten years in the job, Corbyn never once discussed domestic policy with him. Along with Miliband, Corbyn voted against airstrikes targeted at the Assad regime in Syria in 2013. He opposed the renewal of the Trident nuclear weapons system. His views on Russia and President Vladimir Putin were typically unorthodox. At the beginning of the Ukrainian crisis in 2014, when Russia annexed Crimea (but before the bloody scenes in eastern Ukraine), he eschewed the general Western analysis, in which Putin was seen as the aggressor, and suggested instead that the roots of the conflict lay in 'belligerence', by NATO, adding that Russia was 'not unprovoked'.[220]

A keen viewer of Russia Today, the English-language television station owned and run from Moscow by the Russian state, on the day of the royal wedding between Prince William and Kate Middleton in April 2011, he sent a tweet advising his followers: 'Try Russia Today. Free of royal wedding and more objective on Libya than most.' Corbyn was in fact an early adopter of social media, joining both Twitter and Facebook in February 2010, a rather modern approach for a man of his years (and one that would serve him well in the 2015 leadership election).

In March 2014, Tony Benn passed away at the age of eighty-eight. In his public tribute, Corbyn said:

> It was a pleasure and an honour to work with him on causes ranging from the miners' strike to opposition to the disastrous wars in Iraq and Afghanistan. We have his diaries, we have his books, we have wonderful memories, and above all we have an inspiration that we can follow.[221]

Privately, he was greatly distressed. But, in his sixties, Corbyn was blessed with a handful of other strong friendships, particularly that of John McDonnell, his fellow MP who had been his closest comrade in Parliament for nearly twenty years. If Corbyn was still not a popular figure in the House of Commons, nor was he the pariah he had once been when he brought Irish Republicans like Gerry Adams to visit. Virtually unknown personally to newer MPs, his more established peers respected his work ethic and commitment to his many political causes, the London Labour Members in particular appreciating the fact they could always rely on his help. When, a few weeks before polling day, in April 2015, David Lammy realised he had forgotten to ask a fellow MP, as is the convention, to launch his campaign in Tottenham, Corbyn happily scrambled to step in, giving his customary anti-austerity speech. Having spent the day with him, Lammy says that although Corbyn was as committed as ever to his beliefs, he sensed no greater ambition. 'I am absolutely clear that Jeremy had no clue at all at that point that he would be running to be leader a few weeks later.'

Margaret Hodge also benefited from Corbyn's willingness to help out. She says:

> I was fighting the BNP [who captured council seats in her Barking constituency] between 2006 and 2010. Jeremy must have come down two or three times, brought a car full of people from Islington to help me. And that's Jeremy – I think he appeared more often than any other London MP. I was fighting fascism and that would be completely up his street.

Many of those MPs who did know Corbyn considered him a gentleman. 'He's always, always courteous,' Hodge says. 'I've never seen him lose his temper.' Emily Thornberry adds: 'I love Jeremy, he's a personal friend. I have a lot of time for him and a great deal of respect for him. And what I respect about him is that he is pretty uncompromising. He takes stands on things and he fights his corner. I like that about him.'

If his relationship with his fellow MPs had improved, his dress sense had barely changed since his entry to Parliament in 1983. Slightly less shabby than in his early years in the Commons, Corbyn never fully smartened up. During the 2015 leadership election, and following his victory, his unique (in Westminster, at least) sense of style became a subject of much debate; eschewing the smart suits and ties of most male politicians, by the time of the last general election he had adopted a uniform designed more to provide comfort than to convey authority. Usually tieless, he could generally be seen in the Commons wearing an open-necked shirt with a white vest peeping out from under it, bought, he confessed to a Mumsnet web chat, from a stall at Nag's Head Market in his constituency for the princely sum of £1.50.[222] He often sported a corduroy jacket, from which his glasses and a pen invariably poked out of the top pocket. A photograph of Corbyn wearing long shorts and black knee socks, taken during the 2015 leadership campaign, provoked much mirth.[223]

Although Corbyn continued to devote most of his energy to politics, in his seventh decade he began to allow himself a little downtime, loosening up, slightly, from the old Hornsey days when his Labour Party friends remember him being too driven to truly enjoy time away from campaigning. Having spent many years on a council waiting list, in March 2003, the same week that Britain went to war in Iraq, Corbyn was finally granted an allotment in East Finchley, which he referred to humorously as 'Jeremy and the Land'. There he spent many happy hours pottering around, growing vegetables and fruit, which he would later serve up for friends. During a rare break from the 2015 leadership campaign, Corbyn would pass a few peaceful hours making jam from fruit harvested from his allotment. He grew potatoes, beans, soft fruit and apples; produce that doesn't require much watering, he has said. In words which would have amazed the colleagues who had watched him work ceaselessly for years, he told the *Sunday Mirror* hours after his election: 'I enjoy doing other things in life. You can't just do your job. If you just do your job, you don't do it very well.' He went on: 'I enjoy growing things in my allotment and garden. This year the maize has done very well. It's been a great year for maize. I dug in lots and lots of manure in.'

Corbyn's other hobbies include reading, once naming Oscar Wilde, W. B. Yeats and the Nigerian author Chinua Achebe as his favourite writers,[224] and film – he likes *Casablanca* and *The Great Gatsby*.[225] He's a runner, still finding time during the leadership election to pound the streets of Islington, and relishes watching cricket; he enjoyed lengthy discussions about the England team's performance with his friend Mike Marqusee, who, despite being an American, was an avid cricket fan. A devotee of Arsenal Football Club, he is a member of 'In Arsène We Trust', a fan group that supports the often under-fire manager, Arsène Wenger.[226] He is also a devoted cyclist and railway enthusiast; despite his teenaged years spent tinkering with his father's car, for environmental reasons he now refuses to drive himself and travels by public transport wherever possible. When *Railway Magazine*[227] put him on the front cover a few weeks after he was elected Labour leader, the delighted Corbyn tweeted out a photograph of it to his hundreds of thousands of followers. His favourite restaurant is Gaby's Diner, a non-kosher Jewish deli in Covent Garden, where he and John McDonnell liked to retreat after attending rallies in Trafalgar Square. 'The hummus is delicious,' McDonnell has said.[228]

Indeed, in his last years in Parliament before becoming leader of his party, Corbyn seemed in danger of finally developing, in Denis Healey's famous phrase, a 'hinterland' away from politics. On long railway journeys, he told one audience during the leadership campaign, he whiled away the time by writing poetry and drawing sketches, adding that his taste in art runs to new works that are 'abstract beyond belief'.[229] He still has a cat, which he calls El Gato – 'the cat' in Spanish – and even found time to watch a little television, enjoying the BBC's football highlights show *Match of the Day* and historical documentaries. Friends and acquaintances universally describe him as a kind man; both Chris Mullin and the journalist Kevin Maguire have anecdotes about encountering Corbyn on a train and sharing his sandwiches. The former Labour adviser David Mills has said that Corbyn is the only dinner party guest he has ever known who asked if he could take the uneaten pudding of pastries away with him to give to the homeless.

In his family as well as his friendships, Corbyn felt blessed. He remained close to his brothers, particularly Piers, who often came round to dinner, where the family would enjoy spirited but friendly debates. In 2013, Corbyn was awarded the Gandhi Peace Award and his office surprised him by inviting his oldest brother, David, along to the ceremony at the House of Commons to see him pick up the prize. David describes his pride at watching his youngest brother receive such a prestigious international honour:

> It was quite a moving occasion. His office tipped me off that he was getting it and made arrangements for me to be able to go and listen to the presentation. It's not given every year; it's irregular, when they think someone is worthy of it. Completely independent people recognising what he is; he really is trying to make the world a better place.

In their citation, the award's organisers said:

> The trustees of the Gandhi Foundation agreed to offer him our International Peace Award in recognition of his consistent efforts over a thirty-year parliamentary career to uphold the Gandhian values of social justice and non-violence. Besides being a popular and hardworking constituency MP he has made time to speak and write extensively in support of human rights at home and worldwide. His committed opposition to neocolonial wars and to nuclear weapons has repeatedly shown the lack of truth in the arguments of those who have opposed him.[230]

Corbyn, who arrived ten minutes late for the ceremony (he is notoriously tardy, usually squeezing too many meetings into the day) clearly saw much to admire, and perhaps even empathise with, in the esteemed figure in whose name he was being honoured. In his acceptance speech, he said:

> There are people who approach Gandhi from an entirely critical point of view because of things he said and did in the early part of his life and he's sometimes condemned for wearing a suit in London when

> he was a student here, and things like that, but you have to look at the
> totality of his life and the extraordinary contribution that he's made
> in the long run to ideas of peace and justice.[231]

One deep sadness for all the Corbyns was the loss of Andrew, the second oldest brother, in 2001. A mining engineer by trade, Andrew's work took him first to Africa and later to Australia, where he settled with his wife and children and became a lecturer in mining at Murdoch University in Freemantle, in the west of the country. From there he would take lengthy sabbaticals and research trips, sometimes accompanied by students, to exotic places around the world. He had hoped to obtain a pilot's licence to enable him to travel more easily to the remote destinations he explored, but was barred from getting one when it was discovered that he had very high blood pressure. David, Corbyn's oldest brother, says Andrew had an unhealthy lifestyle and 'the strangest of diets', and refused to take medication.

One of the places Andrew had been working was Papua New Guinea. Initially, his family travelled with him, but his wife, whom he met at an Islington North Labour Party function while helping out his brother in the 1980s, found the conditions too arduous, so he returned to the jungle on his own. It was during a visit to town, while in a restaurant in Papua New Guinea's second city of Lae, that he suffered a fatal stroke. He was just fifty-seven. David Corbyn says:

> He used to frequently go off on bush expeditions with students, taking
> them way out into the jungle, looking at things that were interesting,
> mostly geologically related. That's when you would have thought he
> would come to an untimely end, but no. It was no distance from the
> hospital, they got there quickly, but he died, unfortunately. Probably
> his health wasn't 100 per cent anyway because of high blood pressure.

According to Keith Veness, Corbyn used to refer to Andrew, humorously, as 'my really mad brother', as opposed to Piers, who was just 'my mad brother'. 'At the 1987 general election, they both turned up to help, and Jeremy said: "Have you met my mad brother?" And I said: "Who? Piers?" And he said: "No, my really mad brother."' Now Corbyn was tasked with bringing Andrew's body home. Veness says: '[Andrew] was an honorary member of the tribe there and Jeremy had to go out there and retrieve the body. He had to sit out on the veranda for two days while the tribe carried out their ceremonies. He was totally crazy, Andrew.' Corbyn remains close to Andrew's children, as he does to the entire Corbyn clan.

Corbyn is also on friendly terms with his ex-wife, Claudia Bracchitta, and is a devoted father to his three now grown-up sons. While the former spouses remained in their separate flats in the house in Holloway when the boys were younger, he has since moved to a modern home in nearby Finsbury Park worth today around £620,000. Corbyn and Bracchitta's oldest son, Ben, became a football coach, working for five years at the family club of Arsenal, where he was employed in community liaison, and later at Barnet, where he was involved in youth development. He holds a UEFA B Football Association qualification and now coaches junior players at the newly promoted Premier League club Watford. A fluent Spanish speaker, he also sometimes translates for players. Now aged twenty-eight, Ben himself has a son, making Corbyn a grandfather. Corbyn never speaks of his grandson in public, but the little boy clearly has a big place in his heart. Before his move to the rooms belonging to the Leader of the Opposition, his small Westminster office had a drawing by his grandson pinned to the wall in pride of place. Ben's son was allowed to go along to the final rally of Corbyn's leadership tour, held in his Islington constituency, making observers smile as he ran around, clearly relishing the spectacle of his grandfather holding court on stage.

All the Corbyn boys are political, and their politics are those of their parents. Before they made them private during the leadership contest, they would frequently use their social media accounts to promote left-wing and international causes, particularly those relating to Latin America, where their mother is from, and Palestine. Ben was not a Labour supporter until his father entered the leadership contest, writing on his Facebook page: 'I'm completely disillusioned with the Labour Party and never joined but I will vote for the left-wing campaign.' Also on Facebook, Ben displayed a 2007 photograph of himself posing with Gerry Adams and wearing a T-shirt reading: 'Palestine: End the Occupation'. In another posting, he told of visiting a memorial to the hunger striker Bobby Sands.

The most committed of the sons is Sebastian, or Seb, now twenty-four, who, after university, went to work as a researcher for John McDonnell. During the leadership campaign, he played an active and key role; one rather touching photograph of the pair showing the son smoothing his father's wind-tousled hair generated much publicity at the time. More recently, critics have accused Corbyn and McDonnell of nepotism, the latter having given a job to the son of his best friend. As one Labour MP puts it: 'Can you imagine the outcry if George Osborne had employed David Cameron's son as his parliamentary researcher?' Corbyn's former press spokesman Harry Fletcher says in response:

> In all my years working with MPs I have never met a single one who
> employed a member of staff through open recruitment. In this day
> and age, there are just too many people who want to work here [in
> Parliament]. It's impossible to sift through them, and MPs certainly
> don't have the time. So in this place, it's who you know. It's not right,
> it's not an ideal system, but no one has come up with a better one.
> And who is to say that Seb is not the best person for the job? He has
> a 2:1 from Cambridge and is very bright.

Corbyn's youngest son, Thomas, is as politically active as the other boys. He started his own company repairing laptops and PCs while still at school. He left after GSCEs but recently took a foundation course at York University and, having worked as a technical assistant for a number of computer firms, is back working for his own company, Better PC, while volunteering part time for the Labour Party. At the start of the leadership campaign, Harry Fletcher took Claudia Bracchitta and all three boys to a pub near her house to discuss how best they should handle the attention they would receive. They agreed that they would not speak to the media in any way. It is a vow Bracchitta and her sons have stuck to.

And then there is Laura Alvarez, Corbyn's third wife and the woman he was finally prepared to make room in his life for. The couple had an unlikely matchmaker: Tony Benn. In 1999, soon after Corbyn's divorce from Claudia, he went to speak at a fundraiser on behalf of the Fire Brigades Union. There Benn, a fellow speaker, was approached by a Mexican woman called Marcela Alvarez, who had been taken to the event by a friend. She told Benn that her estranged husband had snatched their seven-year-old daughter Jasmin from their home in Crawley, West Sussex, and disappeared. 'Tony, who became a great friend, introduced me to Jeremy and he promised to help,' Marcela later said. 'Tony was like a mentor to Jeremy. They were very close, like family. Jeremy helped find my daughter. He intervened and made calls and did everything he could to help. Without his assistance I would never have been reunited with Jasmin.'[232]

Soon after meeting Corbyn for the first time, Marcela asked her sister, Laura, who at the time was living in Mexico City, to come to England to help in the search. The sisters went along to another fundraiser, this time in Finsbury Park, where they again ran into Corbyn. Marcela said: 'Because of our case he met my sister and they fell in love. Was it love at first sight? I don't know. I think that their love grew slowly.'[233]

Corbyn contacted West Sussex Police and accompanied the Alvarez sisters to meetings at the police station. Marcela's daughter was eventually traced to the United States, to Ogden, Utah, and in 2003, she and Marcela were reunited, arriving home in England on Christmas Day.[234] Following her sister's reunion with Jasmin, Laura returned to Mexico City to study law, but stayed in touch with Corbyn. Marcela said they 'maintained a long-distance relationship for years'.[235]

Twenty years Corbyn's junior, Laura Alvarez is the youngest of five children, and grew up in relative poverty in Mexico City, her father earning money by selling cheese door-to-door. Family and friends say she was an 'ordinary' girl, but she was clearly bright.[236] After law school she worked for two years at a bank specialising in providing funding for local businesses in impoverished, rural areas. Through most of her lengthy long-distance relationship with Corbyn, she was working at the Mexican National Commission for Human Rights. One family friend, Gil Velasquez, has said: 'Laura has always been committed to helping other people. She has a fine social conscience. She is very smart and always very friendly.'[237] By 2011, the couple decided they could no longer live apart. Alvarez moved to London and settled into Corbyn's new home.

Corbyn once said he could never have a relationship with someone whose politics he did not share,[238] and luckily Alvarez's were in order. She quotes the intellectual writer Noam Chomsky on her Facebook page, and has attended rallies and events relating to causes Corbyn holds dear, from Palestine to human rights in Latin America. As he did with Bracchitta, Corbyn was keen to keep Alvarez's profile low. Before the leadership contest, the only mention of her in the British press was as a guest at the London memorial service to commemorate the death of Nelson Mandela in March 2014; her link to Corbyn was not referred to.[239] Indeed, it was not until Piers brought her up in an interview with the *Sun* newspaper well over a month into the leadership campaign that most people in Westminster were even aware that Corbyn had married for a third time.[240]

The wedding took place in Mexico in 2013, at the Hacienda Panoaya, the former home of the revered seventeenth-century writer and nun Juana Inés de la Cruz, which is nestled in the foothills of two volcanoes, Popocatépetl and Iztaccihuatl, and is now a tourist destination complete with a restaurant, zoo and theme park. Gil Velasquez, who was one of the guests, has said that Corbyn brought only one friend with him from England, a journalist whose name he does not recall: 'The wedding was a very small and private affair,' Velasquez added. 'Her parents and brothers were there and a few close friends. It was a beautiful setting and very romantic.'[241] The wedding party enjoyed champagne on the lawn followed by a sit-down meal in the hacienda's restaurant. Although they did not attend the wedding, Corbyn's immediate family are fond of Alvarez. His sons sat beside her to watch Corbyn's first speech to Labour conference as leader, where he eschewed the traditional, somewhat hackneyed custom of bringing his wife onstage to embrace him. As they left the conference hall, Tom was photographed putting a protective arm around Laura to shield her from the media scrum. Piers Corbyn has said of Alvarez: 'She is committed to the cause and is active,'[242] – qualities more important to the Corbyns than to most men, perhaps.

Alvarez made Corbyn happy and, while he was careful to keep her below the radar, he enjoyed taking her along to political events with trusted audiences, and on parliamentary trips. Margaret Hodge met Alvarez at the event she spoke at in Islington North at the start of 2015. She says: 'He introduced me to her and he obviously seemed quite proud of her. I thought that was quite nice, actually. I felt: "Oh my god, he's proud and in love."' After her marriage, Alvarez enrolled on a part-time course in human rights at Birkbeck College, part of the University of London. The couple enjoyed holidays back in Mexico and elsewhere in Latin America.

For a time, after her mother returned to live in Mexico, and before Alvarez had moved to the UK, her then sixteen-year-old niece, Jasmin, lived with Corbyn. They enjoyed a harmonious existence: he turned a study into a bedroom for her, and they took turns to cook dinner. When Alvarez eventually moved into the house two years later, a toxic atmosphere developed, with aunt and niece frequently clashing over matters such as the household chores. Corbyn, Jasmin has said, remained 'neutral'. Despite his pleas for her to stay, she stormed out of the house and found a place in a homeless shelter for young people. Today she describes Corbyn as a 'father figure', telling *The Sun*: 'He was the only man in my life who would listen and be there for me.'

Not long after returning to the UK, Alvarez also set up a small company importing organic, fair-trade coffee from her native Mexico. When, during the leadership contest, the *Mail on Sunday* published an exposé on the firm, claiming that the coffee growers were paid less than the minimum wage,[243] Alvarez was devastated at the thought that she had harmed her husband's campaign, while Corbyn was incandescent at what he saw as the intrusion of the press. A source in the Corbyn campaign team says:

> Laura's company is a very small-scale thing, it never made any profit at all, and this idea that she was exploiting anyone is just ridiculous. She was very upset when the story was published, because she hated the idea that she had done something that would hurt Jeremy. Jeremy was just furious. I think it was his worst time in the whole leadership campaign. He hated that Laura was dragged into it.

After moving to Islington, Laura became a familiar face in the constituency, joining Corbyn on the campaign trail and taking part in CLP events and family get-togethers. Those who know the couple say she has brought great joy to his later years, a calm, supportive presence in a life which for so long had been devoted to causes and people other than himself.

This, then, was Jeremy Corbyn as he prepared to stand for re-election to Parliament on 7 May 2015. Happy in his personal life, secure in his friendships, confident in his role in life politically, and looking forward to many more years as a leading campaigner and activist on the left. If you had told him that in just over four months' time he would be elected Leader of the Labour Party by a landslide on a wave of popularity and excitement not seen in British politics since the early days of New Labour, he would have laughed in your face.

CHAPTER THIRTEEN

FALKIRK

I T WAS TEN o'clock at night and Eric Joyce, Member of Parliament for the Scottish steel-making town of Falkirk, was drunk and getting drunker. As usual at that time of the evening, Strangers' Bar, the claustrophobic pub located at the heart of the Palace of Westminster, was packed. Although the Commons had long wound up its business for the day, MPs have for centuries whiled away the hours away from their families during the week by gathering together to chew over the day's political gossip over a drink. The atmosphere in the Chamber had been tetchy that day, 22 February 2012, with irritable clashes between David Cameron and Ed Miliband at Prime Minister's Questions over the coalition government's proposed NHS reforms, followed by an ill-tempered debate on the scheme. Although the evening had begun in convivial fashion, the mood in Strangers' too soon began to sour.

While Joyce and his friends downed pints in the Labour corner of the bar, a gaggle of Conservative MPs regaled their guest, Andrew Scheer, the Speaker of the Canadian House of Commons, with tall stories. Something was said that Joyce took umbrage at. Lurching over, he declared that the bar was too 'full of fucking Tories' before head-butting Stuart Andrew, the Conservative MP for Pudsey, seemingly at random.[244] During the mêlée that followed, Joyce hit out at several other Tory MPs and their guests. The police were called and the flailing Joyce was handcuffed and thrown into a cell in a nearby police station for the night. He later pleaded guilty to assaulting four people and, after being suspended by the Labour Party, announced he would stand down at the general election in May 2015. Unwittingly that night, the intoxicated Joyce had set off a chain of events that would lead directly to Jeremy Corbyn's election in the Labour leadership contest more than three years later. As the academic Philip Cowley would say after Corbyn's rise: 'You can trace all of this back to Eric Joyce lamping people in Strangers'…'

The roots of Corbyn's victory in September 2015 lie, counterintuitively, in an attempt by his predecessor to stamp his authority on the Labour Party and prove he was no trade union poodle, a process that began with Joyce and Falkirk.

Ed Miliband was elected leader in September 2010 following Labour's defeat at that year's general election and the formation of the Conservative–Liberal Democrat coalition. It was a bruising battle in which Miliband only narrowly beat his older brother, David, the race favourite and candidate of the right. The contest was played out under the electoral college system which had been in place since 1980, with the votes of three groups of electors, one made up of Members of Parliament and Members of the European Parliament, another of ordinary party members, and a third of members of affiliated organisations, including trade unions, given equal weighting. The vote of one MP was therefore equivalent to those of thousands of ordinary members and tens of thousands of affiliated members.

In Ed Miliband's case, while his brother David had come top with both the MPs and party members, an overwhelming victory in the trade union section of the electoral college had swung the entire contest for him. So keen on the younger Miliband brother were some unions that they sent out his campaign literature with members' ballot papers. When first elected, Ed Miliband had no thought of changing the electoral system – why would he, given that he owed his position to it? But throughout his first few years in office he could not escape the accusations both that he had robbed his older brother of his rightful role, and that his victory lacked legitimacy because he had failed to win over the wider party. Changing the rules was his attempt to change that narrative.

The trigger for this transformation was a vote-rigging scandal in Falkirk, in which members of the trade union Unite were accused of trying to fix the selection contest to pick Labour's candidate for the 2015 general election following the departure of Eric Joyce, who had represented the Stirlingshire town, in the Central Lowlands of Scotland, since a 2000 by-election. Joyce would remain in the Commons until 2015, but the process to replace him began within a few months of his expulsion from the PLP in 2012. Then, in March 2013, the contest was suspended amid bitter recriminations and allegations of voter fraud. The claims centred on the suggestion that members of the Unite union had attempted to rig the Falkirk CLP ballot in favour of their preferred candidate, Karie Murphy, a friend of Unite general secretary Len McCluskey. She was also a former office manager for Tom Watson, now the party's deputy leader, who at the time was in charge of the 2015 election campaign, and who went on to stand down from the role as a result of the Falkirk scandal.

Soon after Joyce's resignation, Stephen Deans, chair of Unite in Scotland, also became chair of the Falkirk CLP. Membership, which had stood at around a hundred under Joyce, more than doubled. Many of the new arrivals were workers at the local steel plant and members of the Unite union. Following Karie Murphy's selection, lurid claims circulated of forged membership forms, intimidation and harassment. The contest was suspended and the CLP was reported to the police. Although no criminal proceedings were ever brought, an internal report produced for Labour's ruling NEC later concluded that members were recruited without their knowledge in an attempt to 'manipulate the process'. Murphy was barred from standing (although later cleared of wrongdoing and allowed to return to the Labour fold) and a new candidate, Karen White, was selected. (White would go on to lose the seat by a substantial margin to the Scottish National Party.)

While the toxic situation in Falkirk attracted headlines at the time, it seemed unlikely there would be long-term repercussions from the row. In Westminster, however, the scandal seemed to some to present opportunities. Ed Miliband's inner circle, wary since his election of appearing in thrall both to the left and to the trade unions, had watched events play out in Falkirk with alarm. It seemed like a return to the bad old days of the 1980s, when left-wingers and trade unionists attempted to capture local parties. Having tasked Bob Roberts, his media adviser, and Anna Yearley, his political secretary, with sorting the Falkirk mess out, Miliband and his team wondered if there was more they could do. One senior Miliband adviser says now:

> We fought a relatively bruising battle over Falkirk and got the result we wanted in the end. [But] Falkirk was such an internal thing, there was definitely a view in the office that we ought to use the moment where we sorted Falkirk out ... to make a bigger symbol, a bigger moment, [of] Ed Miliband's changing party. People saw this victory over machine politics as an opportunity to make a wider change in the Labour Party. It wasn't something that was really on our agenda [until then] but there was definitely a feeling that you should use the moment to do something bigger ... and to have a bit of 'Ed reforms the party'.

In stamping his authority on the electoral system, Miliband hoped to prove to his critics on the right that the trade unions did not exert an unhealthy influence over his Labour Party. Corbyn's friend Tariq Ali says: 'That's the irony of it: the left, trying to appease the Blairites, changes the party. That's so funny.'

Miliband's team gathered in the garden of his house in Dartmouth Park, north London, over a weekend in the spring of 2013 to discuss the matter. The outcome of those talks would prove instrumental in creating a new system for electing the Labour Party leader that would hugely favour a candidate of the left in 2015. Was this deliberate? Most Labour people who have considered the matter believe not, although is telling that among those present in Dartmouth Park were two members of Miliband's team, Jon Trickett and Simon Fletcher, who would go on to join Corbyn's campaign, Fletcher in particular taking advantage of the new system to shepherd their candidate to victory. One senior Labour source says:

> [Miliband] created rules which allowed it to happen. It was: 'I can't be seen once again to be being pushed around by Unite. Let's find a way that [shows that] I am the strong man, but I don't utterly piss them off [the unions]. So let's get together in the back of [my] garden, with people who don't understand the Labour Party – and Simon, who does understand the Labour Party.'

Trickett, who was something of a mentor to Miliband, says that while party reform had not been top of the then leader's agenda beforehand, the idea of having an electorate based on 'one member, one vote' immediately appealed to him:

> The idea that as an MP I should have one vote and it's the equivalent of 3,000 members, I always thought it was preposterous. We live in

a twenty-first century, for God's sake, and this whole idea of a political elite steering the country through the good times and the bad, it was never a good idea. If you're going to end the age of deference and introduce a proper era of democracy, it seems to me the MPs ought not to have a special section where their votes count for more than anyone else.

At the conclusion of the garden gathering, it was agreed that Lord (Ray) Collins, the former trade unionist and general secretary of the Labour Party, would be charged with undertaking a six-month review of the leadership rules, with the intention that the new system be based on one member, one vote. Jenny Smith and Declan McHugh from the Labour Party Constitution Unit were co-opted to help him. It was explicit, however, that Miliband and his team would be closely involved with framing the final outcome. McHugh has since said of the review:

> The change was sold by Labour spinners as a modernising moment on a par with Tony Blair's revision of Clause IV. The reform was undeniably significant. But it was not the culmination of a carefully crafted modernising plan. Rather it was the product of political panic, damage limitation and – ultimately – a deal with the unions.[245]

What seems bizarre is that few of Miliband's top team, including the leader himself, appear to have ever realised that they were drawing up a system that would be used to select the person who would replace him in just two years' time. Despite polls which should have given little confidence that Labour would be able to form a majority at the 2015 general election, and the very real possibility that Miliband might either be forced out or choose to stand down as leader, no one seems to have considered that the new system would be tested on the Labour movement, in a contest to decide the most important role within it, as soon as the summer of 2015. Instead, they broadly assumed it would be given a trial run in the competition to select a candidate to become Labour's representative in the 2016 London mayoral election. The oversight would have lasting repercussions.

In his introduction to the Collins Review, which was completed in February 2014, the peer set out his mission, as commissioned by Miliband, thus: 'Ed's central objective is to transform Labour so that it becomes a genuinely mass-membership party reaching out to all parts of the nation.'

The review proposed a simple one member, one vote system, with candidates pre-screened through a nomination process by MPs. Trade unions would have to formally affiliate members who wanted to participate: a significant change from the old system. Jon Trickett says:

> There had ... always been a debate about the legitimacy of the trade union link. Personally, I always wanted [Labour] to be a mass party of working people. And I thought that you could have both the collective affiliation, which we've retained in the new structure, and the possibility of trade unionists individually becoming members of the party.

By removing the direct link between trade union membership and participation in Labour leadership contests, Miliband must also have hoped to shed some of the sense that clung to him of being in hock to the unions.

In introducing one member, one vote, the team around Ed Miliband would at a stroke also remove much of the power of MPs to select the man or woman who would stand in front of them at the dispatch box of the House of Commons and represent them in the media and country at large. It was a profound change, the scale and implications of which few appreciated at the time. A senior Labour source says: 'Ray Collins never devised the system. The people who actually devised the system were very clear that there [had been] a massive parliamentary lock-in. The big prize for them was getting rid of the [disproportionate influence of the] PLP.' Jon Trickett adds:

> There was a big debate about whether the MPs should cease to have a special role. I was clear from the start it was wrong. Under the new rules, that role went. There are two or three hundred MPs, but there are over half a million other members of the Labour Party. That's how I see it – one member, one vote. It's far more egalitarian, it's far more horizontal in its structure.

The Collins Review departed from a pure system of one member, one vote, proposing that non-members be allowed to participate in leadership elections by signing up as 'registered supporters'. His recommendation said:

> Individuals who are not already party members or members of an affiliated organisation may take part in leadership elections by registering with the party as a supporter. This will require them to declare their support for Labour values, provide the party with personal contact details, be on the electoral roll and pay the party a fee.

He did not stipulate what the fee should be, although insiders say it was always envisaged it would be a nominal one. Allowing non-members to participate in leadership elections was seen by those drawing up the new rules as creating a form of open primaries, the system used by the two main American political parties in some states for selecting presidential candidates, and adopted by the Conservatives in this country in a handful of constituencies. The Socialist Party in France has also experimented with open primaries, allowing supporters to take part in the selection of its presidential candidate after paying a €1 (73p) fee.

Ironically, Corbyn and his fellow travellers in the Campaign Group were among those who initially opposed giving 'registered supporters' the right to vote, believing it was unfair to full members. One of those involved in drawing up the new system brushes off suggestions that allowing registered supporters similar rights to those of full members, who currently pay an annual levy of nearly £50, is unfair. 'That is an argument for shrinking your party year after year after year. The job of a political party is to go out and reach new people,' he says. 'There has to be an offer and an enticement to get those people involved, and selecting a leader is a very good one.'

The system was also open to allegations of 'entryism', with suggestions that saboteurs on the right or left would seek to hijack a contest. Rows over this would dominate much of the 2015 leadership race, with claims that Conservative supporters and even Tory MPs were seeking to join in order to vote for Corbyn to thwart a more mainstream and theoretically more threatening opponent. Later, following complaints from Corbyn's rivals, the party launched a 'purge' to weed out supporters of far-left groups. Whatever the truth about entryism, the decision to allow non-members to take part in leadership elections by paying what was eventually set as a £3 fee would inspire a wider public interest in the 2015 leadership contest, ultimately helping to secure Corbyn's victory. Jon Trickett says: 'That was arguably a key moment; changing the electorate and the way that the electorate was decided was a key staging post.' David Lammy adds: 'Once Ed Miliband came up with this £3 primary, there was this movement which could be co-opted in very quickly. The means to organise were certainly there, the tools were there, and Jeremy was always going to be a fantastic figurehead because he'd put in the hours.'

A number of those within the party who deplore Corbyn's election now believe it was a major error not to have a 'freeze' period for recruiting new members and supporters, one which they say should have been set early on in the contest, before the close of nominations, meaning the electorate was not tied to a particular candidate. Doing so would have given the party sufficient time to vet new recruits and, perhaps more importantly for Corbyn's rivals, would have prevented what went on to happen: the phenomenon of a candidate capturing the public's imagination and signing up new members with the specific intention of voting for him. The Corbynistas are not Labour people, his rivals complain, but Corbyn people. John Lehal, who was Andy Burnham's campaign manager, says:

> It was Jeremy Corbyn's chief of staff [Simon Fletcher] who set up this whole process. The Labour Party was woefully unprepared for the whole thing. Let's be honest, you can't have a deadline then two days later be issuing ballot papers. It should be set up before candidates are known. Likewise, you shouldn't then be issuing ballot papers to people before you've done verification. There are all sorts of things the Labour Party didn't manage very well. And it does leave you wondering, if the Labour Party can't organise its own election, should it be entrusted with the economy and our public services?

Tom Baldwin, a former member of Miliband's team, has little sympathy for this view, however. He has said:

> People in the mainstream of the party who are seeking to blame these party reforms of Ed Miliband need to actually look in the mirror if they want to know who to blame. These reforms are open to everybody to go out and sign people up to the Labour Party. They need

> to ask themselves why they spent many of the last months whining about the process rather than recruiting people with the same effectiveness Jeremy Corbyn has.[246]

But was it inevitable that opening the contest to non-members would favour a candidate of the left? Not necessarily. The Collins Review also recommended that MPs retain the power to effectively screen prospective candidates, by requiring that those seeking to stand secure a certain number of nominations from MPs. Before the rule changes, the bar had stood at 12.5 per cent of the parliamentary party, meaning in the 2010 contest, when there were 257 Labour MPs, contenders needed to pick up the backing of thirty-three of their colleagues. Corbyn's friend John McDonnell had failed to meet the target when he stood for the leadership in both 2007 and 2010. The requirement was designed to weed out rogue candidates who could not command the support of the PLP.

With the scrapping of the electoral college and elimination of the MPs' privileged role, the nomination process now became far more important than before. In recognition of the new significance the nominating process would have under the one member, one vote system, Miliband's team proposed raising the bar, to as high as 20 or 25 per cent of the party, a demand that would have severely limited the number of candidates who would have been able to meet the requirement.

Increasing the threshold was opposed by the left, who were unhappy that John McDonnell had twice failed to be nominated and that Diane Abbott had achieved it in 2010 only after being 'lent' votes from more established candidates. Ironically, however, it was in fact the Labour right that saw off the plan to make the nomination process a far more substantial hurdle to entering the leadership contest. During the Collins Review negotiations, a number of figures on the right of the party, including Jim Murphy, who would go on to become Labour leader in Scotland before losing his seat in the 2015 election, negotiated the bar back down to 15 per cent, fearing that a candidate of the right would also struggle to get on to the ballot if it was set any higher. One former senior aide to a shadow Cabinet minister says:

> It wasn't Trickett and that lot who won that argument, it was Jim Murphy and the Blairites. They wanted a Blairite candidate to manage it. That's the fucking stupidity of it. It was the right that were vehement. They actually wanted it at 12.5, then the new proposals came in at 20 to 25 per cent, and they got it down to 15.

By the summer of 2015, with Labour reduced to 232 seats, the 15 per cent bar meant any candidate seeking to get on to the ballot would have to secure thirty-five nominations. Jon Trickett says:

> There was a role for the PLP, which was the nomination process. The idea was, you would have a bar, nobody could stand if they were an eccentric with three mates; Billy-no-mates. You had to get a number, 15 per cent, it turned out it was thirty-five people, so there was a bar you had to get across. That was the role of the PLP, to filter out.

Declan McHugh has said: '15 per cent was judged to be a safe barrier to any outsider – especially someone from the hard left. That judgement proved to be mistaken.'[247]

Whatever level the nomination bar was set at, the plan would work only if MPs understood and accepted their new, somewhat different, role under the system created by the Collins Review. John Woodcock, the MP for Barrow-in-Furness, who helped run Liz Kendall's campaign and is on the right of the party, says that those who blame the Blairites for blocking attempts to raise the bar higher than 15 per cent fail to recognise that it was the MPs themselves who abdicated their responsibilities under the new leadership rules. He claims that Ed Miliband is among those who have attacked his wing of the party, adding:

> What a surprise, who would have thought it from Ed M, he says it's all the Blairites' fault for lowering the threshold. But if that was the case, that wasn't the conversation I was ever a part of. What actually happened was that the original threshold was lower, and it was raised. So we actually increased the sense of responsibility for our role – and then significant numbers completely disregarded that. The system was specifically designed so that people who have worked most closely with their parliamentary colleagues, who have had the best chance to see their strengths and weaknesses as a future leader, were able to have that judgement in the first instance. People chose to ignore that responsibility and give themselves a completely different responsibility, which was to widen the debate, or give the members what they thought the members wanted.

Amid the general post-mortem now taking place among those unhappy at Corbyn's victory, a number of senior figures have expressed the view that MPs failed to understand their enhanced role. One senior Labour strategist says: 'The whole system was designed to stop a figure like Corbyn, who commands no support in the PLP, from getting on the ballot, and the MPs let the party down.' One of those who helped draw up the system adds.

> The system was designed to give the PLP the keys to the gate. That doesn't favour a left-wing candidate, it favours credible candidates which have the support of the PLP. The truth is the PLP decided to open

the gates completely wide. It wasn't the people who designed the system that caused the problem, it was the people that didn't understand the system that caused the problem. They're Members of Parliament, they're meant to be in leadership positions. If they want to do something which is a lousy option, [and] put someone who isn't credible or has the support of the PLP on to the ballot, that is not the fault of the system, that's the fault of the people who did it.

On 1 March 2014, a special conference was held at London's ExCel Centre to debate and vote on the Collins Review. At the time, it was thought that reducing the influence of the trade unions would prove the most controversial aspect of the plan. In the event, however, the recommendations were adopted by an overwhelming majority of the delegates, made up of CLPs, trade unions, affiliated societies and elected representatives, with the backing of 86 per cent of the vote. The country's three most powerful trade union leaders – Dave Prentis of Unison, with 1.3 million members, Len McCluskey, head of the country's biggest union, Unite, with 1.4 million members and Paul Kenny of the GMB, with 630,000 members – gave speeches warning that they would not accept any further watering-down of the link between the unions and the party, but ultimately backed the Collins plan. Only the tiny Bakers, Food and Allied Workers Union, with just over 20,000 members, and Young Labour, voted against the review. Even Ed Miliband's team was surprised by the scale of the victory. One of his advisers says:

In a way we were trying to make them [the reforms] more controversial. We wanted a bit of a fight. Losing the unions' electoral college, we expected a bit more of a bust-up over that, [but] there was an irrefutable logic that the old system wasn't as democratic as it could have been. We essentially won the argument [and] we won on a fairly easy basis.

In the wake of Corbyn's subsequent victory, the Collins Review and the new system that was born from it have come under heavy criticism from those who feel it favoured a candidate of the left. Anna Turley, the newly elected MP for Redcar, is one of those who now believe Collins was a mistake. 'I feel totally naive when I think back to voting for this system,' she has said. Adrian McMenamin, a former Labour chief press officer, has said: 'The system is broken, but that's because MPs were fools and cowards over nominations.' Anna Yearley, however, has since defended the system she helped created. She said: 'I will stand by the electoral system for electing the leader. It's about opening up politics.'

Although Jon Trickett does not believe the new system necessarily favours the left, he does admit he was optimistic at the time that the ideas he believed in could now get a proper airing. Unlike most, he was also confident that the wider membership would prove open to the ideas he, Corbyn and others on the left had been interested in for decades. He says:

> I thought that if there was a proper debate with all tendencies within the party out there, the ideas which I've had all my political life would for the first time see the light of day. I joined the Labour Party in 1969. I think I know the Labour Party as well as anybody. I was absolutely certain that if you got the right person with the right set of ideas, it would resonate with tens of thousands of people – and so it did.

And who were those tens of thousands of people who would go on to form the new electorate? There is a virtually unanimous belief among those in Labour who opposed Corbyn's election that the drift to the left among party members began under Ed Miliband. DJ Collins, a former senior Labour staffer, says: 'The electoral system helped it happen ... and Ed [Miliband] allowed it to happen.' The younger Miliband certainly positioned himself to the left of New Labour in order to win the leadership in 2010, introducing policies, such as the proposed mansion tax on properties worth more than £2 million, which were anathema to the Blairites. In doing so, he attracted new members who, while they might not define themselves as 'hard' left, were certainly somewhat 'soft'. Through the inevitable disappointments of thirteen years in government, particularly in the wake of Iraq, many of these soft left-wingers had drifted away from the Labour Party. After 2010, they began to return. In an insightful essay, Atul Hatwal, the editor of the Labour Uncut website, has written:

> CLP chairs and secretaries are uniformly clear that most new members and supporters [who joined during the 2015 contest] have been involved with the party before. The defining characteristic of the majority in this group is that they are from the soft left. Not the hard left from where Corbyn hails, nor Trotskyite entryists or Stalinist tankies [Communists] from fringe groups outside the party … One of the [2015 leadership] candidates told me that based on their experience of umpteen CLP visits and hustings, the people who've joined 'are the people at the back of the GC (General Committee) who just want it all to be better and feel more right on'.[248]

One Labour source adds:

> The Labour Party had spent thirty years if not getting rid of these people then certainly not being attractive to these people, and suddenly they're given a reason to come back, en masse. [Miliband] opened up a crack in the door for a move to the centre of gravity to the left, then it just went.

Under Miliband's rule, another important change to the party was quietly allowed to take place: the selection of parliamentary candidates who were significantly to the left of their predecessors. Some Labour insiders suggest that Miliband failed to keep a grip on the leader's power of patronage. Where both Tony Blair and Gordon Brown had taken a keen interest in the selection of parliamentary candidates, Miliband abdicated responsibility to Anna Yearley, who was later criticised for failing to find constituencies for senior allies. 'Even in his dying days, Gordon [Brown] was always able to swing selections for whoever he wanted to get into Parliament,' one former member of Miliband's team says. 'Ed couldn't do that. He didn't have the clout and the people around him couldn't deliver. There were some very good people who he promised seats to, who didn't get them.' One adviser to a former member of the shadow Cabinet says: 'He [Miliband] allowed – or failed to prevent – the selection of loads of daft, left-wing candidates … which also helped Corbyn.' A source close to Miliband rejects the accusation, however, saying the left-wing candidates emerged in 'tough selection contests' in CLPs which had already begun to drift to the left. 'It's easy to say someone should have had more control but I don't actually know what more control you could have,' the source says. 'It's an argument for having an excuse for what happened rather than having a proper analysis about why Jeremy Corbyn won.'

In the vacuum left by the Miliband leadership, the trade unions stepped into the selection process in a number of seats, organising on behalf of local left-wingers and ultimately ensuring that the 2015 intake was more left-wing than any since the early 1980s, when Tony Benn was in ascendence and Corbyn himself came to the Commons. A new MP who is not on the left of the party says: 'The process just got away from Ed and all these weird and wonderful people got elected.'

The tectonic plates of Labour politics, to use John Prescott's famous phrase, were shifting in Corbyn's direction.

CHAPTER FOURTEEN

THE CONTEST
BEGINS

THE SUN WAS about to rise on the morning of 8 May 2015 as Ed Miliband stood on stage at his constituency in Doncaster, a broken man, and waited for the result of his election count. Only a few hours earlier, he had held out the hope he would be walking into Downing Street that day. At the very least, he assumed he would be on his way to Westminster for intense talks to form a coalition government. Instead, he had led Labour to its second election defeat in a row, and it would be Conservative leader David Cameron, not him, who would be sleeping in No. 10 that night. When the results of his own seat of Doncaster North came in just before 5.30 a.m., it was of little comfort to learn that he had increased his majority by more than 5 per cent. 'This has clearly been a disappointing and difficult night for the Labour Party,' Miliband told supporters gathered at the count at Doncaster's Metropolitan Council Offices. Nearly 200 miles away, at the Sobell Leisure Centre in Islington, Jeremy Corbyn's result had been declared a few hours earlier; he too had been safely returned, and with an increased majority. After thanking voters 'from the bottom of my heart',

Corbyn addressed himself to the Conservatives' shock victory: 'It's bad news for the poor of Britain, bad news for the health service and bad news for the young.' What each man would now do over the coming hours, days and weeks would shape the future of the Labour Party for ever.

The loss of the 2015 general election was as much of a shock for the Labour Party as 1992 had been under Neil Kinnock. Miliband's confidence was not a blind faith – no one had seen a majority Conservative government coming: not the media, not the politicians, and above all not the opinion pollsters, whose pronouncements everyone else had based their belief on. Although less rosy for Labour than they had been in Miliband's early years, by the start of the campaign proper in March 2015, most polls put the two main parties neck and neck, with virtually all the major pollsters and analysts predicting a hung parliament. Populus, Lord Ashcroft and YouGov predicted a dead heat for Labour and the Conservatives, each on either 34 or 33 per cent of the vote, while Ipsos Mori and ComRes gave the Tories a lead of just 1 per cent, not enough to form a majority government.

As Miliband woke on the morning of Thursday 7 May, he was cheered by a report in *The Guardian* of an ICM poll suggesting a late swing to Labour, with the party enjoying a 1 per cent predicted lead over the Conservatives. Miliband and his wife Justine voted early, leaving their constituency house in Doncaster North just before 8 a.m. to make the short walk to their polling station at Sutton Village Hall, where they cast their ballots. So many well-wishers turned out to give their support that the police had to close the road outside. Miliband spent the rest of the day at home, resting and talking to his aides. They discussed potential Cabinet appointments, and tactics for what they assumed would be a lengthy series of coalition negotiations.

At 9.59 p.m., Miliband and his team gathered around the television set to await the results of the exit poll. Jointly produced by the BBC, ITN and Sky, the survey of 20,000 voters taken as they left polling booths was far more comprehensive than ordinary opinion polls, which are usually conducted by phone or email with around 2,000 people who may not actually go on to vote. Those gathered in Miliband's front room knew the exit poll was likely to give a broadly accurate guide to the election's outcome. With Miliband in his living room that night were his wife and two closest aides, Stewart Wood and Greg Beales. The shock of what followed cannot be underestimated. It was one of those rare moments of political drama when everything changes in a second. As Big Ben struck ten, the BBC's veteran election night host David Dimbleby began: 'Here it is, ten o'clock, and we are saying …' To the horror of those watching with Miliband, an image of a smiling David Cameron next to a Tory blue rosette now filled the screen. Dimbleby continued: 'The Conservatives are the largest party. And here are the figures – which are quite remarkable, this exit poll – the Conservatives on 316, that's up 9 since the last election in 2010, Ed Miliband for Labour, 77 behind him on 239, down 19.' Far from being on course for Downing Street at the head of a new coalition government, the poll suggested that Miliband had failed; Labour had lost. Could it be true? Had Cameron really confounded the pollsters and, after five years in coalition with the Liberal Democrats, would he now be able to form a Conservative government?

'What the fuck?' one member of Miliband's team said as the full horror of the exit poll dawned on them. Ed Miliband himself simply walked out of the room, went to his study and got back to the speech he had been working on in the minutes before the exit poll came out. To begin with, he couldn't face scrapping the version he had hoped to deliver, which referred to Labour winning the most seats and having a mandate to seek to put together a government. As the night progressed, however, the speech changed several times. By the end of the night, it was one of complete concession. Some in the room were amazed at how calm Miliband was; others felt it was in character. 'What else could he do?' one aide said.

At the outset, Miliband's team did not want to believe the poll was correct, but it soon became clear that the Tories had in fact performed even better than predicted. While many of the Conservatives' gains came at the expense of the Liberal Democrats, Labour's virtual wipeout in Scotland, where the Scottish Nationalists won fifty-six out of fifty-nine seats, meant the party's losses were heavy. Ed Balls, the shadow Chancellor, was among the night's victims.

In the grim early hours, as the scale of the disaster became apparent and the time approached for Miliband to head to his count, the team in Doncaster began to discuss what he should do next. His instinct was to stand down immediately and take all the blame for the catastrophic defeat. His wife, who had not enjoyed the forensic focus of a general election campaign, agreed it was time to go. She is reported to have said she could not bear to have to watch him submit to the humiliation of facing David Cameron across the dispatch box at Prime Minister's Questions following the election drubbing.[249] Greg Beales also felt that resigning immediately was the 'dignified' course of action for the defeated Miliband.[250] Arguing against Justine and Beales were key Miliband strategists Tom Baldwin and Spencer Livermore, and Lord Falconer, the former Justice Secretary and close friend of Tony Blair, who as a constitutional expert had been invited there to discuss the legal niceties of any coalition negotiations.

Those arguing that Miliband should stay on thought he should remain as leader at least until Christmas, to give the party time to digest what had happened. It was a view that Jon Trickett, at his own count in Hemsworth, a short drive away up the M18, shared. Through the night and into the morning, he made a series of phone calls trying to persuade Miliband not to quit. 'I looked at the TV exit poll and then we spoke, we spoke several times during the evening,' Trickett says. 'I was a close political colleague, I spoke to him often. I didn't want him to go straight away because I wanted a debate about the future of the party to take place first.'

It was too late; as Miliband left his count in Doncaster and got into his car to make the long journey back to London, he had all but made up his mind to resign. A member of his team phoned to warn Trickett, who was still waiting for his own result in Hemsworth, and who now tried one last time to persuade Miliband to stay on. Trickett says:

> I was phoned from his car to say he was going to resign. I spoke to him and told him that he could stay as leader at least for a time and then I headed straight to London from my count. I met him here [in London], but it was clear he wouldn't stay on. As it happened, he went very quickly.

On his arrival in London, the visibly distraught Miliband briefly addressed party staff at Labour HQ before convening an emotional press conference in front of an audience of supporters. 'I am tendering my resignation taking effect after this afternoon's commemoration of VE Day,' he said. 'I want to do so straight away because the party needs an open debate about the right way forward without constraint.'

Miliband's hasty decision to quit immediately rather than staying on for a few months would have a significant bearing on the course of the leadership contest. It meant little consideration was given to alternative options, such as the prospect of him acting as a caretaker leader while an internal debate was held over the party's future. Although most defeated party leaders have in recent years resigned in the days following a general election loss, it was by no means the only course of action. James Callaghan had remained in office for eighteen months after the 1979 election in his unsuccessful attempt to deliver the leadership for Denis Healey. In 2005, Michael Howard had generously volunteered to remain in office despite a bruising third Conservative defeat while a lengthy contest was held to replace him.

He appointed a new shadow Cabinet, including two MPs elected only in 2001, David Cameron and George Osborne, and candidates were encouraged to set out their wares by using their roles to oppose the Blair government. The contest did not begin in earnest until six months after the general election, and Cameron's victory over David Davis, the experienced shadow Home Secretary who had been favourite at the outset, was not secured until December.

Howard is now credited as paving the way for Cameron's success, both by promoting him to the role of shadow Education Secretary and by ensuring a long enough race that both MPs and Tory members became familiar with his talents. The latter also gave Davis time to flounder, which he did with poorly delivered addresses at both his campaign launch and the party's annual conference on the eve of the contest in October. By quitting the morning after the election defeat, Miliband forestalled the prospect of such a process taking place within the Labour Party. Corbyn himself is, ironically, among those who has said he wishes his predecessor had remained in his post for longer.

Even as the shattered Ed Miliband was making his emotional resignation speech, one senior member of his campaign team was stunned to receive a text message from a would-be leadership candidate asking for his support in the race that would now follow. With the ruthlessness of all politicians, the eager beaver was not the only MP now addressing themselves to that question. Another potential candidate, Liz Kendall, the Blairite MP for Leicester East, began calling round friends to discuss a run. Andy Burnham, the former Cabinet minister who had stood unsuccessfully for the leadership in 2010, also made preparations to announce his candidacy. Shadow Home Secretary Yvette Cooper, at home in Yorkshire, spent the days following the election consoling her husband, Ed Balls, over the loss of his seat and did not get around to seriously considering her own prospects until the following week. The couple had already given much thought to the matter, however, having agreed as long ago as 2010, when Balls ran unsuccessfully against the Milibands and Burnham, that the next leadership contest would be Cooper's fight.

Despite his desire for Miliband to stay on, Jon Trickett is open about the fact that he too had begun to consider the leadership issue well before election night. 'If we were to lose, the question then was what would happen,' he says. 'I was thinking, well, if we don't lose really badly, Ed should stay. If it's a bad defeat then he'll probably go. The thing was then what should we do about a successor?' Trickett spent the hours after Miliband's resignation comforting the departing leader. Together, they listened as a series of Labour MPs took to the airwaves to offer their analysis of the party's defeat, with some suggesting Miliband had been too left-wing. Trickett was appalled by what he heard, his irritation growing over the next few days as the inquest continued.

An appearance on the BBC's *Andrew Marr Show* by the Blairite MP for Streatham, Chuka Umunna, on the Sunday after the election, in which he suggested that 'our business agenda was pro-business but people were under the impression that it wasn't' inspired some on the left to take action, Trickett says.

> [One of] the political milestones, if you like, which has led to the situation we're in [was] partly what happened on the Friday morning and immediately afterwards. Most party activists were pretty well bruised and grieving at the scale of the defeat. While we were doing that, there were senior people who were really out there putting the knife in. It's amazing how many of them at that time of the morning had written-out articles and speeches that looked pre-prepared. Very, very similar language. It was a bad mistake. I think they had a kind of sense

of entitlement; they thought that it was their party, that it would come back to them, and all they had to do was provide their simple-minded narrative. I think the party hated what they did during [those] days.

Trickett vowed to himself that the left would run a candidate to replace Miliband. But who?

Corbyn's friend John McDonnell, who had stood for the leadership in 2007 and 2010, failing to get on to the ballot both times, swiftly told the BBC he would not be running. As he said before the election: 'I've done it enough times and been blocked from getting on. How many times can I be hit by that?'[251] Diane Abbott also seemed unlikely to stand, having come last in the 2010 contest. A few days after the general election, she announced her bid to become Labour's candidate for the London mayoralty, effectively ruling herself out of the leadership race. Corbyn himself was urged to stand as early as the Saturday following the election, when he appeared on LBC, the London radio station, with host Iain Dale. As they discussed who might take part in the contest, 'Sarah from London' called in to say: 'Many people would love Jeremy Corbyn to run.' The idea seemed so far-fetched that the two men laughed. 'She sounds like a wonderful person,' Corbyn demurred. 'I'm not sure the rest of the world would want Jeremy Corbyn to run.'

If he was seriously considering giving the leadership a shot at this stage, he gave no indication of it, although by the time MPs returned to Westminster on Monday 11 May, Corbyn had become convinced that the left should be represented in the contest. 'I think it's essential that there is a left, anti-austerity candidate in the leadership election,' he told the *Morning Star*. 'We're having a discussion about who it's going to be.' Corbyn had also clearly been doing some analysis of the political landscape of his own, and had worked out that, although the Collins Review had on the surface made it harder for a candidate of the left to get on to the ballot, thanks to Miliband's neglect of the CLP selection process, the election of a number of new, left-wing MPs meant it might yet be achieved. 'Looking at the MPs that are there and the new ones that have been elected, it's possible,' he said.[252] But possible for who? At this stage, Corbyn himself had his sights on quite another job, and while he did now begin to ask his colleagues to vote for him, it was not for the Labour leadership. 'When we came back to Parliament, Jeremy said to me would I give him his vote, he was running for the Foreign [Affairs] Select Committee,' David Lammy says.

In the absence of any sign of interest from Corbyn in a run for the leadership, his newspaper, the *Morning Star*, tipped Ian Lavery, the MP for Wansbeck with the impeccable working-class credentials of having been a former president of the National Union of Mineworkers, for the job. Jon Trickett also began to be spoken of as a possible candidate. By now, the race had its first official contestant. Liz Kendall announced her intention to stand on the BBC's *Sunday Politics*, where she opined that Labour had come across like 'the moaning man in the pub'. Chuka Umunna declared his candidacy two days later, 12 May, with a deliberately low-tech video posted on YouTube, designed to counteract claims that he was too smooth to appeal to Labour members.

Burnham entered the fray on 13 May, issuing a video of his own, and was swiftly installed as the favourite with the media, bookies and many in the party. Despite his declaration that 'our challenge is not to go left or right, to focus on one part of the country above another, but to rediscover the beating heart of Labour', the briefing put about by his supporters was that he would be pitching himself as the candidate of the left. Burnham's rivals claim he spent the years running up to the election cosying up to the left and courting the trade unions in preparation for what would be his second shot at the job of leader. It is a charge he denies, although he admits that, like many of his shadow Cabinet colleagues, he felt detached from Miliband's small, tight-knit leadership team. John Lehal, who became Burnham's campaign manager, says:

> Certainly he had done a lot of work in terms of work with the party. He went into the election in a position of strength and he really used that as a platform to get out there, to talk to candidates, to talk to constituency parties, to have a very high media profile. I think anybody speculating at the start of this year that in the event Miliband loses who would go for it, I think Andy's name was definitely up there. So, no surprises on the 13th of May.

So complete was Burnham's journey that few in Westminster thought the left would bother putting up a token candidate as they had done in 2007 and 2010. David Lammy says:

> Andy Burnham had done such a good job of moving politically into the [left of centre] ground, there had been so much chat about the unions supporting Andy. In the run-up to the election, behind the scenes, anyone who was in the Westminster village could see little briefings, little pieces in the *Mirror*, where it was clear that Andy was that candidate. No one ever thought further left than that.

If Burnham's analysis at the start of the race was that a shift to the left would result in victory, he would be proved correct. Unfortunately for him, it was not a plan he would stick to. Burnham would be dogged throughout the contest with allegations of 'flip-flopping'. And even at the outset, while many on the left assumed they would end up voting for Burnham, some were suspicious of his repeated claims that he wanted to get away from the 'Westminster bubble'. A senior Labour figure, who supported Burnham, admits:

> His difficulty obviously was he was ... the embodiment of it, having spent only three years outside of politics, having gone to Cambridge, and having been a special adviser and then an MP for fourteen years, it made it hard for him. He talked about it successfully but ... people said, 'Ooh, no, I'm not sure about the use of that term because ... you are the embodiment of that yourself.'

Jon Trickett adds: 'I thought probably Andy would get the left vote. He [had] this anti-Westminster rhetoric, but at the same time he [was] vulnerable.'

Meanwhile, any hopes that Ian Lavery might be persuaded to be the candidate of the left were dashed when he announced that he was backing Burnham. Some left-wingers, including Owen Jones, the journalist and friend of Corbyn who would go on to help with his campaign, now contemplated getting Lisa Nandy, the MP for Wigan, who had impressed many since entering Parliament in 2010, to stand. A Facebook page was created urging her to run, but having given birth a few weeks earlier, it was too soon for Nandy, and she too would go on to rule herself out of the contest by backing Burnham.

At around the time Burnham was launching his campaign, Labour's ruling NEC was meeting to confirm the rules for the leadership contest. The timescale of the 2010 campaign, which concluded at annual conference in late September, was seen as a disaster, as shadow Cabinet ministers had been forced to deliver conference speeches in posts they would no longer be holding under the new leader, and with all the talk in the bars dominated by the grievances of the losers. There were audible groans at the first meeting of the PLP after the 2015 general election when Harriet Harman, as acting leader, announced that this timeframe was one of the options being considered by the NEC, and relief when it was rejected the following day. Instead, the NEC agreed to proceed on the basis of the Collins Review, and set a timetable that would see the leader crowned on 12 September 2015. As before, the contest would be conducted on the alternative vote (AV) system, also known as the 'instant run-off', with those taking part given the option of selecting second and third preferences.

The NEC set the deadline for nominations from MPs at noon on Monday 15 June. With the number of Labour Members falling to 232 after the election, to reach the 15 per cent threshold agreed in the Collins Review, candidates would have to pick up thirty-five nominations, including their own.

It was also agreed that, for the first time, non-members in the form of registered supporters would be able to vote, after paying the fee, which was now set at £3. Announcing the outcome of the NEC's discussion, Harriet Harman said:

> This contest will be run under the new rules we agreed last year: a broad and open contest with one person, one vote. We want as many people as possible to take part. This is the first time a political party in this country has opened up its leadership contest in this way and I think there will be a real appetite for it out there. [T]his is a new and innovative way of letting the public in on an important decision. And we have changed the rules so that it means one person has one vote regardless whether they are an MP, a shadow Cabinet member, a trade unionist or a registered supporter – everyone's vote is equal, as it should be.

One senior figure close to Harman says that at this stage it was anticipated that between 3,000 and 5,000 registered supporters would sign up. When the membership later began to swell, and amid charges of entryism and fraud, many would be critical of the low financial bar. Simon Danczuk, the outspoken Labour MP for Rochdale, who became a vocal critic of Corbyn, complained: 'Through poor planning, Labour has handed its opponents the chance to undermine the party for the price of a Tesco meal deal.'[253] At the time of the NEC decision, however, there seemed no such concerns. There was no mention either of what would later be a stipulation for registered supporters, that as well as sharing Labour's values they should not be active members or backers of rival parties, including the Greens and the Socialist Workers. Harman also announced some positive news: more than 30,000 people had joined the party since the election loss of less than a week earlier. It was, perhaps, a tiny clue to the mood among a significant minority of the electorate who were clearly appalled at the Tories' return to power.

The leadership field was swelled the day after the NEC's announcement with the entry of Yvette Cooper, who, in an article for the *Daily Mirror*, said: 'We need a Labour Party that moves beyond the old labels of left and right, and focuses four-square on the future.' At this stage, Cooper's team believed that Burnham was the favourite, and that he would win the backing of the major trade unions. No serious consideration was given to a potential threat from the far left. Team strategist Roger Baker says: 'In that first month of May, the landscape that we were thinking about was Andy was going to be stroking the left and moving right, we're going to be in the centre and trying to build out both ways, and Liz will be on the right.' Liz Kendall's team too failed to see the threat from the left, and also believed that Burnham was the man to beat. John Woodcock, who would become one of Kendall's campaign managers, says: 'He was clearly the one to beat at the start, and it was all about how dynamic Andy was. In a contest of mass misjudgements and miscalculations, the original one [was] that nobody saw the Jeremy Corbyn thing coming.'

To the bemusement of some, Mary Creagh, the low-profile Wakefield MP and shadow Environment Secretary, also now announced her candidacy in a newspaper, in her case the right-wing *Daily Mail*, with what the paper described as 'a powerful pro-business appeal to Middle England'. And so, by the end of the first week after Labour's election drubbing, the contest to replace Ed Miliband had begun in earnest, and seemed likely to be a five-horse race. One left-wing MP says his side of the party was unimpressed: 'There was a wave of revulsion in the party [as] the various candidates emerged. They were all like little Sir Echoes of each other, all arguing the party's gone too far to the left, was anti-business, anti-aspiration, didn't win the middle-class vote, all that shit basically.'

Friday 15 May was a day of drama in the Labour leadership contest. Just ninety-six hours after announcing his candidacy, Chuka Umunna withdrew from the race, saying he had not anticipated the 'level of pressure' he would be subjected to, or the impact on his family. It was a feeling that Corbyn, at this stage still uninterested personally in the leadership, would go on to share, finding the glare from the media spotlight as it hovered over his personal life and loved ones almost unbearable. The departure from the stage of the charismatic Umunna was a blow to the Blairites, some of whom were underwhelmed by the remaining candidate of the right, Liz Kendall.

Another potential contender, Tristram Hunt, the shadow Education Secretary, procrastinated for several days before he too decided not to run. A fourth member of the 2010 intake (Kendall, Hunt and Umunna were all elected in the year of the coalition's victory), Dan Jarvis, the former paratrooper and MP for Barnsley Central, was urged to stand but felt he needed to focus on his young family, having recently lost his wife to cancer. Kendall was the immediate beneficiary of Umunna's withdrawal, briefly becoming the media's perceived candidate of change, particularly after some Conservatives put it about that she was the contender they most feared. Andy Burnham's team, however, saw no threat, and remained confident of victory. John Lehal says:

> The whole campaign felt that this was ours to lose. We were clear very early on that Liz would come last. We just felt they backed the wrong candidate, with Chuka pulling out of the race. There could only be one candidate from the Blairite wing of the party and it struck us that the wrong one pulled out.

Amid all the chatter about Umunna, few noticed a letter published on the LabourList website that afternoon. Signed by ten Labour MPs elected for the first time eight days earlier, the letter would have repercussions far beyond any of them could have imagined. It began:

> Having arrived in Westminster as newly elected Labour MPs after speaking to tens of thousands of voters during our election campaigns, we know how important it is for the future of our party to move forward with an agenda that best serves the everyday needs of people, families and communities and that is prepared to challenge the notion of austerity and invest in public services.

In a direct challenge to Liz Kendall and the Blairites, the letter went on:

> As we seek a new Leader of the Labour Party, we are needing one who looks forward and will challenge an agenda of cuts, take on the powerful vested interests of big business and will set out an alternative to austerity – not one who will draw back to the 'New Labour' creed of the past.

The ten signatories included the left-leaning future Corbyn backers Clive Lewis, the new MP for Norwich South; Richard Burgon, from Leeds East; and Cat Smith, who worked for Corbyn before being elected in Lancaster and Fleetwood. It was an explicit declaration by the new intake of a desire for left-wing policies – and a candidate from the left.

One of the few MPs who did notice the LabourList posting, a centrist fellow member of the 2015 intake who would go on to support Andy Burnham, says:

> When I saw that letter I could see what exactly we were dealing with. You would never have had a letter like that from the 2010 intake or the 2005. You usually have one or two people on the left in each intake, but here there are ten of them, and they make a large block vote with a capacity to influence events.

But if few in Westminster paid attention to the letter, away from Parliament it had not gone entirely unnoticed.

CHAPTER FIFTEEN

CANDIDATE CORBYN

I T IS ONE of the ironies of the story of Jeremy Corbyn's rise to power that a key link in the chain of events that ultimately led to him standing for the Labour leadership as the candidate of the left should have come about in two middle-class, solidly Tory, prosperous towns in the Home Counties. Another is the fact that it took the very modern medium of social media to sweep an old-fashioned lefty to office. Yet Corbyn himself credits an online petition dreamed up by a part-time aromatherapist from Worthing in West Sussex and a mother-of-four from Orpington, Kent, for his decision to enter the 2015 Labour leadership contest. The result was a social media campaign that would not have been possible even at the time of the last contest in 2010. And the whole thing was unwittingly helped along by the first of many errors by the race's favourite, Andy Burnham.

Michelle Ryan, who treats elderly people using aromatherapy in care homes near her house in Worthing, describes herself as 'just a very ordinary person who voted Labour'. The 45-year-old had joined the party after the 2010 election in order to vote for Ed Miliband as leader, and although she had grown increasingly interested in politics since then, she confined her activism to the internet, communicating with fellow left-wingers on Facebook and Twitter. Ten days after the 2015 general election, on Sunday 17 May, Ryan read an interview in *The Observer* with Andy Burnham, whom at that stage she had been planning to vote for in the leadership contest. Burnham was asked for his view on Miliband's flagship mansion tax policy, and responded: 'I think we have got to get away from things that look like symbolism. I am going to put the mansion tax in that category ... it spoke to something that the public don't particularly like, which is the politics of envy.' Ryan was unimpressed. She says:

> When the candidates started putting their hats in the ring, initially I was thinking I'd support Andy Burnham. I put him second in the previous leadership election and I'd always quite liked him. It wasn't that I thought, 'Oh, great, I'll go with Andy', it was 'OK, I'll go with Andy'. And then he came out with something that completely switched me off. He was talking about the mansion tax and he described it as the 'politics of envy'. And that was just it for me.

Ryan took to the internet to share her concerns about Burnham's interview with like-minded Labour supporters, and stumbled across the letter by the group of ten new MPs calling for an anti-austerity candidate, which had been posted on LabourList two days earlier. 'It inspired me,' she says. Ryan asked her virtual friends on a Facebook page called Labour Refocused what they thought, and suggested they start a petition calling for a left-leaning, anti-austerity candidate to take Burnham on in the leadership race. One user, Rebecca Barnes, responded saying she would like to help. Barnes had joined Labour as a teenager but let her membership lapse during the Blair era when the first of her four children was born. She was, however, an active trade unionist, having been a railway ticket collector for more than twenty years. Despite re-joining the party at the start of 2015, the forty-year-old had not been an active campaigner at the general election; living in the safe Tory seat of Orpington, she had seen little point. Instead, like Michelle Ryan, she was active online. Before she read Ryan's post on Labour Refocused, Barnes too had been planning to vote for Burnham. 'I was supporting Andy Burnham because he's the best of a bad bunch and he looks quite nice,' she jokes. '[But] I wasn't happy. There was a feeling it was time for real change.' The two women, who to this day have never met or even spoken on the telephone and have only ever communicated via the internet, agreed to draw up the petition that would lead directly to Corbyn's decision to stand.

Written by Rebecca Barnes, the petition began:

> As members, supporters and voters of the Labour Party, we endorse the open letter from the new intake of Labour MPs and offer them our support. We read with encouragement their proposed agenda to best serve the needs of people, families and communities of the UK by challenging the austerity notion and instead promote investment in public services. We too feel this is the best course of action to adopt for the future direction of the Labour Party.

It ended: 'Whilst the leadership contest is under way, we still wait in anticipation for a suitable candidate ready to take on these challenges and bring these much needed anti-austerity ideas to the forefront of the campaign.' The petition was signed in the names of 'Beck Barnes and Chelley Ryan'.

Keen for the petition to get as wide an airing as possible, Barnes and Ryan contacted Red Labour, an organisation founded in 2011 with the aim of promoting socialism within the Labour Party, via its popular Facebook page. Their plea for help was spotted by one of the site's administrators, Naomi Fearon, a 32-year-old teacher from Fleetwood in Lancashire. She too had been disappointed by the way the leadership contest was unfolding. 'When the leadership candidates were announced, we were all feeling a bit flat,' Fearon says.

> We dubbed it 'fifty shades of bland'. Do we vote for the lesser of the evils or do we vote at all? It was all a bit boring, really. I said, what about doing some sort of statement encouraging people that would like to see some different policies or candidate? Anti-austerity had to be on the agenda. We started to draft something then Beck got in contact via the Red Labour page. She said, 'We've done this letter.' Saved me a job.

Fearon decided to give the petition as prominent a display as possible, by posting it to 38 Degrees, a not-for-profit campaigning website which supports 'progressive politics' and has around two million members. It went live on 20 May. At this stage, Ryan, Barnes and Fearon were all unclear who might respond to their plea to run as a candidate of the left. They set their sights on finding a suitable MP to represent their views. 'It wasn't Jeremy,' Fearon says.

> He'd never expressed an interest in the leadership. We all knew Jeremy, he'd been quite a key figure on the left, and his interest was always foreign policy. We talked about possibly Ian Lavery, he's normally seen as quite a left MP, but then he came out and supported Burnham and he ruled himself out, so we thought, 'Oh no.'

Michelle Ryan, meanwhile, wondered if the new MP Clive Lewis might be persuaded to stand, having been impressed by an interview she saw on YouTube in which he unapologetically described himself as a socialist. 'I just wanted somebody who represented our view, and there was nobody, and it was just really horrible to be really unrepresented in the Labour leadership election,' she says. Rebecca Barnes thought John McDonnell might run again, and even wondered if the octogenarian Dennis Skinner could be persuaded.

An experienced user of social media, Naomi Fearon promoted the petition on Twitter and elsewhere, ensuring the message was put out at what she describes as key times of the day, focusing particularly on the journey home from work. The petition took off in a modest way, eventually attracting nearly 5,000 online signatures. It was an early sign of the potential of the internet and social media to build momentum behind a political cause. Activists could now become involved in campaigns, bringing with them significant influence and the power to shape real-time events, without ever leaving their living rooms. Corbyn's team would later successfully harness this amorphous movement, using it to drive their man relentlessly to victory. The consequences of the birth of online people power are still being played out today, with some claiming in the wake of Corbyn's victory and the social media campaigns that continue to support his leadership that the internet has empowered those with loudest voices, who may not necessarily be representative of the wider British public.

As the pressure for a left-wing candidate built, Ryan, Barnes and their online friends began a round-the-clock campaign to promote the petition, directly tweeting MPs urging them to heed the call to enter the race. But was anyone listening? It is now clear that Corbyn was. He was one of the first to retweet one of Ryan's messages, soon followed by John McDonnell. Corbyn later credited Ryan and Barnes with inspiring his decision to run, writing, appropriately enough, on his own Facebook page: 'One of our biggest supporters, Chelley Ryan, who along with Beck Barnes instigated the original petition demanding an anti-austerity candidate in the Labour leadership election[,] essentially sparked this whole thing…' Within a few days he would decide that he should be the candidate those on left were crying out for.

But for a man who would go on to inspire such excitement and devotion, it took a surprisingly long time for Corbyn to officially emerge as the candidate of the left. Even as May turned into June, it was still not yet certain that he – or anyone from his wing of the Labour Party – would run. By the third week of May, the four declared contenders for the leadership – Andy Burnham, Yvette Cooper, Liz Kendall and Mary Creagh – were busy setting out their stalls. While Burnham remained the bookies' favourite, there was a clear sense that the contest was a long one and that both Kendall and Cooper (if not, perhaps, Creagh) were well positioned to change the outcome. Some on the left were growing increasingly depressed by what they were hearing in these early weeks, particularly as the contenders moved to distance themselves from Ed Miliband and the ideas he had offered at the general election (even though all four had served on his front bench).

With the social media campaign for an anti-austerity candidate bubbling away, the small number of left-leaning MPs in Parliament came under ever greater pressure to put themselves forward. Many activists were appalled at the timidity of their representatives, and were determined to force them to act. On 23 May, at a meeting of the executive of the Bennite Campaign for Labour Party Democracy, a decision was taken to demand that reluctant MPs accept their responsibilities. The CLPD's candidate of choice was Jon Trickett, and at this stage, with no expectation of victory, their ambition was a modest one: to push Burnham and Cooper to the left. It was felt that if a left-wing candidate was on the ballot, voicing opposition to the austerity agenda, then the centrist candidates would have to respond by acknowledging their own concerns about the deficit reduction programme. If that voice was not heard, the fear was, they might be tempted to emulate Liz Kendall and the Blairites by tacking right.

In a statement issued by the CLPD after the meeting, the group said:

> There is widespread dismay amongst party activists at the uninspiring nature of the leadership election campaign, with candidates queuing up to apologise for the alleged overspending by the last Labour government, and still failing to challenge publicly the neoliberal narrative on austerity which is the primary reason why Labour was ultimately judged wanting in its handling of the economy. Those on the Blairite wing of the party may well believe that narrative but, like Ed Miliband and Ed Balls, Andy Burnham and Yvette Cooper might not. And yet, with no left candidate putting an anti-austerity case, there is no chance of them showing any more courage than their predecessors ... A left candidate is essential to changing the nature of this election.

Two members of the CLPD executive, Corbyn's old friend Jon Lansman and Peter Willsman, a member of the NEC, were deputed to bring Jon Trickett the good news. 'It was a slight surprise that they came to see me because I'd made it clear I wasn't going to stand,' Trickett says.

> I'd had all these phone calls saying, 'We've got to have a candidate, we're not going to win but we've got to have a candidate to make our case.' [But] I didn't think I could unite the left. I'd been on the front bench for seven years. It needed someone from a completely fresh point of view.

Unfortunately for Trickett, Lansman had already emailed the entire CLPD membership informing them that he was a candidate. He would still be receiving messages of support weeks later.

Having disappointed some with his 'politics of envy' reference to the mansion tax at the start of the contest, Andy Burnham now compounded the error in the eyes of the left when he delivered his first speech of the campaign in the heart of the City of London, to business leaders at the headquarters of Ernst and Young, on 29 May. Jon Trickett was among those who found the tone of the debate, as the centrist candidates repudiated what had gone before, unedifying, feeling it failed to address some of the causes of Labour's defeat such as the rise of the left-wing SNP in Scotland. He says, 'I was surprised that they attacked the manifesto and Ed immediately from the right. It quickly became clear that ... they all assumed that the party would immediately shift to the right. The party didn't like any of that.' One former member of Ed Miliband's campaign team agrees that Burnham blundered by abandoning his plan to appeal to the left in the early stages of the contest. The aide says:

> Burnham's strategy had been to pitch to the left. The election freaked him, so he tacked right. Big mistake. It's also only possible if you don't believe in much in the first place – the New Labour school of realpolitik. Everyone in the Westminster bubble was saying Labour lost [the general election] because it was too far to the left. Andy, despite saying he wanted to go outside the bubble, couldn't see beyond what they were saying.

With the shine already coming off Burnham's campaign in the eyes of the left, the Campaign Group, swollen in number by the arrival of the radical new MPs, including Cat Smith and Clive Lewis, gathered in Room W3 in the House of Commons for its first meeting after the general election. It has become part of the mythology around Corbyn that he was the reluctant candidate, who ended up standing because it was 'Buggins' turn'.

In fact, it was he who was the first to tentatively suggest to his colleagues in the Campaign Group that he should run, only to be persuaded not to by his friends. Alive to the social media campaign out there for a left-wing candidate, Corbyn made the case that someone ought to put their name forward, concluding with the words: 'What about if I stand?'[254] The new MP Clive Lewis later described the response: 'There was a silence around the room. There were some people, for a variety of reasons, who weren't keen on it – some, I think, because they were worried about what would happen to Jeremy.'[255] With his record of more than thirty years of trouble-making, a number Corbyn's colleagues feared he would be too much of an easy target for his rivals and the media. What he did secure from the meeting, however, was a broad agreement that someone from the left should stand. He later said: 'We had a discussion of MPs of the Labour Party who are anti-austerity, and decided it was a good idea to put a candidate up who would be prepared to take that position.'

David Winnick believes that Corbyn had decided to run well before he finally declared. Having never seen Corbyn attend the weekly meetings of the PLP, Winnick was surprised to spot him at the first two gatherings after the election. Looking back, he believes Corbyn's presence was an early clue that he was considering running for the leadership, giving him an opportunity to rub shoulders with colleagues he usually made little effort to mingle among, even if he hadn't yet persuaded his allies in the Campaign Group that he should stand. 'My view is that everything had been decided by then,' Winnick says. 'I don't necessarily take the view that there was this shy, reluctant person who never in his whole life even thought of high office.'

By late May, Harry Fletcher was beginning to despair that a candidate of the left would ever be found, and voiced his concerns to friends including John McDonnell, Matt Foot (son of the campaigning journalist Paul Foot and great-nephew of Michael Foot) and Corbyn himself. He says:

I can remember having discussions late May, early June, about whether the left should put up a candidate. What was going on was simmering discontent with the candidates. John said what a sterile competition this was going to be. Who on earth are we going to work with? My mates were all saying: 'There has got to be somebody, but is it worth the risk of a left candidate being humiliated?' The debate was: 'What if we don't get the thirty-five [nominations] and the left is further prostrated?' I was saying: 'The left has got to stand, but who was going come forward?' The majority view was not to put anyone up. It kind of stalled.

While some on the left were now finally persuaded that a candidate should be found, specifically to make the case against the new Conservative government's austerity measures and cuts programme, many remained unconvinced that Corbyn was the right person. Clive Lewis has said of the arguments at the time:

There was a bit of a split … [there were] those who thought that if we stand and get drubbed and lose, it will basically mean the right of the party would say: 'Get back into your box – you've had your say, you're finished, go away, you came last. You got Ed [Miliband] in, we lost the election, now you've come last' – that was the fear.[256]

With time ticking away until the close of nominations on 12 June, Naomi Fearon, Michelle Ryan and Beck Barnes now stepped up their social media campaign, relentlessly tweeting and emailing those left-wing MPs they knew were opposed to Chancellor George Osborne's austerity measures, urging them to run. Jon Trickett admits that MPs were by now very aware of the feeling among ordinary members that a candidate of the left needed to be found. John McDonnell, as chair of the Campaign Group, agreed to hold another meeting to discuss the matter. The day before, on 2 June, Corbyn ran into Jon Craig, Sky News's veteran chief political correspondent, in one of the Commons' many snaking corridors. Craig later wrote of their encounter:

> 'Why isn't there a left-wing candidate in the contest this time, Jeremy?' I asked him … 'Ah!' he said excitedly. 'We're having a meeting of the Campaign Group tomorrow to discuss that.' And the rest, as they say [is history]. (Although I'm not sure Corbyn expected to be the candidate himself when I spoke to him that day.)[257]

Again, the group gathered in Room W3. While some members continued to argue that the cause of the left might be damaged if a candidate ran and fared badly, the prevailing view seemed to be that without a presence in the contest, their wing of the party – and the policies they believed in, particularly their opposition to austerity – would be viewed as irrelevances. Once it was agreed that someone from the left should stand, it seemed there was no option other than Corbyn. 'It kind of fell to Jeremy,' Cat Smith has said.[258] The Campaign Group numbered only nine MPs elected before 2015, and it was felt that it was too tall an order for the new Members to run. Of the old-timers, three, John McDonnell, Michael Meacher and Diane Abbott, had fared badly in previous contests. A fourth member, Ian Lavery, had already ruled himself out by backing Andy Burnham, and John Cryer, the MP for Leyton and Wanstead, was reluctant to give up his role as chair of the PLP. A sixth member, Ian Mearns, had nominated Cooper. At seventy-two and eighty-three respectively, the veterans Ronnie Campbell and Dennis Skinner were considered a little long in the tooth to take on the demands of a leadership campaign. And so it was left to the relatively youthful Corbyn, at sixty-six, to take up the challenge. 'I'll stand if I've got your support,' he told the meeting.[259]

During the last rally of Corbyn's leadership campaign, a triumphant John McDonnell described the somewhat less than electrifying moment the candidate agreed to stand. 'We were sat around the table, we looked at Jeremy, and he said, "Alright, alright, I'll do it."' Clive Lewis has said: 'The people in the room went, "OK, if you're going to do it, we'll back you."'[260] Ronnie Campbell added: 'I think it was a persuasive argument for Jeremy to stand, basically. Nobody else would. [We told him]: – "Jeremy, have a go, get on the hustings, your turn."' Corbyn was in the race.

Cat Smith and Clive Lewis left the meeting and went on to the Commons Terrace, where they began to spread the word that Corbyn was running. There they saw Kevin Maguire, the well-respected *Daily Mirror* political commentator, who had already tweeted out the news, having been tipped off shortly before the Campaign Group met that Corbyn was likely to throw his hat into the ring (another sign that he was determined to run well before the group agreed to it). Maguire was the first to break the story, and was realistic about the new candidate's chances. 'Jeremy Corbyn running for Labour leader from the left. Widens the debate but suspect he'll struggle for thirty-five nominations,' his tweet read. Maguire's message was retweeted ninety-eight times and favourited forty times, immediately suggesting the strength of the desire out in the country for a candidate of the left. Michelle Ryan was the first to comment.

A few hours later, Corbyn gave an interview to *The Guardian* in which he sounded somewhat less than enthusiastic about his candidacy:

> We had a discussion among a group of us on the left about how we
> might influence future developments of the party … We decided some-
> body should put their hat in the ring in order to promote that debate.

> And, unfortunately, it's my hat in the ring. Diane and John have done
> it before, so it was my turn.

Asked if he needed 'persuading' to run, he added: 'Yeah. I have never held any appointed office, so in that sense it's unusual, but if I can promote some causes and debate by doing this, then good. That's why I'm doing it.'

Like Corbyn himself, no one in the Campaign Group meeting that day seriously believed that he might go on to win; most thought he might not even manage to rack up the thirty-five nominations needed to get on the ballot, particularly as Andy Burnham had already signed up a number of left-wing MPs. Instead, the aim was to influence, perhaps only in a small way, the nature of the debate over Labour's future during the hustings and discussions that would take place over the summer. Ronnie Campbell says:

> With the nominations, we knew he might not get it because of all
> this trouble we had [in 2010] getting Diane Abbott on. We thought
> we would have even more trouble with Jeremy. I didn't expect it.
> The main thing Jeremy was doing as far as I [was] concerned, he was
> putting the left agenda, the socialist agenda, back on the Labour Party
> ballot paper. I'm sure that was his motivation at the beginning.

By coincidence, on the day of the Campaign Group meeting, having reached their 5,000 target, Naomi Fearon had delivered the petition drawn up by Michelle Ryan and Beck Barnes to Jon Cryer, in his capacity as chair of the PLP. She, Ryan and the others were thrilled when news of Corbyn's candidature began to get out. Fearon says: 'People like Jeremy, they to me reflect what it means to be Labour. The fact that we got Jeremy – wow! I wasn't sure anyone was going to step up and do it, so I was really pleased.' Jon Trickett, who was not at the Campaign Group meeting, was also happy:

I thought, well, he is the right person to capture the zeitgeist. Some lefties are sectarian, they see everybody else as the enemy, 'Which side are you on?' He doesn't seem to me like that. He's not like an angry young man type of character. He's been principled, he hasn't been involved in any of the compromises that the rest of us have. I thought he was the right person.

Len McCluskey, the general secretary of Unite, has said of Corbyn's decision to enter the contest:

I was listening to Liz and Yvette and Andy and I reached for the nearest, sharpest object so that I could slit my wrists – because the blandness and the sameness of that was something that was depressing. For someone like me, who's been around the block a few times, it was difficult to come to terms with. And then Jeremy Corbyn arrived and gave us something that electrified everybody.[261]

Harry Fletcher learned of Corbyn's candidacy on a breaking news alert on Sky News. He immediately phoned Seb Corbyn, whom he had been sharing an office with in John McDonnell's rooms in the Commons since the general election. Seb told Fletcher: 'My dad was under a hell of a lot of pressure from constituencies from the broader left.' An official announcement was made later that day to Corbyn's local paper, the *Islington Tribune*. Saying he was standing on an 'anti-austerity platform', Corbyn confirmed that he had been directly influenced by the likes of Ryan, Barnes and Fearon. 'This decision to stand is in response to an overwhelming call by Labour Party members who want to see a broader range of candidates and a thorough debate about the future of the party,' he said. 'I am standing to give Labour Party members a voice in this debate.'

The bookmakers immediately installed Corbyn at 100–1. Many thousands of people are now kicking themselves for failing to take those odds. One of the few canny ones was Kat Fletcher, Corbyn's election agent in Islington North who would become one of his closest aides, who placed a bet in a bookies' on the Holloway Road. Even she did not really believe that Corbyn would win. 'To be honest, the bet was an act of solidarity,' she has said since. 'It was so I could tell Jeremy that I had backed him.'[262] She later spent her £2,000 winnings on hotel accommodation for twenty enthusiastic young volunteers to attend Corbyn's first Labour Party conference as leader.

CHAPTER SIXTEEN

NOMINATION

AT ONE MINUTE to noon on Monday 15 June, Andrew Smith, the 64-year-old long-time MP for Oxford East, made his way down one of the darker, more subterranean corridors of the House of Commons and, to the clear joy of a small clutch of people gathered outside, walked into the tiny room used as the headquarters of the Parliamentary Labour Party. In his hand was a nomination form for the leadership of the Labour Party, and written on it was the name Jeremy Corbyn. It was Corbyn's thirty-sixth nomination, although amid the high drama that had played out over the preceding hour, his campaign team believed it was the thirty-fifth – the magic number for getting the candidate on the ballot – and only began celebrating once Smith made his move. As they shook each other's hands, still unable to believe that the left-winger was on the ballot, Big Ben began to chime twelve times.

The story of how Smith – described by Matthew Norman in *The Independent* as 'a politician of breathtaking obscurity' despite his service as Work and Pensions Secretary under Tony Blair – and others like him came to nominate Corbyn, a candidate whose hard-left ideas they had long opposed, is one of the most intriguing of his entire journey to the leadership. Many would come to bitterly regret their actions, and all would be furiously castigated and even abused by party colleagues dismayed by Corbyn's ascent to the leadership. Even the most charitable of Corbyn's opponents accuse those MPs who nominated him when they did not want him to win of seriously misunderstanding the responsibility placed on them by the changes in the rules drawn up in the Collins Review following the Falkirk scandal. The roots of their error, if error it was, lie with Corbyn's former lover, Diane Abbott, and her unsuccessful bid to run for the Labour leadership in the summer of 2010.

At the outset of the contest, David Miliband was the clear favourite to succeed Gordon Brown as Labour leader. As the race got under way in May 2010, concern began to be expressed that it was shaping up to be not just an all-male affair, but a battle between contenders with remarkably similar backgrounds, careers and outlooks. The Miliband brothers, Ed Balls and Andy Burnham were all in their early forties, had all served first as New Labour special advisers, then as MPs and finally as Cabinet ministers; they were Oxbridge-educated and from backgrounds that ranged from the lower to the upper middle classes. They spoke alike and looked alike. Their views weren't altogether dissimilar, either. Although Corbyn's friend John McDonnell had thrown his hat into the ring on behalf of the left, it was clear that he was struggling to attract the necessary numbers to get on the ballot. So it came as a relief to many, not least the other candidates, when Diane Abbott, the black, feminist, left-wing, long-serving backbencher from Hackney, who was by now in her late fifties, declared that she would join them in the contest. 'We can't go forward with a leadership debate where there is no woman,' she said. 'And, you know, if we are going to have a debate about immigration, I am the child of immigrants. Don't the millions of British people who are the children of immigrants have a voice in this debate also?'[263] (Abbott failed to mention that the Milibands' parents were refugees; Jews who had fled the Nazis.)

Abbott had a problem, however. With few friends outside the tiny Campaign Group and a somewhat abrasive manner, according to one fellow MP she was 'unpopular' in the parliamentary party. Like John McDonnell, she quickly realised she would not be able to pick up the required number of nominations, which in 2010 stood at thirty-three, 12.5 per cent of the PLP. Abbott sought out David Lammy, who was a prominent supporter of David Miliband, and asked for his help. As a fellow black MP, she told Lammy, he had a responsibility to ensure that an ethnic minority candidate was on the ballot. She suggested that in the name of equality, David Miliband, who had the support of more MPs than any of the candidates, could encourage some of his backers who had not yet formally nominated him to 'lend' their votes to her. Lammy agreed to approach David Miliband, who privately was initially reluctant but eventually agreed, even going so far as to transfer his own nomination to Abbott. And so it was that around a dozen Labour MPs, including David Miliband supporters Jack Straw and Phil Woolas, who would not ultimately vote for Abbott in the leadership contest proper, decided to nominate her. On deadline day, as the thirty-third MP came into the PLP office with a form with Abbott's name on it, she and Lammy hugged each other, both of them in tears. Although Abbott would go on to fare poorly in the contest, eventually finishing last, a precedent had been established.

By the time of the 2015 leadership campaign, when Corbyn was seeking to get on to the ballot, many of those supporting his candidature used Abbott's experience to suggest it was the responsibility of the PLP to ensure that all wings of the party were represented, to allow what they described as 'a proper debate'. David Lammy is clear, however, that the argument he had made in 2010 was that Abbott should be in the contest not because she was left-wing but because she was a woman and a member of an ethnic minority. Harriet Harman, the then deputy leader, is among those who explicitly said at the time that they were nominating Abbott as a result of her gender.[264] Lammy says he hoped that thanks to Abbott's stand, Labour would one day elect a member of an ethnic minority as leader. 'I have to say I did it because I believed it was important for Diane to open the door,' he now says. 'I have to be perfectly honest, at the front of my head and hers, we thought we were opening the door that Chuka Umunna would walk through. That was what was going on in our heads. It was having a woman and a black candidate.' Harry Fletcher adds: 'Diane, in 2010, she was tokenistic. The white guys nominated [her] because they wanted a black woman in the contest.'

If most MPs nominating Abbott were doing so in the name of equality, there were concerns even at the time about what had taken place. In a precursor of the protests that would be made following the 2015 nominating process, Paul Richards, who had been a special adviser to the former New Labour Cabinet minister Hazel Blears, tweeted: 'Some of us spent decades fighting the hard left. Now our MPs are falling over themselves to get the Campaign Group on the ballot. Crazy.' Richards felt that MPs should give their nominations only to candidates they considered viable potential leaders, and that, therefore, it was irresponsible to nominate someone they did not plan to vote for in the contest.

In the days after Corbyn finally announced that he would be standing, the Campaign Group remained sceptical that he could emulate Abbott by making it on to the ballot. The assumption in Westminster was that he would end up as the usual 'human sacrifice of the left', as one commentator put it. The delay in entering the contest meant that not only was he three weeks behind his rivals in terms of seeking nominations, he also had just twelve days to hunt them down before the deadline of midday on 15 June. His task was made even harder by the assiduity with which Andy Burnham's team in particular was picking up nominations from the pond in which Corbyn would have expected to fish.

Burnham's team was keen to establish a narrative and a momentum behind him as the front-runner, and eager to get their hands on the official Labour membership lists, which were made available to candidates only once they were on the ballot. The MP Steve Rotherham was tasked with conducting what was described as a 'whipping operation' to get colleagues to nominate early on his behalf. Ian Lavery and Lisa Nandy were not the only left-leaning MPs who were snapped up early on. Burnham's team was forced to deny claims by rival camps that he was calling MPs into his office and offering them jobs in return for their support. The *New States-man* calculated that fifteen MPs whom Corbyn might have hoped to sign up had already pledged their support to Burnham, along with three who were backing Yvette Cooper.

If Corbyn was less than confident about his prospects, others were determined he would be more than a footnote in the history of the 2015 Labour leadership contest. Another unsung social media hero entered Corbyn's story within a few hours of his declaration on 3 June, with the launch of a second online petition, this time urging MPs to nominate him. It was the brainchild of Stuart Wheeler, a 44-year-old father of three who works in the accounts department of a meat processing firm and lives in the small town of St Blazey, Cornwall, a county which, despite being officially the most deprived in England, has long been associated with Liberalism rather than Labour politics. Wheeler had joined the Labour Party in the immediate aftermath of the shocking death of its then leader John Smith in 1994. Over the years he had become increasingly active, serving on his local council and as agent for the (losing) Labour parliamentary candidate at the May election. A fan of Ed Miliband, Wheeler considers himself on the left of the party, saying he supports policies aimed at the 'lower 90 per cent' of the population, and like Michelle Ryan and Rebecca Barnes, he had planned to vote for Andy Burnham until he heard the news that Corbyn was running. Wheeler says:

> As soon as I heard that someone had come forward on an anti-austerity agenda, I thought that was something I could actually vote for. I was worried Jeremy couldn't get the nominations and then the whole discussion would have been quite arid. We would have had three candidates saying very similar things. Nobody would have been saying the key things about austerity. It was quite late in the day, he hadn't come out and announced he was going to stand immediately, so a lot of MPs had already nominated.

'Off his own bat', and without discussing his plan with anyone, Wheeler created an online petition urging MPs to get Corbyn on the ballot. Posted to another campaigning website, Change.org, it read:

> The requirement to have thirty-five MPs nominating candidates in order to enable them to appear on the ballot assumes that the MPs fully reflect the make-up of the party. In the absence of any other way of getting onto the ballot … we see it as essential that the MPs open up the field as widely as possible on our behalf. We ask this simply so that a section of the party is not cut out totally from this process, rather than in the expectation of victory. It is very important that the party discuss the possibility that anti-austerity might be the way forward for our party and our people. We therefore petition Labour MPs to ensure that thirty-five of them nominate Jeremy Corbyn and allow full discussion of the anti-war, anti-austerity wing of the party.

Within twenty-four hours, the petition had picked up more than 2,000 signatures and a mention in the *Daily Mirror*. Naomi Fearon spotted Wheeler's petition and tweeted it out on behalf of Red Labour the day after it launched. Michelle Ryan also began promoting it. 'I wanted to start a petition straight away to get nominations but someone beat us to it – Stuart Wheeler – so I circulated that petition as much as I circulated our petition,' she says.

Back in Westminster, having missed the target himself in 2007 and 2010, getting his close friend Corbyn on to the ballot would be sweet revenge for John McDonnell. Knowing that the self-effacing Corbyn would struggle to ask for votes himself, McDonnell set himself the mission of wooing the PLP, aided by Seb Corbyn, Harry Fletcher and, once again, an extraordinary network of activists, most of whom he had never met, who now worked tirelessly to drum up support among MPs via social media. While Fletcher had not been close to Corbyn prior to the contest, he knew him from his campaigning work, describing him as 'very friendly', and offered his help and support as soon as he heard the Islington MP was running. Although the circumstances appeared less favourable than in 2010, with the threshold raised to 15 per cent, in fact the election of the group of new MPs with left of centre views meant the arithmetic, although tight, was not impossible, despite the loss of a number of left-wingers, including some of the Campaign Group, to Burnham and Cooper. Fletcher says: 'We had then got [only a few] days to work up the nominations. By the end of that week it was about ten.'

Jon Trickett and Ronnie Campbell both claim to have been the first to nominate Corbyn. Trickett says: 'I was the first MP publicly to nominate him. For a few days I think I was the only one then it took fire. It just went like a flame. It just spread.' Campbell insists: 'I was the first to nominate him. I was first in – I pushed [Dennis] Skinner out the way.' Other early nominations came from the new MPs Clive Lewis, Cat Smith and Richard Burgon.

But as the weekend arrived, and rivals Yvette Cooper and Andy Burnham reached the thirty-five mark, meaning they were formally on the ballot, the signs were not looking all that good for Corbyn – and the candidate himself experienced something of a wobble. A member of his team says:

> Over that weekend Jeremy really had second thoughts about whether he should stand. It was about would he get sufficient numbers, would it damage him or his family, all the attention. He was probably mindful about what Ed [Miliband] had been through. Would he have people knocking on his door, bothering his kids?

That Monday, 8 June, the candidates appeared at a hustings held by the PLP. One MP supporting Corbyn sensed that he was at a low ebb, seeming self-effacing as the other candidates made great show of their leadership qualities:

> They [the MPs] were interested in him but they thought he wasn't going to get anywhere. He couldn't bring himself to say words like 'when I become leader' and 'if I become leader'. Once the campaign got started the other candidates tried to define the nature of leadership in a certain way. Yvette in particular was … trying to say, 'Look at me, I look like a leader', then the part of the sentence that wasn't expressed: 'Look at Jeremy, he simply doesn't look like Prime Minister material.'

If the supporter was underwhelmed by Corbyn's performance, others were more impressed. Another person who was at the PLP that night, who is not a fan of Corbyn's, says:

> I remember people were coming out of that PLP hustings and eve-
> ryone was quite ashen-faced and nervously laughing, but saying,

'On that performance, I think Jeremy Corbyn could do it,' because he was the most fluent, he was comfortable in his own skin, he was jovial, he knew what he was talking about, he had an argument, he knows what he believes in, obviously. The others were very all over the place. They were just weak, they didn't sound like they believed in [anything]. They sounded like slightly gradated versions of one another.

A sense of Corbyn's potential appeal to the wider party began to emerge the following day, 9 June, when the five declared candidates travelled to Dublin to address a hustings organised by the GMB union. While the newspapers concentrated on the hard time given by delegates to Andy Burnham and Liz Kendall for failing to condemn the government's proposed welfare cuts, it was apparent to everyone there that Corbyn had received the warmest reception.[265]

In Corbyn's absence in Dublin, John McDonnell, Seb Corbyn, Cat Smith and Clive Lewis continued to work the PLP hard. McDonnell told MPs who had yet to nominate that they owed it to the wider party to ensure a 'full debate' about the causes of the devastating election defeat, with all streams of opinion represented. His argument that left-wing grassroots members would not forgive them if their views were not given voice in the contest was reinforced as Stuart Wheeler's petition took off, reaching more than 5,000 signatures by 8 June when Liz Kendall reached the 35-nomination threshold, confirming that the right would be represented. Wheeler, who had circulated petitions in the past on local issues, said: 'It spread very quickly. I have never had anything go like that.' Michelle Ryan says: 'I was properly chasing MPs and emailing so much it was becoming like a full-time job. I didn't give them a moment's peace, none of us did.' Quick to realise the potential of social media, Seb Corbyn and the team began using a new Jeremy Corbyn for Leader Facebook page and JeremyCorbyn4Leader Twitter account to push out links to Wheeler's petition. When the team published a list of MPs who had yet to nominate, Wheeler sent each what he described as a 'nicely worded' email imploring them to back Corbyn and referencing his petition. But by the end of the day, Corbyn still had just eleven declared nominations.

As his supporters both inside and out of Parliament worked flat-out to get him on to the ballot, Corbyn himself was philosophical about his chances, and happy at what he had achieved so far. '[There were] a number of discussions among left MPs in Parliament about what to do and eventually, a week ago, we said we'd try and put somebody's hat in the ring to try and promote that [anti-austerity] debate,' he said.

> If we get [on to the ballot paper], great. We'll see what happens, but as far as I'm concerned we've already – by the action we took a week ago – changed the terms of debate. There are a lot of people who actually profoundly disagree with me, and have disagreed with me for thirty years, who say, 'Well, at least you're saying something different.' They are kind of appreciative of that.[266]

By 11 June, Corbyn had sixteen endorsements, including the first of those who would help him on to the ballot despite having no plans to vote for him in the final contest. Chi Onwurah, the MP for Newcastle Central, explained why she was giving her support. 'I respect his views,' she wrote in a message to constituents posted on her website.

> He is well known for his strong advocacy of socialist ideals, principles and policies. More importantly in this context, many members share his views or would at least like to hear them debated. I asked members and supporters in my constituency who I should nominate and the overwhelming feedback – including, to be fair, from many who

> do not live in Newcastle Central – was that Jeremy Corbyn should be
> on the ballot. That is not to say I believe he should be the next leader
> of the Labour Party.

Catherine West, newly elected in Hornsey and Wood Green, tweeted: 'I can confirm that I have nominated Jeremy Corbyn this evening as the Labour leadership debate needs to be as broad as possible.'

Jo Cox, new MP for Batley and Spen, told her supporters: 'While I won't personally vote for Jeremy in the final ballot, I'm determined to nominate in a way that will ensure a broad debate and the widest possible choice for party members.'[267] Emily Thornberry, Corbyn's neighbour in Islington South who went on to vote for Yvette Cooper, says:

> I nominated him because I was as annoyed as many at the way some
> people were taking advantage of the election to yank the party to
> the right. It seemed to me that we should have a proper debate, we
> shouldn't be afraid of that. I didn't expect this [Corbyn's victory] to
> happen, but there we are.

Some in the Labour movement are now scathing about the failure of a number of MPs to resist the pressure they came under on social media in the days running up to the close of nominations. 'They are law-makers, they are paid to take the difficult decisions,' says one former senior Labour staffer. 'The whole point of the [Collins] system was that they had a responsibility to think about who would be an acceptable future Prime Minister. Jeremy Corbyn wasn't that, they knew it, yet they weren't strong enough to look like bad guys by keeping him off the ballot.'

Jon Trickett, however, believes that MPs were right to listen to the voices outside Westminster:

A huge amount of pressure was put on MPs on social media to endorse Jeremy even if they didn't agree with his ideas, on the principle of 'Let's have a proper debate'. That did have a big effect. The social media movement probably is what got him on. People say MPs were foolish for nominating him if they didn't agree with him. What they forget is the relationship between the wider society and elected representatives. All this preoccupation with an old-fashioned idea of leadership and an old-fashioned idea of decisions being made in here [Parliament] in isolation is dead in a Google world. A spontaneous movement arose, thousands of thousands of people tweetering [*sic*] their MPs saying, 'You've got to nominate Jeremy', developing quite sophisticated arguments in 140 characters to say that's what should happen. People who are watching politics think that the football game is played in the House of Commons. Actually, I think the ball is outside of here altogether. If you want to watch what's going on you've got to see where politics really is, and that's out in the wider community.

Others in the mainstream of the party blame Ed Miliband for allowing the election of a group of left-wing new MPs who helped get Corbyn on the ballot. A source close to Miliband, however, says:

If those people hadn't been there, those hardcore people, they just would have found other people in the PLP to nominate him, because there was such a momentum about trying to get a left-wing candidate on the ballot paper, the pressure that was being put on people, they just would have found other people to give their vote. It's just an easy thing to say without giving it any proper analysis or thought.

On Friday 12 June, Mary Creagh quit the race, saying she was struggling to attract enough support from her fellow MPs. Andy Burnham's team had hoped to pick up her supporters' nominations and were surprised and disappointed when most instead fell to Corbyn. Media coverage of Creagh's withdrawal referenced Corbyn's failure thus far to reach the magic number of thirty-five, but included the tantalising detail that he had topped a poll by the LabourList website of grassroots supporters. An overwhelming 47 per cent of activists had named Corbyn as their preferred candidate, compared to 13 per cent for Burnham, 11 for Kendall and 9 for Cooper. As the nomination phase entered its final days, the LabourList figures piled further pressure on MPs who were yet to declare. Corbyn's nominations inched up to twenty.

The growing trend for MPs who were natural supporters of other candidates to nominate Corbyn irritated the rival teams, many of whose staffers felt the MPs were either weak to give in to pressure from left-wing CLP members and social media campaigners or had profoundly misunderstood their role. Although Andy Burnham's camp 'weren't taking him that seriously' at this stage, there was disappointment that, thanks to Corbyn, instead of the ninety nominations they had hoped to receive, they ended the process with only sixty-eight. Liz Kendall's team felt that losing nominations to Corbyn hurt her chances. John Woodcock says:

> Once Liz was on the ballot paper, at that stage there were people who were inclined or already committed to Liz who nevertheless decided to back Jeremy, and that annoyed us, in the sense that: you're just doing that because you're getting grief from some email writers in your constituency, and the consequences of that is that Liz's support in the PLP is understated because you've chosen to cast your vote elsewhere.

The weekend before the close of the nominations saw most MPs back in their constituencies, where they were able to hear the first-hand views of grassroots members, who, as many later reported, overwhelmingly urged them to get Corbyn on the ballot. On Sunday 14 June, with fourteen nominations still needed and less than twenty-four hours to go, the Jeremy Corbyn for Leader Facebook page published a list of the forty-six MPs who had yet to declare. Michelle Ryan, Stuart Wheeler and Naomi Fearon leapt into action, directly tweeting every MP on the list. By now, Wheeler's petition had attracted more than 7,000 signatures. John Prescott, the former deputy leader, added his voice to those calling for Corbyn to get on the ballot, writing in the *Sunday Mirror*: 'I may not agree with a lot that left-winger Jeremy Corbyn says. But it's important in this debate for the soul of the party that members get to vote on his views. That's why I hope Labour MPs lend Corbyn their votes.'

Two MPs who were running to become Labour's candidate in the London mayoral elections, David Lammy and Sadiq Khan, now stepped up to nominate Corbyn. They have since been accused of doing so in order to curry favour with the capital's electorate, which tends to be further to the left than the rest of the country. Khan, the eventual winner, certainly benefited from being aligned with Corbyn, his campaign picking up having hitherto been trailing Tessa Jowell. After the contest, the Tooting MP revealed that he himself had voted for Burnham. One member of Corbyn's team describes Lammy's and Khan's nominations as 'a calculated gamble'.

Lammy admits he came under heavy pressure to nominate Corbyn, both from the users of social media and from Corbyn's own allies. He says:

> I didn't really make up my mind until the Sunday night [before nominations closed]. I was well disposed to Jeremy, I just hadn't really given it much thought because I was preoccupied with the [mayoral] campaign. Seb, his son, rang me up, and then Jeremy rang me up, and I said, 'I'll come into Parliament and get you on.' I was a little bit

surprised when Clive Lewis, the new MP, on the Sunday night sent me a message kind of poking me publicly and telling me to nominate, just because we don't tend to do that publicly. He hadn't spoken to me about it, he just publicly put me in it. There are so many social media campaigns that go on that you're aware of, but they don't all have an effect. But I could see there was a strength of feeling about Jeremy emerging.

(Lammy says he later came under heavy criticism for nominating Corbyn from Jews in his Tottenham constituency who claimed he was an apologist for anti-Semites.)

Harry Fletcher, who had been looking after press for Corbyn, spent Sunday 14 June scribbling three alternative press releases in long-hand in a notebook, for use the following day. The first was simple and headlined: 'Anti-austerity candidate makes the ballot'. The second read: 'Jeremy Corbyn narrowly fails, but picks up more support than John McDonnell and Diane Abbott, showing ideas are on the rise'. The third anticipated the nightmare scenario that Corbyn might end up well short of the required number: 'The result is an affront to democracy that MPs can determine who members vote for', it said. By now, Fletcher was growing hopeful that he would be issuing the first release.

That Sunday night, Naomi Fearon stayed up late, throwing everything at her campaign to get Corbyn into the race. 'I worked through the early hours in the morning. We were constantly emailing and emailing and emailing all these MPs who hadn't nominated to get him on the ballot. We were quietly confident that a few MPs would step up to the mark, albeit in the last minutes and hours.' Her work had an effect. The following morning, with just over three hours to go before nominations closed, the Bermondsey and Old Southwark MP, Neil Coyle, sent out a tweet in response to the deluge of messages he had received. 'Emailing re Corbyn/Labour leadership? Please include: how u voted 7 May; if not Labour, why (he was!); & ur plan if he's on ballot but loses', he said. What he heard back convinced Coyle to nominate Corbyn – a decision he would come to rue. (He would later manage to have Corbyn's brother Piers, a constituent, barred from registering as a supporter in order to vote in the contest, on the grounds that Piers had campaigned against Labour locally at the general election.)

By now, Corbyn had 'thirty-one or thirty-two names', Harry Fletcher says. 'Seb was of the view, and Jeremy concurred, that there was a high probability three or four more would come on-side. We told MPs it would be a tragedy to have come so far and be so near [and not get the numbers].' Jon Trickett adds:

> The Monday morning we were still, I think, at thirty-one nominations. People were saying, 'He's not going to make it.' We were at thirty-one and we had six or seven names and therefore I knew we were going to get there, although I must admit when it got to five to twelve I wasn't certain.

One member of a rival team, furious about the timing of the nomination process, later told *The Guardian*:

> To have [the close of nominations] at twelve o'clock on a Monday – we must have been on fucking crack cocaine. You can't get to anyone, so people were wandering in after a weekend of spending time with their bloody constituency secretary or their left-wing wife, they just fucking wander off the train and hadn't even had a cup of tea in the Tea Room by twelve o'clock on a Monday. They go straight down to the PLP office and do something stupid.

With half an hour to go, the Liz Kendall supporter Gareth Thomas, MP for Harrow West and another mayoral candidate, and Margaret Beckett, the former deputy leader who was backing Andy Burnham, joined those nominating Corbyn. Beckett would later publicly flagellate herself for her decision, telling the BBC: 'I probably regard it as one of the biggest political mistakes I've ever made.' Asked to respond to a suggestion by John McTernan, a former adviser to Tony Blair, that MPs who 'lent' Corbyn their nominations were 'morons', she sighed: 'I am one of them.'[268]

Harry Fletcher believes Beckett's decision was considered, however: 'Margaret Beckett thought it would shift the tone of the debate and move the other candidates away from the centre,' he says. Roger Baker, one of Yvette Cooper's strategists, argues that many MPs simply failed to appreciate the greater filtering role they had been tasked with:

> It became apparent during that May and June nominating process, especially [among] the new MPs, no one had explained the MPs' role in the new system. And that isn't just the new MPs, really seasoned old hands did not understand their role in that process. I'm not just saying that's their fault, to be fair to them, no one had made this clear. And the PLP nomination process, in other rule forms, had been a bit of debate, consensual, it had been a lot that. But this was an entirely different system.

Others are less charitable. John Woodcock says: 'It was only retrospectively when we saw the tidal wave that, not just among Liz's team but all the MPs when they were talking, [the feeling] was: what form of punishment was most appropriate for the people who actually abdicated their responsibility in the process.' Campaign Group member Ronnie Campbell is gleeful about the buyer's remorse of Beckett and others: 'I'm sure Members of

Parliament who nominated [Corbyn] are regretting it now because they're getting the finger pointed at them. These other MPs thought, 'It'll make a good debate.' Some of them MPs ... thought he'd raise the debate in the hustings. Obviously [they] know now to their cost.'

As the final minutes ticked down, Harry Fletcher and Jon Trickett decided to go over to the PLP room, where the last stragglers would register their votes. Walking down corridors Fletcher hadn't known existed, he felt the tension mount. Both men were struck by the 'theatre' of the scene that awaited them outside the PLP, where Corbyn, still wearing his cycling jacket and carrying his helmet, John McDonnell, Cat Smith and Jon Lansman had already gathered. As a sideshow to the drama of Corbyn's nomination, there was a separate scramble among the candidates for the deputy leadership to get on to the ballot, after Rushanara Ali, the young MP for Bethnal Green and Bow, withdrew at the last minute, leaving those who had yet to accrue the required numbers scrambling to pick up her supporters. With the five remaining deputy leadership candidates milling around, Tom Watson, the front-runner who would go on to win the contest, offered to give Corbyn his own nomination, before changing his mind.

'An hour to go, we were in the high twenties and nowhere near,' John McDonnell later reminisced. 'Then we got thirty-two and we got to thirty-three and we had five MPs that had promised us that if we got to thirty-four they would nominate. It got to ten seconds and then two of them cracked. I admit I was in tears begging them.'[269] The first to 'crack' was Gordon Marsden, MP for Blackpool South and a backer of Yvette Cooper, after Cat Smith pleaded with him: 'Give us a contest, give us a chance, let us have a debate.'[270] Then, with a second to go, another Cooper supporter, Andrew Smith, stepped forward. As Big Ben struck twelve, Corbyn became an official contestant in the 2015 Labour leadership contest.

Altogether, more than half of the MPs who nominated Corbyn for the leadership would go on to vote for other candidates.[271] As well as those already mentioned, they included Dawn Butler, Jon Cruddas, Rupa Huq, Louise Haigh, Tulip Siddiq and Frank Field. And so it was that the Parliamentary Labour Party nominated for the leadership Jeremy Corbyn, a man they overwhelmingly did not expect – or want – to win.

CHAPTER SEVENTEEN

CAMPAIGN

I N THE FIRST minutes and hours after getting on to the ballot for the 2015 Labour leadership campaign, Jeremy Corbyn found it impossible to adjust to the notion that he was actually a candidate. While MPs who had given him the last, precious nominations were still scrambling to get their excuses out – Andrew Smith explaining he felt the party needed an 'open debate' and Gordon Marsden assuring the Twittersphere that he would be voting for Yvette Cooper – Corbyn did what he had been doing for the past forty years, and went on a demo. And so he began the 2015 Labour leadership contest in much the way he would end it: by attending a rally in Parliament Square in support of those less fortunate than himself.

While John McDonnell was emotional at his friend's eleventh-hour – or, rather, eleventh-hour, fifty-ninth minute – achievement in getting on to the ballot, perhaps feeling some vindication following his own two unsuccessful bids, Corbyn remained calm. Leaving his son Seb to break the good news to his supporters with a text that read simply '36!' he, McDonnell and Harry Fletcher went outside to Parliament Square to join a demonstration of about 200 women protesting against the conditions at the Yarl's Wood

Immigration Removal Centre. As they walked through New Palace Yard on the way out of St Stephen's Gate, they bumped into John Cryer, the left-leaning chair of the PLP, who said admiringly to Corbyn: 'Bloody hell, how've you done this?' The little group laughed in reply. The bookmakers reacted to the news of Corbyn's success in getting on to the ballot by lowering his odds to 20–1. He remained the contest's rank outsider.

After spending some time with the Yarl's Wood women, the trio wandered over to Downing Street. There, outside the Ministry of Defence, on the opposite side of Whitehall to No. 10, they joined a second small demonstration, protesting on behalf of Shaker Aamer, the last Briton to be detained at the Guantanamo Bay prison camp. As Corbyn chatted to a few of the protesters, he had no real belief that in less than three months' time he would be Leader of the Labour Party, heading the fight to replace David Cameron at 10 Downing Street, the famous address he now stood outside amid a group of human rights activists. None of the three men, Corbyn, McDonnell or Fletcher, seriously thought that day that he could win the contest. Instead, having first aimed merely to get him on the ballot, they now set themselves an only slightly more ambitious target: to not finish last.

After that first hour of denial about what they had taken on, it dawned on the little group that they had better get down to work. 'Jeremy was very surprised he got the thirty-six [nominations],' Fletcher says. 'It was: "Christ, what do we do now?" Because there was no infrastructure. Other campaigns had teams and offices.' The three men repaired to the House of Commons, where they hastily convened a meeting to work out a plan of action. Corbyn suggested he undertake a nationwide tour, speaking in towns and cities the length of the UK. McDonnell joked that at their age it might become a '*Last of the Summer Wine* tour',[272] (a reference to the BBC sitcom featuring three accident-prone pensioners from Yorkshire). In fact, the national tour would become a dazzling procession, gathering pace, fans and momentum as it turned Corbyn from a slightly bumbling left-wing, middle-aged politician into something resembling a rock god in the eyes of his adoring supporters. Even as they talked down their prospects, Fletcher says, secretly they could not help beginning to experience a few flickers of excitement. 'We started to get a feel, even then, on that first day, that this was going to be a thing.'

From humble beginnings, the Corbyn camp began to assemble what would turn out to be one of the most ruthlessly effective campaign machines ever put together for a leadership bid. Those at that first meeting at Portcullis House included the MPs Richard Burgon, the late Michael Meacher, Cat Smith (who argued that Corbyn needed to smarten up his appearance), Rebecca Long Bailey, Kelvin Hopkins and Kate Osamor. Researchers working for Meacher and Burgon agreed to help out, and Mark Serwotka, the head of the Public Services and Commercial Union (who would later be barred from voting in the contest) sent along a group of aides. 'It was anyone we could get our hands on,' Harry Fletcher says. Carmel Nolan, another press officer, described it as a 'coalition of the willing and available'.[273]

The main players now assumed their places. First and foremost after Corbyn was John McDonnell, who became campaign manager. Sixty-four-year-old McDonnell is a divisive figure even among those Labour MPs who find Corbyn tolerable. When, as his first appointment as leader, Corbyn made McDonnell his shadow Chancellor, it created a near mutiny among the PLP. Intelligent, organised and 'ruthless', as one MP puts it, unlike Corbyn, who apart from his sojourn on the Haringey Council Planning Committee has spent his forty-plus years in politics in permanent opposition, McDonnell actually has experience of running things. He was chief executive of the Association of London Authorities (which became the Association of London Government); one former colleague has described life under McDonnell at the ALA as, in the words of Thomas Hobbes's

Leviathan: 'nasty, brutish and short'.[274] He then served as Ken Livingstone's deputy at the GLC, running London's budget before the two fell out when even Red Ken found McDonnell too left-wing. 'I had no idea of the bitterness that was about to break around me or that a decade would pass before John or I would get over it,' Livingstone wrote of their disagreement in his memoir.[275] McDonnell was also active in London's Irish Republican circles; after Corbyn was elected leader he was forced to apologise for remarks in which he joked about assassinating Margaret Thatcher and praised the IRA.[276] 'Jeremy is teaching me to be a nicer person,' he has said.[277]

One MP who has known Corbyn and McDonnell since the 1980s, says that while the former is a 'harmless old lefty', his friend is a more hard-edged character. This MP also claims that even before Corbyn made it on to the ballot, it was McDonnell who was driving the agenda, and who continues to run the leadership in Corbyn's name. 'John McDonnell, he was always the shadow in the background, he's incredibly clever, really ruthless, totally Jekyll/Hyde,' the MP says. 'He's the one deciding everything. Jeremy's not. Jeremy is purely the puppet on the string in the hands of John McDonnell.' While the team reject the characterisation of McDonnell as the master manipulator, all agree that Corbyn relies heavily on, and values the support of, the man he describes as his greatest friend in politics. 'John McDonnell [is] the most principled, hard-working and committed colleague I have ever worked alongside,' Corbyn has said.[278] Later, defending his decision to name McDonnell shadow Chancellor, he would say:

> I always knew there was going to be some criticism made of it. He is
> a very close friend of mine, as everybody knows. He is a brilliant guy
> on economics and the ideas that go with it. I think it's very impor-
> tant that the leader and shadow Chancellor are thinking in the same
> direction and we're certainly doing that.[279]

After McDonnell, the most important people on Team Corbyn were the three Fletchers: Simon, Kat and Harry. Unrelated to each other, the shared surname is a coincidence. Of them, it was the widely admired Simon Fletcher who would play the most crucial role. He was the member of Corbyn's campaign whom his rivals would most liked to have had on theirs, and he came on board a day or two after the first meeting. Having acted as Ed Miliband's link-man with the unions, Fletcher had helped draw up the leadership rule changes following the Falkirk scandal, and so perhaps understood the new voting system better than anyone working across the four campaigns. His relationship with the trade unions would soon prove invaluable, as the candidates began to seek their backing. The son of a trade union leader, as a teenager Fletcher was one of Tony Benn's 'Teabags', the affectionate name Corbyn's mentor gave to his young helpers (it stood for The Eminent Association of Benn Archive Graduates). In the 1990s, he helped Ken Livingstone in his battle to be elected Mayor of London as an independent, against the Labour candidate Frank Dobson. And, as his chief of staff, Fletcher is credited with shepherding Livingstone back from the cold, moving him away from the extremist groupings he had been flirting with into a place where he could re-join Labour in time for his re-election in 2004. Four years later, Fletcher was embarrassed when a Channel 4 *Dispatches* programme linked him to the Trotskyite group Socialist Action. Livingstone was relaxed, however, saying: 'Almost all of my advisers had been involved in Socialist Action. It was the only rational left-wing group you could engage with. They used to produce my socialist economic policies. It was not a secret group.'

A singularly effective operator, 45-year-old Fletcher now wielded his vision and organisational effectiveness on behalf of Corbyn, crafting policies – including investing in public services, renationalising the railways and abolishing tuition fees – that sounded seductively fresh and dynamic while remaining true to the candidate's long-held ideals. Speeches were timed to coincide with the 6 p.m. and 7 p.m. news bulletins, and rallies held around the country in the early evening so Corbyn could get the last train back to London. One former Labour aide says: 'Simon is responsible for the winning strategy; nice guy, very decisive, very talented.' Roger Baker, who worked on Yvette Cooper's campaign, adds: 'I've a lot of respect for Simon Fletcher; he knows what he's doing.' One MP who regrets Corbyn's ascension says of the campaign as drawn up by Simon Fletcher:

> It's not like Ed Mili's office, which was all over the place. This is an incredibly efficient operation and you see it in everything they do. It's all thought through. Those early issues – we want to nationalise the railways – well, nobody can argue about that, but what they really want to do is nationalise the banks.

The second Fletcher, Kat, became Corbyn's head of strategy, and was in charge of his soon-to-be vast volunteer army. A former president of the National Union of Students, as a young political activist Kat Fletcher was known for being on the hard left, and won the NUS post in the face of opposition from the more moderate Labour Students, who before her election in 2004 had held the office for more than two decades. One former Labour aide and student politician who clashed with her at this time says: 'Kat Fletcher's roots are in the most extreme, most unpleasant of the left-wing groupings – people who think Putin is doing a great job in Ukraine and that Venezuela is a model for good government.' Now thirty-five, Fletcher got to know Corbyn after moving to Islington, where she served on the council and was elected deputy mayor, becoming his agent. A workaholic like her boss, before she came to work for Corbyn full-time she ran a small chain of gastropubs.

The third Fletcher, Harry, was an experienced press operator. Having served as assistant general secretary of the probation officers' union NAPO for more than two decades, for the past few years he had been a campaigner for victims' rights, working on a cross-party basis in Parliament to tackle internet abuse. After the 2015 election, when Elfyn Llwyd, the Plaid Cymru MP who had been sponsoring Fletcher's Commons pass, retired, he came into the Campaign Group's orbit, when John McDonnell agreed to sponsor him. Fletcher had first got to know Corbyn in the 1970s in Haringey, and later worked with him for the release of the Birmingham Six. He would bring a gentler, less strident tone to Corbyn's public offering, often calming down stories that threatened to spiral into hysteria as Fleet Street's finest pored over Corbyn's record and gleefully reproduced the gems they uncovered.

After a week, Harry Fletcher was joined in the press operation by the ebullient Carmel Nolan. A veteran of the Stop the War movement, Nolan, fifty, was a Liverpool-based former radio journalist who was close to George Galloway; her then eight-year-old daughter, Hope, is said to have come up with the name 'Respect' when he launched his anti-war party in 2004. Both Fletcher and Nolan found it difficult to juggle the demands of the media and a candidate who dismissed virtually all journalists as 'the right-wing press'. Corbyn had never worked with the Parliamentary Lobby before, and he didn't see why he should start now. In fact, his experience of the media over his long years in the Commons had been largely hostile, on issues from Northern Ireland to the monarchy. Corbyn's fellow MPs watched with amazement, and a little admiration, as he refused to take part in the traditional set-piece media ordeals, such as trial by ITV's *This Morning* or the BBC's *Andrew Marr Show*, and conducted only a handful of press interviews with chosen reporters. One former Labour aide says: 'Corbyn can ignore all of what the lobby says. He has already lost 80 per cent, who were never going to give him a chance, why not lose 99.9 per cent?'

Nolan once described handling Corbyn's press operation as like being 'at the reins of a runaway horse'.[280]

Seb Corbyn became his father's personal assistant, his tall figure a familiar sight on the campaign trail as he did his best to ensure he got Corbyn to events on time. It was not an easy task: Corbyn is notoriously tardy and disorganised. Keith Veness, who was his agent for almost a decade, says:

> It's not a job you'd wish on your worst enemy. You used to draw up what he was going to do that day, then he'd say: 'But I'd promised to go to that meeting…' On the one hand, you think that's lovely, on the other hand, it's very irksome when you're trying to keep your act together. People say he's a lovely man, which he is, but he's murder if you want to get him anywhere on time.

Late in the campaign, when Corbyn's rock star tour came to Margate in Kent, where the Venesses now live, he insisted on joining them for fish and chips on the sea front, to Seb's despair making him hours late for a 'Latinos for Corbyn' event that his middle son had organised back in London.

Owen Jones, the 31-year-old left-wing commentator and activist, also came to assume an important role in the campaign, often serving as warm-up man at Corbyn's packed-out rallies and explaining the candidate's thinking in thoughtful articles and blog posts. Richard Murphy, a 57-year-old Norfolk-based accountant and tax expert, provided Corbyn with much of his economic platform, a rejection of austerity including his controversial plans for a national investment bank and 'people's quantitative easing', which would become known as 'Corbynomics'. Other members of the team proved less helpful. Jon Lansman, whom Corbyn had known since their days working together on Tony Benn's 1981 deputy leadership campaign, was forced to lower his profile after being criticised for tweeting a link to a spoof website called Liz Kendall for Tory Leader.[281] Late in the campaign, Lansman would have a spectacular falling-out with Carmel Nolan.

In the second half of June, the group around Corbyn began pulling together a strategy and an organisational structure. They established two campaign headquarters, both provided by trade unions: one by the Transport and Salaried Staff Association (TSSA) at Walkden House, in Melton Street, near Euston Station, the other at Unite's head office, on Theobald's Road, Holborn. The first was Simon Fletcher's fiefdom, where he oversaw campaign strategy and the press operation, while Holborn was run by Kat Fletcher and staffed by volunteers, whom she dubbed the 'super vols',[282] under their banner of 'Jez We Can!', an echo of Barack Obama's 2008 presidential campaign slogan. As well as phone canvassing, the 'super vols' were tasked with jobs ranging from inputting data to responding to queries and stamping envelopes. The team came up with a slogan: 'Straightforward, honest politics'. Harry Fletcher says: 'For the first week, week and a half, it was putting together the infrastructure. We were just hoping for credibility.'

Two days after the contest proper began, on 14 July, Corbyn still didn't seem comfortable in his role as a leadership contender. He gave his first major interview of the campaign to *The Guardian*, spending most of it insisting that he 'didn't do personal', to the extent that the newspaper made it the headline. On being congratulated by interviewer Simon Hattenstone for getting on to the ballot, he responded 'warily': 'Thank you. I'm slightly surprised that we made it through, but there we are.' Corbyn took a long time to learn to associate himself with the concept of leadership. Even a month later, when he appeared on the BBC's *World at One*, he could not reply in the affirmative as he was repeatedly pressed by host Martha Kearney to say if he actually wanted to be Prime Minister.

But if it took Corbyn a while to recognise that he was on course for victory, one or two others spotted the potential for a left-wing insurgency right from the start. Harry Fletcher remembers walking through Portcullis House with Corbyn three days after nominations closed, and being stopped by Graham Allen, the thoughtful Labour MP for Nottingham North, who asked: 'Do you want to win this?' Corbyn replied: 'Of course, of course, of course.' 'If you do, you can win this,' Allen said. 'The other three are all in the Westminster bubble and you're not, and that can attract an awful lot of people.' Corbyn turned to Fletcher and said: 'Harry, do you think I can?' Fletcher responded: 'It's useless asking me, I only thought you'd get twenty-five nominations.' Jon Trickett says of the mood in the team at this time: 'Did we think he'd win at the beginning? I don't think we did. But I did think there would be an explosion of ideas and of membership and I did think that something dramatic was about to happen.'

If, at this stage, few in Corbyn's team really believed he could emerge as leader, certainly none of his rivals saw him as a genuine threat. John Lehal, who ran Andy Burnham's campaign, says there were no concerns about the left-winger joining the race, and that at the outset their team believed he would probably come third. 'At first we were pretty relaxed,' he says. 'We thought this would help frame the context about the "sensible candidate", and that was between Andy and Yvette. We knew that Liz would come last, but we felt it would be between Yvette and Andy.' Another Burnham team member adds:

> I would say there had been a legitimate welcome to him, in terms of being on the ballot, in terms of ideas, although privately I thought it's kind of insulting because you should only be on it if you want this job, and I don't care what he says now, he was making it clear early on that that wasn't why he was going for it.

John Woodcock, from Liz Kendall's team, says: 'We were thinking of it purely in terms of where did it drag the debate, where does it position the other candidates? I think our sense was that probably it would unsettle Andy, because I think he wasn't quite sure where to position himself at the beginning.'

By now, the Labour Party's exhausting and seemingly endless programme of hustings was well under way. It had begun even before the close of nominations at the start of June and would continue through July, leaving all the candidates drained and exhausted. Although there had been a private PLP hustings in Westminster, and two trade union events, including the one held by the GMB in Dublin, the first opportunity most members of the public had to eye up the contenders was on 17 June, when the BBC's *Newsnight* programme held a live hustings from Nuneaton, in Warwickshire, the seat Labour had needed – and failed – to capture in order to form a government. Hosted by Laura Kuenssberg, what followed would come as a surprise to many. As the right-wing *Daily Telegraph* put it under a headline reading: 'Jeremy Corbyn wows audience with left-wing agenda', he was the stand-out performer. The *Telegraph* said:

> Far-left MP Jeremy Corbyn has emerged the clear winner in Labour's
> first major leadership hustings as the party's last-minute drive to get
> him onto the ticket appeared to backfire. The veteran socialist won
> repeated cheers from the audience as he called for an anti-austerity
> economic policy and railed against Tony Blair and the 'illegal war' in
> Iraq as more centrist candidates struggled to connect.

Newsnight confirmed what the rival teams had already become aware of in the earlier hustings: that Corbyn's unorthodox views played well with an audience that seemed jaded and uninspired by his younger, New Labour rivals. Katie Myler, Andy Burnham's head of communications, says:

The first televised hustings was in a church in Nuneaton, a bloody freezing church, with Laura K, and we saw that night Jeremy getting cheered every time he talked about Iraq and Blair. And that continued. He didn't even have to say anything of substance to get that kind of riotous response.

To those on the left, Corbyn came across to audiences from the start as a breath of fresh air, while his rivals seemed stale. One supporter says: 'He was different. The other three looked as though they were using the same language and demeanour. They were trying to protect a decaying political culture.' A source who was working at Labour HQ at the time of the contest adds:

It was tough for the other teams, because nobody saw it coming. Once Jeremy was on the ballot paper and he just took off, the other candidates were just so uninspiring. Andy and Yvette kind of amalgamated to be the establishment figures. There was nothing between them. Yvette's first big message was all about technology and Andy was all about 'I had never been to Westminster before and I'm an outsider' and all this stuff. No, that's clearly not what's capturing the imagination of people. You could see quite early on there was such momentum behind Corbyn, it was just a force bigger than anything.

After the *Newsnight* hustings, Corbyn's odds were shortened to 12–1, still in last place but catching up.

While Liz Kendall's team felt the audience's response was to be expected, both Burnham and Yvette Cooper's camps found it unnerving. John Woodcock says:

I don't think we saw that as particularly remarkable. We saw that as the general predictable sense that it tends to be activists that are more to the left that will make the effort to come to those hustings whereas the members that tend to be closer to the centre, that's not the way they chose to spend their free time.

One member of Burnham's campaign admits that a decision was taken to counteract Corbyn's positive reception by returning once again to the left. 'Ultimately it did push Andy to the left,' the source says.

We were accused of flip-flopping and some of that was a very valid criticism levelled at the campaign. There was a tendency to think, if we're the people trying to win Jeremy's supporters then we can't attack Jeremy, we're going to have to be seen to be supporting a lot of what he's been saying.

While Corbyn's rivals desperately tried to figure out how to handle him, his own team still felt that they were not just outsiders but almost upstarts, with little idea of what they had taken on, compared to what they saw as the professionalism of their rivals. On Saturday 27 June, while Corbyn, Seb and Harry Fletcher were on a train to Birmingham to attend yet another hustings, they spotted Yvette Cooper and her team further along the carriage. As the train pulled into Birmingham Station, Corbyn asked if they needed to get a taxi. Fletcher recalls:

I said: 'No idea, do you know, Seb?' But Seb didn't know either. We had no idea where we were going or what we were doing because there was no diary secretary, no one looking after the itinerary. I said I would ask Yvette – I had seen her a few days earlier at the school our kids go to at an event for people taking their GCSEs – and they said: 'No, she'll think we're incompetent.'

Privately, in the run-up to the Birmingham hustings, Corbyn began to tell his team that he was having doubts about his candidacy, and seriously considered withdrawing from the race. He did not enjoy the early stages of the contest, feeling exposed and uncertain of how to deal with the spotlight after so many years in relative obscurity. He appeared diffident in interviews and was noticeably less keyed-up than his rivals during the early hustings. Ironically, Corbyn's equivocation may well have helped woo early supporters. Many found his almost relaxed manner refreshing in an age when most politicians weigh every word so carefully that they often lose sight of their beliefs. The sense that he would not be devastated if he lost contrasted well with the almost over-wrought impression given at times by Burnham, and the stilted, buttoned-up aura around Cooper. Jon Trickett says: 'He's perfectly happy to go back to his allotment if he loses. He's very attractive. He's not power-hungry.'

Meanwhile, during this early stage of the campaign, both Burnham and Cooper had insecurities of their own. Bruised by a general election in which her husband, Ed Balls, had lost his seat, Cooper's team now admits she was slow to get off the ground. Vernon Coaker, her campaign manager, says:

Most people accept that our campaign got going a bit late. There was a big battle to establish ourselves. There was a sense of: 'What are you, Yvette? What do you stand for? You're everybody's second preference, aren't you?' We spent a lot of time trying to say, no, we're not. But that took a long while before we got to a point were we said … we're a radical, exciting alternative.

Cooper herself has said: 'That first month, every party meeting I felt I needed to lift people up and lift myself up after the disappointment of losing the election. To be honest, it is not part of my style to stand in front of these big banners with my face on.'[283]

A senior member of Burnham's campaign feels that he too was slow to prepare for the contest:

> I'm very clear in my mind that Liz and Yvette were planning these campaigns for months, in terms of infrastructure and getting ready, and so on and so forth. Whereas Andy, he may have done some of the thinking and developed as a politician, been on a bit more of a journey, but in terms of the organisation it was hopeless.

One of the party's most senior staffers at the time describes watching the 'mainstream' candidates Yvette Cooper and Andy Burnham with despair as, in contrast to the dynamism of Corbyn's campaign, they came across as tired and flat. The staffer says:

> Bearing in mind that Andy was the front-runner, and had five years to prepare for his campaign, and Jeremy Corbyn had five minutes, he came up with a much more inspiring campaign than Yvette and Andy did. Andy was just all over the place. Andy flip-flopped left, right and centre, Andy was just blowing whichever way the wind was going.

Despite his misgivings about his candidacy, it was at the Birmingham hustings that Corbyn and his team first began to get a sense that he might be on course for victory. Harry Fletcher says:

> The other teams there were professional, with stalls set up and impressive campaign material. Our team just had a bundle of leaflets which

Seb had taken up in his bag, which we began handing out. After a while we stopped doing that and just listened [to the hustings]. And he was winning every argument. Liz got booed.

After the Birmingham event, the Corbyns and Fletcher returned to London, where they were due to join the Gay Pride march, which was already under way. As they got off the Tube at Oxford Circus and emerged into the street, they spotted a group of familiar faces. 'By chance we saw a banner coming around the corner reading: "Gays and lesbians support the miners",' Fletcher says.

Jeremy spotted people he knew from campaigns of the 1980s. Then a 'Jeremy for Leader' banner came along. He had been due to go straight to the platform, but he decided to take part in the march. As we marched, on twenty, thirty occasions there were spontaneous cheers as he went past. I was walking with Jeremy and Seb and we were so impressed. We said: 'This is phenomenal. There is something phenomenal here that he is going to capture.' It was at that moment that we thought there is something incredible going on here. We got to Trafalgar Square and it kept happening again and again. Jeremy kept trying to get through to make his speech and he kept getting mobbed.

Corbyn went on to Brighton a few days later, where the same thing happened: he dominated the hustings and found himself surrounded by supporters eager to join the campaign. The team now came up with a clever idea: they decided to hold rallies immediately after each hustings, events which quickly turned into packed fan-fests. The band of Corbyn supporters who had been so active on social media, first to get him to stand as a candidate of the left and then by pestering MPs into nominating him, now began to hold 'Twitter storms' to promote his candidacy, agreeing a time at which they would all, simultaneously, send out messages praising him, to get their man trending on Twitter.

The other teams watched on, their bemusement turning to dismay as volunteers working their phone banks began to report a similarly warm response to Corbyn, with those canvassed for support invariably saying they were planning to vote for the left-winger. Roger Baker, who was working for Yvette Cooper, says:

> I don't think anyone was of the opinion: 'This is an utter disaster.' But then almost immediately, we started to get stuff on the phone: 'I think it's good that there's something to vote for on the left', 'I might give you second [preference vote]', 'I'm going to do Corbyn and give you second'. There was a lot of that and that came through almost immediately. And so even then [we] were like: 'Uh oh, what's going on here?'

Even though by the end of June they had begun to realise that Corbyn was a serious contender, Andy Burnham's team was slower to spot the danger. John Lehal says:

> Actually when Jeremy started being seen as a serious candidate, our view was, as a campaign, 'Oh, actually that's not unhelpful because we'll no longer be seen as the left candidate and it will be Andy and Yvette who will be in the centre ground.' So you would have Jeremy at one end of the spectrum, Liz at the other end, and then these guys would be fighting it out. We just had a sense that that's what the race would come down to, that it would be Andy versus Yvette.

Even the growing enthusiasm for Corbyn at the hustings did not panic

Burnham. 'What we were noticing was at the hustings, the support for Jeremy was increasing,' Lehal says. 'But again you convince yourself that's not important, because only 5,000 people are going to go to the official hustings across the country. Jeremy's not going to win, so the audience might agree with him but it doesn't matter.'

By now, the first nominations from constituency Labour parties were beginning to come through. To the surprise of many, Corbyn immediately took a clear lead. As the days passed and Corbyn remained consistently ahead in CLP nominations, with Burnham usually a distant second and occasionally overtaken by Cooper, it became clear that Liz Kendall enjoyed virtually no support in the country at large. The first days of the campaign in mid-May had been her high water mark; by the end of June, none of her rivals would view her as a serious threat. Although the CLP nominations counted for nothing in the eventual voting tally, they were a clear guide to how the grassroots party was feeling. It was yet another early hint to the contest's outcome, but even now, with the signs becoming clearer, it seemed that few could quite believe that the narrative of the left-wing candidate doomed to defeat would not play out again.

Andy Burnham's team, for one, believed that as the membership was not distributed evenly, with declarations by smaller CLPs with few members having the same effect as those from larger, mass membership local parties, they were a poor guide to the state of play. John Lehal says:

> When the first CLP nominations were coming through and Jeremy did do well, even then we didn't take the threat seriously, we were relaxed about it. We thought, 'These are constituency delegates in small moribund CLPs; North Devon will never have a Labour MP and if their constituency party is going to nominate Jeremy, fine, they've only got a handful of members who turn up at meetings, we've got all these

> other places that will hopefully go for us.' [It was:] 'Oh shit, OK, but
> don't worry, these are members on the left of the party, and there-
> fore let's not worry too much about that.' We were thinking, 'It's rank
> and file, ordinary party members that are going to decide this race.'

One senior member of Labour Party staff at the time who did pay attention to the CLP nominations says, however, 'I went to my own CLP
and remember thinking, "Yup, this is going to happen." There was such
a momentum.'

Having had a hesitant start, as June drew to a close it was gradually
dawning on Corbyn's team that they might have something to get excited
about. But they remained cautious. When Ben Soffa, the TSSA's head of
digital operations who was seconded to the team (and is the partner of the
new MP Cat Smith) produced data that suggested their candidate was well
in the lead with members, and performing particularly well with the £3
registered supporters, they couldn't quite bring themselves to trust what
they were hearing.[284] Soffa is credited with two innovations that proved
invaluable: an app that allowed volunteers to make calls from home while
still plugged into the system and able to input data, and a device embed-
ded on Corbyn's website that enabled users to click through to sign up as
registered supporters. By doing so, the team ensured that those interested
in Corbyn could easily sign up to vote for him. The other three camps were
dismayed at their own failure to do the same.

As the contest entered its second month, Corbyn set off on his 'Last of
the Summer Wine tour'. But while the candidate may have been old enough
to claim his pension, those turning up to listen to him in ever increasing
numbers were often young, politically aware and excited by this most unorthodox of politicians. The media dubbed them 'Corbynistas'. Carmel Nolan
has since said that it was at a rally at Birkenhead Town Hall in Merseyside

on 9 July that it first struck her that Corbyn was going to win.[285] Of the 350 people who came to hear him speak, 100 signed up to become volunteers and fifty said they would be joining the Labour Party, overwhelmingly in order to vote for Corbyn. By the end of the campaign, more than 16,000 people would have turned out to volunteer on Corbyn's behalf, an incredible number in an era when political activism had become unfashionable. They ranged from a thirteen-year-old schoolboy to a pensioner of ninety-two.[286]

Shortly before the Birkenhead rally, on 5 July, Corbyn found himself the beneficiary of one of the game-changing moments in the campaign, when first the powerful Unite union and then Unison came out for him. With Simon Fletcher easing the way, many of the country's other major trade unions, including the Communication Workers Union, the RMT, ASLEF, the Fire Brigades Union (FBU) and the Bakers, Food and Allied Workers Union, would go on to back him. Corbyn's odds were tightened again, now standing at 8–1. A spokesman for Betfred speculated that Corbyn had captured a wider zeitgeist, comparing his campaign to the Syriza anti-austerity movement in Greece: 'The events in Greece and the moving to the left-wing side of things there has made people here get behind Corbyn.'[287]

The background to the unions' decision was yet another potential error by Andy Burnham. At the start of the contest, in late May, before Corbyn had even declared and when it was still assumed that Burnham himself would be running as the candidate of the left, he announced that he would not accept trade union money to fund his campaign. Fearful that he was being compared with Ed Miliband, who had, after all, just lost the election, the move was designed to portray Burnham as his own man. Unlike the out-going leader, he would not be dogged by the suggestion that he was in hock to the unions. Given that Burnham had spent the previous few years courting the unions, and with most of the major union leaders assuming they were going to give him their endorsement as well as their cash, the announcement felt like 'a slap in the face', in the words of one ex-trade unionist. A former senior Labour aide who has worked closely with the unions believes that Burnham's error was compounded by the impression that the announcement was rushed out on the spur of the moment, rather than being a position he had properly thought through. It also suggested that Burnham was not wholehearted in his conversion to left-wing politics, aggravating the perception he was a 'flip-flopper'. The aide says:

> The trade union leadership was furious at Andy saying he wouldn't take their money. The implication was that it was dirty. Len McCluskey [the head of Unite] was especially furious. Sending it out in a half-assed press release to make a cheap point just showed it was not a considered view.

By turning his back on the unions' financial support, Burnham left the door wide open for Corbyn to snap them up. This would have huge repercussions, not just because of the trade union members who would follow their leadership's example by voting for Corbyn, but because of the might of the organisational capacity the unions could bring to bear. At Corbyn's two union-provided headquarters, there were computers and iPads and secretarial assistance. The other candidates could only look with envy at the vast phone banks his team was able to command. There were also the platforms the unions could offer. When, a week after the Unite and GMB endorsements, the candidates travelled north for the annual Durham Miners' Gala, an important and symbolic event for the Labour movement, Corbyn was the only one invited to address the crowd. The other contenders were forced to watch in silence as he spoke about inequality, the disgrace of people sleeping on the streets in a wealthy country, the scandal of children in inadequate homes.

John Lehal insists, however, that it was right for Burnham to have turned down the unions' cash. He says: 'Had he won it would have meant he wouldn't have been labelled the union candidate. Not taking the funding I don't think damaged the campaign.' Unite's Len McCluskey disagrees, saying of Burnham's decision: 'The reality is he probably made a mistake because he did not seize the moment to run as an alternative.'[288] David Lammy also thinks that Burnham's actions changed the course of the campaign. He says: 'The general view was because Andy had the unions, [Corbyn's] was a very fringe candidacy. Having said that, Andy then kicked off his campaign almost rebuffing the unions, and opened up a space I guess, in hindsight.' Burnham himself believes he did not blunder. He has said:

> I said at the beginning I didn't want it and that caused me a problem. But the idea was it would make me stronger if I win it without their support. And I think that is a really important thing for the party, actually, because Ed … he looked like he was the puppet of the unions at times.[289]

Rejecting the trade unions' money was yet another of the many mistakes Andy Burnham would make during the 2015 leadership campaign. And now he would commit the error that he believes lost him the leadership to Corbyn.

CHAPTER EIGHTEEN

WELFARE
REFORM BILL

HARRIET HARMAN SAT on a cosy armchair on the set of the BBC's *Sunday Politics* show and prepared to give her party's verdict on the government's planned welfare cuts. It was 12 July 2015, and Harman was two months into her second stint as acting leader, having played the same role when Gordon Brown stepped down following the 2010 general election. After that long summer in which the Miliband brothers had duked it out for the leadership, Harman had been criticised for letting the party drift. Specifically, she was blamed for what was perceived as a fatal error in allowing the Conservative-led coalition to pin the blame for the 2008 financial crisis and the austerity measures that followed on Labour. Harman was determined not to make the same mistake again. Rather than sitting back and waiting for the new leader to emerge, she would provide strong and effective stewardship through the campaign. What Harman would now say to the *Sunday Politics*' million or so viewers, some have claimed, would have a more profound effect on her party than anything she had said and done in her distinguished, 28-year career in Parliament, including many years' service in the Cabinet and shadow Cabinet, eight years as deputy leader and decades as one of the country's leading equalities campaigners.

Four days earlier, in what he described as an 'emergency' Budget drawn up following the Conservatives' shock victory in the general election, Chancellor George Osborne had set out plans to reduce the welfare budget by £12 billion. This was to be achieved, in part, by capping benefits at £20,000 per household (£23,000 in London) and by limiting payments to families, who would now be able to claim for no more than two children. A Welfare Reform Bill would be put before the Commons within weeks. Some have since suggested that Osborne's rush to legislate was designed as a trap for a leaderless Labour Party still reeling from the May election defeat. If it was, it was one Harman now rushed into head first.

Determined to challenge the perception that Labour was not to be trusted on the economy, Harman told *Sunday Politics'* host Andrew Neil:

> We won't oppose the Welfare Bill, we won't oppose the household benefit cap. [We won't oppose] what they brought forward in relation to restricting benefits and tax credits for people with three or more children … We've got to recognise why the Tories are in government and not us, not because [voters] love the Tories but because they didn't trust us on the economy and on benefits.

Harman went on to say that during her travels round the country, she had repeatedly encountered 'hard-working' mothers who would have loved to have more children but could not afford them – and resented people who were helped to support large families with benefits. When asked by Neil if the leadership contenders knew of and were happy with her stance, Harman said: 'I'm the Leader of the Opposition. There is going to be the Welfare Bill and there will be votes in Parliament. I am stating the position that the Labour Party will be taking on that.'

It would later transpire that three out of the four leadership candidates did not necessarily share Harman's view that Labour should support the government on welfare reform. At a meeting on 7 July, the day before the Budget, Harman had told the shadow Cabinet of her strong belief that the party could not be seen to be putting forward 'blanket opposition' to the government, particularly in the area of benefits, which she felt had helped lose them the election. When Andy Burnham had attempted to suggest that Labour should be wary of following the Conservatives' lead on welfare, Harman is said to have slapped him down, snapping: 'You may have noticed we lost the election.'[290] 'She was unspeakably rude to him,' one member of the shadow Cabinet was quoted as saying afterwards.[291] Yvette Cooper is also said to have expressed private doubts about the wisdom of following the government's lead.[292]

Sources close to Harman deny she over-reached in speaking as she did on the welfare cuts. One says:

> She absolutely damn well had the right to do that. She was Leader of the Labour Party at that time. She's the person who has to get up and do Prime Minister's Questions, she's the person who has to go head to head with Cameron. Harriet ... she didn't need to do this, it was put on her by George Osborne, who is a great tactician, knew the Labour Party was in turmoil, and the guy is an absolute genius, and like a bunch of idiots we all acted in exactly the way he wanted us to react. Harriet was ... being incredibly altruistic, like she always is with the party. Her view was it was better for her to take the hit as the interim leader and at least it would clear the pitch for the new leader, whoever he or she was, to make a new decision of whether they wanted to carry on that path.

As Harman was speaking on the *Sunday Politics* show at noon on Sunday 12 July, the candidates were in the midst of yet another hustings, this time in Newcastle. Their teams were soon made aware of what she had said when their Twitter feeds lit up with outrage from Labour members appalled at the suggestion that the parliamentary party would be going along with the benefit caps. All four candidates were taken aback by what Harman had said. But for Andy Burnham in particular, it created serious problems. He had spent the first weeks of the race 'flip-flopping' between framing himself as the candidate of the left and presenting himself as the 'serious' contender who had launched his campaign at Ernst and Young. The decision whether or not to support Osborne's cuts crystallised the dilemma for him: where did he stand? Still at this stage expecting to win the contest, Burnham was determined he would go on to lead a united team and could not, therefore, comfortably defy Harman as acting leader by rebelling, a move that would have entailed him resigning from the shadow Cabinet. Aware of Corbyn's growing appeal, he was also concerned that in a contest that might well come down to second preferences, it could be unwise to offend left-wingers who might be planning to make him their no. 2 choice.

Some in Burnham's team believe that in the space of one ten-minute television interview, Harman handed the leadership to Jeremy Corbyn. John Lehal, his campaign manager, says:

> It was the Welfare Bill that changed the race. Absolutely. It was the one moment in the race we can point to when suddenly we thought, 'This is now going to start slipping.' It was Harriet going on to the Sunday morning sofas and announcing policy without consulting the campaigns. Having just lost an election where immigration and welfare were two of the big issues, I can understand why she felt she had to

do it, but I just feel she should have consulted the leadership teams and there could have been a deal done.

After Harman dropped her *Sunday Politics* bombshell into the leadership contest, Burnham's rivals were relatively clear where they stood. Corbyn, the only contender not in the shadow Cabinet, would do what he always did when told by the whips to vote in a way he disagreed with: he would rebel. At the other end of the spectrum, Liz Kendall would not oppose the cap, believing, with Harman, that to do so would send the wrong message to the electorate. Like Burnham, Yvette Cooper, fighting a campaign from the centre, had misgivings about the Welfare Bill, but was relatively content to be guided by Harman, whom she was close to, seeing the older woman as something of a mentor. This could potentially have placed Cooper in as difficult a position as Burnham, but her team believe she played the situation far better than her New Labour rival. While Cooper deliberately kept a low profile through the entire Welfare Reform Bill saga, Burnham now went off on a very public, Hamlet-esque wrestle with his conscience over whether or not to defy Harman and rebel.

John Lehal makes clear that Burnham was on the horns of a dilemma. He says:

> He's thinking, 'Now, do I lead this rebellion, walk out of the shadow Cabinet?' It's easy to resign and say, 'I don't support this, I've got to do what's right, this is a measure that's going to have a very punitive effect on people in poverty, people with families, so I've got to do the right thing here' … versus does he stay in and therefore have the respect of the shadow Cabinet and the loyalty he wants as Leader of the Opposition? And at this point he's still thinking he's going to be the Leader of the Opposition in mid-September. And it is genuine when he says

he is a party man who has been very loyal to the party, who always believes in arguing internally.

In the hours after Harman's *Sunday Politics* appearance, Burnham's campaign team felt compelled to act. They issued a press release and made their man available for sound bites for the main news channels. But while he addressed some of the detailed concerns he had over the Welfare Reform Bill, Burnham failed to nail his colours to the mast over whether or not he would rebel. 'We were dancing on the head of a pin,' one member of his team admits. Shortly afterwards, Corbyn issued his own response to Harman: 'I am not willing to vote for policies that will push more children into poverty,' he said. 'Families are suffering enough. We shouldn't play the government's political games with the welfare system if children are at stake.'[293] The contrast between his high-minded lack of equivocation and Burnham's dithering could not have been more stark.

Over the next twenty-four hours, Burnham and his team agonised over what to do next. On Tuesday 14 July, he was due to appear at a lunch with the Press Gallery (the group of parliamentary reporters based in the House of Commons). Speakers at these lunches, traditionally high-jinks affairs, are expected to give an amusing speech packed with self-deprecation and jokes. Cooper and Kendall had already appeared before the Press Gallery and had acquitted themselves well. (Corbyn simply skipped the event.) John Lehal says:

> On the Monday he was really wrestling with what to do. We were saying, 'Hang on, you've got this big thing with the Press Gallery, you've got to get your jokes ready,' and he's spending his time worrying what he should do on the Welfare Bill. So he recognised very early on that it could be potentially very, very difficult and damaging for him.

All through Monday and into Tuesday morning, Burnham's team tried to get him to focus on his Press Gallery speech, but he kept coming back to welfare reform. Finally, he decided to bring the two together. Leaving the press wondering where the jokes had gone, Burnham used his speech to announce that he would demand the shadow Cabinet introduce a 'reasoned amendment', a technical motion that allows the Opposition to set out the reasons they oppose a Bill. If the term meant little to most of the seasoned political reporters at the Press Gallery lunch, it would prove utterly meaningless to the wider public. Burnham did not say, but implied, that if the shadow Cabinet did not accept the amendment, he would quit.

Yvette Cooper's team felt that Burnham was committing an error by making his arguments over the Welfare Bill so publicly. A source close to Cooper says:

> Andy was showboating on this and then didn't follow through, so he shot himself in the head. We were doing absolutely the same argument but doing it behind closed doors. We felt: 'We've got to get it sorted and we don't want to do it publicly because it makes it harder to get it sorted.' But also because there's no way Yvette Cooper would be briefing against Harriet Harman.

Burnham went straight from the Press Gallery to the shadow Cabinet, where an ugly scene played out. To his irritation, Harman invited Cooper to speak first, giving his rival the opportunity to suggest the tabling of a reasoned amendment before he could. Some on Burnham's team would later accuse Harman of trying to tip the contest in Cooper's favour. 'Harriet was obviously supporting Yvette,' believes one senior member. In response, Cooper's camp point out that by putting both centrist candidates in a difficult position, Harman's stance on welfare helped no one but Corbyn. A source close to Cooper says:

If Andy or Yvette had resigned, it would have made them unelectable in the country, I think. So a situation was being created that was pushing down a route that the one who won internally was going to lose in the country, and primarily the only beneficiary was going to be the most unelectable in the country: Jeremy.

Sources close to Harman deny both that she was favouring Cooper and that she helped Corbyn to victory by placing the moderate candidates in an impossible situation. 'It wasn't a question of helping Corbyn or not,' one says. 'As the adjudicator of the rules, it wasn't really for her to say, "I'm not going to make this calculation because it could affect the leadership competition." She had to make a decision based on what was the best public policy position for the Labour Party.'

When Burnham finally spoke at shadow Cabinet, he argued that if the reasoned amendment was unsuccessful, which was likely given the Conservatives now enjoyed a Commons majority, the party should vote against the Welfare Bill. He was backed only by Michael Dugher and Lord Falconer, both members of his campaign team, with most of those present taking Harman's line: that they should support the Bill. Harman now pointed out that at the weekly meeting of the PLP, most MPs had also urged her not to oppose the Bill. Burnham and Cooper continued to push for a reasoned amendment. With the shadow Cabinet hopelessly split, an uneasy compromise was agreed. The reasoned amendment was tabled, but because of the tight parliamentary timetable, it was rushed, leaving no one happy with the wording. 'Not only did we end up with a fudge, we ended up with a crap fudge,' John Lehal says.

On the night of 20 July, six days after the shadow Cabinet meeting, the Welfare Reform Bill came before the Commons and, as expected, the reasoned amendment was rejected. Burnham and Cooper were back to square one: would they rebel against the acting Labour leader and vote against the by now hugely unpopular government plans to cap benefits? In the end, they decided on another compromise and, along with the rest of the shadow Cabinet, abstained. For the good it did them, they may as well have voted for it. 'It was meaningless,' Lehal admits of the reasoned amendment and abstention. 'And that was one of the things we were aware of. You just can't sell that.' Corbyn, along with forty-six other Labour MPs, voted against the Bill, the only leadership candidate to do so.

Harman's appearance on the *Sunday Politics* show and the spirited argument she had given for not opposing the welfare cuts now seemed a distant memory. Many, both inside and outside Westminster, were furious at Labour for failing to offer proper opposition to the Bill. And the target of their rage, unfairly or not, was Andy Burnham. One member of his team says: 'It was a mess. But instead of what would normally happen with the PLP, which was to slag off Harriet, they slagged off Andy, who was at that stage still the front-runner.'

Why did Burnham find himself vilified, when Cooper emerged from the vote relatively unscathed? John Lehal suggests that Burnham's high-profile agonising over the Bill and his status as the race's favourite meant it was he who suffered the most. 'Because he always came out quite publicly on this stuff, he did raise his head above the parapet,' Lehal says.

> I think he was in the line of fire because he'd made a bigger deal out of it. Saying you're going to fight for it in the shadow Cabinet, and then being unsuccessful, and us still ending up in a position where it's opposition but it's a reasoned amendment made us a target. [Cooper's] campaign was always going to be: 'Keep my head down, don't offend anyone, play it safe, pick up second preferences.'

Another Burnham supporter adds: 'She [Cooper] got away with murder, and instead of the ire which would have normally been directed at Harriet, a lot of that was directed at Andy. Which meant he was damaged by that. That was a kind of turn in the road for him.'

Burnham's rivals agree with his team that the Welfare Bill proved fatal for him, but most believe it was a problem of his own creation. John Woodcock from the Liz Kendall campaign says:

> His credibility collapsed from that point onwards. There were a number of stories before about flip-floppery and facing both ways, but suddenly that became part of the narrative. Could he have won without it? Well, maybe. But it was entirely a product of his own making. It was utterly idiotic of him to march everyone up to the top of the hill. He made it a key test of whether you were true to Labour, left-wing principles. He was the one who put the press release out there: 'I'll be opposing this.' He made that the test; no one else did it. And then he failed it. Having done it, he should have just grasped the nettle and opposed it. It was one of a series of misjudgements and it was just, I'm afraid, in character with the whole way he did the campaign.

A former member of Ed Miliband's campaign staff agrees:

> For unions it was the money, for the grassroots it was the welfare vote that lost Andy the contest. But they come down to the same thing, which is that you can only make the mistakes that he made if you don't actually believe in anything. That was what was so different about Jeremy. He had a clear set of ideals and everything flowed from that. Andy spent his whole time trying to second-guess where to position

himself and that was because he had no underlying set of principles to work from. And ultimately that caught him out.

Almost as soon as the vote was over, and with Labour supporters vocal in their anger at what had transpired, Burnham's team realised with sickening clarity that his chances of winning the contest had diminished. John Lehal says:

> I feel that, after that, the momentum was just Jeremy's. He voted against, he did the right thing, party members were thinking: 'Well, hang on a minute, we've got a Labour opposition who are supporting a measure that's going to have a punitive effect on these people…' and that just became this head of steam that it was very difficult to overcome.

Cooper's camp, too, were aware immediately after the welfare vote that the contest had swung in Corbyn's direction. One member of her team says: 'Oh yeah. It was absolutely apparent from the debate you were getting here [in Westminster], it was absolutely apparent from what you were getting on the phones [when canvassing], it was clear that this was going to massively boost Jeremy.'

Burnham would spend the rest of the contest being dogged by his indecision over the Welfare Reform Bill, even finding himself heckled and booed on occasion at hustings. On his Andy 4 Leader Facebook page, under a post in which he attempted to explain his thinking in tabling the reasoned amendment and in abstaining on the Bill, one disbelieving supporter wrote: 'How on earth could you abstain??? Your role of opposition is to oppose the government!' It was among the kinder comments. The sense that Burnham was a 'flip-flopper' now took hold. Such was his desire to compensate for his actions that he drew ever closer to the left, from now on becoming, as one

MP told the *New Statesman*, effectively the 'prisoner of Corbyn'. Burnham himself believes that had he acted differently over the Welfare Reform Bill he might today be the Leader of the Labour Party. Towards the end of the campaign, he told the *New Statesman*:

> There's no flip-flop at all. If people are saying I should have resigned and split the party, I could have done, possibly I would have won this contest if I'd done that. But it wouldn't have been me, I've never put myself before the party, ever. I wasn't prepared to do it just to win this contest.

Others disagree that the Welfare Bill lost the contest for Burnham and Cooper. A source who held a senior position at Labour HQ at the time says:

> I can understand they're very bitterly disappointed by what happened, but blaming Harriet, when at that point Jeremy Corbyn had already started gathering a big head of steam… [is wrong.] The Welfare Bill is absolutely part of the story of the summer, it's part of the narrative, but the idea that that is the single cause of why they did so badly and Jeremy won… [is not right.] Jeremy won because of reasons and forces much bigger and deeper than the Welfare Bill. The truth is, and it was pretty devastating and disappointing for all of us, they lost because they didn't run inspiring campaigns.

Corbyn's principled stance on welfare reform would reap rewards not just in the leadership contest, but also following his election in September 2015. Ten weeks later, with Labour now officially staunchly opposed to the tax credit cuts, Chancellor George Osborne was forced to reverse his plan, a major coup for Corbyn and the first big win over the government of his leadership.

Following the welfare vote, any remaining doubts the candidates may have had that Corbyn was now the clear favourite to win the race were shattered when, on 22 July, the first public opinion poll of the campaign was published by YouGov.[294] Its findings sent a shockwave through Westminster. Not only did Corbyn have a lead, it was a huge lead: 43 per cent compared to 26 for Burnham, with Cooper on 20 per cent and Kendall 11. Once second and third preferences were redistributed the poll suggested that Corbyn would triumph over Burnham in the final run-off by 53 per cent to 47. He was on course for victory.

CHAPTER NINETEEN

FAVOURITE

'LABOUR WAR AS Corbyn closes in on victory', read the headline in *The Times* as it reported the findings of the first public opinion poll of the 2015 leadership contest. They were words that neither Jeremy Corbyn nor his three rivals had expected ever to read when he entered the race six weeks earlier. Now he was the man to beat. Yet, although they were alarmed by what appeared to be taking place, Corbyn's fellow contenders were determined not to give up. While the numbers appeared unequivo-cal (and repeated the findings of a largely overlooked poll published in the *New Statesman* a day earlier) there was still time for them to close the gap. There were also doubts about the accuracy of the poll, given the difficulty in identifying the electorate in a rolling contest in which registered supporters were still being signed up. There was the recent chastening experience too of the general election, in which none of the main pollsters had predicted a Conservative majority. While YouGov had got the last Labour leader-ship contest spot on in 2010, its own president, Peter Kellner, now urged caution in interpreting its latest findings, saying: 'Our poll is like a grainy photograph of the Grand National with half the race still to run: we have

a broad sense of the state of play but cannot be sure of the eventual winner.' The bookmakers responded with caution, making Corbyn the joint
second favourite with Yvette Cooper at 5–2. Andy Burnham remained in
pole position, with Liz Kendall the 20–1 outsider.

Corbyn also treated YouGov's findings with a pinch of salt, saying: 'We're
not commenting on polls, because I'm not quite sure how that poll was done,
because unless YouGov were given access to all Labour Party members' and
supporters' phone numbers or emails, which I would be surprised if they
had been, it's unclear how that poll was conducted.'[295] Liz Kendall's team,
however, was all too aware that the YouGov poll was not a rogue result –
even though they were careful not to say so in public. Its findings almost
exactly tallied with a private poll they had carried out a week earlier. John
Woodcock of Kendall's campaign team says:

> The thunderbolt for us was a private poll we got that showed him way,
> way out in the lead. We thought it was accurate, and that meant we were
> really up against it. Our sense was that if that poll was made public or
> something similar was to come out – e.g. what transpired [the YouGov
> poll] – it would completely skew the dynamic of the campaign and it
> would become all about Jeremy Corbyn, whether Jeremy Corbyn is
> going to win, and how to stop Jeremy Corbyn. And indeed that was true.

Kendall herself identifies the YouGov poll as the moment she realised
that Corbyn was going to win. 'It was that initial poll in *The Times* when I
thought, "Well, that's pretty strong,"' she has said. 'But also you could see
in the hustings, right from the start, you could see the kind of reactions
Jeremy was getting.'[296]

Kendall was not the only one alarmed at the prospect of victory for Corbyn. On the same day *The Times* published the YouGov poll, on 22 July,

the man he had spent so many years opposing, most obviously over the Iraq War, entered the fray. Appearing at a conference organised by the Progress think-tank to mark the twenty-first anniversary of his election as Labour leader, Tony Blair made an impassioned plea for the party's electorate not to squander his legacy by abandoning New Labour and returning to their 'comfort zone'. Given the wariness most former leaders of all parties feel about discussing the merits of individual candidates in a leadership contest, Blair's intervention was already remarkable. What he said next was like pouring oil on a roaring fire. Asked if he would support Corbyn if he was elected leader, Blair said: 'I'm not sure that'll actually happen. It's not about an individual, it's about a platform that, in the end, wouldn't work for the country.' Almost as a throwaway, he added: 'When people say, "My heart says I should be with that politics," well, get a transplant.'

Blair's 'heart transplant' remarks proved incendiary for an electorate that had long ago tired of New Labour and had grown increasingly mistrustful of its figurehead. Corbyn refused to respond, as ever retreating to his position that he 'didn't do personal'. But others did so on his behalf. A week later, when the Communication Workers Union, with its 200,000 members, came out for Corbyn, general secretary Dave Ward said as he announced the endorsement: 'There is a virus within the Labour Party and Jeremy Corbyn is the antidote. The grip of the Blairites and individuals like Peter Mandelson must now be loosened once and for all.'[297] John Prescott, who served as Blair's deputy for his entire thirteen years as leader, also criticised his former boss, saying that it was the decision to invade Iraq that had eroded Labour's support. 'To use that kind of language is just abuse,' he added. 'The Labour Party is about the heart as well as the head. To suggest that somebody should have a transplant if they are making decisions by the heart is totally unacceptable.'[298]

The impact of Blair's intervention on Corbyn's campaign was felt immediately, as thousands scrambled to defy the former leader by signing up.

One Corbyn volunteer, Will Armston-Sheret, was reported as saying: 'We noticed a particular spike in donations after Tony Blair came out against the campaign. The bad publicity plays into our hands. It shows that negative campaigning just doesn't work.'[299] Jon Trickett says: 'All that stuff about if your heart's with Jeremy you need a heart transplant. Hang on. There are hundreds of thousands of people who think [like Corbyn]. Was that a very wise thing to do? Blair of all people. He almost delivered the leadership election for him.' Clive Lewis, one of the new left-wing MPs helping with Corbyn's campaign, has said: 'It was just the dignity of it. I think many people thought Tony had lowered himself, and from there the campaign went just like that – *whoosh*. It was massive.'[300]

Two days after the YouGov poll and Blair's intervention, Corbyn secured his 100th CLP nomination by winning the backing of Leeds East. Like Liz Kendall, Yvette Cooper sensed that the poll and Corbyn's lead in CLP nominations spelt danger. Her campaign manager Vernon Coaker says: 'I think we had all woken up to the fact that he was out there, his meetings were attracting loads of people, [CLP] nominations had gone well for him, all of those things.' Another member of the team, Roger Baker, adds: 'Do I think he will get 60 per cent at this point? No. Do I think he would win? I thought it became rather than a possibility almost a probability, but not a certainty by any way shape or form.'

At the end of July, Cooper disappeared to America for a camping holiday with her family. The previous month, while they were waiting in the green room for the Local Government Association hustings to begin, Corbyn had suggested to Cooper and Andy Burnham, who both have young children, that all the candidates take two weeks away from the campaign trail, to give them time with their families. Kendall had agreed to the plan. There was mild irritation among the camps when Burnham now failed to abide by the agreement, which all admit was only tentative. In fact, Burnham had simply got his dates wrong, and went away to Spain in August. When it became apparent that he was continuing to campaign during their truce period, Kendall and Corbyn kept going too.

In the days after the welfare vote, it had become all too apparent to Burnham's team that their campaign had been damaged. Katie Myler, his press secretary, says: 'After that it really did start to turn. I went from lots of calls going on about "It's your guy, it's your fella, he always looks good at things, it's yours to lose"... it went from that to "OK, we've now got to get it back".' A few days after Cooper's departure, a private poll was leaked to the *Daily Mirror* that not only confirmed Corbyn's status as the front-runner but suggested that Burnham had actually fallen to third place, behind Cooper. For the first time, on 29 July, the bookmakers established Corbyn as favourite, at 11–8. 'Jeremy Corbyn is the favourite and this gamble has resulted in the biggest price fall in political betting history,' William Hill spokesman Rupert Adams said.

In a desperate bid to retrieve the situation, Burnham's team now took a calculated decision to move towards the left, to try to capitalise on the wave of enthusiasm for Corbyn. When he came to launch his manifesto on 6 August, Burnham changed the priorities of some of his key policies, making his support for the renationalisation of the railways, which had been somewhat buried, one of his five key 'pledges'. Although Corbyn was now the race favourite, the team calculated that he could not win under the alternative vote system under which the contest was being run, because he was unlikely to pick up the second preferences of people voting for Burnham, Cooper or Kendall, and therefore would never be able to reach the required level of 50 per cent. John Lehal, Burnham's campaign manager, says:

> Earlier in the race we thought he was going to come third, and then
> he started to build up that head of steam and we thought this might

become interesting. But we thought his only game plan was to get over 50 per cent in the first round, because if he didn't, all the second preferences would go elsewhere. We thought Jeremy wouldn't be able to make it past the 50 per cent mark, and that's why we thought we should be OK even if we come second, as long as we're in that final run-off.

With a new aim of coming second in the first round, Burnham's team felt that with Cooper on holiday they had once again become the main rival to Corbyn. Then they noticed they had begun to leak volunteers to the left-winger. Even then, they did not hit the panic button. John Lehal says:

> We went into August thinking, this has been bad, we've felt it, we've taken a hit, but we're OK. We felt it in terms of the volunteers who were moving over to Jeremy and we were seeing it in terms of the social media campaign, but again, our reading was, don't worry, Labour Party members are sensible and they won't go for any of this. So we felt that something was bubbling but we didn't really take it seriously as a threat. We still felt it was OK, we felt it was winnable for us.

Yvette Cooper returned from her holiday, in the words of her campaign manager Vernon Coaker, 'refreshed and with a new sense of purpose'. The team held a meeting where they asked themselves if they wanted to win the contest, and on deciding that they very much did, they set about defining a vision which was to be based on challenging Corbyn from the 'passionate centre-ground'. Coaker says:

> The really important thing is to be a centre candidate against Jeremy: he isn't the only person who owns principle, he isn't the only person who's passionate, he isn't the only person who is exciting. You can

be passionate, principled and exciting and actually be in the centre ground of the Labour Party and actually care about that, and actually marry that with pragmatic policies and credibility, and you can speak to the country as well as the party. That ignited our campaign.

While Andy Burnham continued to court the left, Cooper now began to take Corbyn on in a series of speeches warning of the risks to the party if he became leader. It became a source of irritation that while both she and Liz Kendall urged members to vote 'ABC – Anyone But Corbyn', Burnham, still hoping to pick up votes on the left, refused to advise his supporters how to use their second and third preferences. A member of Cooper's team says: 'He never, as far as I can remember, during the campaign explicitly said that his people should vote for Yvette or for Liz second, it was always, 'Well, it's up to them.' And to us that was always a bit disappointing.' Later in the contest, Cooper would win plaudits for taking a tough stand on the refugee crisis, shaming David Cameron by insisting, in her role as shadow Home Secretary, that the British public understood the difference between migrants and refugees, and would welcome those risking their children's lives to flee Syria. Unfortunately for Cooper, it was too late. Way, way too late. One senior Labour insider says:

Yvette, right at the eleventh hour, got on to the migrant thing. She wasn't around [earlier] when all the Calais stuff [first] kicked off. She was away. The truth is that Yvette had such a big late surge, if Yvette had been much more on it earlier, Yvette would have won.

By mid-August, Corbyn's rock star rallies had become something of a phenomenon, with photographs of the extraordinary scenes at his packed-out events exploding on social media. The mood of excitement was perhaps best encapsulated by a now famous photograph of a group of four teenagers who climbed up the side of a building to catch a glimpse of a Corbyn rally through a window. One of the first rallies to capture the public's attention was held at Liverpool's Adelphi Hotel on 1 August, where it was standing room only in the ballroom to hear him speak, and hundreds more supporters spilled into a second event space. Another was held on a balmy evening in north London, when around 1,500 people turned out to hear Corbyn, supported by Ken Livingstone and the music producer Brian Eno, speak at the Camden Centre. So huge was the crowd that it filled the main hall and an overflow room. In the end, Corbyn went outside, addressing those who had been unable to get inside from the top of a fire engine which members of the Fire Brigades Union (not, as his rivals would point out, currently affiliated to the Labour Party) had parked outside. A photographer captured the scene, creating another of the iconic images of the campaign.

Again and again, in Newcastle, Plymouth, Southampton, Birmingham, Coventry, Edinburgh, Belfast, Leeds, Cardiff, Nottingham, Chelmsford, Norwich, and dozens more towns and cities around the country, people gathered to see Corbyn in vast numbers. Tickets for a meeting in Glasgow were snapped up within five minutes of being offered on the Corbyn for Leader Facebook page. In Bradford, organisers were forced to transfer the event at the last minute from a community hall to a cricket pitch. Five hundred people turned out to hear Corbyn speak in the north Wales seaside town of Llandudno, representing one in forty of the 20,000-strong population. By the end of the summer, attending a Corbyn rally had become the latest craze. People who had never been interested in politics went along; Tories went along; even the supporters of other leadership contenders turned out to hear Corbyn speak. You wanted to say that you had been. Such was the buzz around Corbyn that some highly unlikely voices began to sing his praises. In early September, the right-wing commentator Peter Hitchens attended a rally at Great St Mary's Church, Cambridge. In a blog about it for the *Mail*, he wrote:

> Great St Mary's holds 1,400 people, and was totally full, and … there were at least several hundred outside who couldn't get in. The meeting had been postponed because the original venue had been too small to safely hold the audience who signed up. Most readers of this blog, if they heard the speech without knowing who was delivering it, would have thought it workmanlike and commonsensical, though obviously of the left. It was completely coherent, delivered fluently without notes by a man who obviously still writes his own speeches and understands what he is saying. Every statement in it obviously resulted from a long and considered examination of the subject, and he could have defended every assertion if he had had to. I simply don't think any of his rivals could have done this, not because they're stupid or bad speakers, but because they don't actually have coherent political positions.

Corbyn's rallies followed a similar pattern. Long queues would appear outside hours before the early evening start time, snaking for hundreds of yards down the street. Sometimes stalls would be set up outside, selling copies of *Socialism Today* and other left-wing publications. Stewards, often from the Unite union in high-vis jackets, and ordinary volunteers in wearing 'Jez We Can!' T-shirts, shepherded people to their seats. The atmosphere was friendly. Often there would be one or two toddlers and babies. Although much has been written about the number of young people who flocked to hear Corbyn, there were plenty of older people there too, including many who had put in long service on the left through the '80s, '90s and '00s, and who were thrilled to see their candidate, for once, in the ascendance. At some rallies, food and drink was available, usually tea but sometimes wine, but the ambience was mellow rather than rowdy. People chatted excitedly and listened politely to the warm-up speeches. Jason Beattie, political editor of the *Daily Mirror*, says: 'You could not help but be impressed by how excited and energised the crowd was. There are very few people in politics who have that kind of an effect on people these days.' Kat Fletcher said of those turning out to hear Corbyn: 'This is not just about a bunch of youngsters getting involved, it's across the generations. We're seeing people coming back to the party, or seeing people who've been dormant for a decade or two. And of course a lot of new members too.'[301]

When Corbyn spoke, the audience was rapt, listening attentively and interrupting often with warm applause. At each of the ninety-nine rallies Corbyn held around the country (the 100th was the special conference that declared him leader on 12 September) he delivered a different speech, always without notes. The themes were the same, however: support for the NHS, opposition to the Trident nuclear defence system, the iniquity of the government's anti-austerity measures and welfare cuts, investment in manufacturing, support for the public services, belief in the United Nations and international law. He often criticised or darkly joked about the 'right-wing press', and he boasted that he would not engage in personal attacks on his rivals. If he had still not become an exciting public speaker, he was a competent one, and the crowds seemed not to mind, finding inspiration in what he represented and the issues he raised rather than the manner in which he expressed himself.

Watching Corbyn light up the contest with his sell-out rallies was dispiriting to his rivals, who struggled to gather crowds of more than double figures. Katie Myler from Andy Burnham's team says: 'You couldn't deny the momentum. Just look at his rallies. When we would have events, they were members. When Corbyn would have events he would invite any-body. And that's great, it's impressive to draw any kind of crowd like that, it's great to see people politically engaged.' John Lehal adds:

> Sometimes you struggle to get a hundred people in a church hall and meanwhile he's got five hundred, he's speaking to people from a fire engine. We did big meetings in Nottingham and Leicester and Sheffield, but it wasn't on the scale of his. And his were getting sold out, and ours weren't. So yes, it was hitting the morale a bit.

Roger Baker from Yvette Cooper's team adds:

> It was galling. But equally there was a feeling as well … that there was a curiosity aspect to it. Some of our supporters would go along to these rallies just to see it. Non-members were going along just to see it. Because it had been fed so much. This was a thing, this was a phenomenon. If you were at all interested in politics, why not pop along?

Suddenly, Corbyn had transcended the world of politics and moved into the sphere of celebrity. To his discomfort, the media's gaze now turned squarely on him; long articles were written about his background, family and private life. Journalists and television camera crews attended his rallies and reported back on the near religious experience of being in the crowd. In the dog days of summer, with little else on the news agenda, it seemed that Corbyn was the only story in town. Everyone, not just political nerds, was discussing the Labour leadership contest. At one point, a group of senior BBC News executives convened a meeting to discuss their growing fear that they were fuelling the story by paying Corbyn so much attention.

But the sense that Corbyn *was* the story was inescapable. A member of Yvette Cooper's team says: 'After the Welfare Bill, the big thing that happened was that Jeremy winning suddenly became credible. And in the dearth of the summer, the media went mental. It was wall to wall Jeremy and Jeremy events. They were the only events the cameras were at.'

As with any media sensation, the coverage ranged from the sublime to the ridiculous. Corbyn was mortified when he was asked during an appearance on BBC Radio 4's *Woman's Hour* what he thought of reports that he had become something of a pin-up, with women from the online forum Mumsnet describing him as 'attractive in a world-weary old sea dog sort of way' and 'very sexy ... if you half-fancied Dumbledore [the wizard headmaster in the Harry Potter children's books]'. Corbyn became transatlantic on 3 August, when the *New York Times* devoted a long article to the leadership contest, saying: 'While the consensus of political analysts is that Labour must move toward the center, where most British voters are, wounded party activists are turning toward an old-style socialist, Jeremy Corbyn.' Other publications from Spain to the Middle East followed suit.

As Corbynmania took off, a paper cup he had drunk from at a rally was sold on eBay for £51. To Chris Mullin's delight, his publisher ordered a reprint of his novel, *A Very British Coup*, which had been inspired by Tony Benn but now seemed to be coming true for Corbyn (who appeared on course to becoming Labour leader, if not yet Prime Minister). And now celebrities began to come on board: the singers Charlotte Church and Andy Bell; the outspoken classics scholar Mary Beard; the director Ken Loach; Julie Hesmondhalgh, a former Coronation Street soap star; the actors Maxine Peake, Daniel Radcliffe, Sean Bean and Emma Thompson; the band Primal Scream. Soon rival parties sought to jump on the Corbyn bandwagon, with an eclectic range of politicians, from UKIP leader Nigel Farage to the SNP's Alex Salmond to the Tory Mayor of London Boris Johnson singing his praises. While some Conservatives licked their lips at the prospect of a Corbyn victory, believing it would consign Labour to electoral oblivion, others recognised the challenge that this un-spun man of principle represented. Even Rupert Murdoch, whose Wapping fortress Corbyn had picketed outside in the 1980s, sent a tweet saying: 'Seems only candidate who believes anything, right or wrong.' Each celebrity endorsement led to another story about the Corbyn 'surge', leaving his rivals struggling to get any coverage at all. Andy Burnham's team was initially thrilled when the results of an opinion poll came in showing that most voters saw him as the candidate with the best chance of returning Labour to No. 10; to their frustration, it got barely any coverage.

Corbyn was asked to appear on ITV's flagship mid-morning magazine show *This Morning* for a cosy chat with presenters Eamonn Holmes and Ruth Langsford. When his press officer, Carmel Nolan, spoke to a member of the production staff the night before to discuss the questions he would be asked, she spotted danger right away when she was told they wanted to cover Corbyn's divorce from Claudia Bracchitta. Nolan says:

> I said he's not to talk about that. I'll pull him off if you insist on asking about that. The producer said: 'He'll have to face questions like this if he wants to lead the Labour Party.' So I asked her to put me through to Martin Frizzel [the programme editor] and she refused. So I pulled him. I pulled him at ten o'clock the night before he was due to go on. Within a couple of weeks Frizzel was calling me himself begging me to have Jeremy on, on any terms. But that was it; he just doesn't do personal.

Frizzel later texted Katie Myler, an old friend from their days together at ITV's former breakfast show *GMTV*, to bemoan what had happened. 'Never mind that, when are you going to get Andy on?' Myler asked. 'Get back to me when Andy's the story,' Frizzel told her.

And then suddenly Corbyn began to enjoy it. He was tired and frustrated with the attention on him as a personality, and in particular with what he saw as the intrusive focus on his family and private life. But who could help but be seduced by the headiness of appearing, night after night, in front of adoring crowds lapping up every word you say? After so long in the political wilderness, it must have been intoxicating. That is not to say he had changed. In words designed to tug the tail of the Blairites, he suggested that as leader he might restore Clause IV,[302] allow Militant back into the party, and apologise on behalf of Labour for the Iraq War.[303] And he remained his old modest self. At the height of the contest a photograph did the rounds on social media showing him, exhausted, going home on a night bus. He would continue to travel by bike and public transport even once he was entitled to an official car as Leader of the Opposition. He still wore sandals to some events. But now he began to tentatively speak of himself as a prospective leader. And it seemed as if he quite liked the idea. He described the leadership election as 'the most exciting period of my life'.[304] 'There's something happening out there,' he told one crowd of supporters at London's King's Cross Station. 'The summer of 2015 is like no other in British politics that I can ever remember.'[305] 'He was enjoying himself,' one campaign source says. 'He went completely away from where he was at the early stages of the contest, which was thinking he had made a dreadful mistake.' At the start of August, John McDonnell began to hold meetings to discuss the agenda for when – no longer if – Corbyn became leader. Fearing he could become a target for far-right groups, Harry Fletcher drew up plans for his security.

One of the most extraordinary aspects of Corbyn's success was the sheer number of ordinary people who turned out to help him to victory. By the end of August, Corbyn's phone banks were staffed by 400 people at a time, working out of seven offices around the country. Having so many people willing to canvass on his behalf gave Corbyn an enormous advantage over his rivals, who were forced to rely largely on email to get their messages out to voters. John Lehal says: 'I've never been convinced of anything by reading an email, it's by talking to people. We just couldn't get the volunteers, and Jeremy had the volunteers phoning members and convincing them. We just didn't have the level of support needed to make those calls.'

Those who visited Corbyn's volunteer campaign headquarters met solicitors and schoolboys, a guy from Google, a mother and son, pensioners and twenty-somethings, people of all colours and races. One journalist who visited the Holborn offices which had been provided by Unite contrasted the busy hubbub and vibrant cast of characters in the offices devoted to Corbyn with the 'four thirty-something white guys with indie haircuts' working in the room next door, which had been given to Tom Watson, the deputy leadership candidate who had also been backed by the union.[306] Accidentally, on a much larger scale, Corbyn had recreated a movement similar to that he had taken part in as a young activist in Hornsey in the 1970s, and that he had helped foster at the Red Rose Centre in Islington in the 1980s and 1990s. Volunteers to his campaign would get pizza delivered to the offices as they worked the phones late into the night, before repairing to the pub. The journalist Ellie Mae O'Hagan wrote of them in *Foreign Policy Review*:

> They often stay until late into the evening, drinking, joking, and debating politics. This is the most remarkable and powerful aspect of the Corbyn campaign: it has almost accidentally morphed from a political campaign into a social movement, joining disparate elements of the British left – from students to trade unionists, activists to politicians – together. On the ground, friendships are being formed out of the campaign, connections made, activists born.

On social media too, Corbyn inspired thousands of people to become active, although not always with a positive outcome. Corbyn's rivals, particularly Liz Kendall, complained of being targeted for abuse by his supporters on Twitter; journalists who wrote anything remotely critical also found themselves under fire. Female reporters and candidates in particular came in for unpleasant, sometimes sexually threatening, vitriol. It was an issue Corbyn would later address in his first speech to Labour conference, calling for an end to 'cyber-bullying ... and especially the misogynistic abuse online'.

But the bad was dwarfed by the good – during the campaign at least. Corbyn inspired many activists who might otherwise have sat out the 2015 contest, including the likes of Michelle Ryan, Rebecca Barnes and Stuart Wheeler, to become involved, with thousands signing up to his Jeremy Corbyn for Leader Facebook and Twitter pages, taking part in 'Twitterstorms' to get hashtags such as #JezWeCan and #VoteCorbyn trending on Twitter, and further propelling the sense of momentum behind his candidacy. In a post on his Facebook page in mid-August, the team boasted:

> We now have 56,000 likes on Facebook and 43,000 followers on Twitter. Add to that a FB reach which has peaked at 2 million and Twitterstorms which have mentioned Jeremy's campaign over 20,000 times in an hour, and we can all see that it is just incredible stuff – history in the making. This alone makes it by far the biggest social media campaign ever for a British politician.

By the end of the month, Corbyn's official leadership Twitter feed had swelled to 60,000 followers.

Corbyn's success in harnessing social media to create a mass movement of support would go on to have lasting repercussions for his leadership. Uniquely for a Labour leader, it has allowed him to enjoy a relationship with grassroots members quite separate from the apparatus of the official party. During the difficult time of the Commons vote that split his shadow Cabinet in the late autumn of 2015, members were polled for their views on airstrikes in Syria. While the results, which overwhelmingly backed Corbyn, were dismissed by his opponents as unscientific and unfair, the poll demonstrated Corbyn's ability to reach over – and ignore – his MPs to connect directly with individual supporters. This private army of followers now has a name, Momentum, a group born out of the Jeremy for Labour Leader online campaign. On its newly launched website, Momentum describes itself as 'a network of people and organisations that will continue the energy and enthusiasm of Jeremy's campaign'. At their best, Momentum and social media give the Labour Party a grassroots-driven democracy it has never before enjoyed. At their worst, they potentially give rise to the kind of bullying that saw MPs who voted for airstrikes threatened with deselection and even physical violence.

Along with its ability to attract support online, Corbyn's leadership team also proved remarkably adept at fundraising. While his coup in wooing the trade unions away from Andy Burnham brought him hundreds of thousands of pounds (money which, as his campaign took off, was needed to pay for larger venues and the travel costs of his growing staff), such was the success of his grassroots campaign that much of his cashflow came from ordinary members. At the start of the campaign, the team set themselves the target of raising £50,000 in fifty days; they reached it in thirteen. A second £50,000 was again hit in less than a fortnight. The money poured in, not from wealthy individuals, as it did to the other candidates (Yvette Cooper benefited from £100,000 in donations from Barbara and Ken Follett, the former MP and her novelist husband) but thanks to hundreds of ordinary people who usually gave quite small amounts. The average donation to the Corbyn campaign was just £22, and he received the fewest gifts of more than £500 (the level at which they must be declared to the Register of Members' Interests) of all the candidates. Everyone who gave more than £10 received a letter of thanks. On one post on Corbyn's Facebook page, the team wrote: 'Thank you to all who have donated so far, from £2 to £25, to the young man that didn't order a pizza last night and gave us £10 instead.' Corbyn's coffers were further boosted by the sale of JezWeCan! merchandise, particularly the popular T-shirts.

As the days ticked down to 12 August, the deadline set by Labour's ruling NEC for registering as a supporter in order to vote in the leadership contest, it became apparent that, driven by the cult of Corbyn, a vast number of people would be taking part. With panic setting in among many in the 'mainstream' of the party, wild rumours and accusations began to fly about the nature and character of these new entrants. To begin with, the concern was that mischief-making Conservatives would seek to join up as £3 registered supporters in order to vote for Corbyn, the candidate they boasted would ruin Labour's chances with the wider electorate. Harriet Harman and party chiefs promised to weed out vexatious applicants, by ensuring that their public pronouncements were in line with the statement they signed on registering expressing support for Labour and its aims. The Tory MP Tim Loughton was among those caught out early on seeking to take part.

Corbyn's rivals had for some weeks clung to the hope that, while those turning out at his rallies and hustings were clearly backing the left-winger, the rank-and-file membership who had been in the party for some time might come to their senses and vote for a moderate candidate. Andy Burnham's team in particular had convinced themselves they had a clear idea of the type of people who would decide the election: working-class couples, trade union members but not activists, in jobs like dinner lady or bin man, who were not on social media and could be trusted to vote for the candidate most likely to return the party to No. 10. Crucially, Burnham's team believed that, unlike the 'middle-class London lefties' supporting Corbyn, these people *needed* a Labour government back in power. There were two things wrong with this analysis: one was that, as data seen by both the Liz Kendall and Yvette Cooper camps made clear, nearly half of even the existing members of the Labour Party, not counting registered supporters, had signed up since 2010, meaning they had joined under Ed Miliband and were therefore likely to be to the left of all the candidates bar Corbyn. And, second, as the numbers signing up as £3 registered supporters reached not the thousands that had been anticipated but, thanks to Corbyn, the many tens of thousands, it was no longer certain that capturing the votes of old-time full members would be enough.

It had always been anticipated that the 'three pounders', as insiders called them, would favour Corbyn as the left-wing candidate. Now his leadership rivals, and some on the right of the party, began to wonder just precisely how left-wing these new arrivals were. Could they in fact be some of the very same people older right-wingers and centrists had spent much of the 1980s and early 1990s fighting against and eventually expelling from the party? Having already introduced a few checks to stop mischief-making Tories from signing up, Harman and her team now drew up a new set of criteria to stop these potential so-called entryists, the likes of Militant, TUSC (the Trade Union and Socialist Coalition) and the Socialist Workers Party, from taking part. As well as signing a statement saying they agreed with the Labour Party's aims, applicants would be checked to ensure they had not backed rival parties or been vocal in support for them. MPs were invited to comb lists of would-be applicants to spot local trouble-makers. Suspicious cases identified by a team of Labour staffers based in Newcastle were sent for consideration to a panel of senior party officials, who had the power to disqualify them.

The so-called purge of entryists took up much time and energy among Labour Party operatives, created bitterness in the rival leadership teams and occupied much of the media's attention, which now began to produce wild stories about the thousands of Trotskyites allegedly identified as part of what became dubbed 'Operation Icepick', after the weapon used to kill Leon Trotsky. It also produced a somewhat chaotic situation. Having failed to set a 'freeze period' for signing up registered supporters at the start of the race, the party now had to undertake a vetting process even while more and more applications were being received. In seeking to weed out those who had expressed support for other parties in the past, Labour created far more stringent conditions for its £3 registered supporters than had been imagined in the Collins Review, or even at the outset of the contest. It also led to the bizarre spectacle of a political party turning away floating voters who may have been attracted to Labour for the first time, or who may have wanted to return after a period of time away. Among those barred from taking part were Mark Steel, the left-wing comedian who had previously been in the Socialist Workers Party and voted Green at the last election; Mark Serwotka, the trade union leader who had voted for rival left-wing parties; Corbyn's brother Piers, who stood as an independent against the Labour candidate in the council elections in his borough of Southwark in May 2015; film director Ken Loach, founder of a new party, Left Unity, in 2013 to challenge Labour; and the husband of Beck Barnes, who had previously supported the Green Party. All five – like hundreds of others who would be banned as part of Operation Icepick – would protest that they hoped to re-join the Labour movement under Corbyn having become disenchanted with it in the past.

In the end, around 3,200 people would be excluded from voting in the leadership contest, of whom Greens formed the vast majority. The real story of the scare over the entryists, however, was not the small numbers attempting to infiltrate the system but those legitimately signing up in such overwhelming droves. As Corbyn put it at the time: 'The entryism I see is lots of young people who have hitherto not [been] very excited by politics coming in for the first time and saying, "Yeah, we can have a discussion."'[307] One senior Labour staffer adds: 'Jeremy Corbyn's was the only camp that recognised that if you mobilise the movement, the three quids, you could get a pretty good result.'

As the Corbyn bandwagon rolled on, more and more people came forward to pay their £3 and register as a Labour supporter. Towards the end of the process, the Corbyn campaign took out a full-page advertisement in *The Guardian* inviting people to sign up. The response was overwhelming. The Labour staffer says:

> The thing went off the scale after that. We used to look at the figures of people joining, and people were not joining up to vote for Andy or Yvette or Liz. The momentum behind the figures, you could just see as it got closer and closer and he was building up more momentum, you could tell. I thought, 'He's unstoppable.'

In the final hours before the window to register as a member or registered supporter closed on 12 August, so many people sought to sign up that the Labour Party computer system crashed. The deadline had to be pushed back by a few hours to facilitate everyone who wanted to register. When the window finally closed, it was clear that something extraordinary had taken place over the summer of 2015. More than 600,000 people would be taking part in the leadership election, of whom two-thirds had signed up in the previous three months. Of these, 100,000 joined as full members of the Labour Party, 190,000 signed up through their trade union, and another 120,000 paid £3 to become registered supporters. An overwhelming majority of them were planning to vote for Jeremy Corbyn.

CHAPTER TWENTY

LAST STAND

ANDY BURNHAM WAS finally enjoying some downtime after what had proved to be a long, exhausting and frustrating summer. It was the second week of August and he and his wife, Frankie, and their three children had escaped for a much-needed break in Spain. After a gruelling and ultimately disappointing general election campaign, he had gone straight into a leadership contest in which his hopes and indeed expectations of emerging as the head of his party seemed to be slipping away. Burnham did not just want to be leader of the party he had joined at the age of sixteen: he genuinely believed the best hope of returning Labour to its rightful place in government was with him at the helm. It had been dispiriting to watch as the left-winger Jeremy Corbyn, who had done none of the heavy lifting, the years of loyal service Burnham had put in as a Cabinet minister and member of the shadow Cabinet, captured the attention and imagination of the media and public, leaving him branded a New Labour stooge. While Burnham remained optimistic he could yet win the contest, now he certainly needed a break. His children were already asleep in their holiday villa, and he was planning to join them, when his phone rang. It was

Katie Myler, his head of press, with some bad news. *The Times* was running a second opinion poll by YouGov, and the numbers were even worse than last time.[308] What followed was the most extraordinary week of the leadership campaign, as Corbyn's rivals launched two attempts to halt his bandwagon. When they failed, the contest was all his.

Myler had been working virtually alone in Burnham's campaign headquarters at 83 Victoria Street just after 10 p.m. on 10 August when a tweet popped up on her feed that she knew could spell the end for his hopes of becoming leader. Sent by *The Times'* deputy political editor Sam Coates, it read: 'TIMES/YOUGOV: Jeremy Corbyn has **32 point** lead over nearest rival in first preferences in new Labour poll, up from 17 points 3 weeks ago'. Myler was alarmed. She says: 'I texted Sam and said tell me more. He suggested, "Actually this is not going to be bad for you guys." He thought it would almost … not necessarily panic … but make sensible minds become more focused.' When the full numbers came through, they were sobering for the self-styled moderate candidates. In the first round, Corbyn was predicted to win 53 per cent of votes, against 21 for Burnham, 18 for Yvette Cooper and 8 for Liz Kendall. For the last few weeks, Burnham's team had clung to the hope that if they could keep Corbyn below 50 per cent, then they might ultimately triumph by picking up the second preference votes of Cooper and Kendall. But if Corbyn won outright in the first round, second and third preferences would not even be counted. The bookmakers responded to the poll immediately, cutting Corbyn's odds further still, to 2–1.

Corbyn's rivals were stunned by the YouGov poll. Roger Baker from Yvette Cooper's team says: 'Suddenly he's on fifty-three. That he was over fifty was a surprise. I thought he was on low to mid-forties, and therefore eminently catchable. Fifty-three was a surprise.' Aside from Myler, the main players in Burnham's campaign team had taken advantage of his absence to go on holiday, leaving her in a difficult position. Michael Dugher, the shadow Transport Secretary, John Lehal, his campaign manager, and Phil Hope, her no. 2 in the press operation, were all overseas. Myler telephoned Burnham and broke the bad news. She says: 'I said: "You don't have to worry about this. We've a long way to go," It was just, well, take it in our stride, we keep going. And of course we went out and said [to journalists]: "It's one poll, blah blah blah, this is ridiculous."' A series of international calls now took place between key members of Burnham's team as they tried to work out what on earth they could do to stop Corbyn. John Lehal says:

> Michael Dugher, Andy, myself, were all away at the same time. I managed four days before having to join the morning calls again. We're looking at the poll thinking: 'We refuse to believe this.' We were in absolute denial about it, just looking at the numbers going, 'This cannot be true.' And the crumbs of comfort you give yourself are: well, how can a polling company go and find these people who are rank-and-file members of the Labour Party? We can't even find half of them [to canvass them]. So, let's ignore the poll.

Even now, Burnham thought the situation could be salvaged, and was determined not to give up. He returned to London from Spain for a few days to try to get a grip on the situation. 'He was an optimist throughout, actually,' one senior member of his team says.

> He was up and down at times but generally an optimist. We still thought we had everything to play for. Even those days in August, yes, we felt it turn; yes, we were looking at the welfare vote and thinking, 'Yes, this has hit us'; you're looking at social media, it's hard not to be taken in by that. But again you convince yourself: party members aren't on Twitter, these are the Trots, ignore them.

By the time Burnham returned to his family in Spain, he had stopped the panic in his team, but the group had still not worked out how to turn the contest around. A source close to the campaign says:

> That was a really difficult week, a terrifying week, to try and keep the team together, motivated, when people just weren't around. It was the 'week of shit', it was called. That was the week where we thought, 'Hang on a minute, he [Corbyn] could do this.' I remember thinking, 'What do we do next?' It was absolutely insane. It was pretty hairy at the time. It was just the Wild West.

And then came a call which Burnham's camp believed could yet salvage the situation. In one sense, as the *Times* journalist Sam Coates had predicted, the YouGov poll had focused minds, but not necessarily those of the Labour selectorate. All through the summer, the teams working for the three moderate candidates had kept in touch. Unlike Corbyn's band of outsiders, they were largely made up of people who had years of experience working together, either at Labour HQ or as fellow advisers to Cabinet and shadow Cabinet ministers. They had long-standing relationships, often forged in the heat of crisis. And now, they believed, they faced their toughest challenge to date: the likely takeover of their party by a candidate of the far left whose views on where Labour should be were the antithesis of their own. One senior figure in the party says that by the middle of the summer, the three teams were well aware that their candidates were going to lose, even if some of the contenders themselves could not see it. The source says: 'On Andy and Yvette's side, they refused to entertain the notion that the thing had gone, basically, and in all probability Jeremy was almost definitely going to win. But privately their teams were quite open about it: they knew it was up.'

The three campaign teams began talking to each other about the possibility of launching a last stand against Corbyn, by encouraging two of the moderate candidates to stand aside and unite around a single figure. One source close to the negotiations says: 'We weren't sure [if it would work], but if you cared about the future of the party and thought going in a far-left direction was going to go against the interests of the communities we represent and want to represent, then you have to consider it.' The polling data seemed to suggest that it was Andy Burnham who stood the best chance of beating Corbyn. But how could Liz Kendall and Yvette Cooper be persuaded to stand aside? What followed over the course of the next few days, as a plan was hatched for Burnham to be anointed a unity candidate against Corbyn, would leave his rivals hopelessly divided. Many in the three moderate teams remain bitterly angry at what now transpired.

Over the course of the contest, and despite their years of friendship, first as fellow New Labour special advisers, then as young MPs and finally as ministers and Cabinet ministers, relations between Andy Burnham and Yvette Cooper had become increasingly strained. One MP says: 'There was a huge amount of poison between the Burnham and Cooper campaigns. It was pretty astounding actually, both between the candidates themselves, during this time, and also their respective teams.' Both, however, maintained good relations with Liz Kendall. It therefore was decided by the three teams that someone from Kendall's camp would be best placed to broker the deal to agree a unity candidate. One Kendall supporter says: 'She [Kendall] was on pretty good terms with both Andy and Yvette so we tended to find we became the interlocutor between the Burnham and Cooper campaigns, and tended to be the bridge in terms of communication between the two.' Chuka Umunna, the modernising MP who was backing Kendall, now made a series of international phone calls, discussing the idea first with Burnham and then with his campaign manager, Michael Dugher, before approaching the other two camps.

While Kendall's team believe they were articulating an idea that had already been circulating between the camps, a source close to Andy Burnham says: 'The approach came from Liz's campaign. Chuka made an approach to Michael Dugher to say that Liz is ready to go but we need to get Yvette to go. Unfortunately, Yvette was refusing.' The Kendall camp insists, however, that Burnham's team was already aware of the plan before Umunna made his calls, and that he did so only to help all the camps explore an idea that was already under discussion. John Woodcock, from Kendall's team, says:

> That idea was certainly around. There was a little window where Liz was open to considering it … but I don't think it was fair to say she was one of the instigators of it, and certainly as soon as Yvette said no then she wasn't going to be the one to fall on her sword. Yvette didn't want to go for it.

Cooper's camp insists that no formal approach suggesting she stand down was ever made to them. One member of the team says:

> It just seemed to emerge, somehow, this idea for there to be one anti-Jeremy candidate and that Liz and Yvette should step out. Then it started to go to 'We've got data that shows that only Andy can beat Jeremy'. I think the immediate feeling was: why should the girls get out of the way? Even if it wasn't deliberate, we talk about institutional sexism; it was, here we go again.

Cooper's team was suspicious of Burnham's motives in suggesting she stand aside, believing that, in an alternative vote system, when voters could nominate second and third preferences, it would in any case make no difference to the eventual outcome if Corbyn faced only one opponent.

Roger Baker says: 'With preferential voting, this argument about standing down is utterly irrelevant. Every time Yvette or Liz had to answer a question about standing down, it damaged them. So this was a weaponised story. It wasn't anything actually to do with a moderate victory; this was about killing the other two.' John Woodcock says, however:

> You could tell people about the voting system, that no votes were wasted, until you were blue in the face but they're used to first past the post elections. In the end, it was all academic, [Corbyn] won by a landslide, but Yvette's late surge, and Yvette continuing to punch against Andy, I guess they maybe thought they could leapfrog Andy into second or come a credible third. But Yvette was never in the running.

Cooper and her team felt that, rather than working up the idea of a single candidate, the moderates should stick together and urge their followers to back 'Anyone But Corbyn', something they believed Burnham was irresponsible in failing to do. Having found a new impetus since returning from holiday a week earlier, and with a strategy of her own aimed at attacking Corbyn rather than wooing his supporters, Cooper did not see why it should be she who stood aside. One member of the team says:

> No, we're not pulling out. A, it's sexism, and B, we're saying something different. You [in the Burnham camp are] tacking towards Jeremy because you don't want to pee people off and you can get votes from him rather than lose votes to him, and we're saying a completely different pitch here.

Roger Baker adds:

> To be honest with you, our attitude at that point was not about deals. It
> was: no one has fundamentally taken Corbyn on. We need to take him
> on. The only way a moderate would win, you have to get him below
> 50 [per cent of the vote]. We need to get him back to the low forties.

Determined not to stand aside, Cooper continued with her new strategy
of attacking Corbyn, using a speech in Manchester to declare: 'I feel really
strongly ... that his are the wrong answers for the future. They aren't radical and they aren't credible. And they won't change the world. They will
keep us out of power.' As Cooper went on the offensive, Burnham refused
to follow suit, saying: 'The attacks on Jeremy misread the mood of the
party.'[309] A senior member of his campaign admits that sticking close to
Corbyn was a deliberate strategy:

> Yvette went on the attack, Liz went on the attack and Andy didn't; he
> praised him and praised him and praised him, because we knew that
> our best chance of winning was to pick up the soft support for him
> and try to convert that. It was really difficult at times.

Michael Dugher has said that attacking Corbyn would have achieved little.
'The truth is that every time someone attacked this guy, he went up five
points,' he said. 'I agreed with some of the sentiment but I thought it was
catastrophically unhelpful. I felt you had to engage with Corbyn supporters,
not attack them. Just shouting ever louder at his supporters 'Are you mad?'
was not going to win votes.'[310] Cooper's team believe, however, that, in failing
to criticise Corbyn, Burnham actually fuelled his rise. One member says:

> The real reason Andy's campaign imploded is they chase after Jeremy's
> second preferences and move left, they alienate everyone to the centre

and to the right, and then they're in a cul-de-sac. They were stuck there, and that didn't just have a consequence for Andy's campaign, it had a consequence for the entire campaign. Because any attack on Corbyn was blunted. Imagine if Yvette and Liz pull out and it's Andy, who is validating Corbyn, against Corbyn. Is Andy going to win? No. The only way out of the Corbyn phenomenon was to puncture it, not to validate it. That was the only game in town. [Burnham] made it harder to do that.

Happy with her change in strategy, Cooper was buoyed when Alan Johnson, the respected former Home Secretary, endorsed her, saying if Corbyn won it would mean Labour had 'given up on being a serious party of government'.[311] His words were echoed by Alastair Campbell, Tony Blair's former spin doctor, who said that victory for Corbyn would be a 'car crash' for the party.[312] Charles Clarke, another former Home Secretary, described Corbyn as the 'continuity [Tony] Benn/nutter candidate',[313] and suggested his supporters were 'barking mad'.[314] A senior MP on the Blairite wing of the party is critical of those who attacked Corbyn and his supporters in such harsh terms. 'The moderate parts of the party did not show sufficient emotional literacy,' the MP says.

Lots of people have joined the party, it isn't all a bunch of Militant people, it's essentially people who have all the same values but wanted New Labour to be far more ambitious in delivering them, and how can you really have a go at them for that? The worst thing were these people who just called them a bunch of nutters. Some of the New Labour grandees were saying that. That's not the way to build bridges because we all want the same thing in the end, and that's a Labour government.

Chuka Umunna has made a similar point: 'It sounded like we were dismissing people who were critical of New Labour and saying they were mad ... How on earth are you going to persuade people of a case if you don't meet them where they are?'[315] One senior member of Corbyn's camp agrees that in getting personal, his critics harmed no one but his rivals. 'The lines of attack on him have been silly, have been childish and adolescent, and have made the others look as if they are not serious politicians,' the source says. 'The fact that he hasn't responded to that has made him look dignified.'

Next, the *Guardian* newspaper came out for Yvette Cooper in an editorial which read: 'The right leader is the person who can bring both Jeremy Corbyn and Liz Kendall together in one big, progressive tent, offering enough moral common ground to transcend deep disagreements on policy. The person best placed to do that is Yvette Cooper.' Reports began to circulate that Gordon Brown, the ex-Prime Minister who was close to Cooper and her husband Ed Balls, would also be publicly backing her. A senior member of Andy Burnham's team says of Cooper's decision not to stand aside:

> I can understand from her point of view why. She had Gordon Brown about to come out for her, she had *The Guardian* about to come out for her, she had Alan Johnson about to come out for her. Again, it's kind of cabin fever. You think, 'I can win this thing, I can pick up the second preferences.'

The 'Wild West week' continued as, in a flurry of phone calls across Europe, Burnham's team continued to try to come up with ideas to persuade Cooper to stand aside. At one point, the three moderate camps agreed to unite to co-sign a letter to the Labour Party claiming that, through his trade union links, Corbyn had been obtaining membership data days ahead of them, enabling his team to contact voters before they could. The letter gave Burnham's team renewed hope both that the camps might be able to work together to stop Corbyn, and that something could be done to halt the contest. A second letter was drawn up in the names of the campaign managers of the three moderate candidates, this time expressing concern about the veracity of the verification process as a result of the entryism scare. A source close to Burnham says:

> Even at that stage we may have thought the race was slipping, but it was something we wanted to have confidence in. We could see which way it was going. In order to stay positive and think 'We've still got to fight for this', we would find reasons to discount Jeremy's votes.

At one point, Burnham's team began discussing the viability of a legal challenge based on what they saw as the flawed validation system.

Back in Labour HQ, the letters, rightly seen as largely the work of Burnham's team, were received with bafflement. One insider says:

> It was just ridiculous. In head office we were dismayed whenever a Burnham letter came in. It was just desperate and in fact very stressful and quite distressing – instead of actually going out and campaigning and trying to think 'right, what's a really good way of trying to get a message out to our supporters?' [they were sending letters]. Fair play, Jeremy Corbyn was out trying to have a good message to the public, and Burnham's team were just writing angrily worded letters to head office the whole time. At one point they briefed the press that they were going to bring a judicial review. Basically, Andy's team was focusing on challenging the Labour Party rather than winning the actual [contest].

With the teams now in regular contact, the suggestion that Gordon Brown was about to make his views on the leadership race known in Yvette Cooper's favour gave Burnham's people another idea: if they could pull together a 'grand coalition' of former Labour leaders and other party notables to unite in opposition to Corbyn and, ideally, support Burnham, perhaps the membership could yet be won over. The idea was now floated between the three leadership teams of approaching Tony Blair, Gordon Brown, Neil Kinnock, Ed Miliband, Alan Johnson (seen as one of the most popular figures in the Labour movement) and Margaret Beckett (in her capacity as a former deputy leader). The idea kicked around for a few days but again came to nothing. One member of Burnham's team says: 'What we really needed to do was to get Liz, Andy and Yvette round the table, we needed the grandees to say it, but we just weren't able to get that to happen.' A source close to Liz Kendall adds ruefully that having seen how Blair's early intervention had backfired, her team decided that the scheme could further fuel Corbyn's popularity: 'We realised doing a grand coalition and all that, it was actually going to compound the problem.' Lord Kinnock, who had already endorsed Burnham, says: 'I can understand how and why mischief-makers from various parts of the political spectrum would make such a claim or suggestion but as far as I'm concerned, it's fantasy. If I had thought it useful to take another course at any time I would have done so.' A source from Yvette Cooper's camp adds:

> There was a thought that Kinnock, Brown, Blair should all present a critique of Corbyn. It wasn't around a single candidate. In effect it was what Gordon did, but three of them, making the point that Labour in government is the only thing that matters. Trying to make the question that people were answering at the election 'Who was best placed to win'?

Blair and Brown now made their cases separately. The ever-cautious Brown gave what was billed as a major speech on 24 August, in which he failed to mention Cooper or Corbyn by name, although he made it palpably clear he opposed the left-winger by warning: '[I]f our global alliances are going to be alliances with Hezbollah and Hamas and Hugo Chávez's Venezuela and Vladimir Putin's Russia, there is no chance of building a worldwide alliance that could deal with poverty and inequality and climate change and financial instability.'

While Kinnock and Brown's statements appeared to have little impact on the race, Blair's interventions seemed to inspire ever greater support for Corbyn. Under the headline 'Even if you hate me don't take Labour over the cliff edge', Blair wrote in an article in *The Guardian* on 13 August: 'The Labour Party is in danger more mortal today than at any point in the over 100 years of its existence.' Two weeks later, Blair wrote a second article in which he took a slightly more mollifying tone, saying: 'It's a revolution but within a hermetically sealed bubble – not the Westminster one they [Corbyn supporters] despise, but one just as remote from actual reality.' Even if anyone was listening to the former leader, it was too late for Blair to change the course of the contest. The response on social media to his later interventions was as contemptuous as it had been to his first. More people flocked to register as supporters in order to vote for Corbyn.

Although his remarks clearly backfired, one former Blairite Labour aide thinks he was absolutely right to make them. The aide says: 'He was Leader of the Labour Party for thirteen years, he was Prime Minister for three terms, if he had not spoken people would have said it was strange. I wish more people would have come out earlier. Debate is healthy, and Tony Blair represented part of that debate.' The fact remained, however, that, as Diane Abbott told *Channel 4 News*, 'Tony Blair is entitled to his opinion but he's got to judge if it might be counter-productive.' A source close to Andy Burnham adds: 'By that stage, the more that people stood against [Corbyn] in any sense at all, that was galvanising his support.'

The post-mortems on why the last stand against Corbyn failed will probably continue for as long as he is leader. Yvette Cooper's team believe that, in refusing to join in the attacks on Corbyn, Burnham contributed to the failure of the plan to stop him. A source says: 'This is one of the reasons the Kinnock, Brown and Blair thing did not happen, because how can the argument be made that it would be a disaster for the Labour Party when you've got one so-called candidate saying that Corbyn's fine? You validate Corbyn.' In the other two campaigns, however, the blame is put squarely on Cooper. One senior Labour insider says:

> She [Cooper] just would not budge. Now, who knows what that would
> have done? But I know there was a very great degree of frustration.
> Because we could see what kind of a car crash was coming down the
> track. And there was great frustration that Yvette's campaign, to
> the end, maintained that she could win, which was damaging at times,
> and misleading, frankly, to voters.

A source on the Blairite wing of the party who was close to the negotiations adds:

> Yvette blocked it simply because she was too proud or hubristic to
> stand aside, even in the face of overwhelming statistical evidence from
> all sides that she should throw the towel in for the good of the party.
> It could – possibly – have worked. Everyone else was up for it. Andy
> was only tacking left as a tactical thing to try and defeat Corbyn, and
> this was understood and accepted as a necessary step. There was a
> short moment when it looked like everything was coming together
> and then Yvette scuppered it. [I] guess there is an argument that the
> pincer movement could have just helped Corbyn and looked like

ganging up on him, but this wasn't the reason why Yvette Cooper
said no, and it was worth a shot because by that point the writing was
almost on the wall.

In the past, Burnham had been close to Cooper but had a somewhat frosty
relationship with Kendall, who had served under him on Labour's health
team in the last parliament. Now, following the collapse of the plan for
an Anyone But Corbyn candidate, the Burnham and Kendall teams, who
worked out of the same office building at 83 Victoria Street (Cooper was
round the corner on Greycoat Place), became friendly. At the end of what
Burnham's people describe as their worst week of the campaign, they held
an impromptu joint drinking session. One member of his team says:

> That was not a great week, and I remember going down to Pizza
> Express, which was underneath our building, to get some lunch at
> about four o'clock and having a glass of wine, and for rest of the night,
> the entire team decamped, and Liz's team joined us, we were in reg-
> ular touch by then, and we just went through several bottles of wine
> and several bottles of limoncello. There was a bit of a realisation that
> things were going to be very different from then on.

Ironically, given the panic that set in among his rivals following the publication of the second YouGov poll, Corbyn's team ended the campaign with
less certainty than they had felt during July and the start of August. Immediately the poll was published, John McDonnell sent out a tweet urging
supporters not to be 'distracted' by it. The Corbyn for Leader Facebook page
pointed followers to his message, saying: 'Wise words from John. There's
a long way to go in this leadership election and we have an awful lot more
people to convince, both online and offline. Stick with the plan, people.'

As they came under attack from Yvette Cooper, Corbyn's team became nervous, wondering if they could yet be caught, particularly if second preference votes came into play. The mood, which had always been carefree, instead grew tense. Having long seen Andy Burnham as the biggest threat, now they began to worry about Cooper, particularly after she launched her attack on the government over its handling of the refugee crisis. Suddenly, whereas in the past it had always seemed as if there was nothing to lose, now there was very much something to lose. One campaign source says: 'In the final weeks we were being dragged into the mire. There was a lot of stress. Only Jeremy seemed in a good mood.'

Despite the inevitable pressures on his campaign staff, Corbyn had much to be in a good mood about. The 'Wild West' week in which nothing had seemed to go right for his rivals, with the announcement of the large numbers of new members and registered supporters, the YouGov poll, and the failure of the Anyone But Corbyn plot, was now followed by an equally chaotic period. In response to the letter from Burnham and the others complaining that the party had lost its grip on the voting system, Harriet Harman summoned the teams to a meeting at what was billed as a 'top-secret location'. The candidates were not given the address in advance but were instead provided with cars, which drove them north and west out of the capital. But the media soon found out where they were gathering, at a venue in the Hertfordshire town of Stevenage, and reporters made their way there. Inside the meeting, Harman and Mike Creighton, the party's head of risk management, merely assured the candidates that they had confidence in the integrity of the process. With news of the meeting public, however, Burnham felt he would be accused of sour grapes if he continued to raise questions about the rules of a contest he was clearly losing. He felt obliged to make clear that he would not challenge the leadership result legally. Within days he would be ruefully joking at one of his events: 'This campaign has been so long that I just about remember being the front-runner.'

On 22 August, a group of forty economists wrote to *The Observer* giving their backing to 'Corbynomics', the anti-austerity economic policies drawn up by John McDonnell and Richard Murphy, which now included the suggestion that Labour could renationalise the Royal Bank of Scotland. The economists wrote:

> [The] assertions that Corbyn is a 'danger' who is causing harm to the Labour Party and the public in general is quite surprising and inappropriate ... Many of Corbyn's policies are advocated by prominent economists and commentators ... Corbyn's proposals should be welcomed even by his opponents for stimulating serious discussion of crucial issues such as the role of the public sector in investment, management of debt and money, and how to tackle inequality. It is to Corbyn's credit that he has broadened the policy discussion so that the shared assumptions behind the narrow range of policies advocated by both the Conservative government and the other Labour leadership candidates are now being debated.

As a Corbyn leadership became a serious proposition, he began to find his policies subjected to greater scrutiny. Throughout the campaign, the team had boasted of the democratic nature of their policy formation, with Labour members encouraged to come up with ideas which were then opened out to consultation. Supporters could take part via the Facebook page, or email in their submissions. The downside of this approach became clear now when, as part of Corbyn's consultation on public transport, the campaign suggested that trains might have designated women-only carriages, to make them feel safer travelling at night. The idea was immediately mocked by his rivals and sparked a heated debate in the media and online. Yvette Cooper tweeted: 'Just got off tube. Majority of passengers women. Why should we have to shut ourselves away to stay safe?' Baffled by the fuss, Corbyn's defence, that the women-only carriages idea was not a settled policy but a discussion point, was not understood in a world in which politicians can be defined by the issues they raise, however briefly.

But for the most part, as August passed into September, it was smooth sailing. On 3 September, Sky News held the last hustings of the contest. In a poll of viewers held afterwards, 80 per cent said they thought Corbyn had come out on top. The following week, Harriet Harman took part in her last session of Prime Minister's Questions as acting leader, leaving with a parting shot at Corbyn. 'It was quite surprising to discover I'm not possibly old enough or posh enough to be the front-runner of this leadership election,' she said.

The day after Harman's final PMQs, 10 September, was the date set by the NEC for the final ballot papers and online votes to be received at party HQ. As with registration, the deadline was accompanied by chaotic scenes as thousands complained they had not received a ballot and new ones were sent out. Liz Kendall now gave her last speech of the campaign, all but capitulating, and laying much of the blame for Corbyn's victory on her own, Blairite, wing of the party. She said:

> Modernisers must be honest with ourselves: many people who've joined our party in recent months do not believe we are offering change, and some of them doubt our principles altogether. This is partly because too often in the past we've come across as technocratic and managerial. We've allowed ourselves to be defined as purely pragmatic – concerned with winning elections alone, rather than winning for a purpose – thereby ceding the mantle of principle to the far left.

By now, Yvette Cooper too was belatedly convinced that she had lost. Happy with the way she had ended the campaign, her main regret was that she had been so slow to engage with the contest. Vernon Coaker says: 'We probably got going too late. I wish we could have got it going quicker, and perhaps recognised the way Jeremy was capturing the new people.' DJ Collins agrees, saying: 'Yvette came alive almost when it was too late. The reason why what she said on the refugee crisis worked was she combined interesting, practical policy with the traditions and principles of the Labour Party.' Roger Baker admits, however, that by the end of the campaign, Corbyn had become unstoppable.

> The thing the Corbyn camp got brilliantly right was they determined the question that most people asked themselves. The question voters had in their minds was not 'Who is best placed to win?' It was almost 'Who makes you feel good about being Labour?' You can't win then. He was the only answer to that.

In the final days and hours before the leadership result, Andy Burnham was the only one of Corbyn's rivals who still held out the hope he could be beaten, even if his team wasn't so certain. A source close to Burnham now says:

> I don't think Andy ever did [think it was over]. He still thought he might have, at best, a 20 per cent chance. If Corbyn didn't win on firsts [preferences] we knew we'd have a chance. You would have a day when you would think, 'We can still win, we can still win.' There was never a point when we thought, 'That's it, there's no point.' There was still an outside chance.

Another senior member of the team adds:

> We were looking at the numbers and we knew it was slipping. By September we knew it had gone. There was a [victory] speech kicking around the day before, on email, and there was at one point some conversation about who's printing this off, and my view was: no one needs to print this off. I'm pretty sure Andy printed it off in the end.

Corbyn held his ninety-ninth rally of the campaign back in Islington on 11 September, the night before the leadership result was to be announced. The exhausted team all had bad coughs and were taking homeopathic medicine given to them by Harry Fletcher, but had been boosted by the news that Sadiq Khan had been elected Labour's candidate to fight the 2016 London mayoral election, beating Tessa Jowell, the Blairite who had started the contest as favourite. Fletcher says: 'If Sadiq had won, we knew it was in the bag.' Having spent the day with his team tentatively discussing potential shadow Cabinet elections, Corbyn arrived at the rally half an hour late, looking almost sheepish. The crowd gave him a standing ovation lasting several minutes and could barely contain their impatience when first Len McCluskey and then John McDonnell spoke before him. When he did finally speak, Corbyn thanked the crowd for filling the hall with 'hope and joy'. Winning the competition would be only a 'staging post' for further greatness, he promised. And then he left, to prepare for what would be the most extraordinary outcome of a party leadership contest in living memory.

In his final campaign post on Facebook, Corbyn thanked his supporters warmly:

> Whether you helped us gain the support of your constituency party, were amongst the 50,000 who joined us at one of our ninety-nine rallies and events, the 16,000 people who volunteered or the 9,000 who donated – or most crucially, if you have entrusted me with your

vote – thank you. We entered this contest to ensure there was a real political alternative put to the status quo of austerity and a society skewed towards the super-rich. Every one of us has been part of that – whether by sharing a Facebook post or talking about these ideas with friends and colleagues. We have put the case for the fairer, more democratic and decent society we all strive for. This work must continue. Together, we have achieved so much in just a few short months. I look forward to working together with you, in whatever capacity, to argue for and bring about the change we need not just in our party, but our country and world.

CHAPTER TWENTY-ONE

LEADER

LABOUR PARTY STAFF wore black to the special conference in Westminster's Queen Elizabeth II Conference Centre, where the result of the leadership contest was to be announced on 12 September 2015, a small protest symbolising what they saw as the death of the party they loved under the man who, against all the odds, was about to become their leader. They would later receive a severe telling-off from their new bosses for the prank, but anyone looking at some of the Labour employees' anxious faces on that warm September morning would find it hard not to feel sorry for them. Having had no relationship with Jeremy Corbyn before the leadership race and virtually no contact with his campaign team during it, they felt as if they were about to leap into an abyss. As well as their concerns for the party, they could not help but be worried for their own jobs and future prospects under a leader whose politics few of them shared.

The funereal aspect worn by the Labour staffers helped create an atmosphere inside the QEII that was one of bitterness and disbelief rather than jubilation, in stark contrast to the happy scenes outside, where crowds of Corbynistas had gathered shouting 'Jez We Can!' and waving placards reading 'I voted Jeremy'. In the street, the victory party had already begun. Inside, the invited audience was evenly divided between supporters of the four candidates, and the hostility between the winners and the losers was palpable. MPs and journalists mingled with ordinary members in the entry hall, talking in low voices of their astonishment and anger at how the contest had played out. John Prescott and Harriet Harman were there, but the party's former leaders, Ed Miliband, Gordon Brown, Tony Blair and Neil Kinnock, were conspicuous by their absence. Very few of the PLP were the mood for celebrating the prospect of a Corbyn victory; he was a man many of them had served alongside in the Commons for years without ever dreaming he could become their leader. As David Blunkett, the former Home Secretary, made his way to the hall where the announcement was due to be made, a Corbyn supporter shouted in his face: 'Blairites out, Corbyn in.'

The notoriously tardy Corbyn was for once early; the first of the candidates to arrive at the QEII, he got there before most of the crowd hailing his success. It was clear to fellow early birds that he had smartened up – a little – for the occasion. He wore a crisp, pale blue shirt, navy trousers and a new jacket, which his sons had clubbed together to buy him and brought over to his house in Islington earlier in the morning. True to form, he was not wearing a tie, and when asked by the press after the result to name the jacket's designer he did not know the answer.[316] Corbyn was ushered upstairs to wait in what had been designated as 'the candidates' room', taking with him John McDonnell, his old friend and faithful ally, the man who had stood beside him through long years of left-wing activism and was now about to deliver for him the leadership of the party they loved but which hadn't always loved them back.

Liz Kendall was the next to arrive, accompanied by her campaign manager, the MP Toby Perkins. She had been aware for some time both that

Corbyn would win and that she would come last, and of all the losing candidates was the least upset on the day of the verdict (although some members of her team were less sanguine). John Woodcock says: 'We were 100 per cent certain it would be Corbyn.' Kendall and Corbyn had developed a genuine rapport on the campaign trail. She would later say:

> I think he's wrong, but he has his analysis and he sticks with it. Put politics to one side here – there was a point during the campaign where Jeremy got a really bad throat, and I saw his wife and his sons and I could see this amazing thing happening ... You get concerned about the person and how it's going.[317]

Not long after Kendall, at around 10 a.m., two hours before the result was due to be announced, Yvette Cooper arrived in the candidates' room. She was accompanied by Vernon Coaker. Like Kendall, Cooper was certain that Corbyn had won. Roger Baker from her campaign says: 'Everyone knew, I think. Yvette knew, but was philosophical.' Only Andy Burnham, the last to get to the QEII, clung to the faint hope that he still might sneak through to victory on second preferences, giving himself what he saw as a one-in-five chance of success. He entered the candidates' room accompanied by Michael Dugher. As the other six had already done, Burnham and Dugher surrendered their phones and iPads to party officials so that they could be told the outcome of the contest in secret before it was made public. With over an hour to go until the formal announcement, the eight were kept waiting for another half-hour before they were given the news, and in the interval were forced to make stilted small talk. John McDonnell later recalled the conversation as cordial, saying: 'We talked about the campaign and about our families. It was incredibly friendly.'[318] Others in the room have described the atmosphere as strained, however.

At 10.40 a.m., Iain McNicol, the Labour Party general secretary, entered the candidates' room. A large television screen was switched on, and the group of eight were shown a spreadsheet with the results of the leadership election. From downstairs, they could hear faint murmurs as the last stragglers took their seats in the hall where the public announcement would be made. McNicol now said aloud what they could all see; Burnham's faint hopes of an upset were shattered. No second or third rounds were needed to declare Corbyn the new Leader of the Labour Party – by a landslide. If his success was not a surprise to either Kendall or Cooper, the sheer scale of his victory stunned everyone in the room, including Corbyn and McDonnell. He had won with 59.5 per cent, an astonishing result in a four-horse race. Burnham, in second place, could only manage 19 per cent, with Cooper on 17 per cent and Kendall just 4.5 per cent. An incredible 251,417 people had voted for Corbyn, including more than 120,000 full members of the Labour Party, shattering the myth that he would owe his success to the £3 registered supporters. By way of comparison, the entire mass membership of the Conservative Party, the current party of government, numbers only around 134,000. The silence in the candidates' room was eventually broken by McDonnell, who said simply, 'Wow.'[319]

There was time only for the briefest of congratulations for Corbyn from the losing candidates before he and McDonnell were whisked away to prepare his victory speech. The six remaining politicians stared at each other, wondering what on earth had happened over the proceeding four months, and how they had failed so badly to detect the mood of the party. Twenty minutes later, they joined Corbyn and went downstairs, all four candidates assuming poker faces as they took their seats in the audience and listened as first Tom Watson was declared deputy leader after three rounds, and then, finally, Corbyn's victory was confirmed, to cheers within the hall from his band of supporters, whose cries of 'Jez We Can!' changed to 'Jez We Did!'

The contrast between the excitement and joy of the Corbyn supporters in the hall and the despondency of those he had beaten was stark, however much they had anticipated their defeat. John Woodcock says: 'I was in the audience. I think you were psychologically armoured against some of it. Obviously I was disappointed, but not just for Liz; it was because the Labour Party was turning its back on victory at the next election.' The mood in the other losing teams was similarly philosophical. Roger Baker says: 'I was quite surprised that he got 60 per cent. I thought he'd get less than that. Everybody did.' John Lehal adds:

> For him to win on the first round against three other candidates with 60 per cent of the vote, you just can't argue with that. If that's what the party wants, we're a membership organisation, you can't argue with that. I wouldn't say there were tears. I think we were probably relieved it was over at that point.

With the cameras trained on them, the candidates embraced warmly, before Corbyn clambered on stage, pulled out his glasses and began speaking:

> We go forward now as a movement and a party, bigger than we have been for a very, very long time, stronger than we've ever been for a very long time, more determined than we've ever been for a very long time to show to everyone that the objectives of our party are intact, our passion is intact, our demand for humanity is intact, and we as a party are going to reach out to everyone in this country to go on that journey together, so no one is left on the side, everyone has a decent chance in life, a decent place in our society. That is what Labour was brought about to achieve; that is what we're going to achieve. Our party is going to become, I hope, more inclusive, more involved,

more democratic, and we're going to shape the future of everyone in this country in a way which I think is going to be good for everyone, that brings about the justice we crave, and that is what brought us into this wonderful party, this wonderful movement.

They were not stirring words, or particularly left-wing, but ones his parents, the unlikely socialists David and Naomi Corbyn, and his political father Tony Benn, would have been proud of.

For some, it was all too much. John Woodcock escaped from the building as soon as he felt he could. 'I went to thank the team because I knew I had to, but I just couldn't stay,' he says. 'I had to get out of the QEII Centre.' Back in the green room, where Corbyn had been taken, his team now met the party's paid workforce, the equivalent of Labour's civil service, in uncomfortable near-silence. Roger Baker says: 'There were an awful lot of staff there who were probably thinking very long and hard about what they did next. It was much harder for them [than staff on the losing campaigns]: they then had to go into a room and work with people in a very uncertain situation.' There was anger when it became apparent that no one from the party had bothered to book the new leader a car. Simon Fletcher went off to brief the press, as, outside the QEII, senior Labour MPs queued up to announce that they would not serve in a Corbyn shadow Cabinet. Pundits and commentators, many of them former Labour politicians and advisers themselves, were united in declaring that Corbyn could not win the 2020 general election.

Meanwhile, Andy Burnham's team found themselves lost backstage in the QEII's endless winding concrete corridors as they tried to find their way to the underground garage to pick up his own car, leading to a series of awkward encounters with Corbyn and his entourage, which the new leader used as an opportunity to convince Burnham to join his shadow Cabinet.

Katie Myler says:

> We got in the wrong lift and ended up in the boiler room. We get back upstairs, walk down the hall and straight into the lobby journalists waiting to interview Corbyn. Then I ran into Simon [Fletcher] ... and then we ran into Corbyn. By this time we have arrived at the right lift ... We were trying to get Andy out of the QEII so he could be reunited with his family, and Corbyn's trying to get in the lift, basically with us, pushing the buttons, and then one of his people stepped in front of him and was basically acting as a bodyguard for us between him and us ... and he was kind of shouting over his guy's shoulder: 'Andy, I need you!'

Corbyn's friends from around the world began sending their congratulations. Among the first were Sinn Féin's Gerry Adams and Martin McGuinness, who tweeted their good wishes, Argentinian President Christine Kirchner, Greece's left-wing Syriza party, Spain's upstart Podemos party and a spokesman for Hamas. The official Falkland Islands Twitter account sent a message reading: 'Hi @jeremycorbyn – Quick reminder... We're a British Overseas Territory. Don't even think about it. Cheers.'

Carless, Corbyn and his team walked out of the QEII and through the cheering crowds to celebrate in a nearby pub, the Sanctuary. There, with John McDonnell and his brother Piers beside him, as he had on top of The Wrekin on May Day 1966, as he had with his fellow activists in the Hornsey CLP in pubs across north London, as he had beside Tony Benn at Labour conferences through the decades, and as he had at numerous rallies and protests, events and meetings, he led them in a verse or two of the socialist anthem, 'The Red Flag'. Tears welled in his eyes as his friends and supporters, including his brother Piers, punched the air in victory and whooped with delight.

From the Sanctuary, Corbyn made his way to Parliament Square, the place he had gone in the minutes after he first got on to the ballot to enter the leadership contest, to take part in another demonstration. It was a quintessentially Corbyn way of marking his election. Where another leader might have squirrelled themselves away with advisers, drawing up plans or working out appointments, or spent the hours after victory touring the television studios, or even simply stayed in the pub to savour the moment, the new Labour leader did what he had been doing for so many years: joined a demonstration, the Solidarity with Refugees march. Many of the 100,000 people taking part had voted for Corbyn, and they were thrilled when he celebrated his success with them. Addressing the adoring crowd stretched out in front of him, Corbyn told them that Parliament Square had never looked more beautiful, before making a speech which barely touched on his coronation of three hours earlier. He declared that a Europe-wide 'popular uprising' had begun 'in favour of decency and humanity'. 'We are all human beings on the same planet,' he added. Corbyn was then joined onstage by the singer Billy Bragg for another rendition of 'The Red Flag'.

Corbyn not only refused to conduct any broadcast interviews following his election, his team now informed the BBC that he would not be appearing as scheduled on the following day's *Andrew Marr Show* for the set-piece interview a new leader would be expected to submit to. His refusal to court the media to the extent that he effectively snubbed the main broadcast outlets in the hours after his election was bold and in character: he had won without the mainstream media, why should he dance to their tune now? Instead, Corbyn would spend the day after his victory in his constituency, attending an event highlighting the crisis in mental health services.

As Corbyn addressed the crowds in Parliament Square, the three losing candidates sought refuge in various pubs and restaurants around London. Having finally located his car, Andy Burnham's journey to the bar a supporter had hired for his team in Marylebone was held up by the refugee rally. Katie Myler says:

> It took bloody ages to get there because the rest of London was closed off because of the march. We're sitting in the car with talk radio on, with Andy's brothers around me, all cheering on the Everton game which was on the radio, Andy who was doing OK, [a member of the team] who was not doing OK, and I'm looking through Twitter ... So it was a really bizarre hour.

John Lehal adds: 'We knew we wanted to get out of Westminster. Andy had brought his family; even though some people advised him not to, he kind of wanted them there with him. We went off to a bar in the Baker Street area and spent the afternoon drowning our sorrows.'

Yvette Cooper's team gathered at an Italian restaurant behind County Hall. Roger Baker says: 'The mood was good; as good as a losing party can be.' Liz Kendall also held a gathering, as did all of the winning and losing deputy leadership contenders. Gradually, various members of the groups dotted around Westminster made their way to the Greencoat Boy pub, just off Victoria Street, where the Labour Party staffers had gone straight from the QEII. There, the 'mainstream Labour establishment', in the words of one, held a boozy wake to mourn the loss of their party to a very unlikely coup by a left-winger called Jeremy.

The reasons for Jeremy Corbyn's stunningly unexpected victory in the 2015 Labour leadership contest are many and varied. Some subscribe to a somewhat Marxist view, feeling that historic, underlying forces of generational change were behind the tidal wave that swept him to power. They point to the Wikileaks scandal; the Occupy Wall Street movement; a Scotland so alienated by mainstream British politics that it has embraced the separatist SNP; an England that felt so ignored on immigration that it gave the UK Independence Party 4 million votes; anti-austerity movements across Europe that resulted in similarly unexpected left-wing electoral success in Greece and Spain and Portugal; the rise of the anti-politicians Donald Trump and Bernie Sanders in the United States. Harry Fletcher says:

> Why did Jeremy Corbyn's campaign take off rather than John McDonnell's [in 2007] or Diane Abbott's [in 2010]? It's not because of his film star looks. Incrementally, over the last decade, certain groups in society ... have [developed] a sense of injustice, have felt more and more alienated. Kids are either voting Green or not voting. Whether they're feminists, anti-austerity, anti-nuclear, anti-war, anti-poverty, all these disparate groups, he has brought them together.

Others hold to the 'great man' thesis, identifying a series of accidents, specific circumstances, and mistakes by his rivals in the story of Corbyn's unexpected path to power. The changes to Labour's leadership election rules after the 2013 Falkirk scandal; the particular quirks of fate that led more obvious but ultimately perhaps more divisive characters such as John McDonnell, George Galloway, Diane Abbott or Ken Livingstone to sit out the contest; the last-minute decisions by the centrist MPs Andrew Smith and Gordon Marsden to nominate Corbyn; the lacklustre campaigns run by Liz Kendall, Yvette Cooper and Andy Burnham; Harriet Harman and Andy Burnham's actions over the Welfare Reform Bill; Cooper's refusal to stand aside in favour of Burnham. All perhaps played a part in Corbyn's unlikely victory.

Still more believe both theories are true: the broadly left-of-centre public that forms Labour's support base had come to a place where they were disenchanted with the party and everything it stood for and, through his own good fortune and his competitors' failure, in Corbyn they identified the perfect means through which to register their dissatisfaction. It is now clear that as Corbyn was getting on with his lonely struggle through the early years of the century, and without anyone paying it very much attention, a movement had begun to emerge in the UK characterised by its opposition to – as Andy Burnham endlessly referred to it during the leadership contest – the 'Westminster bubble'.

Roger Baker from Yvette Cooper's team feels that if the left had chosen anyone but Corbyn to lead the charge, they would have failed; in stumbling upon the authentic, principled MP for Islington North, they created a perfect storm of candidate, conditions, electoral system and selectorate. Baker says: 'He was so blank to most people that they could project almost anything on to him. He is an authentic anti-politician, to be fair, and that's part of the sell.' Emily Thornberry agrees that Corbyn is appealing:

> I think it's the attraction of people saying what they mean and meaning what they say. And that is what people want from politicians. He's genuine. He's the real deal. He's the antidote to leaders who have become so self-conscious, so scripted, that people just don't believe that they mean it. The way that Ed [Miliband] moved away from his core and over-thought what he was doing, not only did he not really believe, it was obvious that he didn't believe, and people could see that.

Lord Harris adds:

> It's partly the whole anti-politics, anti-Westminster bubble stuff, which Andy Burnham rather bizarrely has been trying to claim he's not part

of. That means there's a seam of frustration amongst existing party members or party supporters that in the name of electability we have had to give up things we've always wanted to see happen in policy terms. There are people of that persuasion or even not that persuasion who think for a period at least we deserve – almost are owed it – to have Jeremy as Leader of the Labour Party.

According to a number of theorists, many Labour supporters, often on the 'soft left', lent their backing to Tony Blair in order to get him into power in 1997, only to feel betrayed by what followed. Jon Trickett, who backed Corbyn for the leadership, says:

> I don't know how anybody can be surprised that this has happened. The British political establishment have fundamentally misunderstood the nature of the country. They think that the political culture of the country is conservative with a small c, and that the way to win at elections is to play to that conservatism. Of course, there is a strong strand of caution and even nostalgia about our country's past and I certainly don't say that everybody is a radical. I wouldn't argue for one second that everyone is a socialist, but there is nonetheless a profound discontent about how the country works.

Some Blairites believe, however, that first Gordon Brown and then Ed Miliband encouraged soft-left members to move on to territory that was less appealing to the wider electorate, abandoning the ultimate New Labour credo, which holds that being in politics without being in government is meaningless. One adviser on the Labour right says: 'The lesson which many on the soft left of the party drew was that Ed M had betrayed their cause by tacking to the centre when the reality was more complex.' DJ Collins agrees that Brown and Miliband tempted the membership to dream of policies that were unacceptable to the wider public; however, he says, modernisers share the blame for failing to inspire the party:

> A project which was unassailable for ten years collapsed within a year. The process started with Gordon from the moment he got to the steps outside Downing Street. The successors to Tony Blair disavowed New Labour, which ultimately led to Jeremy Corbyn by providing an intellectual justification for the left to say New Labour was a mistake. But we share some of the responsibility by not renewing, and allowing the left to say New Labour was all about power and not about principle. It's a false argument but we let them make it. There was a build-up of pressure. This was always going to happen. It was either going to be this time or next time. It's no surprise we now have a left-wing leader.

Vernon Coaker, who ran Yvette Cooper's campaign, says that by the time those in the mainstream identified what was happening over the course of the leadership contest, it was too late to change. 'Even people in my own [constituency] party who would never regard themselves as Jeremy Corbyn supporters in terms of his politics, and would regard themselves as on the right of the party, voted for him because they wanted to put a shot of electricity into the system,' he says.

> My own sense is the anti-politics thing, the sense of disillusionment and despair, it does tend to impact more on the centre, centre-left parties. They're supposed to be more idealistic. Culturally, you aspire to a moral sense of purpose, rooted in Methodism, rooted in Christian Socialism, rooted in the Levellers and these sorts of people, who talked about 'the world can be better'. When people lose that language

or don't have the ability to connect with ordinary people, so ordinary people say, 'I don't believe that guy, or believe that woman.' When they say that, it's very untenable. But Jeremy's got that, at the same time as other Labour people have lost it, and there's been that growing sense of despair and disillusionment and the idea that people want something different.

David Lammy takes a more optimistic view of Corbyn's success, saying that while he does not share his politics, what the new leader inspired over the heady summer of 2015 should not be underestimated – and could provide the means for the party returning to power.

When I think about what's happened, I think that the energy, the inno-vation, the youth, the dynamism, the grassroots, the social media, the sense of a campaign beyond the party, all of that is very healthy for the long-term prospects of the Labour and it's part of the Labour Party [return] to power.

Those drawn to Corbyn were people, often but by no means exclusively young, who were disgusted by the 2009 expenses scandal and attracted by the anti-austerity Occupy movement. They were students who felt betrayed by the Liberal Democrats' 2010 broken promise on tuition fees – accord-ing to a YouGov poll released after the leadership result, a startling 18 per cent of Corbyn supporters voted Lib Dem at the 2010 election compared to only 9 per cent for Burnham and Cooper and 15 per cent of the country at large. And they had marched in huge numbers in 2003 against the Iraq War, only to have their plea for peace ignored by Tony Blair. They were utterly fed up with mainstream politics and politicians. And they found an outlet in Jeremy Corbyn.

As the contest went on, with his quaint lefty ways and unconventional dress sense Corbyn became a kind of celebrity; a left-wing Nigel Farage or Boris Johnson. But he was an anti-politician with a huge base outside of Westminster, who, when the time came, was able to mobilise supporters in such vast numbers that his rivals could only look on with envy. It is remarkable how many people it is possible to meet and engage with on marches and demonstrations over forty years of activism. These were the members of CND and Amnesty International he had toiled alongside, these were veterans of the miners' strike and Wapping, Stop the War and justice for the Guildford Four and Birmingham Six. In later years, they were individuals Corbyn had interacted with on Twitter and Facebook, who threw themselves at the campaign to elect him. At the height of the 2015 contest, when his attention would be expected to be otherwise occupied, Corbyn's friend Tariq Ali recalls spotting him in the background of a tiny demonstration by staff protesting at the privatisation of services at the National Gallery. Who else but Corbyn would have bothered? Such loyalty would be rewarded when he asked those whose causes he had championed for all those years to do so for him.

Why did Jeremy Corbyn win the leadership of the Labour Party? Vernon Coaker perhaps puts it best: 'There's been a convergence of the stars, a convergence of the galaxies around it, and he's been able to capture the distinct political time in which we live.'

CODA

J EREMY CORBYN STOOD on stage at the 2015 Labour Party conference to deliver his first speech as leader. It seemed fitting that the gathering was once again being held in Brighton, the place where, despite Corbyn's best efforts, his mentor Tony Benn had his heart broken by his narrow failure to capture the deputy leadership, and where the IRA had come close to wiping out the Thatcher government. In the front row of the auditorium, Corbyn's wife, Laura Alvarez, was seated alongside the lanky figures of his three sons, Benjamin, Sebastian and Thomas. Further along the row from them was a somewhat shell-shocked-looking shadow Cabinet, including the one-time favourite for the leadership, Andy Burnham, who had agreed to serve as Corbyn's shadow Home Secretary. A few seats down from Burnham sat John McDonnell, the new shadow Chancellor, and along from him was Corbyn's former lover and long-time friend Diane Abbott, now shadow International Development Secretary.

A lot had happened in the two weeks since Corbyn's unlikely election as Labour leader, much of it aggravating, but more of it uplifting. The day following the special conference at the QEII, a Sunday, had begun well as, rather than share a sofa with the BBC's Andrew Marr, Corbyn had mingled with his old friends and constituents at the mental health event in Islington. But it had ended in farcical scenes as he struggled to put together a shadow Cabinet. Although his middle son Sebastian, who continued to play a key role in the team, believed that the line-up had been agreed the evening before the leadership result, by the Sunday afternoon, and with Rosie Winterton, whom Corbyn had retained as Chief Whip, now involved, it had begun to unravel.

As Corbyn himself had anticipated, the appointment of John McDonnell as shadow Chancellor, an 'utter Trot', in the words of one disgusted MP, was always going to be controversial; an 'act of war', as another senior Member describes it. Many in the PLP had hoped that Corbyn would begin his leadership by building bridges with the right and centre of the party, perhaps giving the economic brief to a uniting figure such as the well-regarded Rachel Reeves, whom Burnham had planned to make shadow Chancellor, or even Burnham himself. But those who knew Corbyn understood that he was always going to give the most important job in his shadow Cabinet to his old friend and ally. McDonnell had got him on the ballot in the first place and, ably guided by Simon Fletcher, had helped deliver the leadership for him. He wasn't going to be disloyal now. Corbyn's decision to appoint McDonnell as shadow Chancellor created difficulties, however. Coming from a wing of the party with such a tiny base in the Commons, Corbyn needed MPs from other schools of thought to come on board, if only to make up the numbers. The appointment of McDonnell made many reluctant to do so.

The press had been briefed that the shadow Cabinet line-up would be completed and announced on the afternoon of Sunday 13 September. In the event, the process dragged on late into the night. When most political reporters at the Commons gave up and went home, an intrepid couple of broadcast journalists, Sky News's Darren McCaffrey and Eleanor Garnier from the BBC, stayed up past midnight, listening outside the door of the Whips' Office as they could clearly hear an anguished series of phone calls being made, all but begging reluctant MPs to come on board. Particular sticking points seemed to be the new leader's positions on membership of the European Union and NATO, as well as his opposition to the Trident nuclear deterrent, which made finding a shadow Defence Secretary somewhat tricky.

McCaffrey wrote afterwards:

> Behind a not-very-thick door, we could hear conversations which often spiked in volume and were clearly audible. 'Andy [Burnham] is IN, Hilary [Benn] is IN, Angela [Eagle] is IN,' was the line Rosie [Winterton] would use in an attempt to win people over and get on board with Jezza's shadow Cabinet … The phone calls continued but defence seemed like it had been settled. It had been offered to Chris Bryant. 'Jeremy was up for it,' Rosie said on the phone, but then it fell apart after Bryant insisted on 'a thirty-minute conversation about what would happen if we had to invade Russia'. That was a conversation Jeremy clearly wasn't prepared to have. Bryant was out. 'Oh, maybe Jack Dromey would be good at defence.' But no, Rosie had to get back to her 'defence problem'. A laugh ensued; it was 'the defence of the realm, after all' … Rosie was back on the phone, we couldn't tell who with. 'Now, this might be a bit of an outside idea, how do you feel about being shadow Defence Secretary?' A pause. 'Just what are your views on Trident?' A much, much longer pause. 'But, are you willing to engage in a debate?'[320]

By now, the 'Big Four' had been settled and announced: Corbyn as leader was supported by McDonnell as shadow Chancellor, Burnham at home affairs and Hilary Benn as shadow Foreign Secretary. Then Labour MPs eagerly monitoring the journalists' Twitter feeds to find out who their new leaders would be noticed something. The top jobs had all been filled by men. McCaffrey continued:

> All the shadow Cabinet top positions had gone to men, Labour MPs started to complain online, this is surely not what a Corbyn shadow Cabinet was meant to look like. Then a male voice, it sounded like Simon Fletcher. 'We are taking a fair amount of **** out there about women. We need to do a [Peter] Mandelson [who was First Minister to Gordon Brown]. Let's make Angela [Eagle] shadow First Minister of State. Like Mandelson was. She can cover PMQs. Tom [Watson] knows about this. Do the Angela bit now.' Minutes later a text from a Labour source. Angela Eagle was to be shadow First Minister of State. She would deputise at Prime Minister's Question Time. Was this the plan all along, or a last-minute reaction to outrage on Twitter and private message?

The chaotic scenes that accompanied the formation of the shadow Cabinet and front-bench team were followed by a first meeting of the PLP on the Monday evening which was described as 'frosty'.[321] The events were still being chewed over when Corbyn found himself in the middle of another media storm, after taking part in one of his first ceremonial duties as the Leader of Her Majesty's Most Loyal Opposition: attending a memorial service at St Paul's Cathedral to commemorate the seventy-fifth anniversary of the Battle of Britain. As he stood alongside veterans, senior members of the Royal Air Force in full battle dress, and the royal family in all their regalia, and for once wearing a tie, when the time came to sing the national anthem, 'God Save the Queen', Corbyn's lips remained sealed.

It was perhaps to be expected from a man who was an avowed republican and was at this stage still chairman of the Stop the War Coalition. But the frenzy that followed was also easy to anticipate. Five of Corbyn's new shadow Cabinet immediately denounced his failure to sing along with the national anthem, with Kate Green, who had been made shadow Equalities Minister just thirty-six hours earlier, stating that his actions would have 'offended and hurt many people'.[322] Downing Street helpfully remarked that David Cameron had been 'very proud and willing' to join in the singing.[323] Nicholas Soames, a Conservative MP and grandson of Winston Churchill, added: 'It was an extremely disrespectful thing and I think he needs to make his mind up whether he is a grown-up or not.'[324] A Labour spokesman's explanation, that Corbyn had remained in 'respectful' silence while thinking about his parents and others in London during the Blitz, failed to calm the nerves of many Labour MPs at their new leader's refusal to fall into line with conventions and customs he did not believe in. A promise from Corbyn that he would 'show my respect in the proper way'[325] at future events did little to ease their fears.

But if the first few days of Corbyn's leadership proved somewhat rocky, what followed next was a triumph. On the morning of Wednesday 16 September, as he prepared to stand across from David Cameron at his first ever session of Prime Minister's Questions, his new deputy, Tom Watson, had some good news. On the day of Corbyn's anointment as leader, an astonishing 14,500 more people had signed up to become members of the Labour Party. By the Monday morning two days later, that figure had grown to 30,000, and as they awaited PMQs it had reached an incredible 40,000. Total Labour membership had hit more than 350,000 for the first time since the early years of Tony Blair's first government, and continued to rise, reaching more than 370,000 by the end of the week.

A few days after his election, Corbyn had come up with the novel idea of 'crowd-sourcing' his first PMQs, by inviting members of the public to submit questions they would like him to put to David Cameron. It was a clever move, designed to finally achieve what so many former leaders had claimed they wanted to do but had singularly failed to act upon; taking 'Punch and Judy politics' out of the session. An astonishing 40,000 people responded with questions. With an equally impressive one million viewers watching on television, when PMQs began on Wednesday 16 September, Corbyn stood up and told Cameron he wanted to try out a 'different style' for the session. Some MPs watching were surprised by his calmness and sense of authority. Maybe they should not have been: after all, Corbyn had spent more time in the Commons Chamber than virtually all of them. After more than thirty years on the back benches, however, the step up to the dispatch box for the very first time was a daunting one. Corbyn's poise was remarkable. He went on to ask Cameron a series of interesting and insightful questions, including on housing, tax credits and cuts to mental health services. Because the questions had been posed by ordinary voters, Cameron was forced to respond respectfully and was unable to deploy the vast array of clever putdowns he would have had at his disposal. The session received rave reviews, with many of those watching describing the exchanges between the new Leader of the Opposition and the Prime Minister as refreshing and informative, a welcome change from the abuse and snide remarks that usually characterised the weekly bouts. More people flocked to join the Labour Party.

By the time Corbyn arrived at Labour conference in the last week of September, he had begun to feel more settled, despite the warning from a senior serving general that there would be a 'mutiny' from the armed forces if a future Labour government sought to cut defence, withdraw from NATO or scrap Trident.[326] In the words of one long-standing MP, Corbyn had already 'grown to it', and was relishing his new job, telling the *New Statesman* in an interview conducted in the official offices of the Leader of the Opposition:

'It's fascinating: a lot of pressure, a lot of different things to do all the time. And I'm enjoying it.' He committed himself to remaining as leader until the 2020 general election. Addressing the TUC conference a week before Labour's gathering in Brighton, Corbyn promised to oppose George Osborne's welfare cap, which Harriet Harman had fought so valiantly to support.

For his speech to Labour conference in Brighton at 2.30 p.m. on Tuesday 29 September, Corbyn was introduced by a nineteen-year-old constituent, Rohi Malik, a medical student whose immigrant parents had fled persecution in Pakistan, who told the crowd: 'We have always seen how committed and honest he is, how hard he fights for the things he believes in and stands up for the people of Islington North.' Then Corbyn walked on stage wearing a beige jacket, white shirt and red tie. With Iran's Press TV among the international media taking his speech live, he spoke:

> I've been given a huge mandate, by 59 per cent of the electorate who supported my campaign. I believe it is a mandate for change ... First and foremost it's a vote for change in the way we do politics. In the Labour Party and in the country. Politics that's kinder, more inclusive. Bottom up, not top down. In every community and workplace, not just in Westminster. Real debate, not necessarily message discipline all the time. But above all, straight talking. Honest. That's the politics we're going to have in the future in this party and in this movement.

It was the first time that Corbyn had ever used an autocue, making the gaffe he now committed somewhat understandable. Inadvertently, he read aloud the helpful stage direction that had been inserted by a member of his team: 'Big Message Here.' Corbyn concluded: 'Don't accept injustice, stand up against prejudice. Let us build a kinder politics, a more caring society together. Let us put our values, the people's values, back into politics.'

As his entire campaign had been, the first major speech of his leadership proved divisive, welcomed by his supporters as radical, decried by his detractors as both banal and insubstantial. The universal theme of the criticism was that the speech preached to the converted and made little attempt to reach out to the Conservative voters it was said Labour needed in order to win the next election. As Jonathan Freedland put it in *The Guardian*:

> He came to toast a remarkable victory, to celebrate an extraordinary electoral success. In his debut address, Labour's leader referred to it often, speaking of the mandate he'd won – its sheer scale, finding new ways to count the colossal votes he'd racked up. This was a triumph to savour, one that heralded a new politics. The election result Jeremy Corbyn had in mind was, of course, the one that had made him his party's unexpected leader. Of an earlier ballot, the small matter of the general election that handed David Cameron his first overall majority, there was no mention. For a glorious hour, 7 May was erased from history, its place overwritten by 12 September ... And because 7 May had been eclipsed by 12 September, there was no need to explain what went wrong at the general election or how it might be reversed.

In the days and weeks that followed his first Labour conference as leader, Corbyn would experience more highs and lows as the political establishment struggled to come to terms with this most unorthodox of politicians. First, lengthy sections of his speech were revealed to have been written by a former adviser to Denis Healey, Richard Heller, who had unsuccessfully submitted them to Ed Miliband four years earlier.[327] The following week, in a coup timed to coincide with Conservative conference, Chancellor George Osborne announced that the Labour peer and former adviser to Tony Blair, Lord Adonis, would be resigning his party's whip in order to head a government review of major infrastructure projects. A few days later, Corbyn was accused of 'snubbing' the Queen after he went on a walking holiday with his wife rather than attend the first meeting of the Privy Council since his election, where he had been due to be sworn in on bended knee as a member of her group of advisers entitled to hear state secrets.

On 14 October, Corbyn found himself in the strange position of being not the rebel in the Commons but the rebelled against, when twenty-one Labour MPs refused to follow the whip by opposing George Osborne's fiscal charter, which commits the government to running a Budget surplus by 2020. Another Labour peer, Lord Warner, became the next to leave the party, saying that under Corbyn's leadership Labour faced an 'existential threat'.[328] The appointment of Seumus Milne, a far-left commentator from *The Guardian*, as Labour's head of communications and strategy, was greeted with raised eyebrows among many in the mainstream of the party.[329]

Perhaps Corbyn's toughest time in the short period since his election came in late November and early December 2015, as he struggled to hold his shadow Cabinet together while maintaining his determined opposition to airstrikes against ISIS. By the time of the Commons vote on 2 December, the row had become far more than a debate about the rights and wrongs of taking military action in Syria. Swept up in it were the numerous insecurities and grievances held both by Corbyn's detractors and his supporters; indeed, at times it seemed as if the Syria furore was an ugly re-run of the leadership election itself. At its nub, the disagreement laid bare the incongruous situation in which the Labour Party finds itself: led by a man of the far left who enjoys enormous loyalty in the wider movement but little in the parliamentary party. Having been forced by sheer lack of fellow thinkers in the PLP to appoint a shadow Cabinet that fails to see eye to eye with him on many issues, Corbyn lacked the strength to impose his will over Syria, and was forced to grant a free vote to avoid mass resignations.

In the end, sixty-six Labour MPs, including eleven members of the shadow Cabinet, supported the government motion approving airstrikes; eleven more abstained. As well as Benn, Corbyn was defied by his deputy Tom Watson, shadow Defence Secretary Maria Eagle, shadow Education Secretary Lucy Powell, shadow Culture Secretary Michael Dugher, and such respected figures as Alan Johnson, Chuka Umunna, Harriet Harman, Hilary Benn, Liz Kendall, Margaret Beckett, Tristram Hunt, Yvette Cooper and Dan Jarvis. They were greeted with rage from those grassroots activists who felt Corbyn had a clear mandate to lead and should have been given the respect due to the head of the party. Amid allegations of bullying, both Corbyn and John McDonnell urged supporters to tone down their social media attacks on Labour MPs, to little avail. The name-calling and even death threats hurled at MPs including Stella Creasy and Neil Coyle are a consequence of a social media tiger that Corbyn rides but has not yet tamed.

There will be many more controversies swirling around Jeremy Corbyn in the months and years to come. For now, though, let us leave him in Brighton to savour his moment of glory. Addressing the 5,000-strong audience as leader of the party he had joined as a teenager and spent so many years battling both for and against was the crowning moment of his life. All those rainy days spent knocking on doors and delivering leaflets, all those endless meetings and fratricidal arguments, the thousands of miles marched, the speeches given to crowds large and small, the broken relationships, the late nights, the early starts; it all came down to this moment, and it had all been worth it. Comrade Corbyn was transcendent.

A YEAR IS A LONG TIME IN POLITICS

9 JULY 2016

THE ANNUAL DURHAM Miners' Gala remains the most important social-ist gathering of the political year. For 132 years, brass bands, miners, trade unionists and socialists from across the north of England and fur-ther afield have marched proudly through the ancient streets of the city of Durham, behind colourful banners bearing the names of local collieries. As the brothers and sisters gathered as usual at the town's race track to hear their hero, Jeremy Corbyn, speak at the 2016 event, many were in bullish humour. Corbyn was facing the biggest challenge of his short leadership to date; two weeks earlier, two-thirds of the shadow Cabinet and dozens more front-bench MPs had resigned, ostensibly in protest at his under-whelming performance during the referendum on Britain's membership of the European Union. Days later, a vote of no confidence had passed by 172–40, with 80 per cent of the parliamentary party turning against the leader. In Durham, as Corbyn prepared to speak under leaden skies, he digested the news that talks led by his deputy, Tom Watson, to resolve the crisis had broken down. Then, just before 1 p.m., word came through that his former shadow Business Secretary, Angela Eagle, was preparing to challenge him for the leadership.

Secure in the adoration of the crowd before him, confident of the strength of his personal mandate, Corbyn shrugged the crisis off. Without mentioning Eagle by name, and with a vehemence critics said was lacking in his public statements for the Remain campaign, he began:

> There's a lot of debate about what's happening in the Labour Party at the present time. And I am inundated with questions, questions, questions all the time. And I have patience that is infinite to answer questions, questions and questions. But one I got today really did puzzle me. They said: 'How are you coping with the pressure that's on you?' I simply said this: 'There is no pressure on me, none whatsoever.' Real pressure – real pressure – is when you don't have enough money to feed your kids, when you don't have a roof over your head, when you are wondering if you are going to be cared for, when you are wondering how you can survive, you are wondering how you are going to cope with the debts you have incurred, you are wondering if your lovely employer is going to give you a call to give you a couple of hours work or not bother, or change their mind when you are on the bus on the way to do that job.

Corbyn was not for quitting. The response was wildly enthusiastic – but, then, this was a curated crowd. Twelve months earlier, Corbyn's three opponents for the Labour leadership had been told he would be the only candidate given a platform to speak at the gala. This year, some Labour MPs who were in conflict with Corbyn claimed they had been asked to keep away altogether, in letters sent in the name of the late Dave Hopper, then leader of the Durham Miners' Association, which they felt had 'disinvited' them from the event. (Hopper and the Association insisted the MPs had not been barred but were told to keep away only from the official functions and platforms organised by the DMA.) Corbyn stood beside Hopper, who had described the MPs as 'traitors',[330] to watch the march from the balcony of the town's County Hotel. The Sedgefield MP Phil Wilson was among a handful to have received letters who defiantly attended anyway, marching with the Fishburn banner – representing the colliery his miner father had toiled in. Around him, huge flags and placards bearing Corbyn's name and face were waved alongside those of other socialist heroes, including the Soviet leader and mass murderer Joseph Stalin.

The 132nd Durham Miners' Gala came at a time of crisis for the entire political establishment. Politicians of all parties, those who had supported both Remain and Leave, were still reeling from the unexpected outcome of the Brexit vote two weeks earlier. David Cameron had resigned as Prime Minister, triggering a contest in the Conservative Party to replace him. With the strong possibility that a new leader might seek to take advantage of Labour's poor showing in the polls by calling an early general election, the rebel MPs seeking to topple Corbyn were motivated by fear for the future of the party – and their own seats. It was clear to everyone in the Labour family, both those who marched in Durham and who those who stayed away, that the movement was not in a good place.

The hardback edition of this book bade farewell to Jeremy Corbyn in September 2015, as he stood triumphant onstage at Labour conference for his first speech as party leader. We re-join him as he battles to make it to his second. It is an understatement in the extreme to point out that a lot has happened in the intervening twelve months. Corbyn stands today as the wounded leader of a party which is all but broken. Yet for all the speed with which Corbyn's leadership has descended into chaos and division, it is fascinating to observe how many of the rare triumphs and near-constant tribulations of his first year as head of his party can be traced back to long-established aspects of his character and the history of his strange journey to office. His peculiar position as a leader who largely lacks the support of the parliamentary party he leads has its roots both in his forty years of opposition to previous leaderships within the Commons and in the unique circumstances of his candidacy, particularly the unlikely manner in which he got on the ballot in the first place. The appointment of long-time fellow travellers such as John McDonnell and Diane Abbott to senior positions, the reliance on a tiny circle of like-minded advisers, including such divisive, unpopular figures as Seumas Milne, Ken Livingstone and Jon Lansman, his tendency to preach to the converted, all come naturally to a man long mistrustful of the mainstream, and for whom the term 'broad church' must seem anathema.

Corbyn's more controversial policy decisions and the manner in which he has conducted himself as leader will also have come as little surprise to close followers of his life story. Singing the national anthem at the Battle of Britain commemoration was always going to be a challenge for a life-long republican. Opposing the bombing of Syria was self-evident for one of the founders of the Stop the War movement. The anti-Semitism row of the spring of 2016, in which Corbyn was accused of failing to act against party members, including Livingstone, who voiced opinions many considered anti-Semitic, was perhaps predictable given his long-standing and well-known views on the Middle East. Equivocation over the renewal of Trident is hardly a shock from a man who joined the Campaign for Nuclear Disarmament as a teenager. His lukewarm support for the Remain cause in the EU referendum debate, the trigger for many Labour MPs to move against him, was utterly predictable from a long-time Eurosceptic who voted 'No' during the last referendum in 1975 and who would probably have preferred to have done so again in 2016.

There were early indications too of the toxic tone of the debate around Corbyn's leadership in the manner of his coming to office. The side-lining of mainstream journalists and the use of below-the-radar social media campaigns, deployed by Team Corbyn to such devastating effect in the summer of 2015, have continued during his leadership, with more limited success. Online activism has allowed for a far more direct relationship between the membership and leadership than ever before, but it is questionable how well Labour has been able to reach out to the wider electorate. There are serious negatives, too, with the rise of an alarming trend, first seen in some of the treatment dealt out to candidate Liz Kendall during the 2015 campaign, of online bullying, often of a misogynistic, sometimes threatening nature.

The anonymity provided by social media can serve to embolden or even encourage users to voice opinions with a stridency they would be unlikely to display in person. Occasionally, this rage worked up online escalates into potentially dangerous scenarios in real life. The tendency for political discourse to turn ugly is writ large in Corbyn's Labour Party, where some MPs and others, both those opposed to his leadership and his supporters, have been the recipients of serious abuse, including death threats. Some of those who have found themselves on the receiving end of such treatment feel Corbyn and his allies have failed to do enough to address it. Detractors claim that the Momentum group, founded by Corbyn's long-time ally Jon Lansman as the successor organisation to the Jeremy Corbyn for Leader campaign, equates to a personal army dedicated to sustaining leader, not party. Both sides accuse each other of focusing on fighting those within Labour whom they disagree with, rather than concentrating their fire on the Conservative government.

Corbyn's stubborn determination to remain in post in the teeth of over-whelming opposition from the parliamentary party also comes as no great shock to those who have followed his history closely. The image he likes to portray, of a modest, self-effacing figure who wears the mantle of leader-ship reluctantly, has been somewhat undermined by recent events. But it never quite chimed with the reality of a man who has always been more ambitious than he lets on. The local activist who became a leading light in Bennite circles; the councillor who allowed himself to be persuaded to stand for one of the safest Labour seats in the country; the MP who grad-ually took over the leadership of the left, helped found the Stop the War Coalition and led the global opposition to the conflict in Iraq; the Cam-paign Group member who himself first suggested to his comrades he stand for the Labour leadership, who was then surprised yet delighted when he won the contest last summer, certainly has no intention of relinquishing it without a fight.

In the days after David Cameron stood down, as panicked Labour MPs, fearing an early general election, voted against Corbyn by a margin of four to one, many assumed he would 'do the decent thing' and follow suit. There was never any chance he would comply. Followers of his early life and sub-sequent political career understand that Corbyn's higher loyalty was never to his country, or even to his party, but to the ideals and principles of the hard left, which he was first attracted to as a left-wing school boy out of step with his Tory neighbours in rural Shropshire. That allegiance was indelibly imprinted during his life-changing experiences in Jamaica and Latin America in his formative late teens and early twenties. And it was cemented through his years in the hotbed of left-wing intellectualism in north London in the 1970s. Since entering Parliament in 1983, his lode star has been to advance the cause, not to achieve a Labour government. Quit-ting office, allowing in a successor who did not share those ideals, even if they offered more broad electoral appeal, would, in Corbyn's world view, be a betrayal of the cause.

And so Corbyn remains in place – for now. At the time of writing, in August 2016, he is facing a leadership challenge. Whatever the disastrous state of the party in Westminster, as Corbyn travels around the country seeking to recreate the heady atmosphere of the summer of 2015, he receives every indication that he retains the adoration of the membership. They shout his name, wear T-shirts bearing his image, cheer his speeches to the rafters, demand selfies, that he sings them happy birthday, kisses their babies. Even a Jeremy Corbyn colouring book was a sell-out. Unless a political upset occurs (and there have been plenty of those in the past twelve months) the probability seems to be that Corbyn will address the 2016 Labour conference in Liverpool as leader. Perhaps when he does, he will take a few moments to reflect on his extraordinary first year. Let us continue that story where we left off, at the end of December 2015.

Jeremy Corbyn began 2016 feeling comfortable. He had ridden out the Syria vote crisis, making it a test of strength against his shadow Cabinet, flexing his muscles by showing the power of the support he continued to enjoy in the membership with an online poll backing his position. He had stood firm against Hilary Benn, the son of his great mentor and the man he would go on to sack six months later, triggering the greatest crisis of his leadership. But for now Benn remained in place and, on the surface at least, loyal to his leader. And as Corbyn settled into the job, he began to feel at home, even to enjoy it. After forty years in the wilderness it was still exhilarating to be calling the shots, to enjoy the funding and resources that come with the leadership and all that means in terms of being able to hire a loyal team of advisers, to have secretarial support, to control the party apparatus. Asked in an interview for the left-wing *Red Pepper* magazine at the turn of the year if he was enjoying leadership, he said: 'Yeah, I was pushed into this, but I'm happy I was.'[331]

In his personal life, too, Corbyn was content. Although before his election as leader he had assured his wife, Laura Alvarez, he would stand down from Parliament in 2020, there was no question that she fully supported his role as leader – indeed, revelled in it. She took to hanging around the office of the Leader of the Opposition and attending interviews, meetings and rallies with him. At one point, according to an insider, she even asked Corbyn if she could be given a formal role within the leadership structure, a suggestion greeted with horror by members of the inner circle, who were already grumbling to one another about having to take turns to 'babysit Laura'.

But despite Corbyn's good mood at the turn of the year, there were consequences to the bad feeling in the parliamentary party around the Syria vote and the 'revenge reshuffle' which now followed it. In a forerunner of the reaction to Corbyn's sacking of Benn in June, a number of shadow Cabinet ministers and senior Labour figures publicly aired their unhappiness at the dismissal of Michael Dugher as shadow Culture Secretary and Pat McFadden from the shadow Europe post. Three shadow ministers resigned in protest. To the consternation of many within the PLP, such as the Copeland MP Jamie Reed, who has warned that the British electorate will not elect a unilateralist party, the pro-Trident Maria Eagle was replaced as shadow Defence Secretary by Emily Thornberry, an opponent of the missile system. A review into Britain's independent nuclear deterrent was set up. Benn stayed in post as Foreign Secretary only after, it was claimed in briefings by the Corbyn team, he agreed not to make any further criticism of the leadership. While Benn denied he had been 'muzzled', there were reports that any attempt to dislodge him would have resulted in mass resignations from the front bench – a scenario that would indeed play out a few months later. In public, however, Corbyn continued to maintain that all was rosy. Asked on breakfast television about reports of ructions, he insisted: 'We are making progress as a party ... everybody is getting along just fine.'[332]

Corbyn had never taken the opportunity to reach out to the wider party after his election; now he retreated entirely into the comfort of his inner circle, drawing particularly close to his chief adviser Seumas Milne, long-time allies Kat Fletcher and Cat Smith, and, of course, his closest friend and comrade, John McDonnell. Such is McDonnell's power and influence over Corbyn's Labour Party that many of their fellow Labour MPs describe the leadership as a 'duopoly', despite persistent rumours – much denied by McDonnell – that he seeks the top job for himself. The Corbyn inner circle is characterised by many who come close to it as one of intense paranoia and mistrust. Those who do not toe the line, such as the veteran political operator Neale Coleman, who was forced out as Head of Policy at the end of January following a series of clashes with Milne, are sidelined.

On policy too, Corbyn frequently found himself at odds with much of the PLP. From his suggestion in March that prostitution be legalised, greeted with alarm by leading female Labour MPs such as Harriet Harman, to the announcement in April, denounced as 'student politics',[333] that the fast-food chain McDonald's would be banned from sponsoring a stall at conference, to his continuing opposition to Trident, leading a party that, by and large, did not share his world view was never straightforward. In March, the *Times* newspaper obtained a list, allegedly written by Corbyn's political secretary Katy Clark, categorising most of the PLP into five groups: 'core group', covering nineteen members of the Corbyn inner circle, 'core group plus', made up of another fifty-six names, 'neutral but not hostile', amounting to seventy-two MPs, 'core group negative', numbering forty-nine, and 'hostile' of which there were thirty-six.[334] Listed among the 'hostile' were the Chief Whip, Rosie Winterton, who had remained publicly loyal to Corbyn throughout his leadership, and Sadiq Khan, at the time Labour's candidate to be Mayor of London. The list was greeted with equal measures of alarm and glee from Labour MPs, most of whom refused to accept a flat denial from the leader's office that it had been drawn up there.

Also in March, to mark his six months in the job and presumably in an attempt to sidestep what they saw as the negative prism of the mainstream media, the Corbyn leadership team invited a camera crew from Vice News, the iconoclastic online television station, to spend eight weeks filming him at close quarters. The results, in the form of a documentary called 'The Outsider',[335] give an illuminating glimpse into the group's psyche. Presented by a young journalist, Ben Ferguson, who described himself as a Corbyn supporter at the outset, relations between the leadership team and the Vice crew deteriorated as the weeks passed. At one point, after filming preparations for Prime Minister's Questions, the reporter expressed disbelief at the leader's refusal to press David Cameron over the resignation of Iain Duncan Smith, a key Cabinet minister who had quit purportedly in protest at the welfare cuts proposed in the recent Budget. Corbyn responded by saying: 'It's not up to me to throw in, other than a couple of lines about "the government's in a mess".'[336] Interviewed shortly after PMQs, Seumas Milne then made the astonishing claim that a Labour Party staffer present at the meeting had briefed the media, and therefore the opposition, on the lines Corbyn planned to take at the session. The allegation was greeted with outrage and disgust by the staffers themselves.

The incident highlighted the scepticism with which Corbyn and his allies viewed the ranks of the paid Labour bureaucracy, many of whom were first employed during the eras of Tony Blair and Gordon Brown. The feeling was mutual. One staffer who sat in on meetings held by the inner circle described to the *Daily Mirror*[337] the negative atmosphere in the room, with Corbyn himself contributing little, chewing on a granola bar: 'We had strategy meetings, but they were just hours of rambling discussions where nothing was decided. It would mainly be paranoia. Most of the observations were dominated by who might be making moves against Jeremy, who had said stuff that may be unhelpful.' Another staffer added: 'The aides were always incredibly paranoid about members of the shadow Cabinet. They would systematically not trust them. I can't think of a single element that the leader's office actually does well – apart from to be paranoid.'

Elsewhere in the Vice documentary, the antagonism felt by Corbyn personally towards the media was made clear. 'The one thing I've learnt over the past six months or so is how shallow, facile and ill-informed many of the supposedly well-informed major commentators are in our media,' he said at one point.[338] He launched into a long diatribe against the Labour-supporting *Guardian* newspaper, over an article which questioned his record on anti-Semitism, and accused the internationally respected BBC of bias. Corbyn's hostility towards the BBC has been gleefully taken up by his loyal followers. The Corporation's highly regarded political editor, Laura Kuenssberg, has become a hate figure for Corbynistas. After she was booed by Corbyn supporters at one event, Labour MPs publicly criticised their leader for smiling indulgently, rather than swiftly seeking to quiet his fans.

Kuenssberg was not alone in receiving abuse from supporters of the Labour leader, both online and in person. MPs who opposed Corbyn faced demonstrations outside their offices; their staff complained of harassment. A bizarre conspiracy theory suggesting that Blairites working for the communications firm Portland were behind attempts to dislodge Corbyn in the summer of 2016 led to one employee being sent by post a typed threat to 'Cox' him, a reference to the murder of the Labour MP and Remain campaigner Jo Cox, who was killed a week before the EU referendum. On the day after she launched her leadership challenge in July, a brick was thrown through the window of Angela Eagle's constituency office in Merseyside.

Luciana Berger is another Labour MP who was told she could end up like Cox, who had been a close friend before her death. Other female MPs, including Jess Phillips and Stella Creasy, have received threats of rape and other sexual violence.

Recipients of such abuse complain that the occasional statements from Corbyn and the Momentum leadership calling on supporters to be respectful are both insufficient and often tardy, coming days or weeks after troubling incidents. Following the attack on Eagle's office, Corbyn called for the leadership battle of summer 2016 to be conducted in a civilised manner. A day later, Johanna Baxter, a member of the NEC, wept on live radio as she accused Corbyn of failing to protect her and her colleagues from 'bullying and intimidation' as they gathered to decide the contentious issue of whether he would be automatically allowed on to the ballot.[339] Calling the meeting (which approved his candidacy) 'an utter disgrace to our movement', she disclosed that she and other NEC members had begged for votes to be cast in secret. "The leader of the Labour Party voted against the proposal that we conduct our vote in private in order to protect NEC members who were receiving threats, bullying and intimidation,' she told *The Guardian*.[340]

> He voted against it. He endorsed bullying, threats and intimidation, by the fact of that vote. The only reason to vote against that is so the intimidation can continue. It's the most shameful act I have ever seen. He showed his true colours in that vote. I have had people tweet and post my personal mobile online, directing people to me, directing their mob at me.

Those on the receiving end of abuse from Corbynistas often describe the Momentum group as a malevolent influence. Nurtured by Jon Lansman, Momentum continued to grow through the first months of 2016, spawning branches in around fifty constituencies and reaching a membership of approximately 12,000. It currently has more than 42,000 Twitter followers. Momentum members gained influence on national Labour bodies, including the NEC, as well as within local CLPs and university labour clubs. The organisation, which allows members from rival socialist groups and other political parties, has an overt agenda of protecting Corbyn's leadership. Lansman has raised the prospect of introducing many of the reforms he first worked on with Tony Benn, including mandatory re-selection and greater influence over policy formation for the grassroots. Tom Watson, Labour's deputy leader, has acknowledged the divisive nature of the group, describing its membership as a 'rabble'. Corbyn himself seems to embrace it, addressing its events and remaining close to Lansman, who sometimes works out of the leader's office.

One of the uglier internal ructions under Corbyn arose in the spring of 2016, with the anti-Semitism row. The first signs of trouble emerged in February, when a Jewish co-chair of the Oxford University Labour Club quit, claiming some members were hostile towards Jews. The row prompted Ed Miliband to pull out of a proposed lecture. An investigation into the Oxford Club under the stewardship of Baroness Royall was broadened to include the entire party, following incidents involving the Bradford MP Naz Shah, and Corbyn's old friend and ally Ken Livingstone. Livingstone was eventually suspended after repeatedly suggesting that Hitler had supported Zionism. Prominent Jewish members of the party, including Rabbi Baroness Neuberger and Lord Levy, complained that Labour had 'a problem with anti-Semitism'. Amid rising anger and a growing sense of crisis, Corbyn was accused of failing to respond swiftly or firmly enough, and of rejecting requests to meet backbench MPs to discuss the crisis. The row was an unwelcome distraction, at a time when Labour could have been taking advantage of David Cameron's own troubles following the release of the

Panama Papers, which revealed the use by some UK citizens, including the Prime Minister's father, of offshore trusts.

Corbyn eventually responded to the crisis by commissioning the former head of the civil rights group Liberty, Shami Chakrabarti, to lead the wider review, but not before some supporters, including many Jewish members, had resigned from the party in protest. By the time Chakrabarti reported at the end of June, concluding that while 'toxic' situations had arisen, the party was not riddled with anti-Semitism, the row had been somewhat overtaken by the crisis facing Corbyn's leadership. Corbyn was criticised for remarks he made at the launch of the Chakrabarti report in which he appeared to compare Israel to terrorist groups such as Islamic State, saying: 'Our Jewish friends are no more responsible for the actions of Israel or the Netanyahu government than our Muslim friends are for those of various self-styled Islamic states or organisations.' The Jewish MP Ruth Smee, who was reduced to tears after being verbally abused at the event by a Momentum supporter, would go on to accuse the leader of failing to come to her aid. Both Corbyn and Chakrabarti were pilloried a few weeks later when she was named as Labour's only nominee for a peerage in Cameron's resignation honours list, with the Chief Rabbi, Ephraim Mirvis, suggesting that the credibility of the report 'lay in tatters'.

The disquiet in the party continued with the results of the local elections in May. Labour's performance was unimpressive. Although Sadiq Khan captured the London mayoralty and the party successfully defended a by-election in Sheffield, the broader results were the worst for any opposition leader for more than thirty years, with a net loss of eighteen councillors, the loss of the Welsh Assembly and the virtual collapse of the Labour vote in Scotland. At a comparable stage in the electoral cycle, Tony Blair won nearly 2,000 seats, and even Ed Miliband gained 857. The newly elected Khan was among those who voiced criticism of Corbyn, saying: 'There's no point in us just speaking to Labour voters. What we need to do is speak to everyone.'

In public, Corbyn was contrite, saying in a speech a few days after the elections: 'Let's be clear. The results were mixed. We are not yet doing enough to win in 2020. This is only the first stage in our task of building a winning electoral majority, attracting voters from all the other parties and mobilising those who have been turned off politics altogether.' However, to the alarm of the Vice reporter Ben Ferguson, who filmed his private response, Corbyn insisted he was 'very happy' with the outcome, on the grounds that it was far better than the media had predicted.[341] In a forerunner of his conduct during the EU referendum, Corbyn was accused by several of his own backbenchers of failing to work hard enough, critics highlighting his failure to make any visits to Wales during the course of the campaign.

And then came the European referendum. Long suspicious of the EU, by the time he came to the leadership Corbyn's hostility had lessened but not disappeared. At the start of the year, some within the PLP had been concerned that their leader might side with Leave. To their relief, it was not a battle he decided to pick, announcing he and his front bench would campaign to remain within the Union. He launched his own campaign in April, with a speech in which he outlined his 'personal journey', from Eurosceptic to Remain supporter, and promised to make the 'socialist case' to stay in by highlighting the EU's role in protecting workers' right, helping industries such as steel, and tackling tax avoidance.

From the start, however, those working on the Labour In campaign, headed by Alan Johnson, complained that the leader's heart was not in it. Early on, Corbyn had declared he would not share a stage with David Cameron, fatally undermining attempts to create a cross-party movement. According to a Remain insider, the campaign was exasperated when an offer from a wealthy benefactor to pay for the highly effective senior Labour staffer Ayesha Hazarika to assist Johnson was quashed by the leader's office. There was criticism too of Corbyn's decision to take a week's holiday at the height of the campaign. Gradually, the In campaign came to feel that Corbyn and his team were not just being ineffective, they were veering towards deliberate obstruction. Previously unreleased footage taken from the Vice documentary, issued by the broadcaster following the referendum result, showed a meeting between Kat Fletcher and Alan Johnson in which the former agonised about the struggle she was having persuading Corbyn to play a fully engaged part of the campaign.[342] Johnson himself suggested later that meetings were cancelled or curtailed, speeches watered down and promises of greater action broken. He accused Corbyn and those around him of seeking to sabotage his work. A public glimpse of Corbyn's indifference to the EU was given the week before the vote, when the leader told the Channel 4 comedy show *The Last Leg* that his enthusiasm to remain within the Union was running at a 'seven, or seven and a half' out of ten. His answer gave the Remain campaign apoplexies – and his lukewarm support for the attempt to persuade Labour voters to back Remain would prove the tipping point for his shadow Cabinet.

During a debate on Sky News not long before the referendum, Corbyn had proclaimed: 'I am not a lover of the EU,' and insisted he would not take the blame if the vote did not go Remain's way. But in the days of bitter recrimination that followed the surprise vote to quit the EU on 23 June, and despite the leader's insistence that he had done all he could, the backlash against Corbyn and his team was swift and furious. With many Conservatives naturally hostile to the EU, the Labour In campaign had always known that the actions of Labour voters would be crucial to its success or failure. Perhaps more importantly, most Labour MPs felt that the less well-off communities they represented had both benefited from membership of the EU and would be negatively impacted by the economic chaos they believed would follow a no vote. Rumours (later denied) swept Westminster in the gloomy hours after the Brexit vote that Corbyn himself had voted to leave. He was seen that morning laughing with his closest aides as they breakfasted together.

The following evening, Saturday 25 June, Corbyn received word that Hilary Benn was organising a mass resignation of the shadow Cabinet. In a telephone conversation at 1 a.m. described as polite by both sides, he sacked the son of his close friend and mentor. Later that morning, Ian Murray quit his post as shadow Scottish Secretary in solidarity with Benn. He was followed in close succession by two-thirds of the shadow Cabinet and, the next day, by dozens more front-bench MPs. A vote of confidence was held, in which Corbyn won just forty votes out of 212. Corbyn's response was unequivocal. He released a statement reading: 'I was democratically elected leader of our party for a new kind of politics by 60 per cent of Labour members and supporters, and I will not betray them by resigning. Today's vote by MPs has no constitutional legitimacy.'

What followed was full-scale civil war. Groups were founded on social media dedicated to both attacking and defending Corbyn. New members were signed up in their thousands, on both sides of the argument. A series of senior party figures, from Ed Miliband to Tony Blair, Alan Johnson to Margaret Beckett, Kezia Dugdale to Neil Kinnock, begged the leader to resign, to no avail. Corbyn had been given a mandate by the membership less than twelve months earlier. He was going nowhere. John McDonnell insisted Corbyn was 'enjoying' the fight. Tom Watson publicly acknowledged that the leader had no mandate, and began talks between the leadership, trade unions and senior party figures including Chief Whip Rosie Winterton and John Cryer, chair of the PLP, in an attempt to resolve the impasse.

On 5 July, with the crisis still unresolved, Corbyn took a step which in any other circumstances would have represented one of the highlights of his political career. Following the long-awaited publication of the Chilcot Report into the war in Iraq, Corbyn apologised on behalf of the Labour Party for the invasion and the subsequent errors made by the British government. In a measured statement in the House of Commons, he criticised the leadership at the time of the war, but did not mention Tony Blair by name. He was less circumspect at an event held after the Commons exchanges, at which he was given a standing ovation by an invited audience which included families of some of the war dead, and later implied that Blair should face trial at the International Criminal Court. It was a development even he would have found far-fetched had he been told of it during his days leading the campaign against the war in 2003. But Chilcot would serve as only a brief reprieve from the maelstrom now engulfing Labour.

For twenty days after the EU referendum result, while, in David Cameron's words, the Conservatives held 'resignation, nomination, competition and coronation' by overseeing the smooth instalment of Theresa May as his successor, within Labour, the warring sides continued to fight for the very soul of the party. The battle lines were clear: ranked behind the rebels were those who hoped to see another Labour government as soon as possible; with Corbyn stood those whose mission was to reshape the party before launching the longer-term project of winning the country over to socialism.

On 9 July, as Corbyn spoke at the Durham Miners' Gala, Watson announced that his talks had broken down as a result of the insistence by some trade union leaders that Corbyn's leadership was not up for debate. Watson now added to the calls for Corbyn to go – and was denounced by his former flatmate, the general secretary of Unite, Len McCluskey, for doing so.

Having delayed her move by two weeks, partly to get Chilcot and the Watson talks out of the way, Angela Eagle made clear she would now finally strike. Her official launch was held two days later, just as May learned she would be Prime Minister, her final rival, Andrea Leadsom, having unexpectedly dropped out of the race. To Eagle's horror, journalists began to peel away from the event to report on where the real power lay: with the Tories. She was reduced to begging for questions from a series of senior correspondents, her humiliation complete when those she namechecked, including the entire BBC political staff, ITV's Robert Peston and Michael Crick from *Channel 4 News*, turned out to have abandoned ship. Eagle's campaign never recovered. She would go on to drop out of the contest on 19 July. Meanwhile, at the exact moment Leadsom was quitting and Eagle dying on her feet, Corbyn was pictured addressing a meeting of the Cuba Solidarity Movement.

Two days later, Owen Smith, who had resigned as shadow Work and Pensions Secretary in the swathe of resignations following the referendum result, threw his hat into the ring. Showing timing just as poor as Eagle's, he made his official announcement on the day that May was formally installed as Britain's second female Prime Minister. Unlike Eagle, Smith decided to stay the course, and became Corbyn's only challenger in the 2016 contest.

The previous day, during a heated and emotional meeting of the NEC, Corbyn had successfully argued that he should automatically be on the ballot without the need to gain the nominations of fifty of his fellow MPs and MEPs – a bar he would undoubtedly have fallen short of. Thanks to a poorly drafted set of words in the 2013 Collins Review, which had changed the procedures for electing a Labour leader, the rule was equivocal, and Corbyn's supporters had not been certain the NEC would decide in his favour. So delighted was he at the outcome that he rushed out of the room to give media interviews, thereby failing to vote on a series of subsequent and potentially key motions. On a tied vote, the NEC agreed to introduce a six-month freeze period on new members being permitted to take part in the contest, and increased the fee for registered supporters from the £3 set for the 2015 contest to a hefty £25. Registered supporters were also given just forty-eight hours to sign up. These decisions, which stood in stark contrast to the rules governing the 2015 race, were seen as helping Corbyn's opponents. Nonetheless, Corbyn and McDonnell expressed delight at the outcome of the NEC meeting. Plans were made for yet another rock-star summer tour of the country. 'Save Labour from JC' and 'Keep Corbyn' campaigns began immediately; social media flared into life.

Not content with the outcomes of the NEC meeting, first Michael Foster, a wealthy party donor, and then a group of five new members, took to the courts. At the end of July, a High Court judge rejected Foster's argument that the NEC had broken the party's own rules allowing Corbyn on to the ballot automatically, saying that the decision had been 'correct in law'. Ten days later, the High Court again ruled in Corbyn's favour, the judge, Mr Justice Hickinbottom, agreeing that the group of five – representing an estimated 130,000 new members who had joined the party between January and June 2016 – had been illegally disenfranchised. Team Corbyn's celebrations were short-lived, however. Just four days later, the ruling was successfully challenged at the Court of Appeal by Iain McNicol on behalf of the NEC. The five new members announced they would not appeal, and the extraordinary spectacle of Labour's ruling body and its leadership fighting each other in the hallowed halls of the highest courts of the land came to an end.

And so, less than a year after Corbyn's election, the rules of the game are again in play, and the Labour Party finds itself in the grip of another leadership battle. A series of bad-tempered hustings have taken place, CLPs and trade unions have made their nominations (with Corbyn receiving the overwhelming majority of both), hundreds of thousands of words have been written both decrying and celebrating the two candidates, and all the while the opinion pollsters and the bookies both predict an easy Corbyn victory. The song is familiar; the outcome apparently all but inevitable.

The official result of the contest is due on 24 September 2016. Meanwhile, the permanent revolution that is maintaining Corbyn as leader continues. Where other leaders tremble in the face of internal strife, Corbyn seems to thrive on it. It is hard not to conclude that he seems more at home fighting his own party than he ever did leading it. Most leaders could not cling to power having lost the support of their MPs. Indeed, most leaders would not seek to. But then, Jeremy Corbyn is not most leaders.

Corbyn continues to enjoy a personal loyalty any political leader would envy. Labour Party membership has risen to more than 500,000, with many new joiners saying they did so in order to vote for Corbyn should he face a leadership challenge (a smaller number is estimated to have signed on precisely to do the opposite). The freeze period means that, unless they paid the £25 registration fee, tens of thousands of them will have been disappointed. Among the wider public, however, Corbyn's personal ratings are in free-fall. After ten months in office he has an overall rating of -41. At the same period in their leaderships, Tony Blair stood at +29, Ed Miliband at -7. Even Michael Foot, hitherto considered Labour's most unelectable leader, fared better, on -32. Among non-Conservative voters, including Labour supporters, Theresa May is preferred to Corbyn as Prime Minister by a significant margin.

Whatever the outcome of the 2016 leadership contest, the future seems ominous for the Labour Party. Should Corbyn survive, with little or no relationship between the leadership and the bulk of the PLP he will find forming an effective opposition problematic. On a political level, in a post-Brexit world he faces a resurgent Tory Party eager to unify around Theresa May. On a practical level, he struggles even to muster enough front-benchers to respond to the government on behalf of the official opposition, with dozens of vacancies, and remaining shadow ministers forced to double up in jobs. One Labour MP suggests that each parliamentarian will now, in effect, become an independent, choosing their own way to vote on legislation on a case-by-case basis, taking up causes which interest them and focusing on their constituencies. Identical, in fact, to the approach that Corbyn himself took to life as a Labour MP for most of his time in Parliament.

ENDNOTES

1. Piers Corbyn interview, John Davis, 2010
2. Ibid.
3. 'Jeremy Corbyn, the boy to the manor born', Robert Mendick, *Sunday Telegraph*, 22 August 2015
4. '"It's been 30 amazing years" says veteran Labour MP Jeremy Corbyn', John Gulliver, *Islington Tribune*, 14 June 2013
5. 'Jeremy Corbyn: "I don't do personal"', Simon Hattenstone, *Guardian*, 17 June 2015
6. 'Revealed: the evil monster haunting Jeremy Corbyn's past', Caroline Wheeler, *Sunday Express*, 20 September 2015
7. 'I am much too old for personal ambition', Huw Spanner, *Church Times*, 18 September 2015
8. Mendick, *Sunday Telegraph*, op. cit.
9. Spanner, *Church Times*, op. cit.
10. 'Jeremy Corbyn's day: from national anthem "disloyalty" to "brilliant" PMQs battle with David Cameron', Michael Wilkinson, *Daily Telegraph*, 16 September 2015
11. Davis, op. cit.
12. Times Diary, Kaya Burgess, *The Times*, 15 September 2015
13. Davis, op. cit.
14. Ibid.
15. Ibid.
16. Ibid.
17. *Stanton St Bernard and Its People*, Naomi Corbyn, date unknown, early 1980s
18. Ibid.
19. Spanner, *Church Times*, op. cit.
20. Davis, op. cit.
21. Ibid.
22. Ibid.
23. Ibid.
24. 'Making of Comrade Corbyn', Quentin Letts, *Daily Mail*, 13 September 2015
25. Mendick, *Sunday Telegraph*, op. cit.

26. 'Posh past of the "Sexpot Trot": how Corbyn was brought up in a seven-bedroom house, went to prep school and even played polo', Andrew Pierce, *Daily Mail*, 4 September 2015
27. Davis, op. cit.
28. Pierce, *Daily Mail*, op. cit.
29. Ibid.
30. 'Shropshire lad who became the left's Duracell Bunny', Tim Rayment, *Sunday Times*, 13 September 2015
31. Davis, op. cit.
32. Ibid.
33. Mendick, *Sunday Telegraph*, op. cit.
34. Rayment, *Sunday Times*, op. cit.
35. Pierce, *Daily Mail*, op. cit.
36. 'Jeremy Corbyn: a question of substance over style?', Mark Andrews, *Shropshire Star*, 24 August 2015
37. Ibid.
38. Ibid.
39. 'Very red, much wed, union led', Ben Griffiths and Polly Graham, *The Sun*, 12 July 2015
40. 'Labour leadership hopefuls quizzed on everything from favourite TV to heroes and political priorities', Jason Beattie, *Sunday Mirror*, 9 August 2015
41. Davis, op. cit.
42. Hattenstone, *Guardian*, op. cit.
43. Davis, op. cit.
44. Spanner, *Church Times*, op. cit.
45. Rayment, *Sunday Times*, op. cit.
46. Davis, op. cit.
47. Ibid.
48. Rayment, *Sunday Times*, op. cit.
49. Andrews, *Shropshire Star*, op. cit.
50. Hattenstone, *Guardian*, op. cit.
51. Rayment, *Sunday Times*, op. cit.
52. 'Jeremy Corbyn Interview: On the Housing Crisis, Media Plurality, Climate Change, Religion, Bolivia and "Corbynistas"', Paul Waugh, Huffington Post, 21 December 2015
53. 'Jeremy Corbyn: "I think we have to think in terms of the disillusioned who didn't vote"', Jason Cowley, *New Statesman*, 29 July 2015
54. 'Beards: diary', Jack Malvern, *The Times*, 19 January 2002
55. LBC Labour leadership hustings hosted by Iain Dale, LBC, 22 July 2015
56. 'Jeremy Corbyn: a very middle-class revolutionary on the verge of becoming Labour leader', Dominic Midgley, *Daily Express*, 10 September 2015
57. 'Jeremy Corbyn interview: the leader strikes back', George Eaton, *New Statesman*, 23 September 2015
58. 'Jeremy Corbyn is not a serious politician. I should know', Leo McKinstry, *Daily Telegraph*, 16 June 2015
59. Rayment, *Sunday Times*, op. cit.
60. 'What I learned from singing with Jeremy Corbyn in the Young Socialists', Nick Rosen, *Guardian*, 14 September 2015
61. 'Jeremy Corbyn's ex-wife: "I donated to Yvette Cooper's campaign"', Rosa Silverman, *Daily Telegraph*, 12 September 2015

62. Ibid.
63. 'Jeremy Corbyn and Diane Abbott were lovers', David Brown and Dominic Kennedy, *The Times*, 17 September 2015
64. 'Labour's Corbyn says voted "No" to Britain's EU membership in 1975 vote', Reuters, 10 September 2015
65. Davis, op. cit.
66. Rayment, *Sunday Times*, op. cit.
67. Ibid.
68. Silverman, *Daily Telegraph*, op. cit.
69. 'Ex-wife: "Jeremy used to eat cold beans rather than take me to dinner"', Tamara Cohen, *Daily Mail*, 16 August 2015
70. 'A cold fish relishing his red-hot moment', James Bloodworth and Bobby Friedman, *Sunday Times*, 16 August 2015
71. 'Corbyn, the outsider who could land leadership he didn't want', Sean O'Neill and Laura Pitel, *The Times*, 18 July 2015
72. Silverman, *Daily Telegraph*, op. cit.
73. 'Diane Abbott: "Cambridge was the making of me"', Naomi O'Leary, *Cambridge Student*, June 2010
74. Andrews, *Shropshire Star*, op. cit.
75. 'Exclusive: Jeremy Corbyn's first wife reveals how their marriage really ended after his lover Diane Abbott made a "hostile" home visit and told her: "Get out of town"', Nick Craven and Sanchez Manning, *Mail on Sunday*, 20 September 2015
76. Ibid.
77. 'Labour's moderates have a duty to serve in the shadow Cabinet', Roy Hattersley, *Guardian*, 13 September 2015
78. Eaton, *New Statesman*, op. cit.
79. 'Jeremy Corbyn quizzed over alleged electoral expenses infringements', Lynn Davidson, *The Sun*, 20 September 2015
80. *You Can't Say That*, Ken Livingstone, Faber & Faber, April 2012
81. Ibid.
82. *Ken: The Ups and Downs of Ken Livingstone*, Andrew Hosken, Arcadia Books, September 2008
83. 'Labour leadership election: MPs prepare to resist Corbynistas', Daniel Boffey, *Observer*, 6 September 2015
84. 'Jeremy Corbyn, Tariq Ali and the Battle of Hornsey', Alex Goodall, Medium, 27 September 2015
85. *The End of an Era: Diaries 1980–90*, Tony Benn, Arrow, September 1994
86. 'Jeremy Corbyn's world: his friends, supporters, mentors and influences', Daniel Boffey, *Observer*, 16 August 2015
87. 'Falklands war was Tory plot – and jobless men died for Thatcher, says Jeremy Corbyn: Labour leadership hopeful refused to offer "loyal support" for British troops fighting to liberate the islands', Simon Murphy and Ian Gallagher, *Mail on Sunday*, 30 August 2015
88. Rayment, *Sunday Times*, op. cit.
89. Benn, *The End of an Era*, op. cit.
90. Rosen, *Guardian*, op. cit.
91. *A Very British Coup*, Chris Mullin, Serpent's Tail, January 2010
92. 'Obituary: Michael O'Halloran', Tam Dalyell, *Independent*, 2 December 1999

93. Ibid.

94. Ibid.

95. 'Why I'm standing down from Parliament: Jack Straw, MP for Blackburn', Rosa Prince, *Daily Telegraph*, 13 February 2015

96. 'Labor MP quits party', *Globe and Mail*, 9 September 1981

97. 'When Michael Foot was making progress, Tony Benn pushed us back … just like Jeremy Corbyn is doing now', Rachael Bletchley, *Daily Mirror*, 3 August 2015

98. Gulliver, *Islington Tribune*, op. cit.

99. Philip Cowley, Revolts.co.uk, 24 July 2015

100. 'Jeremy Corbyn: Labour's Earthquake', *Panorama*, BBC 1, 7 September 2015

101. Hattenstone, *Guardian*, op. cit.

102. 'Corbyn: Chris Williamson losing Derby North was "the worst result of that night"', *Derby Telegraph*, 11 February 2016.

103. Griffiths and Graham, *The Sun*, op. cit.

104. 'Left to fight Kinnock's bid for the yuppy vote', Jill Hartley, *Sunday Times*, 11 October 1987

105. 'Parliament: teachers' pay Bill approved after all-night debate', *The Times*, 12 December 1986

106. Benn, *The End of an Era*, op. cit.

107. '400 gay rights protesters back ballet-ban teacher', Dominic Kennedy, *The Times*, 9 February 1994

108. 'About me – Jeremy Corbyn MP', jeremycorbyn.org.uk

109. 'New attack on Corbyn for "inaction" over child abuse', Steven Swinford, *Sunday Telegraph*, 24 July 2015

110. 'A blind eye to child abuse', Guy Adams, *Daily Mail*, 1 August 2015

111. Swinford, *Sunday Telegraph*, op. cit.

112. *Free at Last: Diaries 1991–2001*, Tony Benn, Cornerstone Digital, December 2009

113. 'Short hits at "dark forces" behind Blair', Colin Brown, *Independent*, 8 August 1996

114. 'Fuck the rich: a portrait of Jeremy Corbyn', Alwyn W. Turner, alwynturnerblogspot.com, 20 August 2015

115. 'As Jeremy's excellent adventure continues, who are his fellow travellers?', Jon Craig, *Total Politics*, 27 August 2015

116. Benn, *Free at Last*, op. cit.

117. 'Adams plans book launch in Commons', John Burns, *The Times*, 15 September 1996

118. Ibid.

119. 'Blair slams Labour MP for Adams invite', Reuters, 16 September 1996

120. Benn, *Free at Last*, op. cit.

121. Ibid.

122. 'Adams stays in media firing line with verdict on shooting', David McKittrick, *Independent*, 27 September 1996

123. 'Kinnock is appalled at visit of IRA bombers', Geoffrey Parkhouse, *Glasgow Herald*, 17 December 1984

124. Ibid.

125. 'Labour anger over Adams invitation; Sinn Fein speech storm', Richard Ford, *The Times*, 30 September 1989

126. Atticus, John Burns, *Sunday Times*, 11 October 2015

127. 'How Sinn Féin strolled through Westminster', Colin Brown, *Independent*, 22 November 1996

128. Jeremy Corbyn interview, *Andrew Marr Show*, BBC 1, 27 September 2015

129. 'Eileen Paisley: "I can't wait to see the film about Ian ... I'm sure they'll do an excellent job"', Suzanne Breen, *Belfast Telegraph*, 10 October 2015

130. Livingstone, op. cit.

131. 'Labour's extreme left idealists who never wised up with age', Eilis O'Hanlon, *Belfast Telegraph*, 15 September 2015

132. Jeremy Corbyn interview, *Andrew Marr Show*, op. cit.

133. Ibid.

134. Benn, *The End of an Era*, op. cit.

135. 'IRA prisoner weds', *The Times*, 13 February 1988

136. 'Appeal reform hint as Hill is free on bail', Richard Ford, Edward Gorman and Stewart Tender, *The Times*, 21 October 1989

137. 'Labour fury as Speaker bars "security risk" researcher with Irish links', Michael Jones and Jim Cusick, *Sunday Times*, 4 October 1987

138. Jeremy Corbyn interview, Stephen Nolan, BBC Radio Ulster, 6 August 2015

139. Jeremy Corbyn interview, *Andrew Marr Show*, op. cit.

140. Chris Mullin, *A Walk-On Part: Diaries 1994–99*, Profile Books, June 2012

141. 'Politics gets personal – How a point of principle tore our lives apart', Andy McSmith, *Observer*, 16 May 1999

142. 'Doing right by the child – Interview – Claudia Bracchitta', Margarette Driscoll, *Sunday Times*, 16 May 1999

143. Ibid.

144. Ibid.

145. Ibid.

146. Ibid.

147. Hattenstone, *Guardian*, op. cit.

148. McSmith, *Observer*, op. cit.

149. Ibid.

150. Ibid.

151. Ibid.

152. Hattenstone, *Guardian*, op. cit.

153. McSmith, *Observer*, op. cit.

154. Ibid.

155. Driscoll, *Sunday Times*, op. cit.

156. *The House of Commons: An Anthropology of MPs at Work*, Emma Crewe, Bloomsbury Academic, June 2015

157. *The Rebels: How Blair Mislaid his Majority*, Philip Cowley, Politico's Publishing, October 2005

158. Diary, Matthew Norman, *Guardian*, 20 December 2001

159. Crewe, op. cit.

160. 'Why Labour should end the madness and elect Yvette Cooper', Alan Johnson, *Guardian*, 4 August 2015

161. *Panorama*, op. cit.

162. Ibid.

163. Hattenstone, *Guardian*, op. cit.

164. 'Left-wingers force vote on airstrikes', Sarah Schaefer, *Independent*, 20 April 1999

165. 'Jeremy Corbyn: let taxpayers opt out of funding the Army', Ben Riley-Smith, *Daily Telegraph*, 5 September 2015

166. 'Voice of student protest reduced to mere whisper', Alan Hamilton, *The Times*, 27 November 1999

167. 'Straw rules Pinochet extradition can go ahead', Jamie Wilson, Nick Hopkins and Ewen MacAskill, *Guardian*, 10 December 1998

168. 'Dome should be Queen's new home', Melissa Kite, *The Times*, 5 July 2000

169. The Sunday Stirrer, *Daily Star Sunday*, 31 March 2003

170. 'Chosen one faces brutal baptism with four days of huge decisions', Francis Elliot, *The Times*, 12 September 2015

171. Lucy Powell interview, Sky News, 14 September 2015

172. 'Hard-left MP mulling over Labour deputy bid', Matthew Tempest, *Guardian*, 20 December 2006

173. 'Whatever happened to Tigmoo?: I am a Labour party member – a useless one. This week I attended my first meeting since 1974', Ian Jack, *Guardian*, 13 June 2009

174. 'Islington North MP Jeremy Corbyn was the lowest expenses claimer in the country', Meyrem Hussein, *Islington Gazette*, 9 December 2010

175. Hattenstone, *Guardian*, op. cit.

176. Hussein, *Islington Gazette*, op. cit.

177. Jesse Jackson interview, *We Are Many* documentary film, Amir Amirani, 2015

178. Benn, *More Time for Politics*, op. cit.

179. 'Britain may be seen as "yes-person of the USA"', *Birmingham Post*, 24 September 2001

180. *Voices Against War: A Century of Protest*, Lyn Smith, Mainstream Digital, April 2011

181. Ibid.

182. 'Another coalition stands up to be counted', John Vidal, *Guardian*, 19 November 2001

183. Ibid.

184. 'Jeremy Corbyn: 9/11 was "manipulated"', Peter Dominiczak, *Daily Telegraph*, 25 September 2015, quoting Socialist Campaign Group newsletter, 1991

185. 'Thousands including NRIs participate in anti-Iraq war rally', HS Rao, *Press Trust of India*, 22 September 2002

186. 'British anti-war lobby to go on the offensive', AFP, 25 September 2002

187. *We Are Many*, op. cit.

188. Hansard, 29 January 2015

189. Ibid.

190. *We Are Many*, op. cit.

191. Ibid.

192. See *Standing Down: Interviews with Retiring MPs*, Rosa Prince, Biteback Publishing, May 2015

193. Hansard, op. cit.

194. Ibid.

195. 'I'm backing Jeremy Corbyn for Labour leadership, despite his unsavoury "friends"', Peter Tatchell, *International Business Times*, 3 September 2015

196. 'US designates five charities funding Hamas and six senior Hamas leaders as terrorist entities', US Department of the Treasury press release, 22 August 2003

197. *What Does Islam Say?*, Ibrahim Hewitt, Muslim Educational Trust, June 1998

198. 'Corbyn pal hate cleric', Michael Hamilton, *The Sun*, 25 July 2015

199. 'Jeremy Corbyn says antisemitism claims "ludicrous and wrong"', Rowena Mason, *Guardian*, 18 August 2015

200. 'Fanatics let into UK during G20', Ian Kirby, *News of the World*, 5 April 2009

201. 'Dutch court fines Muslim group for Holocaust-denial cartoon', Johnny Paul, *Jerusalem Post*, 28 August 2010

202. 'On my link to Jeremy Corbyn and the smear campaign against me and him in the UK', Abou Jahjah, aboujahjah.org, 18 August 2015

203. Jeremy Corbyn interview, *World at One*, BBC Radio 4, 19 August 2015

204. Raed Salah, *Sawt al-Haq w'al-Huriyya*, 5 October 2001

205. Raed Salah interview, Jalal Bana, *Ha'aretz*, 2003

206. Mason, *Guardian*, op. cit.

207. 'Sizer: I am ready to meet the Board of Deputies any time', Marcus Dysch, *Jewish Chronicle*, 20 August 2015

208. Mason, *Guardian*, op. cit.

209. 'Don't vote for Jeremy Corbyn, urges new Labour Friends of Israel chair Joan Ryan', Marcus Dysch, *Jewish Chronicle*, 10 August 2015

210. 'Jewish Chronicle accuses Corbyn of associating with Holocaust deniers', Rowena Mason, *Guardian*, 12 August 2015

211. Tatchell, *International Business Times*, op. cit.

212. 'Last house on the left: following Jeremy Corbyn's campaign trail', Taylor Parkes, The Quietus, 9 September 2015

213. 'Corbyn, friend to Hamas, Iran and extremists', Andrew Gilligan, *Sunday Telegraph*, 19 July 2015

214. Jeremy Corbyn, Press TV, May 2011

215. Jeremy Corbyn, Russia Today, June 2014

216. 'Jeremy Corbyn will make Iraq War apology on behalf of Labour if he wins contest', Arj Singh and Alex Britton, Press Association, 20 August 2015

217. 'David Cameron: Jeremy Corbyn would undermine Britain's security', Ben Riley-Smith, *Daily Telegraph*, 21 August 2015

218. Hansard, op. cit.

219. Hattenstone, *Guardian*, op. cit.

220. 'NATO belligerence endangers us all', Jeremy Corbyn, *Morning Star*, April 2014

221. Tributes to Tony Benn 1925–2014, stopthewar.org.uk, 18 March 2014

222. 'Why this man's tops are simply the vest for Corbyn: market trader reveals Labour leadership frontrunner's favourite item of clothing costs just £1.50', Jayna Rana, *Daily Mail*, 29 July 2015

223. 'As Jeremy Corbyn steps out in shorts, black socks and trainers – our style editor's verdict', Dinah Van Tulleken, *Daily Mirror*, 11 September 2015

224. 'Jeremy Corbyn's world', Boffey, *Observer*, op. cit.

225. Ibid.

226. 'Jeremy Corbyn votes for law to officially recognise Arsenal as the "best team in the world"', Callum Davis, *Daily Telegraph*, 12 August 2015

227. *Rail 784*, October 2015

228. 'Jeremy Corbyn's world', Boffey, *Observer*, op. cit.

229. 'Jeremy Corbyn: the secret poet and abstract artist', Michael Wilkinson, *Daily Telegraph*, 2 September 2015

230. The Gandhi Foundation International Peace Award 2013, The Gandhi Foundation, gandhifoundation.org, 9 January 2014

231. Ibid.

232. 'And how did Labour leader Jeremy Corbyn find wife number three? Via Tony Benn and a kidnap plot', Caroline Graham, *Mail on Sunday*, 20 September 2015

233. Ibid.
234. 'Bittersweet reunion in parental kidnapping case', Jed Boal, KSL.com, 18 December 2003
235. Graham, *Mail on Sunday*, op. cit.
236. 'Why did the Sexpot Trot keep so quiet about his (MUCH younger) third wife? An insight into the marriage of Jeremy Corbyn and Laura Alvarez', Tom Rawstorne and Paul Thompson, *Daily Mail*, 3 October 2015
237. Ibid.
238. Hattenstone, *Guardian*, op. cit.
239. 'Memorial: Nelson Mandela', *The Times*, 4 March 2003
240. Griffiths and Graham, *The Sun*, op. cit.
241. Graham, *Mail on Sunday*, op. cit.
242. Griffiths and Graham, *The Sun*, op. cit.
243. 'Wake up and smell the coffee, comrade', Ben Ellery and Martin Beckford, *Mail on Sunday*, 16 August 2015
244. 'Labour MP suspended by his party after "headbutting and punching Tories in brawl at Commons bar"', Larisa Brown, *Daily Mail*, 23 February 2012
245. 'Why did Labour use this system to elect its leader?', Declan McHugh, *New Statesman*, 8 September 2015
246. *Panorama*, op. cit.
247. McHugh, *New Statesman*, op. cit.
248. 'The soft left made Corbyn leader. They're Labour's swing vote and need to be won back for the centre', Atul Hatwal, Labour Uncut, 25 September 2015
249. 'The undoing of Ed Miliband – and how Labour lost the election', Patrick Wintour, *Guardian*, 3 June 2015
250. Ibid.
251. 'John McDonnell: Miliband will have to backtrack on spending cuts', George Eaton, *New Statesman*, 30 March 2015
252. 'Miner Lavery tipped for leaders' race', Luke James, *Morning Star*, 12 May 2015
253. 'Simon Danczuk: why Labour should pause this "disastrous" leadership race', Simon Danczuk, politics.co.uk, 12 August 2015
254. 'The Corbyn earthquake – how Labour was shaken to its foundations', Patrick Wintour and Nicholas Watt, *Guardian*, 25 September 2015
255. Ibid.
256. Ibid.
257. Craig, *Total Politics*, op. cit.
258. Wintour and Watt, *Guardian*, op. cit.
259. Ibid.
260. Ibid.
261. 'Len McCluskey said Kendall, Cooper and Burnham made him want to "slit his wrists"', Alan Tolhurst, *The Sun*, 11 September 2015
262. 'How Jeremy Corbyn went from the no-hope candidate to the brink of victory', Ewen MacAskill, *Guardian*, 11 September 2015
263. 'Diane Abbott joins Labour leadership race', Helene Mulholland, *Guardian*, 20 May 2010
264. 'Harriet Harman nominates Diane Abbott for Labour leader', Allegra Stratton, *Guardian*, 8 June 2010
265. 'Andy Burnham is booed by trade union delegates over welfare cuts', Rosa Prince, *Daily Telegraph*, 9 June 2015

266. 'Jeremy Corbyn: clear alternative to Tory austerity needs to be presented', Frances Perraudin, *Guardian*, 11 June 2015

267. 'Labour leadership: John Prescott leads calls to keep left-winger Jeremy Corbyn on ballot', Andy McSmith, *Independent*, 14 June 2015

268. Margaret Beckett interview, *World at One*, BBC Radio 4, 22 July 2015

269. Wintour and Watt, *Guardian*, op. cit.

270. Ibid.

271. 'Half of the Labour MPs who backed Jeremy Corbyn desert to rival candidates', Christopher Hope, *Daily Telegraph*, 22 June 2015

272. 'Labour leadership candidates: how have their reputations fared?', Patrick Wintour, *Guardian*, 11 September 2015

273. 'Who's who in Team Corbyn?', *New Statesman*, 27 August 2015

274. 'Who are Jeremy Corbyn's main allies in the Labour Party?', Iain Watson, BBC News, www.bbc.org, 13 September 2015, quoting Thomas Hobbes, *Leviathan*, 1651

275. Livingstone, op. cit.

276. *Question Time*, BBC 1, 17 September 2015

277. 'Jeremy Corbyn is teaching shadow Chancellor John McDonnell how to be a "nicer person"', Matt Dathan, *Independent*, 18 September 2015

278. Beattie, *Daily Mirror*, op. cit.

279. Eaton, *New Statesman*, 23 September 2015, op. cit.

280. Watson, BBC News, op. cit.

281. 'Corbyn campaign supporter in Kendall "Tory spoof" picture', Ross Hawkins, BBC News, www.bbc.org.uk, 24 July 2015

282. Wintour and Watt, *Guardian*, op. cit.

283. Ibid.

284. Ibid.

285. MacAskill, *Guardian*, op. cit.

286. Ibid.

287. 'Jeremy Corbyn backed by Unite as future Labour leader', Mary O'Connor, *Islington Gazette*, 6 July 2015

288. MacAskill, *Guardian*, op. cit.

289. 'Corbyn's a nice man. He will be a disaster', Stephen Moyes, *The Sun*, 11 September 2015

290. Wintour and Watt, *Guardian*, op. cit.

291. Ibid.

292. Ibid.

293. 'Budget move exposes Labour division', David Hughes, Press Association, 12 July 2015

294. 'Labour war as Corbyn closes in on leadership', Sam Coates, *The Times*, 22 July 2015

295. 'Corbyn: "My duty to Islington will not waver if I become Labour leader"', Mary O'Connor, *Islington Gazette*, 30 July 2015

296. Wintour and Watt, *Guardian*, op. cit.

297. 'Another union backs Corbyn as the antidote to a Blairite "virus"', Isabel Hardman, *New Statesman*, 30 July 2015

298. Lord Prescott interview, *Today* programme, BBC Radio 4, 23 July 2015

299. 'Labour leadership race: how has Jeremy Corbyn galvanised so many people – young and old?', Joseph Charlton, *Independent*, 6 August 2015

300. Wintour and Watt, *Guardian*, op. cit.

301. Charlton, *Independent*, op. cit.
302. 'Jeremy Corbyn to "bring back Clause IV": contender pledges to bury New Labour with commitment to public ownership of industry', Jane Merrick, *Independent on Sunday*, 9 August 2015
303. 'Jeremy Corbyn to apologise for Iraq War on behalf of Labour if he becomes leader', Ewen MacAskill, *Guardian*, 21 August 2015
304. 'Jeremy Corbyn hails Labour leadership bid "most exciting" time of his life, as party membership surges', Ned Simons, Huffington Post, 7 August 2015
305. 'Jeremy Corbyn hails "summer like no other" as huge support propels him towards Labour leadership', Jack Blanchard, *Daily Mirror*, 18 August 2015
306. Charlton, *Independent*, op. cit.
307. Jeremy Corbyn interview, *Andrew Marr Show*, BBC 1, 26 July 2015
308. 'New poll has Corbyn on course for huge victory', Sam Coates, *The Times*, 22 August 2015
309. Andy Burnham interview, BBC News, 13 August 2015
310. Wintour and Watt, *Guardian*, op. cit.
311. Johnson, *Guardian*, op. cit.
312. 'Alastair Campbell: choose anyone but Jeremy Corbyn for Labour leader', Rowena Mason, *Guardian*, 11 August 2015
313. Charles Clarke interview, LBC, 26 August 2015
314. *Panorama*, op. cit.
315. 'Chuka Umunna: "We shouldn't be seen as an opposition to Corbyn – we want to feed ideas in"', Mary Riddell, *Fabian Review*, 23 September 2015
316. 'Jeremy Corbyn says "party backs me, I have jacket from my sons and I'm ready to be PM"', Vincent Moss, *Sunday Mirror*, 13 September 2015
317. Wintour and Watt, *Guardian*, op. cit.
318. Ibid.
319. 'Jez we did: the day Labour was hit by a political earthquake', Toby Helm, *Observer*, 13 September 2015
320. 'Corbyn's Cabinet chaos: the inside story', Darren McCaffrey, Sky News, 14 September 2015
321. Wintour and Watt, *Guardian*, op. cit.
322. 'Jeremy Corbyn's shadow minister claims he "offended and hurt people" by not singing national anthem', Dan Bloom, *Daily Mirror*, 16 September 2015
323. 'Jeremy Corbyn "will sing national anthem in future"', BBC News, BBC.org.uk, 16 September 2015
324. Ibid.
325. Wilkinson, *Daily Telegraph*, 16 September, op. cit.
326. 'Corbyn hit by mutiny on airstrikes', Tim Shipman, Sean Rayment, Richard Kerbaj and Jamie Lyons, *Sunday Times*, 20 September 2015
327. 'Jeremy Corbyn embarrassed after it emerged passages of speech were written in the 1980s', Peter Dominiczak, *Daily Telegraph*, 29 September 2015
328. 'Lord Warner resigns Labour whip, saying party is "no longer credible"', Patrick Wintour and Ben Quinn, *Guardian*, 19 October 2015
329. 'I wanted to believe in Jeremy Corbyn. But I can't believe in Seumas Milne', Oliver Bullough, *New Statesman*, 23 October 2015
330. 'Labour "traitors" who voted against Jeremy Corbyn barred from Durham Miners' Gala', Peter Yeung, *Independent,* 30 June 2016

331. '"What we've achieved so far": an interview with Jeremy Corbyn', Hilary Wainwright and Leo Panitch, *Red Pepper*, December 2015
332. *This Morning*, ITV, 25 January 2016
333. 'Labour McDonald's ban slammed as "student union politics"', Tom Belger, *Liverpool Echo*, 18 April 2016
334. 'Chief whip on secret Corbyn list of "hostile" Labour MPs', Sam Coates, *The Times*, 23 March 2016
335. 'Jeremy Corbyn: The Outsider', Vice News, 1 June 2016
336. Ibid.
337. 'Life inside Jeremy Corbyn's "paranoid" HQ laid bare as Labour staffers blow the lid on leader's top team', Jack Blanchard, *Daily Mirror*, 5 July 2016
338. 'Jeremy Corbyn: The Outsider', op. cit.
339. *World at One*, BBC Radio 4, 13 July 2016
340. 'Corbyn "endorsed bullying by voting against secret ballot"', Jessica Elgot, *Guardian*, 13 July 2016
341. 'Jeremy Corbyn: The Outsider', op. cit.
342. 'Exclusive footage reveals Jeremy Corbyn's insiders struggled to get Labour leader to fight Brexit', Vice News, 29 June 2016

INDEX

"A welcome shot of optimism in difficult times."
SHAMI CHAKRABARTI

THE
ALTERNATIVE

TOWARDS A NEW
PROGRESSIVE POLITICS

EDITED BY
LISA NANDY MP, CAROLINE LUCAS MP
AND CHRIS BOWERS

368PP PAPERBACK, £12.99

"A thoughtful and original intervention at a time when creative thinking in politics is rare and desperately needed."

– Rafael Behr, *The Guardian*

The 2015 election result was a disaster for progressives in British politics, delivering a majority Conservative government at Westminster. And the outlook for the next election is not auspicious either, particularly amid the aftershocks of the momentous 2016 EU referendum result and with possible boundary changes in the offing.

There is a growing recognition, however, that cross-party cooperation among the progressives could reinvigorate politics and inspire a credible alternative to the Conservatives.

The Alternative sets out a base of core values around which progressives can unite, proposes a number of big policy ideas that embody those values and, crucially, explores an urgently needed new form of politics to achieve them.

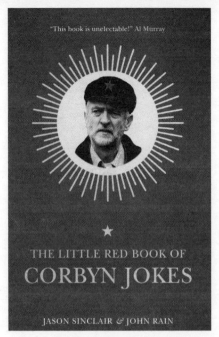